HISTORIANS

OF MODERN EUROPE

HISTORIANS
OF MODERN EUROPE

Edited by

HANS A. SCHMITT

LOUISIANA STATE UNIVERSITY PRESS   BATON ROUGE

ISBN 0-8071-0836-7
Library of Congress Catalog Card Number 71-140961

Copyright © 1971 by Louisiana State University Press
All rights reserved

Manufactured in the United States of America
Printed by Vail-Ballou Press, Inc., Binghamton, N.Y.
Designed by J. Barney McKee

The editor and contributors dedicate this volume
to their colleague, friend, and teacher

S. William Halperin.

INTRODUCTION

HANS A. SCHMITT

New York University

S. WILLIAM HALPERIN was born in Lithuania in 1905 and brought to this country early in life. He received his higher education at the University of Chicago and earned his highest academic credentials there in 1930. Called to the State Teachers College at Pittsburg, Kansas—an appointment he could not decline at a time when any kind of respectable employment was a prize—he was pleasantly surprised by the last-minute award of an instructorship in the department which had just granted him the Ph.D. Except for sabbatical absences and visiting appointments, which have included such faraway places as India, he had found his academic home. Upon his retirement in 1970, William Halperin could look back on forty years of uninterrupted teaching and writing under the aegis of the Rockefeller legacy.

When that moment arrived, thirty years separated me from my first graduate class, Halperin's "Italy since 1815." The young assistant professor I met there in 1940 was a portly, cheerful man, more gregarious and extroverted than the mentor whom the post-war generation of graduate students came to know. From this first encounter with graduate study and the man who directed so much of my own subsequent progress, I retain not only an uncommonly vivid recollection of the subject matter—courses on modern Italian history were a rarity then—but also the memory of extracurricular association with the instructor unusual in the University of Chicago of that day. Without any invidious comparison, I recall being drawn to the rising scholar because he offered in addition to expertise what every beginning graduate student seeks in a faculty: an open door and a patient ear. This happy coincidence may have resulted from Halperin's relaxed frame of mind, following the completion of his prodigious *Italy and the Vatican at War*. Perhaps it was in part a result of that terrible year of 1940, when France fell as the class bell rang in another steamy summer session and we all needed reassurance from each other in the face of catastrophe. In any case, I sought a professional to whom I could talk about history, and S. William Halperin started me on my way by listening and responding. As I acknowledge the resulting debt, I speak for those colleagues and students whose efforts have been brought together in this volume, written and edited in his honor.

Mathematicians at age thirty-five have usually had their say. They are elder statesmen in their discipline. Physicists and chemists have proclaimed their theories, completed their major experiments, and published their most significant papers. Students of uncontrollable nature, unfathomable society, and unpredictable man are then only beginning to formulate their contributions to knowledge. At this stage in his career, however, William Halperin had already staked his claim to authority in the realm of church-state relations in Italy. Although he had written his dissertation on the beginnings of Anglo-German naval rivalry, his first book, *The Separation of Church and State in Italian Thought*, traced the evolution of the separation of church from state in the thought of Italian national leadership from Cavour to Mussolini. Lucidly and with care he dissected the views of the founding fathers; the conflicting theses of separatists and their opponents in the early national period; the continuing discussions during the long interim from 1878 to 1919 when much continued to be said, but little done to resolve the problem; and concluded with the Fascist era and the equivocal Lateran accords. Without wrath and without passion he presented what men said and thought, content to be the self-effacing chronicler of "the theoretical discussion of this question." [1] At the end of his exposé he put down his pen and left the reader to draw his own conclusion. A host of Italian partisans held the floor in the

[1] Halperin, *The Separation of Church and State in Italian Thought from Cavour to Mussolini* (Chicago, 1937), vii.

pages of this slim, finely wrought monograph, but the author himself maintained a scrupulous silence, except for the introductory promise that a treatment of the practical, political side of the controversy was being "reserved for special treatment in a forthcoming series of monographs on Italo-papal relations from 1870 to 1929."

The first installment of this special treatment appeared two years later. It covered the eight years from the outbreak of the Franco-Prussian War to the death of Pius IX. Meticulously reconstructed from the archives of the French Foreign Office, the Haus- Hof- und Staatsarchiv, memoirs, and newspapers, it reflected the same rigorous commitment to convey only what the sources revealed. Because these could not include the documents from the depositories of the major protagonists themselves, the intricate and detailed web of narrative disclosed the author, for all his self-effacing modesty, to be a master at his trade. Much material had been beyond his reach, but he had extracted every iota of information from the testimony at his disposal. This time, however, he could not entirely conceal certain personal preferences. In the introduction one senses a strong hint of sympathy for the Cavourean position which favored the separation of church from state. One of the heroes of the subsequently unfolding story is clearly the Italian Foreign Minister Visconti-Venosta, as he seeks to chart his nation's course without either exploiting unduly French distress in 1870 or the papacy's tactical and moral weakness under the narrow, dogmatic Pius IX. General Cadorna is granted a substantial moment of honorable glory when the author describes the Italian commander's reluctance to occupy part of the previously inviolate Leonine city, whose inhabitants protested their continued separation from Italy. Nor does Halperin deny the pope a sympathetic portrayal as he charts the trials and justifications of his partially self-imposed imprisonment.[2] The historian sides here with the men who prefer service to posturing. He responds to moderation, and as one looks at the date of publication of *Italy and the Vat-*

---

[2] Halperin, *Italy and the Vatican at War: A Study of their Relations from the Outbreak of the Franco-Prussian War to the Death of Pius IX* (Chicago, 1939), 30–31, 64–69, 113–26, 381–90.

ican at War, one cannot help speculating whether the author could entirely resist the temptation of comparing the diplomacy of Visconti-Venosta with that of Mussolini.

Halperin's effort to maintain a high level of detachment must have been extremely difficult. He lived in full awareness of his time and even though he kept its deafening tumult down to a whisper in the pages of his books, they reflect that he, like any historian of modern times, could not isolate himself from the present. *Italy and the Vatican at War* closed with the sketch of a world waiting for a pontiff to be named. Again, there was no attempt to summarize, conclude, or interpret. In fact, everything in these closing pages pointed to the sequel, the next installment in that "forthcoming series of monographs" which he had promised the reader of *The Separation of Church and State in Italian Thought.* But that sequel has yet to appear. In 1946, seven years after the publication of *Italy and the Vatican at War,* the established historian of modern Italy presented instead to his colleagues and students, returning from the battles of World War II, a history of the Weimar Republic.

It turned out to be a remarkable venture for three reasons. To begin with, the book signaled Halperin's capacity for partisanship. The preface left no doubt where he stood: "The story of the German republic makes depressing reading. It records the rise and fall of a venture in democracy. Had this venture succeeded, World War II might never have taken place. Its failure plunged a nation into slavery. Democracy, like peace, is indivisible. What happened in Germany had profound repercussions throughout the world. These repercussions are still with us." The Allies, he continued, had treated the new democratic Germany as an enemy. As a result they encouraged the reactionary subversion supported by military, big agrarian, and big business interests. Hitler's inauguration as chancellor was at this point the moment of supreme triumph for these irreconcilables. Allied statesmen and the German exploiters of their blunders figure as the villains of Halperin's story.[3]

Second, Halperin's gallery of heroes consists less of moderates

[3] Halperin, *Germany tried Democracy: A Political History of the Reich from 1918 to 1933* (New York, 1946), 103–105, 109–53, 256, 279.

than of men who lived their convictions. Courage and perseverance, rather than restraint, are the virtues touted here. To be sure, there is a passing salute to Count Hertling, "that benign and cultured statesman," [4] which creates the shortlived illusion that *Germany tried Democracy* will likewise exalt the modest toiler in high office over the aggressive activist. But only four pages later the author finds equally warm words for the leadership of Independent Socialism, the representatives of "the outraged workers of Germany." Uncharacteristic sympathy for political extremes is the reaction of a historian himself outraged by the events and the then continuing discoveries of the barbarities committed by Germany's totalitarian masters. He is no less sympathetic to the men who must accept the peace settlement on Germany's behalf and who later muster the courage to agree to fulfill the obligations imposed by the victors.[5] The courage to face the wrath of inflamed nationalism is, of course, one characteristic which these forlorn initiators of the ephemeral First German Republic possessed to an even more marked degree than Visconti-Venosta and the hesitant Cadorna.

Finally, *Germany tried Democracy* improved with age. Initially the book received little acclaim. A widespread reaction seemed to be that it was premature. When one reads it now, after literally hundreds of monographs have attempted to illuminate those dismal fourteen years, one must indeed marvel at the boldness of an historian who was painstaking caution personified and who would yet write a book of almost five hundred pages on so polemic a subject. His problem was well illustrated by the treatment of the closing phase after the election of 1928, which was seriously handicapped by its almost exclusive dependence on the Reichstag debates. But there were other difficulties that may have accounted for the cool reception. Blaming the Allies for 1933 had ceased to be a popular viewpoint. As the late forties resounded with the rehabilitation of German generals, aristocrats, and other conservatives, on the grounds that they had led the resistance against Hitler, other components of Halperin's interpretation came in for criticism. Blaming the SPD, finally, for not joining forces with

[4] *Ibid.*, 45.
[5] *Ibid.*, 138, 203.

German communism in order to prevent Papen's 1932 coup d'etat in Prussia still raises many eyebrows. In any case, *Germany tried Democracy* earned little except silence. It was not even reviewed by the *Journal of Modern History*.

Still, Halperin eventually experienced an impressive vindication. The book was reprinted, first in 1963, then a second time two years later. Gordon Craig reviewed the second edition in the *Journal* and found, almost two decades later, that "it has held its position as the best of the single-volume histories of the republic in English." Craig concludes, "Even as it stands, the work is the clearest and most comprehensive introduction to the politics of the period," the limitation of the available sources notwithstanding.[6]

This sally into *Zeitgeschichte* appears as a divide in William Halperin's productive career. After publishing three monographs in less than a decade, he remained all but silent for the better part of fifteen years. In part this was probably because of the development of a new interest in the history of France. This shift may have been abetted, at least, by a stint of teaching at the "GI University" in Biarritz immediately after the war. It resulted in Halperin's offering new courses in French constitutional history and French political thought. There were rumors that he was working on a constitutional history of France since 1815, but all that appeared in print was a brief appreciation of Léon Blum, another characteristic Halperin hero, distinguished by honest, unsuccessful toil for defeated convictions.[7] Beyond that, this concern has, above all, produced a number of works by Halperin students.[8]

The Roman question, likewise, seems to have been put aside. A short essay on the ideological phenomenon of Italian anticlericalism [9] and a brief discussion of the persistent problem under the

---

[6] Craig, review in *Journal of Modern History*, XXXVI (1964), 106–107.

[7] Halperin, "Léon Blum and contemporary French socialism," *Journal of Modern History*, XVIII (1946), 241–50.

[8] Jack J. Roth, "Revolution and Morale in Modern French Thought: Sorel and the Sorelians," *French Historical Studies*, III (1963), 205–23; Edward R. Tannenbaum, *The Action Française: Die–Hard Reactionaries in Twentieth Century France* (New York, 1962); Hans A. Schmitt, *Charles Péguy: The Decline of an Idealist* (Baton Rouge, 1967).

[9] Halperin, "Italian Anti-clericalism," *Journal of Modern History*, XIX (1947), 18–34.

pontificate of Leo XIII [10] fell short of Halperin's original plans for a multivolume history of Italo-Vatican relations.

Actually, Halperin had not turned his back on Italy. The late 1950's found him working in those very Italian archives which had been closed to him earlier. The initial results of these visits revealed that his earlier interests had not been abandoned. They had merely been secularized. Halperin's next monograph, published in 1963, portrayed Visconti-Venosta wrestling not with the papacy, but the problems of war and peace in the summer of 1870. The account—a virtuoso reconstruction almost exclusively from unpublished sources —of Italian foreign policy in the midst of supreme crisis, revealed William Halperin seemingly recovered from the passions engendered by world holocaust. This analysis of the diplomacy of a neutral was not merely an important contribution to the diplomatic history of the Franco-Prussian War; it was a portrait of the statesman whose virtues he had discovered when writing *Italy and the Vatican at War.*

The account did not retouch the warts. The Italian foreign minister admittedly was not only "deliberate" but "sluggish," as well as "slow, timid, and hesitant." Yet Halperin quoted with approval Chancellor Bernhard von Bülow's famous verdict: "I do not believe that he ever did a stupid thing in any sphere during the whole of his life." [11] Slowness and timidity "served his country well" in 1870.[12] These mixed attributes composed the modus operandi of a diplomat who had not been deceived into embracing extravagant dreams of glory by his nation's emergence. New nations are ambitious, the energies mobilized by the quest for statehood seek immediate outlets, and new-found identity at once demands extreme recognition of the newly won status. But, as a rule, these new polities are also weak. Visconti-Venosta knew this and his diplomacy of neutrality rested on the assumption of Italian weak-

[10] Edward T. Gargan (ed.), *Leo XIII and the Modern World* (New York, 1961), 101–24.

[11] Halperin, *Diplomat under Stress: Visconti-Venosta and the Crisis of July 1870* (Chicago, 1963), 2–3. Part of this book appeared earlier in "Visconti-Venosta and the diplomatic crisis of July 1870," *Journal of Modern History,* XXX (1959), 295–309.

[12] *Diplomat under Stress,* 189.

ness. It was successful, but it was in the nature of things that the achievement of keeping the nation out of trouble had to wait almost a century for historical recognition.

Halperin was now in pursuit of more than justice for a man of undramatic competence. The work in Italian archives continued, to be followed by journeys to Paris, Brussels, London, and Vienna, all in hot pursuit of the whole story of international diplomacy and the Franco-Prussian War. "Great crises are a source of perennial interest to a historian," Halperin had confessed in his introduction to the Visconti-Venosta book, and the extent of that crisis in 1870–71 was only partially revealed by the war itself. Conflict had given it a deceptively limited aspect. How was the potential European war avoided? Visconti-Venosta's "prudence, sang-froid and unfailing realism" provided one explanation. But other governments were involved. What saved them from belligerence? Historians have been allowed a few brief glimpses of Halperin's quarry since then, but they are still awaiting the entire story.[13] No doubt they will get it in the author's own good time.

Meanwhile, Professor Halperin has not been silent on other matters. In 1964 he published a slim paperback, *Mussolini and Italian Fascism*.[14] Here, as in *Germany tried Democracy*, his position was quite explicit, but naturally everything emerged on a far smaller scale. Mussolini was a nonhero: "cynical," the "least committed of recent dictators," giving "the movement tremendous rhetorical dash . . . but also . . . its extraordinary intellectual poverty." The entire narrative was laced with such infusions of disapproval. After Mussolini had identified himself with the left wing of the Socialist Party, he "trumpeted its gravamens to all who would listen." [15] But yet the author never played dirty. For the benefit of his student audience he put to rest the myth that "foreign gold" prompted the later Italian dictator to forsake non-

13 Halperin, "Bismarck and the Italian envoy in Berlin on the eve of the Franco-Prussian War," *Journal of Modern History*, XXXIII (1961), 33–39; "Italy and the Genesis of the League of Neutrals of August, 1870" in *Mélanges Pierre Renouvin: Etudes d'Histoire des Relations Internationales*, Publications de la Faculté des Lettres et Sciences Humaines de Paris, Série "Etudes et Méthodes," Tome 13 (Paris, 1966), 149–57.
14 Halperin, *Mussolini and Italian Fascism*, (Princeton, N.J., 1964).
15 *Ibid.*, 3, 19.

intervention in World War I. Mussolini was temperamentally incapable of neutrality; he was an Austrophobe, an understandable position for any Socialist to take, and, with even more impressive logic, the blacksmith's son recognized war as the promoter of social revolution.[16] The dynamic of their faith persuaded many Italian Socialist and Syndicalist leaders of that day to follow the same path. The real betrayal of principle commenced when another villain entered the piece. Not foreign, but domestic gold contributed to the assumption of yet another new position during the restless peace that followed. The first Fascist meeting on March 23, 1919, took place in a hall provided by a local association of industrialists and merchants. In 1922 Mussolini abandoned the rest of his political convictions when he accepted the monarchy and in return received the support of the army. As in Germany, the powers of money and the military combined to doom democracy, to be joined here much more clearly by the Church, whose complaisance regarding fascism comes in for particular censure.[17] As in the case of the Weimar Republic, Halperin forces himself to tell a story that "makes depressing reading." Unlike Visconti-Venosta, who quietly kept Italy out of war, Mussolini "forced a basically pacific nation to act out . . . his own addiction to violence." [18]

Such is Halperin's published work to date. He has written of politics and of ideologies, and he remains deeply immersed in the study of diplomatic crisis. He has at times been completely self-effacing, and he has at other times reached the brink of polemics. His distaste for noisy posturing pervades all of his work. His sympathy for men who labor in silence or who chose failure in preference to betrayal is another constant in his writings. From his rare and fleeting comments on history and from his own example, one gathers, however, that much of this brief program is reflex rather than design. His colleagues and students cannot help but be aware of his almost unquestioning belief in parliamentary democracy as a system under which men may not necessarily flourish, but without which they will invariably meet disaster and suffer enslave-

[16] *Ibid.*, 24–25.
[17] *Ibid.*, 67–68.
[18] *Ibid.*, 88.

ment. But his choice of heroes, I suspect, is more an unconscious identification with kindred spirits than a conscious selection. An essay in praise of his teacher Bernadotte Schmitt and an appreciation of Pierre Renouvin would lead to such a conclusion. In his mentor he praised the man who had *trained* him.[19] He admired in Renouvin "the detachment of a scientific historian" and in his work "a true blend of science and art." [20] Furthermore, both introduced him to the excitement of writing history one has lived to witness.[21] This simple accolade explains to a considerable extent the tone and range of Halperin's own work. He has practiced with tremendous conscientiousness the science of research. His careful, neat prose testifies to his devotion to stylistic literacy. And he has certainly indulged the fascination with the history of his own time. However he may have sought and found his ideals, he has served them unswervingly.

But that is not all. William Halperin's service to history was not confined to teaching and writing. In 1944 he first became involved in the editing of the *Journal of Modern History* as assistant to his teacher Bernadotte Schmitt. Since Schmitt had by then left Chicago to work for the government, it is fair to assume that the bulk of editorial labor came to rest on Halperin's shoulders. In 1946 he became editor in name as well as in fact. Three years later, illness forced his resignation, but he resumed the post in 1959 and held it through 1967. Thus he has been the *Journal's* most persistent guiding influence during the second half of its forty-year history.

One aspect of Halperin's editorial contribution can be gleaned from a comparison of Schmitt's valedictory as an editor with the distinctive content of the publication in a representative year of Halperin's editorship. In his farewell, Schmitt demonstrated almost excessive pride in the *Journal's* contribution to knowledge in areas and on subjects where he himself had established his international fame. In his words, under his direction the *Journal* made a special point of publishing articles and of calling attention to scholarship "based on documents and memoirs dealing with World War I and

---

[19] Halperin (ed.), *Some 20th Century Historians* (Chicago, 1961), vii–xxi.
[20] *Ibid.*, 153, 170.
[21] *Ibid.*, 147.

its origins." Hence, "today more is known about the war of 1914 than about the causes of the Crimean or the Franco-German War."[22] Halperin's "special points" rested on more eclectic assumptions. The issues he prepared contained a large number of contributions of an interpretive, historiographical, or bibliographical nature.[23] Almost invariably these were commissioned, so that the *Journal's* dependence on the vagaries of a contributing public was reduced accordingly. The range of the subjects covered by these request performances was as wide as "modern history." It included the diplomatic history of Europe since 1870 and, with appropriate frequency, articles by none other than Bernadotte Schmitt. But volume XXXIII, for instance, contained Paul Hardacre's "Writings on Oliver Cromwell," Eric W. Cochrane's "Machiavelli: 1940–60," Peter Topping's "Greek Historical Writings on the Period 1453–1914," and Paul W. Schroeder's "Metternich Studies since 1925," a telling illustration of how Halperin implemented this particular goal of the *Journal* under his aegis. For the rest, he followed his own broad preferences which a friend recently characterized as encompassing "meticulous, dispassionate research" and "interpretive . . . work." His own output embraced the meticulous, the dispassionate, and the interpretive. It is to be expected that these were the categories of scholarship he sought to encourage as editor and that he was content beyond this point to let the term "modern history" provide the framework within which such contributions must be sought and made.

William Halperin's forty years as an active member of one of the great history faculties in the United States have been productive, and the end is not in sight. The appraisal of those years offered in this introduction is happily an interim report not a final accounting. True, he has retired from editing and his mandatory retirement at age sixty-five lies just behind us. But there is no indication that the scholar is seeking the pastures of idleness, because the teacher has exchanged the familiar scenes of Chicago's Quadrangle for the urban campus of Wayne State University in Detroit.

---

[22] Schmitt, "Valedictory," *Journal of Modern History*, XVIII (1946), 194.
[23] *Ibid.*, XX (1948), 194–95. As a result the *Journal* published in 1949, for instance, five monographic, five review, and three bibliographic articles.

For those of us who have collaborated on this volume, the moment of formal departure from tenured professorship nevertheless provides a fitting opportunity to pay full tribute to S. William Halperin and to his service to Clio, to his friends, and to his students. We think that the form is particularly appropriate. The *Festschrift* with a theme is a Chicago tradition.[24] The contents in this instance reflect no less the range of Professor Halperin's own interests. In this connection the appreciable contributions to Italian historiography are particularly gratifying. May everything in this joint endeavor stand as a token of gratitude to the colleague, teacher, and scholar in whose honor it was undertaken, and also as evidence in its own right of how historians in our time committed themselves to discover and defend truth, always with their pens and, as several of these essays testify, often at the risk of their lives.

[24] See the last two: Halperin, *Some 20th Century Historians*, "To Bernadotte Schmitt, Scholar, Teacher and Friend, from his former students"; and Richard Herr and Harold T. Parker (eds.), *Ideas in History: Essays Presented to Louis Gottschalk by his Former Students* (Durham, 1965).

CONTENTS

HISTORIANS

OF MODERN EUROPE

PART ONE

ANGLO-AMERICAN PERSPECTIVES

ARNOLD J. TOYNBEE
The Paradox of Prophecy

EDWARD WHITING FOX
Cornell University

IN THE INTRODUCTION to his *Reconsiderations,* Mr. Arnold J. Toynbee sums up the vast accumulation of criticism of his *Study of History* as two charges; first, that he forced his facts to fit his theories, and second, that he abandoned scholarship for prophecy. To answering the first he devotes the rest of this remarkable volume, dealing exhaustively with virtually every scholarly comment on his work that has appeared in print. To the second, however, he merely replies that the next most awkward thing to saying "I think I am a prophet," is to say "I really don't think I am one." The evasion is so deft that the unwary reader might easily miss the fact that Toynbee has not only denied the charge, by implication, but has sidestepped the entire issue.

This is a curious and unfortunate course for him to follow. It is curious because on all subjects save this, he has not only welcomed criticism but eagerly sought to profit from it. It is also curious because he has repeatedly expressed the greatest admiration and reverence for the original prophets. Finally, it is unfortunate because this evasive denial rejects what would appear to be the essential thesis and ultimate purpose of his work. If his long and scrupulous explanation of his motives in undertaking the *Study* establishes anything, it is that he set out to restore meaning as the main goal of historical endeavor. That he believes he has succeeded and that the meaning he has discovered is fraught with urgent significance for all, he has hardly kept a secret. Instead, he has clearly accepted the responsibility, as a historian, not merely to discover but to urge on his fellow mortals the lessons of the past. And what

[5]

is this but prophecy? The important question, however, is not whether Toynbee has committed prophecy but why he should deny his hard-won achievement by panicky rejection of the charge.

The most obvious answer would seem to be sheer, overwhelming modesty. Mr. Toynbee is a remarkably unassuming man. In addition, he nurtures a deep abhorrence of the pretentions to importance, which he believes are the inherent flaw of every self-conscious human being, particularly as he sees their manifestations in himself. His very reverence for the original prophets would make it difficult for him to accept the comparison implied by the title. And self-appointed prophets, he pleads, are regularly taken as figures of fun. He well might feel that pretensions on his part to such a position would be ludicrous, but it would not be like him to deny a conviction or reject an obligation for fear of ridicule.

In a final effort to extricate himself from his embarrassment he adds that, in any case, he could not be guilty of prophecy because he does not believe the future can be predicted. It is difficult to imagine what would drive Toynbee to such a palpable *non sequitur*. Not only will he explain in a later passage that the original prophets acquired their reputation for prediction unintentionally and incidentally, but he began his entire *Study* in an effort to establish the possibility of prediction in human affairs. It would seem worthwhile therefore to examine his treatment of both phenomena—the prophets and historical prediction—to search for clues to his behavior.

The word "prophet," Toynbee reminds his reader, did not originally carry its now common connotation of prediction. The prefix "pro" means "forth" as well as "forward" and the original Hebrew prophets were "speakers forth," or preachers who denounced forthrightly the social evils they saw about them. Utterly convinced of the urgency of their message and embittered by the disinterest with which it was received, they gradually, perhaps unconsciously, began to reinforce their remonstrances with threats of retribution, thus preparing the way for the momentous transition effected by the Babylonian captivity. As the Hebrews began to recover from the shock of defeat and transportation and to reflect on the magnitude of their disaster, they inevitably began to recognize in the prophets' exhortations clear warnings of impending doom. What they had spurned as moral denunciation they now recalled as inspired foretelling. But the same concatenation of moral judgment and historical development also transformed the Hebrew tribal deity into a universal God. To Toynbee and countless others, this still stands as the major revelation of human experience. Indeed, it was so momentous as to completely overshadow the simultaneous metamorphosis of prophecy into prediction. If, in retrospect, it is not in the least surprising that this should have happened, it does account for the fact that the methods and purpose of the prophetic tradition have tended to be misunderstood but not that they should be misrepresented by Toynbee.

Prediction, as he himself explained, was neither an original nor essential element of prophecy. Indeed, a wholly predictable world would have no need of prophets to exhort hapless victims to struggle against a knowable, inevitable fate or future. It is, however, just in the relationship of predictability in human affairs and the freedom of the will that Toynbee has produced his most important insights.

When he undertook the *Study of History*, as we all know, he set out to discover new intelligible fields of historical investigation. He was, along with many others of his generation who had just experienced the First World War, distrustful of the nation-state. But his purpose was not merely to discredit that dominant and dangerous institution of his world, but also, by extending the field of his observation, to attempt to introduce the methods of empirical science into his subject. We can "know," Toynbee explains, only what we can compare with something similar; and the "unique" is, by definition, unknowable unless, by extending our field of vision, we can find other examples of the same phenomenon. It was for precisely this purpose that he abandoned the traditional unit of the nation-state for the more ample area of civilizations.

The object of his study was, like that of any other scientific undertaking, to find "regularities" in his material. Both the component parts of civilization and the civilizations themselves, he began to discover, exhibited identifiable patterns of behavior, which seemed to raise the prospect of scientific prediction in human affairs. The concept of a science of society or of scientific history which had seemed to promise so much to the nineteenth century was by this time mired in determinism. What was predictable, it had come to be accepted, was necessarily predetermined and causation was assumed to carry the same implication. Historians, therefore, found themselves contending with a frustrating dilemma; if they "made any sense of history" either to explain the past or project the future, they committed themselves to a neo-predestination. Some, notably the Marxists, were ready to pay this price; but the majority found it unacceptable on moral, psychological, or pragmatic grounds. Any significance in history came to be looked upon askance. History, it was said, taught nothing save that history taught nothing with useful certainty.

This reaction was due not so much to any deep commitment to the freedom of the will as to the cumbersome character of Marxian or Spenglerian predictions. Things simply did not happen that or any other systematic way. What was observable was not order but isolated facts and in the pursuit of these, the large majority of professional historians sought salvation. Toynbee himself explains their vigorous reaction to his early efforts as an instinctive defense of the "*uniqueness* of historical events and human personalities." In point of fact, he threatened only the uniqueness of the events, not the persons.

Spengler, in endowing civilizations with an organic development, forced them into a fixed life span thus leading to his prediction of the imminent and inevitable decline of the West. Toynbee, while he saw "regularities" in the histories of civilizations, did not find them fixed to any such rigid pattern. Moreover, his basic conviction that the human will was free made it impossible for him to accept the concept of an inescapable doom. For Spengler's determinism he substituted his most famous formula, "challenge and response."

Civilizations, and human beings too, Toynbee proposed were confronted by a series of challenges, that is, critical situations in which they would have to make a choice. Those who made the right response survived and prospered; those who did not suffered or died. In searching for his scientific uniformities in history, he discovered that certain challenges seemed to be repeated with predictable regularity, but that the responses they elicited, while tending to follow a pattern, were not in fact determined. This raised the problem of intermittent causation which was universally accepted as a contradiction in terms. If any one event could be proved to have caused another, it was held, a totally caused or determined system was established; and since both predictability and causation could be demonstrated in the physical world, the suspicion prevailed that they must also exist in human affairs, although perhaps on a scale of complexity beyond the grasp of the human brain. But Toynbee, in the best empirical tradition ignored the logic and concentrated on the phenomena of the case. The more closely he observed his civilizations, the more convinced he became that he could recognize predictable regularities in their behavior which were occasionally interrupted. To explain this anomaly, he had recourse to the new field of psychoanalysis from which he borrowed the distinction between *sub-* and *self-*conscious action. Most human activity, he pointed out, was carried on at the subconscious level. Men normally reacted instinctively to most situations, or challenges, and when they did, their behavior was predictable, as the new social sciences were beginning to demonstrate. On the special occasions when men made self-conscious decisions, however, their actions, or responses, were free and could not be foretold. Not only did this appear to resolve the dilemma of determinism, it separated history from social science at the level of human consciousness. No life lived below this surface could be free; but any emerging self-consciousness had the capacity to choose, thus reintroducing the element of free will into what had become an otherwise determined universe.

Toynbee, that is, succeeded in raising his investigation to a scientific level by extending his field of observation; but in so doing, he moved away from history into the social sciences. Although he never directly discusses this transition, he is obviously aware of its implications. On the one hand, he expresses much more than casual interest in the social sciences and is clearly impatient with historians who refuse to use them as new tools or accept their results as new materials. On the other hand, he recognizes that history deals with the unique actions of self-conscious human beings responding to the challenges of a predictable society.

One of the corollaries of Toynbee's distinction between social science and history would seem to be that all history must be consciously created. The historian who probes old patterns of collective subsconscious actions is using the methods of the social sciences; only when he follows the course of conscious human purpose in action is he practicing his own special art of history. Obviously this brings us close to the activities of the prophets. Reading the record of social abuses committed by their fellow Jews, they denounced the evil they found, proposed courses of action to correct existing inequities, and warned of the dangers of complacent inaction. Their analysis of the prevailing situation was an exercise in social science, but their proposals for reform were historical in intent. Their apparent predictions of doom were based on extrapolations of the subconscious reactions of their fellow Jews. Even if their original intent had not been to forecast the future, they instinctively recognized that, unless interrupted by the creative effort of a new conscious response to the existing challenge, the established patterns of behavior would continue until they ended in disaster.

The element of prediction in this process, it is worth noting, derived directly from their investigation of subconscious reactions —that is, from the area of social science. As historians, the prophets were not foretelling a fixed future but urging conscious actions to avoid otherwise predictable catastrophies.

If we turn from the example of the prophets to that of Toynbee's work, the similarities are striking. In his *Study of History* he found, among many patterns, the tendency of civilizations after periods of anarchy, or "times of trouble," to produce "universal states." These, like the Roman Empire with its *Pax Romana*, ended the plague of civil war but did it by military conquest. Our own civilization, he believes, is also in a time of trouble, and the great military adventures of both Napoleon and Hitler were frustrated attempts to create a universal state. Because of the escalating power of modern arms, we obviously cannot sustain endless strife, and we have even less chance of surviving an ultimate struggle for total victory. With the invention of nuclear weapons, our need for a universal state has become desperate, but the possibility of establishing it in the traditional manner—by force—has vanished. Since such a confrontation could end only in nuclear holocaust, our one hope, it would seem, is to create a universal state by mutual agreement. But there are neither precedents nor indications to suggest that this is possible. It is no exaggeration to say that Toynbee has been obsessed by the problem. He has directed most of his writing to warning us of our peril and urging us to take the necessary steps to avoid it while there is still time, and surely this is prophecy in the great tradition. But why then, if its character is so obvious, does Toynbee continue to deny it?

One possible explanation of this contradictory behavior can be found in his ambiguous attitude toward human consciousness. By limiting predictable regularities of human action to the subconscious, he places the responsibility for original responses to the challenge of existence squarely on the self-conscious mind and will. Only a fully conscious mind will be able to grasp the significance of the challenge—by reading the record of the past— and only the free and conscious will can make the necessary decision to act in an unprecedented manner. The capacity, that is, to make history as well as to read its lessons are the exclusive prerogatives of the self-conscious mind. By overwhelming implication Toynbee not only gives credit for the creation of civilizations but also responsibility for their future to this "unique" phenomenon.

Any who are familiar with Toynbee's work, however, are all too well aware of his horror of the tendency of the human consciousness to see itself as the center and focus of the universe. Even though he argues that only the self-conscious human will is capable of an undetermined and creative response to the challenge of existence, his distrust of human self-centeredness drives him to a profound distrust of *self* in consciousness as well. Clearly the temptation to escape from the agonizing experience of watching fallible human beings grapple with the atomic challenge is more than he can resist. But the price of exorcising the curse of *centeredness* by sacrificing *self* would be the loss of consciousness and the freedom it implies. Nowhere does Toynbee attempt to resolve this implied dilemma in explicit terms. To do so he would have to choose between his belief in the freedom and creative possibilities of the will and his desperate distrust of the fatal tendency to centeredness in the self of human consciousness.

To accept the responsibility of prophecy would commit him to this choice. The prophet, that is, reads the record of self-centered actions and extrapolates their logical conclusions. These he presents to the self-conscious element of his society in the form of challenge. For the response he can only wait in anguish bereft of hope and faith. Total faith in mortals would involve self-worship, which Toynbee never could accept. But what of hope? Does not the vast panorama of the past which he has managed to survey and assess with such persuasive vision demonstrate that, at least so far, men have in fact risen to the fatal challenges by at least the necessary margin?

In his efforts to escape the responsibility of his prophetic role, Toynbee sacrifices the logical conclusion of his argument, namely that history is intrinsically prophetic. The historian, by concerning himself with conscious human actions, is committed to the scrutiny of human purpose and its consequences. History, Toynbee has insisted, involves moral judgment; and by judging past actions, the historian like the prophet, is formulating for his audience the nature of the peril in which they live. Although each begins with the established patterns of instinctive or subconscious reactions, each addresses himself to the self-conscious elements of his society, to a reading of their past achievements and present purposes. A knowledge of what has happened in history does not foretell the future. The social sciences, not history, repeat themselves; and it is from their predictable projections that men of consciousness, or conscience, must defend their civilization by the deliberate and free creation of their own purpose or history.

All of this obviously requires the freedom of the will. Toynbee himself takes this as an article of faith, something he believes deeply and instinctively but which, he suspects, is not susceptible of proof. Perhaps, but in this context it could be described as a necessary attribute of self-consciousness. The possibility of sensing *self* depends on the capacity of focusing consciousness first on *self* and then on aspects of all that is *not self*. A consciousness permanently fixed on either *self* or *not-self* would lack the essential quality of self-knowledge which can be derived only from the distinction between and comparison of *self* and *non-self* and the free-doom to shift conscious attention from one to the other at will. It is in this exercise of consciousness that man is free; without the awareness of *self* he would be incapable of any but instinctive actions. The freedom that derives from this control of conscious-ness might seem inconsequential. It can neither control nor suspend the "laws of nature." It is by no means master of its own subconscious, and it enjoys no "safe conduct" against acts of Fate. Its means are human and therefore puny and precarious but still impressive in human terms. By constant focus, or singleness of purpose it can, on occasion, climb the highest mountain or bring low a hated tyrant.

So far, therefore, from there being any conflict between prophecy and free will, the one would have no meaning without the other. But here, as elsewhere, Toynbee's horror of self-centered-ness has led him to attempt to escape its consequences by the abnegation of self in consciousness as well. And yet the purpose of his own *Study of History* was to extract meaning from the totality of human experience, and his accomplishments in that direction are impressive. His conclusions, if one dare attempt a summary of so vast an undertaking, are that man himself has gradually transformed societies of the sort that abound in the animal and insect worlds into civilizations, purposeful organi-zations that have raised his collective capacities to the point of taking over responsibility for his own future. It is, as Toynbee obviously recognizes, a hazardous transition. But it is not a plight from which we can extricate ourselves by retreat or abdication. Toynbee's greatest achievement may well be that he has shown, in the manner of the early prophets, the imminent consequences of ignoring the challenge implicit in our situation. Only by under-standing the nature of our civilization and applying the lessons of our history can we escape the doom he fears and bring our civilization to the next higher stage which, in his famous figure of the cliff, lies out of sight beyond the ledge above.

In his *Study of History*, Toynbee has resolved the impasse between total determinism and total chaos that had bedeviled his predecessors. By doing this he has accomplished his purpose of restoring "meaning" to history, which in turn restored to us responsibility for our future. Further, he has urged with vigor the ominous import of the "meaning" he discovered and the awesome weight of responsibility it entails, He has, that is, in his effort to raise history to the level of a science, transformed it into prophecy. To many this will present a challenge. To others, his desperate refusal to accept responsibility for this achievement will be even more difficult to understand. The paradox of prophecy in the work of Arnold Toynbee is not that he has revived the prophetic tradition in his history but, that having done so by a lifetime of dedicated labor, he now denies it like a modern Peter.

CARLTON J. H. HAYES

CARTER JEFFERSON
University of Massachusetts, Boston

THE LATE Carlton J. H. Hayes is remembered today chiefly for two things—his pioneer studies of nationalism and his widely read, influential textbooks on European history. Despite his contributions to the study of history, however, and despite his early acceptance as a leading member of what might be called the historical establishment, he ended his career an embattled figure, alienated from many of the colleagues whose praise had brought him recognition. His later estrangement from these men is not surprising for, basically, he did not share their views; the fact that they accepted him so fully in earlier days is more difficult to explain. In this essay, therefore, I hope not only to outline the development of a scholar's ideas but also to indicate something of the nature of prevalent attitudes in the historical profession as it existed in the United States in the past half century.

Hayes was born in Afton, New York, in 1882. Both his parents came from old and respected families that had been in New York since before the American Revolution.[1] His father was a physician, his mother an accomplished musician. Hayes led his class in high school, then attended Columbia University, where he remained the rest of his life. In 1904, just before he finished college, he made a significant decision: he left behind his Baptist upbringing and became a Roman Catholic.

When Hayes entered Columbia, the study of history there was dominated by James Harvey Robinson, leader of the "Columbia School" of historians and proponent of the "New History," essen-

[1] Hayes to Carter Jefferson, March 30, 1955.

[15]

tially a demand for new interpretations that would use the insights of the rapidly developing social sciences to explain historical events. Robinson was a medievalist and his own studies had led him to reinterpret the Reformation as "the Protestant Revolution." Hayes was strongly influenced by Robinson's views, particularly his views on the development of Protestantism. "My choice," he wrote, "was between complete skepticism and full, that is, Catholic Christian belief." [2] He chose Catholicism and, from then on, his religious attitudes increasingly influenced his life and works. His conversion did not alter his plans, however; he continued his studies under Robinson, becoming a lecturer at Columbia in 1907, and received the Ph.D. degree in 1909. He became an assistant professor in 1910, an associate in 1915, and a professor in 1919. He retired in 1950 and died in 1964.

Thus, Hayes began his career as a medievalist; he did not develop his interest in nationalism until the outbreak of the First World War. *An Introduction to the Sources Relating to the Germanic Invasions*, his dissertation, was to be his only monograph in medieval history.[3] It was well received and is still useful. His next book, *British Social Politics*, a collection of speeches and other sources relating to the social legislation passed under the aegis of the Liberal Government between 1905 and 1912, grew out of a suggestion made by Charles A. Beard, who was one of Hayes's slightly older colleagues at Columbia.[4] This book marked his entrance into the field of modern history, but it did not mean that he had forgotten his medieval studies. Later it became clear that his interest in modern social legislation stemmed at least partly from his fascination with the medieval economy. Guilds, the just price, and other aspects of medieval market activity fascinated him; untrammeled free enterprise did not. His editorial comments were quite unbiased but, by choosing the subject he did, he indicated that he was too interested in the problems of his own day to remain immersed in the more esoteric studies he had pursued in graduate school.

[2] *Ibid.*
[3] Hayes, *An Introduction to the Sources Relating to the Germanic Invasions* (New York, 1909).
[4] Hayes, *British Social Politics* (New York, 1913).

In his next work, his first textbook, A *Political and Social History of Modern Europe*,[5] Hayes began applying some of the lessons he had learned from Robinson and Beard. Simply to write a textbook was not then the commonplace move it is today, and to write a textbook that claimed to be a *social* history was to break new ground. Robinson had assured himself a place in American historiography by developing the New History, but Hayes was the first to publish a history of modern Europe that followed the new principles. Harry Elmer Barnes, one of the strongest proponents of social science principles on the historical scene, wrote that Hayes's book was "the first important [history] textbook to appropriate something of the sociological point of view."[6] Reviewers praised it, although one suggested that it really did not contain enough social history to merit its title.[7] A greatly expanded revision, issued in 1932 as A *Political and Cultural History of Modern Europe*,[8] went far toward invalidating that criticism because Hayes increased the "social" content considerably. For years it was one of the most widely used college history texts, and it is still in print, much revised by later collaborators. Hayes and Parker T. Moon, one of his earliest Ph.D. students and later a colleague at Columbia, carried the new technique to high schools in 1923 with their *Modern History*, and then wrote other high school textbooks in later years.[9]

The author's *Political and Social History*, published in 1916, had little to say about nationalism, but Hayes's interest in what became his life work had begun to develop. He had first discussed nationalism in a review article in the *Political Science Quarterly* in 1914. There he spoke of the growth of nationalism as one of the most impressive political and spiritual elements in the "old regime" of the nineteenth century. "Taking definite form in the

[5] Hayes, A *Political and Social History of Modern Europe* (2 vols.; New York, 1916).

[6] Barnes, *The New History and the Social Studies* (New York, 1925) 373n139.

[7] *Nation*, CIV (1917), 554.

[8] Hayes, A *Political and Cultural History of Modern Europe* (2 vols.; New York, 1932).

[9] Hayes and Moon, *Modern History* (New York, 1923); with John W. Wayland, *World History* (New York, 1932). All of Hayes's textbooks were published by the Macmillan Company.

days of the French Revolution under the fair name of Fraternity,"
he said, "it appeared as a revolt of a self-conscious people against
the tyranny or inefficiency of contemporaneous divine-right institutions." [10] Nationalism spread through Europe, often combined
with democratic tendencies, but in Germany it joined with militarism and imperialism and worked against parliamentary democracy. Science, particularly Darwin's evolutionary theory, was constantly misused in the cause of nationalism. Hayes blamed "the
intellectual class" for fashioning nationalist doctrines and "directing the events that have led straight to the present war." [11]

In 1914, judging by the article just quoted, Hayes was pro-
French and anti-German but not particularly warm toward the
English. Two years later, when President Wilson was facing the
necessity of somehow preserving American interests in the face of
German submarine attacks, Hayes proposed that the United States
declare an "Armed Neutrality" rather than enter the war.[12] But
Wilson chose otherwise; when war was declared, Hayes joined the
army and served two years as an intelligence officer with the General Staff.

Upon his discharge, Hayes returned immediately to Columbia.
In 1920 he published a meticulous military study entitled, A Brief
History of the Great War.[13] Preserved Smith, writing in the Nation, said that it "outclasses all rivals" and praised its objectivity,
although he detected a religious bias in the last few pages.[14] Hayes
opened the book with a full-scale attack on nationalism, called
"The General Cause: International Anarchy." This section of the
first chapter closely followed the argument of his 1914 article, except that it complicated matters by including a Hobsonoid discussion of imperialism as a contributor to the growth of nationalism.
Hayes also compared the international political anarchy to the
anarchy of domestic economics, discreetly reaffirming his distaste

[10] Hayes, "The War of the Nations," Political Science Quarterly, XXIX (1914),
687–88.
[11] Ibid., 702.
[12] Hayes, "Which? War without a Purpose? Or Armed Neutrality with a
Purpose?" Survey, XXXVII (1917), 535–38.
[13] Hayes, A Brief History of the Great War (New York, 1920).
[14] Smith, "A Photograph of the Great War," Nation, CXI (1920), 46.

for the market economy. This background chapter could, in fact, be used as a brief outline for his later work, A *Generation of Materialism*.[15] "Competition in big business," he wrote, "gave manner and tone to the whole age." [16] He blamed Germany for precipitating the war, not because of any flaw in the German national character, but because Germany was "the most perfect exemplar of nationalism, imperialism, and militarism, and therefore the most viciously anarchic in international relations" of all the Great Powers.[17] In his conclusion, which reviews the effects of the war, Hayes struck another note that was to be characteristic of all his future work. Among significant economic tendencies, he thought he saw "guild socialism" becoming increasingly popular as a means of ending economic anarchy.[18]

Hayes's support for guild socialism was evident not only in his history of the war, but was also reflected in Moon's Ph.D. thesis on *The Labor Problem and the Social Catholic Movement in France*, written under Hayes's direction and published in 1921. Guild socialists sought public ownership of industry, as did Marxists, but they likewise advocated worker control of production, as did syndicalists. As Moon pointed out, Social Catholics, particularly in France, had fought for several decades to replace laissez-faire capitalism with a system under which capitalists, technicians, and workers would share control of the industries in which they were active.[19] Numerous Social Catholics thought of guild socialists as allies. Although the Catholics opposed state ownership of industrial enterprises, the two programs otherwise were similar. Thus, compromise ought to be possible, especially in view of the great new threat of communism. In France, Germany, and Italy tentative steps toward the development of industrial guilds had taken place during the two years following the war, and in England guild socialists such as G. D. H. Cole, the eminent propagandist and historian, had gained considerable influence. A general reaction was to demolish guild socialism, along with most other

[15] Hayes, A Generation of Materialism (New York, 1941).
[16] Hayes, A Brief History, 1.   [17] Ibid., 7.   [18] Ibid., 467.
[19] Moon, The Labor Problem and the Social Catholic Movement in France (New York, 1921), 390-99.

movements for social reform, in the next few years, but in 1920 and early 1921 supporters of the new movement could still believe that they had at least a chance of success.

Hayes's support of guild socialism was a logical development. The American intellectual community was seething with opposition to capitalism: they held it responsible for the war, for poverty, and for political corruption. The Bolsheviks were immensely popular, and socialism of one kind or another seemed the only solution to many current ills. Hayes, however, was largely immune to this new surge of protest. Thanks to Robinson and Beard, he already had undergone his intellectual transformation: he had become an opponent of capitalism, but he had found his ideal society in the Middle Ages. His socialism was not Marxist, but Catholic. Yet, because he supported guild socialism and because he attacked nationalism, Hayes was accepted by most rebels among liberal intellectuals as part of the wave of the future. That acceptance lasted for nearly two decades.

The scattered ideas on nationalism that Hayes had first enunciated in his 1914 article and then developed in his history of the war became in 1926 the basis of his first major interpretive study. *Essays on Nationalism,*[20] short and provocative, is a devastating refutation of nationalist myths. What Hayes said has become common property; it is the content of everybody's freshman lecture on nationalism. He argued that neither economic rivalry nor man's pugnacious instincts (then being blamed for a number of unpleasant developments) really caused war: "Economic imperialism may create a situation favorable to war. The unrestrained combative instinct may make war possible. But war is not fought without idealism in the hearts of the masses and shibboleths on their lips." [21] The masses developed that idealism, he argued, because nationalism is a religion, intolerant, militaristic, all pervading. In his conclusion Hayes did not hesitate to tell his readers that nationalism as a belief "is evil and should be cursed—and cured." [22] He was willing to concede that nationalism has a certain value as a safeguard against individual selfishness and as an agent for the

[20] Hayes, *Essays on Nationalism* (New York, 1926).   [21] *Ibid.*, 128.
[22] *Ibid.*, 246.

preservation of desirable cultural variety, but he deplored it nevertheless: nationalism was in his eyes too exclusive. Further, it placed a premium on conformity, produced docility in the masses, and popularized war. He urged his readers to help mitigate nationalist sentiment, primarily by denationalizing education.[23]

Reviewers were pleased and Hayes became a figure of some importance to various antiwar and liberal circles. J. A. Hobson's favorable review in the *Nation* was a significant accolade.[24] His next work, *France: A Nation of Patriots*, reinforced his reputation both as student and enemy of nationalism.[25] In it Hayes carefully traced the agencies through which nationalism was planted in the minds of Frenchmen in the late 1920s. The French school system and its textbooks, the press, the system of military training, and the patriotic activities of churches and various other voluntary societies and pressure groups were analyzed to show exactly how the nationalist idealism of the masses was brought into being and nurtured.

Hayes's painstaking study of contemporary France was an excellent preparation for the writing of his most significant single book, *The Historical Evolution of Modern Nationalism*.[26] This essay, dealing not with popular attitudes or the propagation of nationalism but with nationalism "as a body of doctrine," was an attempt to trace the origins of modern nationalism by following its development in the works of significant thinkers.[27] In his first chapter Hayes contrasted the non-national entities of medieval Europe, the Empire and the body of Christendom, with the dynastic states that superseded them as the focus of men's loyalties after the Reformation. Dynastic states, he argued, were not nations in the modern sense: they lacked linguistic homogeneity, they included minority nationalities, and their interests excluded the idea of self-determination of peoples. Only in the eighteenth century did the modern idea of the nation begin to arise, and with it came "humanitarian nationalism." Such thinkers as Boling-

---

[23] *Ibid.*, 248–52, 258–59, 273–74.
[24] Hobson, "The Religion of the State," *Nation*, CXXIII (1926), 378.
[25] Hayes, *France: A Nation of Patriots* (New York, 1930).
[26] Hayes, *The Historical Evolution of Modern Nationalism* (New York, 1931).
[27] *Ibid.*, v.

broke, Rousseau, and Herder were important exponents of this doctrine, which stressed each nation's uniqueness and evinced a desire for the well-being of all of them. This humanitarian doctrine lacked the intolerance and exclusivism that was to become the mark of "Jacobin nationalism" during the wars of the French Revolution.

Hayes analyzed the writings of Barère and Carnot in order to delineate the major characteristics of Jacobin nationalism, attributing the attenuation of the humanitarian side of the doctrine to the fact that the French revolutionaries were under pressure from determined enemies. In the *cahiers* drawn up for presentation at the meeting of the Estates General in 1789, humanitarian nationalism was conspicuous. The federation movement of the early years of the Revolution was equally humanitarian: Frenchmen wanted to inspire other peoples to cast off their chains, but they were not interested in conquest. Only after the war began in 1792, and other nationalities began to develop nationalist ideas of their own, did humanitarian nationalism begin to disappear. Nationalism took on a new character: it became suspicious and intolerant, relying on force and militarism, and it developed all the zeal and trappings of a religion, including a missionary urge. Once that metamorphosis was complete, the basis for Bonapartism was laid.

Out of the upheavals of the revolutionary period came yet another doctrine—"traditional nationalism." Jacobin nationalism was revolutionary and secular; supporters of monarchy, aristocracy, and religion sought to develop a counternationalism to buttress the old regime. Here Hayes drew on the works of Burke, Bonald, and Schlegel to build a picture of traditional nationalism which he could contrast with the nationalism of the Jacobins. While Jacobin nationalism was based on natural rights, was democratic and revolutionary, and made the state the highest symbol of national loyalty, traditional nationalism was based on historic rights, supported aristocracy and evolutionary progress, and demanded loyalty to church as well as to state.

Neither Jacobin nor traditional nationalism met the needs of the triumphant middle class, however, so it followed that a new nationalist doctrine would arise among the English liberals. As in so many other areas, Jeremy Bentham took the lead in outlining the basis of the new "liberal nationalism." It was utilitarian, hence it ignored both natural and historic rights; it was evolutionary, but more progressive than traditional nationalism; it was bourgeois rather than democratic or aristocratic; it supported the absolute sovereignty of the national state, but limited the exercise of the sovereignty in order to preserve liberty. On the surface, it appeared to be a pacific version of nationalism, and some of its major exponents, Guizot for example, kept it so. It supported self-determination, however, and thereby opened the way for both civil and international war. Mazzini, among others, could hardly forego struggle if he wished to free Italy, and the sympathy of independent nations for "oppressed peoples" led them into wars for national independence.

These nineteenth century doctrines were replaced, Hayes argued, by the bellicose attitude that Charles Maurras, its foremost apostle, dubbed "integral nationalism." He quoted Maurras' definition of integral nationalism: "the exclusive pursuit of national policies, the absolute maintenance of national integrity, and the steady increase of national power—for a nation declines when it loses its military might." [28] Hayes traced the rise of this doctrine from Comte's materialist philosophy through Taine's utilitarian apology for Catholicism and Barrès' racial theories.

Hayes argued that nationalist doctrines carried all before them because the Industrial Revolution succeeded in changing the face of civilization. Because markets are worldwide, he suggested, modern economic life ought to be cosmopolitan but, in fact, the differing speeds at which nations industrialized led to national controls over economic life. Liberal economists, who should have been antinationalist, supported wars that would benefit their economies. Socialism, internationally oriented, failed as an international movement and won all its success within the framework of national states; in the end, it promoted nationalism. Christian socialists, perhaps motivated by economic conservatism, had little success. In summary, he argued that the Industrial Revolution was of itself neither nationalist nor cosmopolitan, but that the ideas of sup-

[28] *Ibid.*, 165.

porters of national economics such as List and Rodbertus could be used effectively by nationalist politicians. Taken together, nationalist politics and nationalist economics resulted in integral nationalism.

Finally, Hayes said that nationalism could not be explained simply as the expression of an instinct of the masses, as the result of modern economic trends, or even as a corollary of democracy. He believed that the decline of religion produced a void that nationalism had filled, and that most men had decided that the national state is "the medium through which civilization is best assured and advanced." [29] He ended his book with a pessimistic dismissal of the possibility that "the will to peace," apparently so strong at the time he was writing, could prevent war. Only international education—as opposed to the nationalist education prevalent everywhere —could bring a halt to the development of integral nationalism and the wars it produces. "It is for thoughtful Americans, *par excellence*, to turn their attention to schools, publications, and societies within the United States and to endeavor to make them agencies of a nationalism that shall be humanitarian and truly enlightened." [30]

His chronological classification of types of nationalism has won Hayes the plaudits of later scholars.[31] Obviously, his presentation has flaws. The significance of his "traditional nationalism," except perhaps in England, is difficult to accept; it obscures the extreme antinationalist position that was for several decades so characteristic of conservative continental opponents of the French Revolution. Hans Kohn's specific division between the nationalism of western Europe, which grew from indigenous roots, and that of central and eastern Europe, which developed as a reaction, is more sophisticated. Much can be said, too, against Hayes's interpretation of the economic foundations of nationalism or of the relation between liberalism and imperialism. Nevertheless, what mattered was that Hayes was breaking new ground: he was the first American to make nationalism an object of widespread and serious study. That was an important accomplishment.

[29] *Ibid.*, 302.   [30] *Ibid.*, 321.
[31] See, for example, Louis L. Snyder, *The Meaning of Nationalism* (New Brunswick, 1954), 115–17.

One other characteristic of these books on nationalism should be mentioned, for it was part of Hayes's personal style and is noticeable in almost everything he wrote after 1920—that is his tendency toward unnecessary aggressiveness, sometimes couched in language that fell below usual literary standards and occasionally approached the vulgar. When, for example, he discussed one rival interpretation of the development of nationalism, he did not simply question its validity; instead, he wrote, "All of which may be true, and all which may be buncombe." [32] His *Essays on Nationalism* are heavily freighted with such flippant expressions. In his later years he apparently recognized this fault, for in his last book, *Nationalism: A Religion*,[33] long passages based on earlier works are toned down considerably. Long before he was willing to temper his language, however, his predilection for the blunt statement got him into difficulties.

The *Political and Social History* of 1916 was relatively free of such harshness, but by 1923, when his high school *Modern History* appeared, it was in full flower. If anyone noticed, nobody commented publicly until 1930, when *Modern History* suddenly became notorious. In the spring of that year an Episcopal clergyman complained to the New York Board of School Superintendents that *Modern History* supported "some visionary scheme of internationalism" and that it tended to break down "respect for political democracy, patriotism, and everything that pertains to nationalism." He also described the book as "out and out propaganda" for the Roman Catholic Church.[34] The board quietly dropped the book from the approved list but Hayes publicly denied the charges. A second cleric, this one a professor of religion at St. Stephen's College of Columbia University, said that the passages in question were "truisms." A school official then complicated the controversy by explaining that the book had been dropped not because of the religious or political views it pro-

---

[32] Hayes, *Essays on Nationalism* (New York, 1926), 261.
[33] Hayes, *Nationalism: A Religion* (New York, 1960).
[34] *New York Times*, May 2, 1930, sec. 1, p. 1; for the rest of this story, see the *Times* for May 3, sec. 1, p. 11; May 4, sec. 1, p. 21; May 6, sec. 1, p. 27; May 7, sec. 1, p. 30. The Reverend Lefferd M. A. Haughwout of Staten Island was the priest whose objections started the argument; the Reverend Dr. Bernard Iddings Bell was the professor who defended Hayes.

pounded, but because of its objectionable statements concerning the American economic system.

Hayes and Moon, while protesting, decided to revise the book. Some of the passages revised illuminate the nature of the authors' sins:

Old: Calvin was . . . [Geneva's] religious oracle and political "boss." (p. 110)
Revised: Calvin was . . . [Geneva's] religious and political leader.

Old: . . . the spirit of national patriotism was everywhere broadened and deepened. It went so far as to produce in the twentieth century the bloodiest war in the whole recorded history of mankind. (p. 113)
Revised: . . . the spirit of national patriotism was everywhere broadened and deepened.

Old: Political democracy is only a fairly recent experiment, and if the experiment does not work well, it will probably be abandoned, as other institutions have been abandoned. (p. 145)
Revised: Political democracy is a comparatively recent experiment.

Old: For an aristocracy of titles we have substituted an aristocracy of capital. (p. 823)
Revised: Besides, fear has been expressed that a new aristocracy of wealth threatens to take the place of the old aristocracy of birth.[35]

One passage that apparently was not outrageous enough to merit notice in the *Times* is worth quoting as an example of Hayes's continuing devotion to medieval economic forms. In the *Political and Social History of Modern Europe* he blamed the deterioration of the guild system primarily on "various internal diseases" that sapped the guilds' vitality.[36] Seven years later, in *Modern History*, the guild system—"probably a nearer approach to social and industrial democracy than the world has ever known before or since" —was depicted as "slowly crumbling away" because of the competition it faced from the domestic system and the new capitalism.[37]

[35] Revised passages cited from *Modern History*, rev. ed. (New York, 1930). About forty controversial passages were altered, among them all of those that the *Times* had reported as the subjects of complaints.
[36] Hayes, *A Political and Social History of Modern Europe*, I, 41.
[37] Hayes and Moon, *Modern History* (1923 edition), 35, 73.

Hayes's new and expanded edition of the *Political and Social History* appeared as *A Political and Cultural History of Europe* two years after the *Modern History* revisions had been made. Its tone was noticeably milder than that of other works Hayes was then completing. The *New Republic*, no friend of Catholic propaganda, said it was written with "complete impartiality." [38] That was perhaps a little strong because enthusiasts of laissez-faire undoubtedly found it a little too leftist in outlook.

By the late 1930s, despite his problems with the school board, Hayes had built a solid reputation as an historian. His invitation to join the authors writing volumes in the highly regarded *Rise of Modern Europe* series was a form of recognition; and his contribution to that series, *A Generation of Materialism, 1871–1900*, gave him an excellent opportunity to express the view of history he had developed over his long career. The central theme of the book was the emergence of what Hayes called "sectarian liberalism"—a "much more narrowly urban and bourgeois" political philosophy than the "ecumenical liberalism" of an earlier day. That older liberalism, he said, was actuated by a desire to free and dignify the individual; it was supported by every social class, by nobility, clergy, bourgeoisie, peasantry, and proletariat. Of sectarian liberalism, he wrote that it placed its primary stress upon economic liberty; therefore, it demanded free trade, opposed labor associations insofar as they might interfere with freedom of contract, and fought any governmental restriction on commerce or industry. It still favored old libertarian ideas such as freedom of thought and speech, but it placed too much emphasis on the liberating blessings of technology, science, and secular popular education. "Its horror of possible ecclesiastical dictation was prodigious." And it was afflicted with a "curious kind of nationalism." [39] The liberals dug their own graves, he said, by building the nationalism that came to overshadow their own individual interests and by fostering an industrialism that produced huge corporations and labor unions. He continued: "But what clinched the fate of the Liberal parties was the emergence of the masses, and to this the Liberals themselves contributed by espousing political democracy, by legal-

[38] *New Republic*, LXXIII (1932), 80.
[39] Hayes, *A Generation of Materialism*, 49–50.

izing trade-unions and co-operative societies, and most momen-
tously, by fostering that secular national education which by the
'80's was rendering almost everybody in central and western Europe
literate and peculiarly amenable to journalistic propaganda." [40]
The clergy looked better to Hayes than it has to some other historians; the liberals looked worse.

There was also a kind of semiobscurantist, antiscientific thread
running through this book, particularly showing in the attacks upon
Darwin. Hayes assailed Darwin's theory of the inheritance of acquired characteristics and glossed over vastly more significant aspects of Darwin's discoveries, such as the action of natural selection, which have survived the criticism of later scientists. [41]

Liberals were offended. But the particular facets of Hayes's
thought that offended them were merely more obvious in this
book than in his previous works—they were by no means new. In
teaching and writing about modern European history, Hayes had
always measured modern life against the medieval model he had
constructed during his apprenticeship under Robinson. Though
he was not blind to the less pleasant aspects of life in the Middle
Ages, he seemed to see the Reformation as a catastrophe because
it destroyed the unity of Christendom. He had listened to Robinson and read Max Weber, *parti pris*, and had come to believe that
a remarkably innocent society was ruined when its fledgling capitalists flocked to the Protestant standard because Calvin approved
of usury. He looked at modern life, called it materialistic, and attacked nationalism as its characteristic heresy. From this viewpoint,
it followed that secular schools were incubators for nationalists
and precious little else. Unlike the great majority of liberals of the
1930s, who put their trust in improvement of the schools, Hayes
had concluded that improvement was impossible.

Like other liberals, he deplored nationalism and war, but he
held liberalism accountable for both. Like other liberals, he attacked capitalism, but unlike them he opposed it on religious
grounds. There, perhaps, lay the problem; this was Hayes's first

[40] *Ibid.*, 196–97.
[41] This was not a new idea for Hayes; see, for example, *Essays in Nationalism*,
105.

real "Catholic" book.[42] His bias was not the crude, warped view espoused by the mass of poor, ill-educated Catholics of his day, for he belonged to a different tradition. In Europe he would hardly have attracted attention, for liberal Catholics had long flourished there, despite frequent setbacks. In the United States, however, he was a rare kind of Catholic, for at that time the liberal, intellectual Catholic tradition had only begun to develop. Hayes was, in fact, one of the men who helped to build it. An educated convert from an old patrician family, he had moved up rapidly in Catholic intellectual circles. It just happened that during the years of his rise, the attitudes of those circles partly coincided with those of the secular liberal milieu. By 1940 the fact that in reality they diverged significantly was once more becoming obvious.

Hayes had begun to take his position as a Catholic intellectual seriously almost as soon as he was converted. One of his earliest articles, written in 1912, was a calm criticism of a violent pamphlet attack launched against the eleventh edition of the *Encyclopedia Britannica* by the New York County Federation of Catholic Societies.[43] The federation had accused the *Britannica* of perpetuating "ignorance, bigotry and fanaticism in matters of religion," backing its charge by citing numerous cases of alleged unscholarly practices. It had questioned, among other things, the accuracy of a statement describing the harshness of monastic rules in the days of Charlemagne, certain remarks about the church's use of the Donation of Constantine, and an author's use of the term "Dark Ages." Hayes pointed out that in these cases, the *Britannica*, not the federation, was correct and went on to urge his fellow Catholics to be more careful of their own scholarship when they were attacking that of others. But he also suggested that the federation was not entirely wrong because, he believed, the editors of the *Britannica* indeed had libeled Catholicism in some cases, particularly in some of the articles carried over from earlier editions. He urged the publishers to obtain more advice from Catholic sources on religious matters.

[42] See, for example, the review by Franklin C. Palm, *American Historical Review*, XLVII (1942), 852–54.
[43] Hayes, "The Encyclopedia Britannica and Catholicism," *Independent*, LXXII (Jan.–June, 1912), 22–25.

Other articles on Catholic subjects and in Catholic publications followed. Hayes wrote numerous book reviews for the *Catholic Historical Review* and was an occasional contributor to *Commonweal*, the leading American liberal Catholic journal. He also served in other ways: in 1919 he was chosen to be the first secretary of the Catholic Historical Association and in 1931 he was elected its president.[44] As a Catholic layman, he was cochairman of the National Conference of Christians and Jews from 1925 to 1945, and he cooperated in the writing and editing of a book promoting religious toleration.[45] Thus it is clear that although he was surely a liberal of a sort, he was not a "sectarian liberal" in the sense in which he used the term in his works.

Hayes's split with the secular liberals was already in the making when *A Generation of Materialism* appeared, for he could not accept popular liberal attitudes toward the Spanish Civil War. He had demonstrated his opposition to Franco in 1937 by resigning from the editorial council of the pro-Franco *Commonweal*. However, he had signed a Catholic protest against certain statements published in the United States that apparently condoned the killing of priests by partisans of the Republic.[46] His position was not really ambiguous but neither was it easy to maintain.

Because Hayes was a "moderate" on the Spanish question, he was an eminently logical candidate for the post of United States ambassador to Spain during the tense days of 1942. President Roosevelt, compelled for strategic reasons to treat Franco with consideration and under pressure from many of his own supporters to treat him with contempt, obviously appointed Hayes his ambassador in order to try to escape from his dilemma. The choice was generally praised, but American enemies of Franco soon found fault with Hayes, who persisted—in accordance with his instructions—in trying to promote amity between the Spanish government and his own. He argued that his main function was to keep Spain from joining the Axis powers against the United States and Britain. His critics claimed, however, that by the time he arrived

[44] Obituary, *Catholic Historical Review*, L (1965), 677–79.
[45] Hayes, Roger W. Strauss, and Newton D. Baker (eds.), *The American Way* (New York, 1936).
[46] Hayes, *Wartime Mission in Spain, 1942–1945* (New York, 1945), 5n1.

in Spain that danger was past, and they argued that his generally pleasant relations with Franco's government only served to buttress an odious and shaky regime.[47] Short of a careful examination of General Franco's private files, which is currently not feasible, little of significance can be done to settle the dispute. Whatever may be the truth of the matter, Hayes's attitude toward the Franco regime ruined what was left of his reputation as a liberal. In his memoir, *Wartime Mission in Spain*, he asserted that Franco's government was not fascist in the sense that Hitler's was—a reasonable statement—but that it "has been more in the nature of a military dictatorship traditionally to Spanish-speaking people." [48] Dogmatic liberals would not accept that. In his later work, *The United States and Spain: An Interpretation*, Hayes argued that the republican government was under the control of Communists during the Civil War and that a republican victory would have given Russia a new satellite.[49] Such a position is tenable, but its rejection has been in the United States a touchstone of liberalism.

Criticisms of Hayes were so strong and feeling against Franco was running so high in this country that even the usually quiet business of the historical establishment just missed becoming involved in what undoubtedly would have been a major scandal. Hayes was chosen by the nominating committee of the American Historical Association as its candidate for the presidency of the association for 1945. It was an unexceptionable choice. Hayes had headed the European history section of the A.H.A. committee on the planning of research in 1931, and he was certainly as highly reputed as many of the association's presidents before and since. Moreover, he was first vice-president during the year prior to his nomination and the normal procedure was to move officers up the ladder of dignity. Nevertheless, a group of association members tried to prevent Hayes's election by nominating Sidney B. Fay, an equally eminent historian, from the floor. Fay, the nominating

[47] See, for example, T. J. Hamilton, "Hayes Tells All," *Nation*, CLXI (1945), 692–94; and Percy Winner, "Special Pleader," *New Republic*, CXIII (1945), 718–20.

[48] Hayes, *Wartime Mission*, 103.

[49] Hayes, *The United States and Spain: An Interpretation* (New York, 1951), 121.

committee's candidate for vice-president, hotly refused to run, but the election was held despite his attempt to withdraw. Hayes won, 110–56.[50]

The whole Spanish episode obviously hurt Hayes's reputation, and it probably hurt his feelings just as badly. Even before he went to Spain, Hayes was sensitive to anti-Catholic attitudes; he remarked feelingly about them to his classes.[51] His conduct in the battle over *Modern History* showed that he reacted strongly to criticism. Obviously some part of the agitation against him was simply anti-Catholicism in action, but liberals who were not anti-Catholic could also be bitter about his support for Franco. Hayes's Catholicism, plus his rosy picture of the medieval social structure, certainly made him more sympathetic to Franco than the average militant supporter of American-style liberalism, not to mention the Marxists. Still, a supporter of Americanism for Americans should be able to look kindly on a different system in a foreign state without being classed as a traitor to his principles. Numerous unsophisticated partisans of Stalin have been forgiven, and Hayes was less naïve than many of them were; he was certainly no friend of Serrano Suñer and his Falangist gangs. Pragmatists of the 1960s ought to be less dogmatic than Hayes's critics of 1945, but whatever one may conclude now, there is no doubt that his defense of Franco marred Hayes's later years.

Hayes ended more than four decades of teaching when he retired in 1950 at the age of sixty-eight. A generation of students had heard him give lectures so dramatic that he acquired almost an actor's renown. One admiring listener has called Hayes "a great teacher of undergraduates at a time when Columbia College was enjoying a Golden Age." [52] Hayes was equally at home with graduate students, directing "some sixty or seventy" doctoral dissertations during his tenure at Columbia.[53]

To Hayes, retirement did not mean disappearance. He continued to divide his time between the family home in Afton and his New York apartment, near the Columbia University

[50] *American Historical Review*, L (1945), 695.   [51] Author information.
[52] Edward Meade Earle, preface to Earle (ed.) *Nationalism and Internationalism: Essays Inscribed to Carlton J. H. Hayes* (New York, 1950), xii.
[53] Hayes, *Nationalism: A Religion*, v.

library.[54] He had the energy to write two more books, one a general statement of his philosophy of history, the other the short summary of his work on nationalism that was mentioned earlier.

Christianity and Western Civilization, published in 1954, was both credo and sermon. In it Hayes argued that Christianity, or at least the Judaeo-Greco-Christian ethical system, is the foundation of Western Civilization and must be preserved if that civilization is to live:

> Being a historian and not a prophet or soothsayer, I make no pretense of knowing what the future holds in store for us. . . . I unblushingly persist in believing that our Western Civilization has long been and still is a great liberal and progressive civilization— the greatest that the world has ever produced—and that, having survived other troubled ages, it is likely to survive the present one.
>
> This depends primarily, it seems to me, on whether our civilization retains its association with, and continues to draw inspiration from, the historic religion of the West, or whether, by substituting new gods for old, it is subverted and transformed.[55]

He said also: "Personally, I must confess a conviction, derived not only from faith but from historical study, that wherever Christian ideals have been generally accepted and their practice sincerely attempted, there is a dynamic liberty; and that wherever Christianity has been ignored or rejected, persecuted or chained to the state, there is tyranny." [56]

Nationalism: A Religion added little to what Hayes had written before on the subject. Much of it was taken from his earlier works, polished, and used again. The tone still has in it a little of the old pugnacious Hayes, but generally the book is much more calmly written than were the efforts of his early maturity. One point he insisted upon: he refused to accept the suggestion that nationality and nationalism can be separated from linguistic homogeneity.[57] His remarks on the new nationalism in Africa and Asia were no more than a logical extension of statements made thirty years before, but they still seem fresh and provocative.

[54] Hayes to Jefferson, March 30, 1955.
[55] Hayes, *Christianity and Western Civilization* (Stanford, 1954), 1–2.
[56] *Ibid.*, 21.   [57] Hayes, *Nationalism: A Religion*, vi–vii.

He had little faith in the longevity of multilingual nations such as India and the various artificially contrived African states. "When we recall that it has taken a century and a half and a succession of deadly wars to redraw the political map of Europe along approximate lines of linguistic nationality," he write, "we may well wonder how long and what human holocausts it will take really to nationalize the far more extensive and complex continents of Asia and Africa." [58]

Hayes died in 1964, after he had made a significant contribution to his profession. He was a pioneer, the outstanding American worker in his chosen area for more than a decade. His textbooks reached thousands of students, many of whom read no further in history; his essays on nationalism reached dozens of scholars who have gone on to become more knowledgeable about nationalism than he was. His was an honorable career. But to suggest that his work is comparable to that of Friedrich Meinecke, as has been done, is to be mistaken.[59] Others rapidly surpassed his knowledge of nationalism; despite his interest in "social" history, he never digested much of the vast amount of anthropological work done in his field since 1930. His works are rapidly being superseded, although his scheme of classification of nationalisms by period and type has been assimilated into the literature of the subject. Hayes's place in the annals of the world's historians is secure but he does not belong among the great.

His bias and his aggressiveness will be forgotten, but they strongly influenced the development of his career. During the years between the wars, when Hayes was building his reputation, history in American was a liberal Protestant preserve. Historians could, and did, preach objectivity and detachment, particularly in religious matters, because the essentially secular view they embraced looked to them like a cool and rational reconstruction of history as it really was. Yet Hayes was able to impose himself and his militant Catholicism on them because World War I and its aftermath had opened the way to attacks on the American *status*

[58] *Ibid.*, 163; cf. Hayes, *The Historical Evolution of Modern Nationalism*, 309.
[59] Earle, *Nationalism and Internationalism*, xiv.

quo. For a long time, Hayes's religion looked like a mere eccentricity; when he made scorching attacks on nationalism and capitalism, he seemed simply to be another of the young liberals who was flailing away at reaction—and to do that was to be "objective." But times change; and Hayes wrote more provocatively as he grew older. In the late 1930s, when religious issues once more became important, Hayes's colleagues finally realized that religion was the key to his whole outlook. Some of them took the first opportunity to denounce him publicly; others preferred to exhibit a faint embarrassment in their reviews of his books. Many refused to acknowledge any chagrin but Hayes somehow was no longer really accepted as part of the "establishment." His last years could hardly have been pleasant.

It seems likely that in this case religious zeal and pugnacity reinforced the drive that produced so much. On many subjects, for many years, Hayes's attitudes coincided with those of his liberal colleagues, and thus it was possible for him to build, at least temporarily, a reputation perhaps somewhat greater than his work merited. It was a simple misunderstanding. That, however, is an irony to be savored, not deplored.

OSCAR HALECKI

KENNETH F. LEWALSKI
Rhode Island College

THE CHANGE which has taken place in Oscar Halecki's historical perspective, interest, and emphasis since he began his career more than fifty years ago serves as a reminder that the consciousness of the historian is significantly determined by his experience and that his fate is closely enmeshed with the historical process. In a career overshadowed by war, disrupted by exile, saddened by permanent separation from his colleagues and his nation, and complicated by isolation from the original sources of Polish history, little stability prevailed. Only his irrepressible optimism and his firm commitment to the profession of historian have remained constant.

From 1891—the year of his birth—to the present, circumstances and sometimes accident conditioned Oscar Halecki's career and thought. His broad range of interest, extraordinary linguistic facility, and wide perspective are the result of an unusual cosmopolitan orientation from the beginning of his life. Son of a Polish officer serving in the Austrian army, he was born in Vienna and received his early education there. In 1909 he went to Cracow and enrolled at the Jagiellonian University, where he completed his doctoral training in medieval and Renaissance history one year before World War I began. This war did not greatly disrupt his career; in Warsaw he served briefly as a research assistant to Bronislaw Dembiński, the dean of prewar Polish historians, and obtained a teaching position in 1915 as a docent at his alma mater. As the war drew to a close, he was appointed to a chair of East European history at the newly reorganized University of Warsaw.

The first disruption in his career came after the Armistice was signed when he consented to become secretary-general of the committee of consultants attached to the Polish delegation at the Paris peace conference.

This disruption in Halecki's academic career was to last for an entire decade. For most of this time he was associated with several international agencies of the League of Nations: as secretary of the Committee on Intellectual Cooperation at Geneva from 1921 to 1924 and as director of the university section of the Institute of Intellectual Cooperation at Paris from 1925 to 1926. However, he did not sever his professional ties or abandon scholarly interests during this period; he wrote a large number of articles, lectured extensively in Europe, and delivered numerous papers at professional meetings. After this ten-year absence, he returned to his professorship at the University of Warsaw. Halecki's professional prospects and his reputation in both Poland and in Europe were never higher than in this interwar period. In 1935 he celebrated his twenty-fifth anniversary as a scholar and was presented with a *Festschrift* paying tribute to his brilliant record of publication and his distinction as a representative of Polish historiography abroad.[1] Unfortunately, the advent of World War II aborted his career and radically changed his professional and private life.

When the invasion of Poland occurred, Halecki was attending a conference of Catholic intellectuals in Fribourg. Naturally, he did not return to Poland and in fact never has. He took refuge in Paris where he organized a Polish University in exile, edited an emigré periodical, *La Voix de Varsovie*, and served briefly as a professor at the Sorbonne. After the Nazi invasion of France, he came to the United States under the auspices of the Kosciuszko Foundation. The outcome of the war in eastern Europe shattered his political expectations and professional plans. Unwilling to return to Communist Poland, he reconciled himself to teaching permanently in America—as a professor of East European history at

---

[1] *Księga ku czci Oskara Haleckiego wydana w XV-lecie jego pracy naukowej* (Warsaw, 1935), 1–22, gives a complete bibliography of his publications (262) and his lectures (55) delivered abroad from 1909–34. A selected bibliography of his writing down to 1958 appears in *Teki Historyczne*, IX (1958), 96–99. Since then he has published two books and more than twelve scholarly articles.

Fordham University, with an adjunct appointment at Columbia University. In 1947 he became a naturalized United States citizen. It was only to be expected that these vicissitudes of public service and exile would profoundly affect Halecki's thought and writing. What is remarkable is that he has produced a substantial body of scholarly literature on Polish and European history. His early writings on Jagiellonian Poland possess the greatest amount of unity and scholarly originality. Between 1920 and 1950, as a result of the new interests and perspectives he acquired, he wrote on a great variety of topics. Since 1950 he has defined his objectives more sharply and has concentrated on ecclesiastical research and the philosophic interpretation of history.

Halecki's initial interest was exclusively in Polish medieval and Renaissance history. In 1915, two years after he completed his doctorate, he made a sensational scholarly debut by publishing simultaneously three monographs totalling almost a thousand pages. Within the next five years he finished his major work, the two-volume *History of the Jagiellonian Union*.[2] In addition, he had written more than twenty articles on medieval and Renaissance topics by 1920. He attributed this phenomenal productivity to the rigorous methodological training he received at the Jagiellonian University, the stimulation he derived from study and association with some of the most eminent historians in prewar Poland, the access to source materials in his field, and the vast opportunities to publish at one of three flourishing historical centers—Cracow, Warsaw, and Lwow. In spite of the war, Halecki noted, he was entirely free from political distraction and involvement.[3]

Two of his mentors, Wacław Sobieski and Stanisław Krzyżanowski, strongly influenced Halecki's decision to specialize in the Jagiellonian period and also determined many of his views. His basic orientation to Polish history, which he has often described as "historical optimism," was derived from the revisionary spirit among Cracow historians, after the turn of the century, which was

---

[2] *Halecki, Dzieje Unii Jagiellońskiej* (2 vols.; Cracow, 1919–20).
[3] See his brief autobiographical sketch in *The Book of Catholic Authors*, edited by W. Romig (3d ser.; Grosse Pointe, 1945), 157–63. In several letters to me he has provided additional information and clarified specific details.

directed toward placing a more positive construction on Polish history than that which prevailed in nineteenth century historiography. According to Halecki, the dismemberment of Poland had seriously distorted the perspective on the entire course of Polish history. After the partitions, he argued, European historians had arbitrarily excluded Poland from Europe and denied it a legitimate place in historiography. He frequently referred to Ranke's identification of Europe with the Romance and Germanic nations as an illustration of this tendency.[4] As a result, Poland's past was either completely ignored or treated negatively in the light of the collapse of the Polish Commonwealth in the eighteenth century. For Halecki, the fundamental issue was whether the Jagiellonian Commonwealth distintegrated or whether it was partitioned out of existence. He lamented, but did not find it surprising, that German and Russian historiography, rationalizing the political motives of the partitioning powers, emphasized the intrinsic weakness of the commonwealth and regarded its collapse as natural and inevitable. But he was greatly distressed that the historiography of the Old Cracow School, which dominated Polish thought from 1870 to 1900, was similarly negative in its interpretation of the Jagiellonian Commonwealth. He attributed this fact to the influence exerted by the founder and titular head of the school, Michał Bobrzyński.[5]

Modern Polish historiography could not grow in the auspicious climate of political success and optimism that was provided in Jacksonian America, Bismarckian Germany, or Victorian England. It had originated, Halecki pointed out, amidst the failure of the 1863 uprising and after the creation of the German Empire and the Dual Monarchy confirmed the partitions anew. Michał Bobrzyński reflected this political disillusionment and the scholarly disenchantment with the historiographical tradition of Joachim Lelewel which had idealized Poland's past and interpreted it in terms of nineteenth century liberal ideas. For Halecki, Bobrzyński's

[4] Halecki, *The Limits and Divisions of European History* (New York, 1950), 90; *The Millennium of Europe* (South Bend, 1963), 347.

[5] In "Problems of Polish Historiography," *Slavonic and East European Review,* XXI (1943), 226–33, he discusses the various historical schools and his attitude toward Bobrzyński. See Józef Dutkiewicz and Krystyna Śreniówska, *Zarys historii Historiografii Polskiej: 1900–1939* (Lodz, 1959), 105–108 and 161–66 for a comparison of the historiography of the Old and New Cracow Schools.

Outline of Polish History was a virtual condemnation of the entire course of Poland's development.[6] The dismemberment of Poland was seen as an inevitable consequence of the absence of strong monarchical leadership and of *szlachta* parliamentarianism; external pressures and foreign intervention which culminated in the eighteenth century partitions were greatly minimized. The end of Poland was regarded to have been inevitable as early as the sixteenth century when the Jagiellonian Commonwealth came into existence.

The New Cracow School rejected Bobrzyński's interpretation as an outgrowth of his monarchical political bias and as a distortion of historical facts. They insisted that the decline of Poland was not inevitable but rather that it resulted primarily from misrule in the Saxon period and from foreign intervention in the eighteenth century. Maintaining that Bobrzyński's focus upon the partition issue had abridged the entire course of Polish history and had created an astigmatism which prejudiced the study of the early period, the New Cracow historians sought to examine the medieval and Renaissance periods in their own contexts. These stressed the political and cultural achievements of the Jagiellonian "golden age" and emphasized Poland's liberal and democratic institutional development. Halecki inherited these attitudes and identified himself with the "optimists" of the New Cracow School. His particular interest was the structure of the Jagiellonian Commonwealth and its evolution down to the end of the sixteenth century.

Three highly technical monographs published by Halecki in 1915 analyzed some of the specific problems which confronted the Polish Commonwealth. The first of these dealt with the internecine conflict within the Jagiello dynasty and its collateral Swidrygiello branch over the succession to the Grand Duchy of Lithuania and the allegiance of Volhynia; this conflict plunged the two states into civil war in 1432, brought about the intervention of the Teutonic Knights, and threatened to destroy the Polish-Lithuanian union.[7] At the expense of seven years of strife, the

[6] Bobrzyński, *Dzieje Polski w zarysie* (2 vols.; Cracow, 1877–78).

[7] Halecki, *Ostatnie lata Świdrygiełły i sprawa wołyńska za Kazimierza Jagiellończyka* (Cracow, 1915).

issue was temporarily resolved by Casimir Jagiello who became Grand Duke of Lithuania, thereby not only preserving the union but also strengthening the relationship of its multiple parts by reaching new constitutional agreements. Halecki's second mono-graph showed the practical and logical reasons why Podlasia, Volhynia, and Ukrainia—long associated with Lithuania—chose to become part of the Jagiellonian Commonwealth in 1569 rather than risk absorption by Russia.[8] *The Consensus of Sandomierz in 1570* explored an entirely different topic, namely the efforts among Polish Lutherans, Calvinists, and Czech Brethren to reach a com-mon doctrinal agreement in order to forestall counter-Refor-mation pressures.[9] In this book, the first examination of the subject since 1731 and his initial work in ecclesiastical history, Halecki showed that although these efforts did not produce a single con-fession of faith, they did result in a *modus vivendi* among Protes-tants and an agreement to act in political concert. The consti-tutional guarantee of religious liberty by the Polish Diet in 1573 abated Protestant fears and established the most enlightened re-ligious policy in sixteenth century Europe.

The culmination of a decade of intense and thorough research, Halecki's *History of the Jagiellonian Union* was a synthesis of his earlier writings and the accumulated scholarship of his predecessors and contemporaries on the Jagiellonian era.[10] In this sense it was a definitive study. The first volume traced the evolution of the Polish-Lithuanian union from its inception in the Act of Krewo (1385) to the sixteenth century. The charter of Krewo, which proved difficult to interpret even after the marriage between Ladislas Jagiello of Lithuania and Queen Jadwiga of Poland, needed to be revised. But the conversion of Lithuania to Catholi-cism, the adoption of the Polish language and customs by the Lithuanian nobility, and the common interest of the two states in resisting the territorial expansion of their neighbors provided a more substantial basis for the agreement at Horodlo in 1413, which

[8] Halecki, *Przyłączenie Podlasia, Wołynia i Kijowszczyzny do Korony w r. 1569* (Cracow, 1915).

[9] Halecki, *Zgoda sandomierska, 1570* (Warsaw, 1915).

[10] In place of a traditional bibliography he wrote two essays on his sources (*Dzieje Unii Jagiellońskiej*, I, xv–xvi, and II, 354–63).

set forth the principles that guided the federation throughout its existence. Periodic disruptions of the union occurred in the fifteenth century, Halecki noted, but the frequent renewals of the union illustrated that Polish and Lithuanian interests remained closely interwined. The second volume was devoted to the separatist disputes which jeopardized the formation of a permanent and stable federation. Half of this volume treated the negotiation, ratification, and implementation of the Union of Lublin in 1569 which provided the Polish Commonwealth with a single sovereign and a consolidated diet. However, the principle of separate administrative institutions for the two states was preserved. For Halecki the chief significance of the Jagiellonian Commonwealth was precisely this—that it was a federation and not a unitary state. The simultaneous incorporation of Lithuania's three dependent principalities gave the Commonwealth a multinational and a pluralistic religious character.

Monumentally conceived and constructed, Halecki's *History* wove into his analysis of these federative negotiations a synopsis of Poland's internal development, military reforms, and foreign relations with Prussia and Russia, as well as an examination of Habsburg policy in eastern Europe. Throughout these volumes he stressed the advantages of the union for both Poland and Lithuania in resisting the expansion of the Teutonic Knights, the Duchy of Muscovy, and the Tartars. Religious and cultural factors, though subordinated to the constitutional focus of the work, were shown to be relevant and operative in binding them together. Halecki's main argument was that Polish policy was based on negotiation and on the principle of voluntarism rather than on conquest or aggression, and that the various constitutional agreements consistently guaranteed local autonomy and cultural pluralism to the Lithuanian principalities and legal rights for the Orthodox Christians. In the concluding section—refuting Michał Bobrzyński's negative verdict—he defended Jagiellonian statecraft and paid special tribute to the political ability of Sigismund Augustus. He emphasized that the commonwealth endured for two centuries without internal disruption and that it not only survived but grew stronger in the face of Swedish, Russian, and Turkish interventions in the seventeenth century. Finally, he contended that the Polish Commonwealth still possessed renovative vitality in the eighteenth century as evidenced by the reform movements during the Enlightenment and the Constitution of the Third of May.

Halecki has not altered his interpretation of Jagiellonian Poland throughout his career. In subsequent books and articles, however, he enlarged upon some aspects of Jagiellonian diplomacy and religious policy.[11] His major addition was a complementary study of the religious union at Brest in 1596, seventeen years after Lublin, which led to the creation of the Ukrainian Uniate Church; this union brought about a closer religious relationship with Catholic Poland but preserved the ecclesiastical integrity of Orthodox Christians in the federation and the principle of pluralism.[12] The "Jagiellonian Idea" of multinational federalism came to hold a special significance for Halecki in the larger context of European history, as providing the basis for a permanent solution to the political organization of eastern Europe.[13] In an effort to make his conclusions available to general scholarship he has written numerous summaries of his research on the Jagiellonian epoch.[14] It is significant that most of the criticism directed against his inter-

[11] Halecki, "La politique scandinave des Jagellons," *La Pologne au VIe Congrès Internationale des Sciences Historiques* (Warsaw, 1930); "La Pologne et la question d'Orient de Casimir le Grand à Jean Sobieski," *La Pologne au VIIe Congrès* (Warsaw, 1933); "Unia Polski z Litwa a Unia Kalmarska," *Studia historyczne ku czci Stanisława Kutrzeby* (Cracow, 1938), I, 217–32; "Die Österreichisch-Polnischen Beziehungen zur Zeit der Union von Lublin," *Perennitas*, edited by H. Rahner and E. von Severus (Münster, 1933), 322–34; "The Defense of Europe in the Renaissance Period," *Didascaliae: Studies in honor of Anselm M. Albareda*, edited by Sesto Prete (New York, 1964), 121–46.

[12] Halecki, *From Florence to Brest, 1439–1596* (Rome, 1955); also see "L'Etat polonais et l'Eglise ruthène: les origines de leurs relations historiques," *Le Monde Slave*, IX (1925), 462–68.

[13] Halecki, "Idea Jagiellońska," *Kwartalnik Historyczny*, LI (1937), 486–510; "The Historical role of Central-Eastern Europe," *Annals of the American Academy of Political and Social Science*, CCXXXII (1944), 9–18; "Federalism as an Answer," *ibid.*, CCLVIII (1948), 66–69.

[14] Halecki, *Geschichte der Union Litauens mit Polen* (Vienna, 1919); "L'évolution historique de l'union polono-lithuanienne," *Le Monde Slave* (1926), 279–93; *The History of Poland* (London, 1942); *Borderlands of Western Civilization: A History of East Central Europe* (New York, 1952). He was one of the editors and contributed several chapters on the Jagiellonian period to *The Cambridge History of Poland from the Origins to Sobieski* (2 vols.; Cambridge, 1950).

pretation has been based on the popularizations which abridged his argument and omitted the evidence he had amassed in his scholarly studies. In response to some of his critics who felt that he stressed only the positive features of Jagiellonian policy, he has subsequently taken into account the practical political consider-ations governing Polish policy, the existence of limitations in re-ligious liberty, and the inadequate provision for the autonomy of the Ruthenian provinces within the federation. In particular, he readily admitted that tripartite status for Ruthenia, such as was eventually agreed upon but not implemented at the Union of Hadziacz in 1658, would have been politically wise and a logical extention of the federative principle. As recently as 1963, however, he contributed to a symposium an article entitled "Why Was Poland Partitioned?" defending the Jagiellonian Commonwealth as a viable political unit and restating his view that it had every prospect for survival.[15]

The works of Halecki written before 1920 have not been trans-lated. The fruit of his exhaustive research has thus been available to most historians only in inadequate and misleading popular-izations. The *History of the Jagiellonian Union* is unquestionably his *magnum opus* and his most important contribution to his-toriography. It has remained the definitive study of the evolution and constitutional development of the Polish Commonwealth. His *Consensus of Sandomierz* has also retained its value and has in fact acquired additional significance in the light of present interest in ecumenical theology. Few of his later works are as thoroughly grounded in research, as free from subjective elements, or as impressive in displaying his formidable analytic capacities.

Halecki did not carry forward his plan to write a comprehensive eighteen-volume history of the entire Jagiellonian epoch. In the period between the two world wars a fundamental transformation of his interests and perspective caused him to turn away abruptly from his earlier specialized research and his exclusive concern with Polish history. The resumption of Poland's statehood after World War I was an important factor inducing a major change in his

15 Halecki, "Why Was Poland Partitioned?" *Slavic Review*, XXII (1963), 432–41.

outlook. The creation of the republic in 1919 marked a fresh political departure for Poland and suggested to Halecki the necessity for a corresponding change in historiography. During the partition period he felt it natural that Polish historiography had acquired a distinctly introverted character; concerned mainly with preserving Poland's moral identity when all political realities denied its formal existence, the historian at that time could hardly avoid a sense of Poland's isolation from the ongoing development of European life. But the new historiography ought to accord with the present reality—to face outward and assert Poland's place in European history. His main interest now became the interpretation of Poland's relations with Europe, accenting the continuity of this relation across the disruptive interlude of partition. In particular, Halecki's interest in the Jagiellonian period was now focused upon its international significance.

An equally influential factor in the formation of Halecki's new historical outlook was his extensive work with the League of Nations which brought him into contact with a large circle of European and American historians. Halecki frequently commented on the pleasure he derived from this experience and attributed the enlargement of his perspective and interests to his association with some of the most notable scholars of the period: H. F. Schmid, Alfons Dopsch, Charles Diehl, Pierre Renouvin, Henri Pirenne, Francesco Ruffini, Arnold Toynbee, and R. H. Lord. Suddenly and fortuitously he was introduced into the mainstream of international historiographical debate on periodization, methodology, historicism, economic and social causality, the role of ideas and religion in culture, the relation between western and eastern Europe, and the philosophical interpretation of history. Halecki remained concerned with historiographical developments throughout his career and contributed to the discussion and controversy on these issues. His subsequent scholarship shows that he had become as much a European as a Polish historian.

Halecki's intense interest in religion also stems from his post-World-War-I experience. He had always been a devout Roman Catholic, but he had carefully separated his religious beliefs from his scholarship in his early writings. Work in the international

field with the League of Nations, he noted, led him to a profound realization of the significance of Catholicism in history and
greatly affected his professional orientation.[16] He was influenced by
the Swiss Catholic historian Gonzague de Reynold and inspired by
the way Toynbee and Christopher Dawson placed religion at the
center of cultural development. Halecki's ambition to produce
a spiritual interpretation of Polish and European history based on
their religious development dates from this period. In addition, he
acquired specialized interests in ecclesiastical history; in 1928 he
began research in the Vatican Archives and at the Pontificio
Istituto Orientale in Rome on the reunion of Roman and Byzantine Christendom.

By 1930 it was evident that Halecki had radically departed from
what he called the empiricist or *fachhistorische* approach characterized by strict philosophical neutrality and confined to technical
investigation. Heir to the tradition of nineteenth century scientific
historiography, he did not, however, abjure it entirely; he always
retained the scholarly discipline and the devotion to documentation which this training instilled. Moreover, he recognized that
scientific history had made invaluable contributions to historiography by perfecting research techniques, by systematically com-
piling documents and sources, and by producing a substantial body
of significant monographic literature. Nevertheless, his new interest led him to cultural history, which placed primary emphasis
on interpretation and recognized if not the necessity at least the
validity of a philosophic framework for the historian. His essay
Kulturgeschichte und Geschichtsphilosophie, written for a *Festschrift* in honor of Alfons Dopsch in 1938, sums up his thought
on the conflicting tendencies in modern historiography, advances
his arguments for the necessity of developing a systematic philosophy of history, and reveals his interest in the use of *Gestalt*
methodology.[17]

Halecki saw *Kulturgeschichte* as an antidote to the restrictive
scope and severely analytic methodology of the scientific school.
He lauded it for restoring interest in general and universal themes

[16] Romig, *The Book of Catholic Authors*, 159.
[17] G. P. Bognetti, H. Cam, A. Domanovslsy, et al, *Wirtschaft und Kultur:
Festschrift zum 70. Geburtstag von Alfons Dopsch* (Leipzig, 1938), 484–96.

and for initiating a more humanistic historiography which encom-
passed the full range of human experience, recognizing the causal
role of ideas and the centrality of ethical and moral issues. He considered the synthetic or Gestalt approach of cultural history as a
major historiographical advance. The analytic methodology of
the scientific school, he contended, was eminently suited to in-
vestigative and descriptive purposes but yielded only a fragmentary
historical understanding and limited generalizations. Gestalt
methodology by contrast, operating within a large conceptual
framework and striving to crystallize rather than to isolate historical
phenomena, broadened the context for inference and accepted
intuition as a legitimate historiographical instrument. Most important, it enabled the historian to apprehend the total configura-
tion of an entire civilization, nation, or period, and to determine
the meaning rather than merely the causal structure of history. The
Gestalt approach thus produced more creative results and a unified
historical knowledge. Finally, Halecki looked upon cultural history
as providing the basis for supplanting socioeconomic interpretation
of history which he regarded as materialistic, mechanistic, and
deterministic—a misdirected effort to fill the intellectual vacuum
created by the scientific historian's rejection of a philosophy of history. In the concluding section of the essay he argued the necessity
and logic of advancing beyond *Kulturgeschichte* to the adoption
of a Christian philosophy which recognized the divine presence in
history.

Halecki's popular *History of Poland* dates from this interwar
period, marked by extraordinary religious intensity and methodological experimentation. Although it was written five years prior
to the article on *Kulturgeschichte*, it represents his first major
effort to write a lengthy interpretive account utilizing the new
perspective he had been acquiring since 1920. Its original title—
La Pologne de 963 à 1914. Essai de synthèse historique—indicates
that it was not a traditional survey.[18] The introduction clearly de-

[18] Halecki, *La Pologne da 963 à 1914. Essai de synthèse historique* (Paris
1933). Besides the translation into English in 1942, this work has been translated
into Finnish, Spanish, Polish and German. Frequent new editions and printings
provided Halecki with the occasion to revise and add a new section on the interwar years in 1942, on the period after World War II in 1955, and an epilogue in
1961 bringing it up to date.

fined synthesis as "interpretation," a distinct type of history occupying an intermediate place in historiography between a purely factual account and a theoretical interpretation. Halecki recognized that philosophic history was an ambitious undertaking and that it was regarded as chimerical by most professional historians. Several years earlier in an exchange with Henri Sée in the *Revue de Synthèse Historique,* he conceded the danger of introducing abstractions in history and of losing "le terrain solide de l'histoire concrète." [19] Halecki felt that these dangers could be circumvented by starting with a synthesis grounded in fact and concrete in nature. In the *History of Poland* he attempted to show the continuity of Polish history, the providential and historical forces which shaped its destiny, the contributions of Poland to the common patrimony of European civilization, and its indelible Christian, European, democratic, and heroic character. He hoped that this would provide a point of departure for a wholly theoretical treatment of the philosophy of Polish history at some future time.

Although this book was far from satisfactory as a whole, as a general history it was reasonably and perhaps even remarkably successful. It conveyed a vast amount of accurate and detailed information and it integrated political and cultural history skillfully. Brilliantly written and compactly organized, it maintained throughout a balance of fact and generalization, narration and interpretation. Its chief limitation as a general history was the slight treatment of economic development, one of Halecki's major shortcomings. On the interpretive level it was considered more vulnerable. Entirely too subjective, the treatment of religious and moral phenomena pointed backward to Michelet rather than forward to Dawson or Toynbee. The frequent recourse to terms such as "soul of Poland," "providential mission," and "national conscience" indicated that Halecki had not yet developed an adequate conceptual framework for conveying Gestalt ideas or a sufficient discipline in this new type of history, so completely different from his earlier writings.

[19] Halecki, "Moyen age et temps modernes," *Revue de synthèse historique,* XLII (1927), 69. The article was a reply to Henri Sée's "La division de l'histoire en périodes," *ibid.,* XLI (1926), 61–67.

It is fair to point out that Halecki wrote the book for a general rather than a scholarly audience and that its subjective character was explicitly set forth in the introduction. Nevertheless, it was a premature venture into interpretive history, revealing his personal religious intensity more than his scholarly skills. It is entirely likely that had it been written a decade later, or even after he had thought out his position as clearly as he had in the article in the Dopsch *Festschrift*, it would have been a considerably better book. Ironically, the *History* of Poland is Halecki's best-known work and has proved therefore to be damaging to his reputation. Few of its readers have had the perspective on his total scholarly production to recognize it as an experimental book written in a period of great personal and intellectual ferment.

Halecki wrote on such a vast range of subjects during the interwar period that it is difficult to find any underlying unity. Judging from the numerous articles he published on ecclesiastical and historiographical subjects, however, it is evident that these were becoming his basic and permanent concerns. Since World War II, his interest in the rapprochement between western and eastern Christendom has intensified and has become the area of his research. The various theoretical studies he wrote on periodization and the intellectual characteristics of Europe prepared him for and led logically to a systematic philosophical interpretation of Western civilization. Four years after the war, Halecki produced the first of two books which can be said to comprise his "study of history," *The Limits and Divisions of European History*; the second one, *The Millennium of Europe*, appeared more than a decade later. In the former he examined the geographical and chronological components of European history and in the latter he interpreted its transcendent and operative ideas. These two books are structurally related and united by a common purpose: to discover the intrinsic meaning of European civilization and its place in universal history. To achieve this end Halecki made extensive use of Gestalt and comparative methodology.

The interpretations of Arnold Toynbee, Gonzague de Reynold, and Christopher Dawson served as his point of departure.[20] Much

---

[20] Dawson, *The Making of Europe* (London, 1932); the first four volumes of Reynold's *La Formation de l'Europe* (7 vols.; Fribourg, 1944–57); and the first

as he admired and agreed with Toynbee and Reynold on basic premises, he was keenly aware that his own vision and convictions were quite different. Halecki's thesis was constructed around five dominant themes: the concept of a European Age in world history; the continuity of Europe as a moral and historic community; the integrity of western and eastern Europe; the cultural coterminality of western and eastern Christendom; and the idea of unity in diversity. He was thoroughly familiar with speculative historical writing, supremely conscious of the controversial nature of his opinions, and cognizant of his departure from traditionally accepted views.

The Limits and Divisions of European History is Halecki's most mature and cogent book, crystallizing more than twenty-five years of speculation on space and time factors in European history.[21] The European Age in history was defined as the period from the latter part of the tenth to the first half of the twentieth centuries, or more specifically from 962 to 1945. In sharp opposition to Toynbee he argued that this period was an eminently intelligible Gestalt. "All that has been said about Europe as a field of study intelligible in itself," he emphasized, "refers only to that European Age. . . . The very fact that this age is now closed makes the interpretation of European history easier, more instructive, and perhaps also more urgent than before." [22] Toynbee conceded that this chronological limitation had strengthened Halecki's case for the intelligibility of Europe as a civilization but did not grant that it was a valid one.[23]

From the perspective of universal history, the European Age was preceded by a Mediterranean Age and was followed by an Atlantic Age. Ancient and contemporary history were thus axiomatically excluded from the European Age and from any direct considera-

---

six volumes of Toynbee's A Study of History (12 vols.; London, 1934–61) were available at the time Halecki wrote Limits and Divisions but both studies were completed when he published The Millennium of Europe in 1963.

[21] The most significant of his preliminary articles are: "L'histoire de l'Europe orientale—sa division en époques, son milieu géographique et ses problèmes fondamentaux," La Pologne au Ve Congrès (Warsaw, 1924), 73–94; "La division de l'histoire en périodes chronologiques," La Pologne au VIe Congrès (Warsaw, 1930); "Moyen age et temps modernes," ibid.; "Qu'est-ce que l'Europe Orientale?" Bulletin d'information des sciences historiques en Europe Orientale (Warsaw, 1934), VI, 83–93.

[22] Halecki, The Limits and Divisions of European History (New York, 1950), 10.

[23] Toynbee, A Study of History, VII, 726.

tion in this study, but this universal framework served to clarify the relation of the European Age to Europe's total history and to the history of Christianity. The European Age corresponded to the second millennium of both European and Christian histories because they began at approximately the same time, namely with Caesar and Christ. Europe and Christianity were therefore closely identified from the start—more intimately in the first than in the second millennium—and vitally associated throughout the European Age. For Halecki the Christian imprint on the European mind was indelible. "Even if and when that mind seemed to reject Christian doctrine," he maintained, "it remained more than *naturaliter Christianus;* it remained faithful, even if unconsciously, to the Christian species of culture." [24] One of the specific functions of the European Age in world history was the defense of Christendom and the expansion of Christianity to its truly universal proportions.

The selection of 962 as the beginning date of the European Age was not arbitrary. After carefully weighing the arguments of Dopsch, Pirenne, Reynold, and Dawson he accepted the conclusion of the latter that the formation of Europe was completed in the Ottonian rather than the Carolingian period. The division of time in European history, Halecki insisted, must be based on a chronology relevant to all of the distinct nations. As the dividing point between the Mediterranean and the European Age, the Ottonian era was to him most fully in accord with this principle. For western Europe, the importance of the coronation of Otto I in 962 was that it marked the decisive renewal of the Holy Roman Empire which endured, albeit with significant mutations, for eight of the ten centuries of the European Age. The conversion of Poland, Hungary, and Scandinavia to Roman Christianity and of Kievan Russia to Orthodox Christianity at approximately the same time made the Ottonian demarcation relevant for eastern Europe.[25] By the end of the tenth century, Europe had expanded

[24] Halecki, *The Limits and Divisions,* 15.
[25] *Ibid.,* p. 40. He expanded on this point in "The Place of Christendom in the History of Mankind," *Cahiers d'histoire mondiale,* I, No. 4 (1954), 927–50, and in "The Significance of the Christianization of Poland in European History," *Polish Review,* VI, Nos. 1–2 (1961), 3–17. Halecki's most recent book, *Tysiąclecie Polski Katolickiej* (Rome, 1967), sums up his thought on Poland's Catholic heritage; unfortunately this work was not available at the time this article was written.

eastward and thereby reached its "natural geographic limits." As the formation of Europe was completed before the Cerularian Schism of 1054 divided western and orthodox Christendom, Halecki considered them as coterminal parts of a single culture in the European Age. The auspicious dawn of the European Age was heralded by Otto III's vision of the *Respublica Christiana*, a universal and supranational community comprising four constituent parts—Roma, Gallia, Germania, and Sclavinia.

Halecki's geographical classification was somewhat different but was based on a fourfold division: western Europe (Italy, Spain, France, the Lowlands, Britain); west-central Europe (Germany, Austria, Switzerland, Scandinavia); east-central Europe (Poland and Lithuania plus the Baltic, Danubian, and Balkan states); eastern Europe (Ukrainia and Byelorussia). This classification was highly controversial for what it included as well as for what it excluded. Halecki was completely out of accord with de Reynold who maintained that although some parts of eastern Europe were culturally related to the west, they were nevertheless not integral parts of "Europe européenne." He vigorously opposed the tendency in German historiography—explict in Ranke—to confine European history to the Romance and Germanic nations, and in Russian Pan-Slavic thought to regard all Slavic nations as a separate cultural entity.

The most controversial issue, however, was his sharp division between Kievan Rus and Muscovite Russia and his exclusion of the latter from Europe. Halecki granted that all of Russia had initially been geographically and culturally linked with Europe. But as a result of the Mongol invasion in the thirteenth century, he argued, Muscovite Russia became alienated from European cultural influence and acquired an Asiatic character which, in spite of superficial ties in the St. Petersburg era, separated her permanently from Europe.[26] The Ukraine and Byelorussia, however, because of their long association with the Jagiellonian Commonwealth, were considered integral and constituent parts of Europe. No view of Halecki's has been as widely and justifiably contested as this. The implications of this argument for Polish history are apparent: po-

[26] Halecki, *The Limits and Divisions,* 88–101.

litical realities in eastern Europe from the Treaty of Andrusowa in 1667 to the Yalta Conference have from this perspective been out of accord with the geographical and historical principles of the European Age.

The inclusion of distinctly Orthodox Christian territories in the structure of Europe has been similarly disputed. Radically disagreeing with Toynbee and the Czech scholar Jaroslav Bidlo, Halecki claimed that religion was not a sufficient criterion for determining cultural differentiation and in fact maintained that western and eastern Christendom constituted a single culture.[27] He contended that neither the Muslim invasion nor the 1054 schism alienated Byzantium permanently from Europe as the Mongol conquest had alienated Russia: Byzantium did not succumb to the cultural influence of her conqueror and the Cerularian Schism was not regarded as final by either party. Furthermore, relations between Rome and Constantinople were improving up to that point; negotiations to resolve the conflict began almost immediately afterward; and the possibility of a religious rapprochement leading to cultural reunification always existed. Halecki still remains hopeful that the ecumenical efforts of Rome resumed by John XXIII will result in reunion.

He supported these conclusions in numerous research articles and in two lengthy monographs—*Un empereur de Byzance à Rome: vingt ans de travail pour l'union des églises et pour la défense de l'empire d'orient, 1355–1375* and *From Florence to Brest, 1439–1596*.[28] The first efforts at reunification, based on dynastic

[27] *Ibid.*, 107. Halecki and Bidlo had been carrying on a debate on the definition of eastern Europe since the Fifth International Historical Congress at Brussels in 1923; see their exchange, "Qu'est-ce-que l'Europe Orientale?" *Ibid.*, 82–119. Toynbee refuted Halecki's thesis in A *Study of History*, VII, 726–29, to which Halecki replied in the epilogue of the German translation of *The Limits and Divisions: Europa—Grenzen und Gliederung seiner Geschichte* (Darmstadt, 1957), 187–201.

[28] His monograph on Emperor John V Palaeologus was published in *Rozprawy Historyczne Towarzystwa Naukowego Warszawskiego*, VIII (1930). Other important articles on the subject are: "Le problème de l'Union des Eglises," *La Pologne au VIᵉ Congrès*, 119–40; "Two Palaeologi in Venice, 1370–1371," *Byzantion*, XVII (1944–45), 331–36; "Isidore's Tradition," *Miscellanea in honorem Card. Isidori Kioviensis (1463–1963)*, (Rome, 1963), 27–43; "Sixte IV et la chrêtienté orientale," *Mélanges Eugène Tisserant, Studi e Testi* (Vatican City, 1964), II, 241–64.

marriage by Charlemagne, Otto II, and Otto III, he regarded as unproductive. Conciliar negotiation from the Second Council of Lyons in 1274 to the Council of Florence in 1439 was more successful. Reunion was in fact proclaimed by both of these councils; although not generally implemented, these proclamations did lead to partial reconciliation between Rome and the Armenian, Coptic, Syrian, Chaldean, and Maronite churches. Halecki emphasized the efforts of the Polish clergy on behalf of reunion and pointed out the successful coexistence between western and orthodox Christians in Poland since the Treaty of Krewo in 1385 and the creation of the Ukrainian Uniate Church in 1596. In *Un empereur de Byzance* he noted the remarkable record of the Avignon papacy in ecclesiastical reunion and the fact that their efforts were unfortunately nullified by the Great Western Schism in 1378.

Halecki attributed the failure to achieve a general reunion to several other factors besides the schism: increased tension which developed after the Fourth Crusade and King Ladislas III's Varna expedition; [29] rivalry between Moscow and Constantinople; personal animosities between the patriarchs and the emperors in Byzantium; inability to develop grassroots support among the regular orthodox clergy and laity; and obstructionism on the part of secular nobles. Finally, the fall of Constantinople in 1453 not only interrupted the achievements of the Council of Florence but permanently jeopardized further negotiations throughout most of the European Age. However, he maintained that Orthodoxy after the fall of Constantinople gravitated toward the West rather than toward Russia's "self-styled" *Third Rome,* as was evident from the ecclesiastical separation of Kiev from Moscow in 1458 and the Union of Brest.[30] While Halecki's thesis on the unity of western and eastern Christendom remains disputed, he has supplied sub-

[29] In *Crusade of Varna: a Discussion of Controversial Problems* (New York, 1943) he defended the personal integrity of Ladislas and published new documents to exonerate him of the charge that he had betrayed Murad II and the Crusaders by launching the Varna expedition.

[30] Halecki, "The Ecclesiastical Separation of Kiev from Moscow in 1458," *Wiener Archiv für Geschichte des Slaventum und Osteuropas,* II (1956), 19–32; "Les Trois Romes," *Le Flambeau,* XXXI (1948), 277–90; "Rome, Constantinople et Moscou au temps de l'Union de Brest," in L. Beauduin (ed.), *L'Eglise et les églises,* 1054–1954 . . . (2 vols.; Chevetagne, 1954–55), I, 441–74.

stantial documentation for his position based on detailed research and original investigation.

The principal reason for Halecki's inclusion of such diverse components within a single culture was his adamant belief that the essence of European civilization was its inherent pluralism. "Whatever is colossal and uniform is definitely unEuropean," he insisted; "that is the secret of all the refinement and distinction of European civilization." [31] The physical basis of European diversity is its heterogenous racial and ethnic structure. Historically, European culture derived from the fusion of Hellenic, Roman, Christian, and barbarian elements in the Mediterranean Age. For Halecki, Christianity was the most important of these components because it imparted to European culture its supranational and universal character, its proclivity to embrace variety and to transform it into a deep spiritual unity, and its vision of a harmonious order based on the idea of *caritas*. These four constituents endowed European culture with its richness but they were not perfectly fused and were perhaps irreconcilable in nature. Accordingly, they gave rise to certain dichotomies which generated conflict and tension. The first of these was the fundamental opposition between Graeco-Roman anthropomorphic humanism and the Christian idea of piety. The second antinomy was between the Greek concept of diversity and freedom and the Roman concept of uniformity and compulsion. In *The Millennium of Europe*, the second part of his "study of history," Halecki examined the ideological structure of the European Age in terms of the dialectical relationship and the continuing tension between these basic elements throughout the second millennium of Europe.

In this work Europe is treated as a moral and historical community not identical with but nonetheless occupying the central place in universal history from the tenth to the twentieth century. Halecki's thesis is that Europe was animated by the transcendental and operative idea of unity in diversity, which, however, was in perpetual conflict with the antithetical idea of uniformity or empire. The idea of empire, according to Halecki, was not a European concept and was in fact inimical to the European tradition.

[31] Halecki, *The Limits and Divisions*, 12.

Nor was it of Greek or Roman origin but had been absorbed by Rome during her expansion and contact with the Orient and transmitted to European culture. Though it was repeatedly rejected in the European Age, it frequently reappeared in the form of conquest, centralization of authority, political domination, and uniformity.

The nearest approximation to a genuine supranational community was the *Respublica Christiana* composed of separate nations governed by two universal and coordinate authorities and based on an unusual philosophical *communis consensus*. Though far from harmonious, the *Respublica Christiana* remained closest to the Ottonian and Christian vision; it was destroyed in the fourteenth century when strife between the two coordinate powers was renewed, the idea of empire was reasserted, and the unity of one of the powers was destroyed by the Great Western Schism. This rupture undermined the *Respublica Christiana* but the idea of supranationalism was preserved—with major and significant mutations—throughout the rest of the European Age.

In the second or transitional phase of the European Age (1400–1600), which Halecki treated as a "time of troubles," the idea of unity in diversity found expression in the conciliar movement which endeavored not only to heal the religious schism and its grave political consequences but also to reunify western and eastern Christendoms. In contrast to Paul Hazard, he regarded the Renaissance as the fundamental "crise de conscience européenne," because it reasserted anthropomorphic humanism, produced a violent clash with the Christian concept of piety, and led to an entirely new dualism between Protestant and Roman Christianity. The development of nationalism in this period enriched European diversity but at the same time threatened the correlative principle of unity. Nevertheless, the idea of unity in diversity found new manifestation in the idea of federalism and the idea of the balance of power. The former was closer in spirit and structure to the *Respublica Christiana* and was embodied in the Jagiellonian Federation, the Swiss Confederation, and the Scandinavian Union of Kalmar, while the idea of the balance of power was merely an adequate means of achieving tranquility rather than true union.

The early modern period (1600–1800) represented for Halecki

the recovery of the idea of Europe as a community. He regarded the development of natural law as an effort to establish a new philosophical consensus and saw Sully's *Grand Dessin* and Voltaire's *Grande République* as reasonable though wholly theoretical substitutes for the *Respublica Christiana*. In the Enlightenment, in spite of its avowed hostility to Christian doctrine, the tension between anthropomorphic humanism and Christian piety reached a climax that resulted in a new synthesis in which humanism became more Christian and Christianity, by renouncing methods of coercion and involvement in power politics, became more human.[32] The eighteenth century revolutions affirmed the principle of voluntarism; the American republic, though it was outside the geographic structure of Europe, offered the most significant example of the idea of *diversitas in unitate*, and prepared the way for the Atlantic Age.

The conflict between freedom and force, however, was not resolved. Napoleon's vain effort to create a European community by compulsion grew out of the failure of the idea of the balance of power which had never possessed a constructive philosophical foundation and which lost even its operative value in eighteenth century colonial and continental competition. After 1814 the unity of Europe was preserved only by artificial or outright mechanistic means such as the Concert of Europe or the Alliance and Entente System. The last genuine and noble effort to preserve the supranational principle in the European Age was the League of Nations; its initiation outside Europe already signified the transition to the Atlantic Age in which Europe had ceased to occupy the central place in history. The European Age came to a tragic end with World War II. Ironically, Halecki noted, Europe's condition after World War II was reminiscent of the chaotic situation in the tenth century when the European Age began; still more ironic, the Soviet Empire, after the war, reduced the frontiers of Europe to what they had been at the time of Charlemagne before the making of Europe was completed.[33]

[32] Halecki, *The Millennium of Europe*, 387–88.
[33] *Ibid.*, 364–66. His hostility to Russia after World War II is also evident in "The Two World Wars: A Comparison," *Thought*, XXI, No. 80 (1946), 21–44, and in "Imperialism in Slavic and East European History," *American Slavic and East European Review*, XI (1952), 1–26.

Halecki's "study of history," is a remarkable interpretive achievement that commands admiration for the universality and wisdom of his vision. Even those who will not agree with his argument would not deny his scholarly responsibility and intellectual honesty. Of the two parts, *The Limits and Divisions of European History* is the more original and therefore, the more provocative; it is also the most erudite, disciplined, and precise of his speculative writings. What *The Millennium of Europe* lacks by way of succinct definition, precise terminology, and structural compactness it compensates for by brilliant insights and intellectual excitement. These two works represent the fruition of half a century of scholarly study and reflection and the culmination of an ambition acquired as early as 1923, when Halecki first advanced the idea of the Atlantic Age. He recognized that philosophic interpretation was a professional risk, subject to criticism of its premises and its bold generalizations. He succeeded, however, where many have failed, namely in retaining a firm base in "le terrain solide de l'histoire concrète."

The passing of the European Age was for Halecki a logical historical development implicit in European expansion since the Renaissance. He was vigorously opposed to the view that Europe, because it had lost its dominant place, would cease to play an important role in history. In 1963 when he wrote *The Millennium of Europe*, he was optimistic about the future of Europe: she had made a remarkable material recovery, had achieved political stability, and had began to rebuild a supranational community based on mutual interests. The revolutions of 1956 encouraged him to believe that eastern Europe would resume ties and eventually be reintegrated with the West. The ecumenical efforts initiated by John XXIII represented for Halecki the most exciting prospect since the fifteenth century conciliar movement for the reunification of western and eastern Christendom. Much like William H. McNeill, he felt that European culture had made an indelible mark on human history and that subsequent civilizations would be intelligible only in terms of the achievements of the European Age.[34]

[34] Cf., Halecki, "The Place of Christendom in the History of Mankind," *ibid.*, 929–30 and William H. McNeill, *The Rise of the West: A History of the Human*

Nothing was more central to or more controversial in Halecki's interpretation than his belief in the providential direction of history. The Marxist denunciation of his conception of history as "fideistic" prompted him to defend his convictions in his presidential address to the Catholic Historical Association in 1956 on *The Moral Laws of History*.[35] In one of his rare agreements with Marxism he conceded that the ideographic approach to history was completely unsatisfactory and that there was a nomothetic element in historical development. But he rejected socioeconomic laws as the basis for historical development because of their implicit and sometimes explicit determinism. He cited Toynbee as an example of a nomothetic approach to history which successfully combined law and freedom. In an effort to clarify the relationship between divine law and human freedom, Halecki distinguished between two kinds of divine laws: those which God gave to nature and those he set down for man. While the former are inexorable physical necessities, the latter, to which the laws of history belong, are divine directives or "elements of order" implicit in the natural law and explicitly formulated in the law of love in the Sermon on the Mount. While they are *moral necessities* they need not be followed, and accordingly there is a provision for free will, contingency, accident, and chance in human history. In *The Millennium of Europe* he asserted that "in the Christian interpretation of history there are no inescapable laws of development,

---

Community (Chicago, 1963), 806-807. In *The Limits and Divisions*, pp. 57-60, Halecki strongly opposed Eric Fischer's view in *The Passing of the European Age—a Study of the Transfer of Western Civilization and Its Renewal on Other Continents* (Cambridge, Mass., 1943) that Europe would play only a diminished role in future world history. J. Godechot and R. R. Palmer, "Le problème de l'Atlantique du XVIIIᵉ au XXᵉ siècle," *Relazioni del X Congresso Internazionale di Scienze Storiche. Roma 4-11 Settembre, 1955* (6 vols.; Florence, 1955), V, 175-239, dispute the optimism of Halecki and other proponents of an Atlantic civilization.

[35] *Catholic Historical Review*, XLII (1957), 409-40. J. Tazbir's polemical article "Fałsz Historyczny i Zdrada Narodu w pracach O. Haleckiego," *Kwartalnik Historyczny*, LX, No. 3 (1953), 172-95, accused Halecki of falsifying history and of betraying Poland. In his address Halecki defended Toynbee against a similar attack by Maria Borucka-Arctowa, "Idealistyczna historiozofia A. J. Toynbiego narzędziem Amerykańskiego imperializmu," *ibid.*, LX, No. 1 (1953), 181-91 and in a subsequent article, "The Validity of Toynbee's Conception of the Prospects of Western Civilization," in *The Intent of Toynbee's History: A Cooperative Approach*, edited by E. T. Gargan (Chicago, 1961), 201-16, he lauded Toynbee's explanation of the relationship between freedom and divine law.

and nothing is predetermined in the historical process except its ultimate outcome: the triumph of the kingdom of God and the end of time." [36] Halecki's conception of the interaction of sacred and profane forces in history is strongly Augustinian. The *terrena civitas* he felt would be far from perfect, but it could through human and divine cooperation achieve a tenable reconciliation of the antinomic forces in human nature and in history. This was for him the spiritual meaning of Europe.

Oscar Halecki has been an exceptionally provocative historian throughout his career. This has been intentional. The general tenor of Polish historiography and the New Cracow School in particular taught him that the business of the historian was to confront rather than evade disagreement, to challenge prevailing attitudes, to dispute accepted conclusions, and if possible to reverse the established judgments of historians. He rejected the pedestrian approach to history and valued interpretation as the highest historiographical function. The indispensable obligation of the historian for Halecki was responsible judgment based on exhaustive research.

His Catholic viewpoint and specialized interest in eastern European history has tended to place him at the periphery of contemporary historiography. Yet it was his intense religious concern that prompted the ecclesiastical research which substantially enriched the literature on ecumenism and the relations between Byzantium and Rome. Only a relatively small circle of eastern European specialists have benefited from and can fully appreciate his contributions to medieval and Renaissance studies. Halecki's Polono-centric approach to eastern Europe has offended Russian and some Slavic historians. Western scholars too have perhaps been irritated by the prominent place he assigned to Poland in European history. There was national pride on the part of Halecki, of course, but there were genuine scholarly motives as well. He felt that European history had too often been written from the perspective and interests of the great powers, and that western historiography had relegated eastern Europe to a remote and tangential place. As a corrective he emphasized the historical importance and contributions of the lesser states and of eastern Europe. He has undoubt-

[36] Halecki, *The Millennium of Europe*, 12.

edly pressed his case hard and has often given the impression that Polish history was singularly exempt from aggression and self-interest. But he has never defended the mistakes in Polish history: if he overlooked some of them, or refused to dwell on them, or hesitated to admit them, it was because he felt that there was already too much negativism in European treatments of Polish history and in the Marxist historians' rejection of Poland's Christian and "bourgeois" past.[37] His entire scholarly effort was directed toward placing as positive a construction on Polish history as the facts would allow.

Halecki's fulfillment as a person was intimately bound up with his identity as historian. His determination to be both a scholar and a philosopher stems from the inseparable relationship he saw between personal and professional life. His approach to history is one of total engagement, combining a wealth of specialized knowledge with a passionate concern for human destiny and bringing them both to bear on the meaning of human experience. There is a prophetic dimension in his writings—not in a predictive sense but in his endeavor to record the moral nobility of man and the frustrations he encountered in the pursuit of spiritual vision. For Halecki, what mattered in history ultimately was not that or how often man had failed, but how much he had strived and the degree to which he succeeded in establishing the conditions for a civilized existence.

[37] In "What is Realism in Polish History?," *Journal of Central European Affairs,* III (1943), 322–28, he rejected the plea of Olgierd Górka and W. J. Rose for a new revision of Polish history as signifying a return to Bobrzyński's "condemnatory" spirit. On the encouraging side he saw Gotthold Rhode's *Die Ostgrenze Polens: Politische Entwicklung, kulturelle Bedeutung und geistige Auswirkung* (Cologne, 1955) as evidence of a more favorable treatment of Poland in German historiography.

HANS KOHN
Historian of Nationalism

LOUIS L. SNYDER

*The City College of New York
of the City University of New York*

ANS KOHN was born in Prague in the province of Bohemia
on September 15, 1891, to a family which had lived for
generations in the Czech countryside. He entered the Al-
städter *Gymnasium* in 1902 and passed from *Prima* to *Octava*
from his eleventh through his nineteenth year. During this school-
ing he obtained a thorough grounding in classical languages and
literature, a training of some consequence in his later career as a
scholar.

The young man was reared in an atmosphere of explosive nationalism. Since the critical year of 1848, many attempts had been
made to assert the independence of Bohemia in the old Austro-
Hungarian Empire. The Bohemian national question was eventually solved by the collapse of the Habsburg monarchy and by the
success of the Czechoslovak movement. Early in life Kohn became
aware of the power of nationalism in human affairs—it was a lesson he never forgot during his long career.

In 1910 Kohn was enrolled in the faculty of law and political
science at the University of Prague. His main interests at this time
were philosophy, literature, and theology:

As I grew older, I gained a new and deeper understanding of . . .
Kant, later Nietzsche. Kant's sober enthusiasm for individual liberty
and for the moral forces, represented for him in the Enlightenment
and in the French Revolution, his categorical imperative that no
utilitarian consideration could justify a deviation from the moral law
and that every human being must be treated not as a means for
one's own progress but as an object of infinite worth, seemed to me

to accord with Nietzsche's concept of a moral elite. It may seem strange to link Kant, the small-town scholar, who led a life of exemplary regularity, and Nietzsche, the homeless wanderer, who was at bottom an artist but thought of himself as a prophet. But both were rigorously ethical beings who cared deeply for the independence and dignity of the individual, and both were daring intellectual revolutionaries.[1]

After receiving the degree of Doctor of Laws, the twenty-three-year-old Kohn at the outbreak of World War I joined an infantry regiment composed mostly of Czechs and was sent to officers' training school at Salzburg. During the Carpathian campaign he was taken prisoner by the Russians. From March, 1915, to January, 1920, he remained in Russia in a continuing personal encounter with war and revolution, including a forced march as a prisoner of war along dusty Galician roads from the Carpathian Mountains to Lemberg. He studied the Russian language and civilization and witnessed the transition from Tsarism to Leninism. In a prisoner-of-war camp in Siberia he organized a series of cultural activities to exercise the minds of captives endangered by apathy and ennui. In February, 1916, he escaped and tried to make his way to Afghanistan, only to be captured after three days and exiled as a "dangerous prisoner" to a fortified outpost near the border of Chinese Turkestan.

From 1920 to 1931 Kohn lived in Paris, London, and Jerusalem. He was in Paris for fifteen months, but there he was alienated by the intellectual poverty and venality of the metropolitan press and the near police-state atmosphere which included censorship of the press. For four years in London he worked at the British Museum on various problems of nationalism. There followed six productive years in Palestine, where he completed several books on the Middle East and on the process of modernization of non-Western lands. He also produced a study on Martin Buber.

Kohn left Palestine for the United States in the fall of 1933 and began an active career of teaching and publishing. His first post was at the New School for Social Research. In 1934 he became professor of modern history at Smith College, where he

[1] Kohn, *Living in a World Revolution* (New York, 1964), 60–61.

held the Sydenham Clark Parsons Chair for fifteen years. In 1949 he accepted a call to The City College of New York, where he remained until his retirement in 1961. He was visiting professor at many institutions, including Harvard University, Mount Holyoke College, the Universities of California, Colorado, and at Minnesota, Yale, Bowling Green, and Wesleyan universities, and universities at Denver, Pennsylvania, and Texas. In 1948 and again in 1955 he was a member of the Institute for Advanced Study at Princeton. He frequently lectured on behalf of the United States government throughout Europe and North Africa. He has received numerous grants by scholarly foundations and was awarded several honorary degrees. Unlike his early idol Kant, who never traveled more than forty miles from Königsberg, Kohn preferred the opposite approach: his restless mind and temperament could be satisfied only if he went to see for himself. He was never the armchair historian.

Added to classroom teaching was an extensive publication record. From 1922 to 1965, a period of forty-three years, Kohn wrote and published books—at the rate of one per year.[2] At the same time he wrote numerous articles for scholarly journals and many book reviews. This tended to place him in the category of "prolific writer," for some historians a term of disapproval. In the view of some scholars the "great" colleague is the one who vegetates in libraries for a lifetime, finally producing a two-volume examination of the background of each member of the House of Commons, replete with thousands of footnotes heckling the text. Kohn's extraordinary output notwithstanding, much of his work bears the mark of able scholarship.

Kohn's work is distinguished by careful organization, an easy, fluid style, and by evidences of the solid classical training of the early days in Prague. His publications are concerned with four major areas: (1) nationalism; (2) modern European intellectual history; (3) issues of modern times; and (4) Zionism and related Jewish problems. His first book, published in Vienna, com-

[2] For a chronological bibliography of books by Hans Kohn from 1922 to 1963, see Kohn, *Reflections on Modern History: The Historian and Human Responsibility* (Princeton, 1963), 357–60.

bined nationalism with Judaism as subjects for analysis. Then came a series of studies concerning Jews, Judaism, and related topics. These were followed by volumes on national movements in the Orient, Near East, and the Soviet Union. Kohn came to the United States with a solid reputation as a historian of nationalism; along with Carlton J. H. Hayes, Seth Low Professor of History at Columbia University, he became known as an outstanding scholar of that often vague, paradoxical, and mysterious ism. In 1944 Kohn published his major work, *The Idea of Nationalism: A Study in its Origins and Background*, which went through eight printings and was translated into Spanish, German, Italian, and other languages.

After *The Idea of Nationalism* came a succession of studies, including the well-known *Prophets and Peoples* (1946; fourth printing, 1957), as well as examinations of German, Swiss, and American nationalism. In 1962 appeared a summing up, *The Age of Nationalism*.

Along with his studies on nationalism, Kohn devoted much attention to the intellectual history of the major European countries. His *The Mind of Germany: The Education of a Nation* (1962) was translated into many languages. There were similar studies, on a more modest scale, of the Russian and French minds, as well as volumes on Austrian history and Pan-Slavism. Always interested in contemporary affairs, Kohn published many books on phases of current history.

Kohn's productive capacity was shown also in his many articles published in scholarly journals and in papers delivered before the American Historical Association and other organizations. These include such diverse topics as Ernst Moritz Arndt and the character of German nationalism, Germany's role in the New Europe, United States policy in the Cold War, the Atlantic Community, and changing Africa.

In intellectual disputations Kohn has remained the scholar and gentleman. He refused to join the widespread and somewhat malicious assault on Toynbee, whose prodigious *A Study of History* was denounced by critics as "filled with conjuring tricks," "intellectual hanky-panky," and "a terrific perversion of history." As an established student of nationalism, Kohn agreed with Toynbee's position that nationalism in the twentieth century had often degenerated, politically and spiritually, into a danger to individual liberty and international peace, to the human mind and man's well-being. Kohn saw riches in Toynbee's massive volume, "He broadens the horizon, as no other historian has done, to include the whole panorama of past and contemporary civilizations." [3] However, at the same time Kohn expressed this criticism:

In his sweeping condemnation of nationalism, Toynbee disregards, however, the fact that nationalism began in eighteenth century Western society as striving for the protection of the rights of the individual citizens against the power of the government and the dogmatism of religion. In the atmosphere of the Enlightenment it was a liberating movement from the fetters of a deadening tradition. From Milton and Locke to Jefferson and Condorcet, this early nationalism helped the growth of man's stature. But in the course of the nineteenth century, when nationalism spread from the shores of the Atlantic eastward, into lands with an entirely different political and cultural tradition and social structure, nationalism turned more and more into a desire for collective power and self-assertion and tended to subject the individual to the political, intellectual, and moral authority of the collectivity.[4]

Kohn's distinction as a historian rests primarily upon his work on nationalism. With his Prague background in the old Austro-Hungarian Empire, his knowledge of many European languages, his wide travels, and with what Carlton J. H. Hayes called "his knowledge of research and flair for synthesis," he produced a series of studies which has had an important effect upon examination of "the preponderant factor in modern history."

Although Kohn has investigated every conceivable phase of nationalism, he had made special contributions in two specific approaches—meaning and classification. Both are vital to any understanding of nationalism.

By some linguistic quirk the use of the suffix "ism" has led to obfuscation and confusion. The words seem innocent enough in print—capitalism, imperialism, racialism, fascism, international-

---

[3] Kohn, "Faith and Vision of a Universal World," *Christian Register*, CXXXIV (1955), 12.
[4] *Ibid.*, 9–12.

ism, socialism, communism. Each represents a historical movement of significance in modern times, yet each has been obscured in a fog of miscomprehension. Nationalism has been beclouded with vagueness, inconsistency, and paradox.

In eliciting the meaning of nationalism, Kohn set up a framework of reference that has become standard. Nationalism, he said, "is first and foremost a state of mind, an act of consciousness." He saw human beings as subject to both ego- and group-consciousness: with the growing complexity of civilization, the number of groups, unfixed and changing, increases. With these plural kinds of group consciousness, there is generally one recognized by men as the supreme and most important:

> The mental life of man is as much dominated by ego-consciousness as it is by group-consciousness. Both are complex states of mind at which we arrive through experiences of differentiation and opposition, of the ego and the surrounding world, of the we-group and those outside the group. The collective or group consciousness can center around entirely different groups, of which some have a permanent character—the family, the class, the clan, the caste, the village, the sect, the religion, etc. . . . In each case, varying with its permanence, this group-consciousness will strive toward achieving homogeneity within the group, a conformity and likemindedness which will lead to and facilitate common action.[5]

In effect, Kohn directed attention to the importance of social psychology in extracting the meaning of nationalism. It was a plea for an interdisciplinary approach to a complex subject which goes far beyond the range of the historian—a plea to the psychologist, the sociologist, the psychiatrist, and the psychoanalyst to direct their energies to the clarification of nationalism. That relatively little attention has been paid by these disciplines to nationalism is to be regretted, but that is another subject.

Second, and more within the sphere of the historian, Kohn contributed a challenging theory to the classification or typology of nationalism. Scholars of nationalism have presented dozens of forms, but the two most widely accepted are those by Hayes and Kohn.

The formula proposed by Hayes may be termed a vertical con-

[5] Kohn, *The Idea of Nationalism* (5th printing; New York, 1951), 10–11.

ceptualization which treats the classification of nationalism on a chronological basis. He presented the evolution of modern nationalism in these successive forms: humanitarian (Bolingbroke, Rousseau, Herder); Jacobin (Robespierre); traditional (Burke, Ambroise, von Schlegel); liberal (Bentham, Mazzini); and integral (Barrès, Kipling, D'Annunzio, Treitschke, Plehve). At the beginning there was nothing in the national state which contradicted libertarian and humanitarian ideals. But the idea of national states took on a more and more lurid complexion. Under the integral form the national state began to assume functions far beyond the military and police powers of earlier states. This led to a type of nationalism which stressed "all or nothing at all." It was in some respects a reversion over thousands of years of civilization and a return to primitive pagan tribalism.

Although Kohn also saw nationalism as the outcome of a long historical process, taking its coloration from the political climate as well as historical conditions in which it is engendered, he preferred to judge the same set of historical facts from a different angle. He applied a horizontal measuring rod on the assumption that at any given time one type of nationalism might not be the same as another. From this premise he derived a major dichotomy in the typology of nationalism, presenting a fundamental distinction between two types of nationalism: (1) nationalism in the Western world (England, the British colonies, the Netherlands, and Switzerland); and (2) nationalism outside the Western world (central Europe, eastern Europe, and Asia). The two areas are the poles around which the new age with its multiplicity of shadings and transitions revolves. In each of the two areas there was a centrifugal tendency which gave to nationalism a distinctive kind of character. At the same time Kohn recognized the dangers of generalization and admitted that there are always exceptions to rules set up as historical guides.

In presenting this classification, Kohn organized his approach along three lines—origins, characteristics, and development. In the matter of origins, Kohn agrees generally with Hayes, but he makes a distinction between the origins of nationalism in the Western and in the non-Western world. In the West, Kohn says, the emer-

gence of nationalism was mainly a political occurrence: nationalism was preceded by the formation of the national state or coincided with it. This was in direct contrast with the experience of
non-Western areas, where nationalism arose much later and also at
a more backward stage of political development. Nationalism in
the non-Western world arose as a kind of spontaneous protest
against the existing state pattern. Its first expressions were culturally oriented. There was some chaos as rising nationalities moved
across the borders of existing states.

There is a similar contrast in historical motivation. Kohn sees
in the early modern history of the Western world at a time when
the roots of national sentiment were being nourished, enormously
vital developments (Renaissance and Reformation) which extended far beyond the usual cultural and religious spheres. Both
Renaissance and Reformation contributed to the development of
a new society in which the secularized bourgeoisie was flexing its
muscles and gaining political as well as economic power. Nationalism in the Western world was a product of indigenous forces
which came to fruition in the eighteenth century.

According to Kohn, in the non-Western world, the Renaissance
and Reformation did not result in profound changes. In the German states these two great movements of modern times were more
precisely scholarly and theological in nature, even if there were
some politicoeconomic overtones. But Russia, the Near East, and
Asia remained virtually untouched. Here the old divisions, such
as that between Roman Catholicism and the Greek Orthodox
Church, between the relics of the Western and Eastern empires,
still persisted. A kind of ephemeral universalism, closer akin to the
Middle Ages than to modern times, continued in the non-Western
world. When nationalism rose in the non-Western world, it was
a product of cultural contact as well as a mistaken interpretation
of the past.

In the Western world, Kohn sees nationalism as a product of the
Age of Reason. Here there emerged an open, pluralistic society,
stressing the ideas of liberty, equality, and fraternity, as well as
such concomitants as constitutionalism, parliamentarianism, liberalism, democracy, tolerance, and free speech. In the non-Western

world, Kohn sees the Enlightenment rejected as unreasonable, even foolish. Here the natural form of society is to be found in authority, in a union of state and faith. Nationalism here meant not freedom but duty to serve the state—the authoritarian or closed society.

Kohn sees a similar dichotomy in the historical development of each major area. Western nationalism was in a very real sense an outgrowth of the Enlightenment. Relying on the autonomy of the individual and on voluntary association, it was the outcome of a rationalistic and humanitarian regard for one's fellow man. The secularized Stoic-Christian tradition lived on in both Protestant England and Catholic France. The growth and development of nationhood was to a large extent the product of internal forces. Throughout the nineteenth century the original stimulus to nationalism on a libertarian framework was shown in the persistence of liberal nationalism, even if in increasingly diminished form.

Quite different, says Kohn, was the development of non-Western nationalism. Originally impelled by and dependent upon outside forces, it proceeded along two contrasting lines. One accepted the Western form with all its characteristics displayed in British parliamentary institutions, the French bourgeois republic, and the Industrial Revolution. The second branch placed emphasis upon national peculiarities and regarded itself as outside the periphery of cultural contact with alien civilizations. Non-Western nationalism insisted upon using history for national ends, thus invading the ground of historicism. Deeply attracted by the past, by tradition, it was fascinated by the mysteries of ancient times. It re-created a sense of tribal solidarity and always tended toward isolation.

The value of the Kohn classification lies in its clarification of the many inconsistencies and contradictions that have surrounded the meaning of nationalism. It explains the variations in definitions of nationalism by directing attention to the intellectual climate at certain times and in places where nationalism functions. It shows how the meaning of linguistic terms depends upon the historical milieu.

There have been many explanations of why German and Russian nationalisms took on a quality different from that of the

West. Kohn describes the original acceptance of the Enlightenment by a small group of German and Russian intellectuals and
its later rejection as alien by policy-shaping enemies of the liberal-
democratic tradition. Discarding the Western idea of nationalism,
Germans and Russians geared themselves to the type of authoritarianism they found traditional in their own development.

The Kohn formula further encompasses the process of cultural
influence and resistance in non-European areas. For too many
years the appearance of nationalism in non-European areas has
been regarded as a kind of sporadic, accidental phenomenon. Kohn
shows how the idea of nationalism may be communicated by cultural diffusion, but its particular meaning and form in most cases
will take on characteristics dictated by the aims and aspirations of
each people concerned.

Critics have attacked Kohn on the ground that his typology is
far too favorable to the Western world. He is accused of cleansing
Western nationalism of tribal impurities and of disregarding the
manifestations of antidemocratic or non-Western nationalism in
the East. The criticism is understandable but it is unreasonable.
In his long series of studies, Kohn never described Western nationalism as a blessing and the non-Western form as a curse. He
carefully pointed to non-Western types of nationalism which accept the Western form. He is well aware of its unattractive features in the West as well as in non-Western nations. Nowhere
does he intimate that the open society is perfect.

Another criticism holds that Kohn's geographical typology tends
to discount the manifestations of democratic (Western) nationalism among the nations which he places in the non-Western category.[6] Yet, Kohn spoke carefully of a non-Western branch of nationalism which accepts the Western characteristics.

The Kohn dichotomy has served a generation of historians well
and there have been no significant attempts to annihilate, alter,
or modify it. It has many of the advantages of the multidisciplin-
ary approach to the study of nationalism in that it takes into account a combination of political, social, cultural, economic, and

[6] See the review of Kohn's *The Idea of Nationalism* by H. H. Gerth, in *American Journal of Sociology*, LI (January, 1946), 341.

psychological factors. Most of all it clarifies the basic framework in which modern nationalism operates; in this respect it provides a most useful guide for the study of a most difficult historical phenomenon.

Throughout his career Kohn revealed his interest in nationalism wherever it has appeared, but his special attention has been paid to its development in Germany.[7] He sees German nationalism as characterized by two interwoven strands: an emphasis upon liberal constitutional rights after the Western pattern, and a struggle for national power strengthened by authoritarianism. He judged it to be unfortunate that the second strain became dominant in the decisive moments of German history: the War of Liberation, 1813; the Revolution of 1848; and national unification in 1871. "It was Germany's misfortune that she had a Bismarck and not a Gladstone, not even a Cavour."

Kohn points out that German nationalism arose in the nineteenth century as a newly awakened response against Napoleon and French missionary nationalism. Inside Germany the struggle against Napoleon was led by intellectuals, who saw German nationalism not only as a rejection of Napoleon's rule but also of all the principles upon which the American Revolution and the French Revolution had been based. In essence this was a rejection of humanitarian and liberal nationalism.

Some of Kohn's best work has been done in clarifying the nature of German romanticism, which gave German nationalism its strongest impetus. He shows how German romanticism, poor in creative genius, mobilized the totality of the past to struggle against the principles of 1789. German romanticists revealed a longing for the organic folk-community which would immerse the individual in an unbroken chain of tradition. They saw the nation-state not as a societal organization based on law, but as an organic personality. This was expressed in the Hegelian dictum: "All the worth which the human being possesses—all spiritual reality, he possesses only through the State."

Kohn shows how the German professors of 1848 attempted to

[7] See especially Kohn, *German History: Some New German Views* (Boston, 1954), and *The Mind of Germany: The Education of a Nation* (New York, 1960).

achieve national unification on a liberal basis, only to be smothered in defeat. The eventual result was a nationalism based on Bismarck's *Eisen-und-Blut*. Germany's unification was achieved through militarism and authoritarianism. German nationalists tended to regard liberalism and equality as brief aberrations, "against which the eternal foundations of societal order would prevail." Bismarck reversed the temporary rebirth of liberal nationalism. Few Germans rejected the Bismarck ethic or doubted its wisdom.

Bismarck's Second German Reich, a product of war, collapsed just two decades after the chancellor's death in 1898. The Prussian monarchy disappeared in 1918 after defeat in World War I. The Weimar Republic, "a republic with few republicans, a democracy with few democrats," was unwanted, unloved, misunderstood. There came a frenzied revival of integral nationalism in Hitler's Third Reich, "which revived, expanded, popularized, and vulgarized the glories of the Second Reich." Hitlerism and its perverse nationalism collapsed in the debacle of 1945.

As a historian of German nationalism, Kohn sees the course of German history as clothed with tragedy. There has been polarity in German history, a dichotomy of ideas and procedures that has never been resolved. The history of Germany has been a story of the long struggle for a working compromise between uniformity and disruption. As A. J. P. Taylor shows, at no time has there been a central power strong enough to crush the centrifugal tendencies of the component parts. At no time were the individual parts weak enough to allow themselves to be submerged in a centralized body. Uniformity seemed to be contrary to the cultural and political divergencies of the German people.

Kohn sees another tragic element in the German misconception of *Geist* (spiritual depth) and *Macht* (authoritarian power). Eighteenth century Germans underrated the importance of power and correspondingly overrated purity of spirit. There came a change in the nineteenth century, from one extreme to another. From a life of the spirit they turned to the pursuit of power. They raised the nation, state, and economy to supreme concepts, and regarded history as the unfolding of ultimate and self-justifying reality. There emerged an almost mystical veneration of power. Power and State became popular symbols as even the most humble of Germans assumed a sense of belonging to a superior order. In a kind of higher sense of spirituality, Germans found a compensation for their country's allegedly national misfortunes.

In recent years Kohn has shown an optimism regarding the Bonn Republic, an attitude which has brought him into conflict with other observers of the contemporary German scene. The key to Germany's future, Kohn believes, lies in her close contacts with the West. He sees remarkable progress in the politicoeconomic development of postwar West Germany. He senses a new opportunity for the creative contribution of today's Germans to a common civilization based on a common heritage. Safely anchored to the West, the new German generation finds inspiration and social solidarity in a return to the principles of human freedom. Granting that Germany's two hegemonial wars of the twentieth century brought both Germans and Europeans to the brink of catastrophe, Kohn nevertheless sees one great gain—a democratic Germany finally taking its rightful place in Western society.

The economic miracle is well-known: West Germany rose rapidly to the top of the European economic structure, with German goods once again flowing to the markets of the world and the Mark recognized as one of the most stable of the world's currencies. Kohn, deeply attracted by intellectual history, is more interested in changes in the German mentality than in her economic success. Contemporary Germans, he says, are far less addicted to metaphysics, to a vague *Weltanschauung*, than in the past. Noting that national character is always in process of change, Kohn believes that the Germans have taken on an unprecedented sober, practical quality. They now are more influenced by political and social realities than by daring nationalistic zeal.

Above all, Kohn sees the German mind as finally attuned spiritually toward the West and the free world. This is the culmination of a long era in which the German mentality oscillated between the West and East. To Kohn this is one of the more promising developments of the twentieth century. German alienation from the West has come to an end. The First World War inflamed militarist passions in Germany at a time when rapprochement with Western liberal democracy seemed to be on the way. Kohn sees the situation changed after World War II, when the defeat of Germany resulted in the preservation of liberty and civilization not only in the greater part of Western and Central Europe but also in Germany itself.

Kohn's optimistic view has been challenged by other observers of the current German scene who point to repeated outbursts of pro-Nazi sentiment. These critics recall the tragedy of Hitler, and ask how confidence can be placed in a people who react irrationally at critical moments in their history.

Kohn is not impressed by this skeptical view. He sees the new German trend to the West as more decisive than the old tendency to give in to totalitarian tyranny. He regards the Bonn Federal Republic as the first real attempt in German history to create a Western-oriented liberal and democratic state. The chances for a free Germany in the Western sense, he believes, are far greater today than at any time in the past century. We should not be blinded by spotty manifestations of older forms of German nationalism.

Kohn's basically optimistic view on recent German developments reflects his general attitude as a historian. He is well aware of the imperfections of the human animal in both thought and action. But he refuses to put on the cloak of a prophet of doom and describe all civilization as heading straight for the abyss. He speaks with a moderate voice in an era of gloom.

Kohn has always had the utmost respect for his discipline. He categorizes the historian as one who tries to find out what has happened in the course of time and who correlates the events, within the limits of the available material on the one hand and his intelligence, imagination, and ethical understanding on the other, into a meaningful sequence. In his view, the writing of history means something more than regarding events as isolated phenomena, but rather the important task of placing events in the context of time.

This attitude reminds one of the famous Rankean formula of "wie es eigentlich gewesen ist,"—as it actually happened. Kohn sees the first task of the historian to find out by patient and painstaking research the true facts of the past. "Scholarly research, like all scientific endeavor, carries its reward in itself in the joy of discovering unknown facts, of finding new interpretations, of shedding light on obscure relationships." [8]

For Kohn the discipline of history—in this way differing from the sciences—contains an essential element of art. It is for this reason that great historical works retain a permanent value. History does not serve society but instead serves man, enriching his knowledge, equipping him with a deeper understanding of himself, of his fellow man, and of the situations in which humans find themselves. This was expressed by Kohn in a challenging passage:

> [History] can tell us as much about man and the human condition as the best novel or the greatest drama. In this way too, then, history has much in common with art. Beyond this function, it should give us a critical awareness of ourselves and of our own time by providing perspective through comparison and distinction. Persons, events, and situations are always different and never the same: but they are never entirely new or unique. That is the truth, the partial truth, in the Greek attitude toward history, which saw in history a morphology of human behavior, or as Florus, the Roman historian of the time of Trajan and a disciple of Livy, put it pithily, *"ut qui res eius legunt, non unius populi, sed generis humani facta discant"* ("so that those who read its story, do not learn the facts about one people but about the whole human kind").[9]

Kohn sees the historian not only as a scholar and to some extent an artist but also a teacher. This is obviously an important function, for the correct teaching of history may be fundamental to the moral and political wisdom of peoples. Historians, says Kohn, have responsibilities, not to nations or classes, to dogmas or creeds, but to truth and humanity. It is their training which can help them understand the genesis of events and movements and to evaluate their relative worth and importance by comparison with similar attitudes in other peoples, climes, and periods. Kohn feels that this should make their approach more critical and more cautious. They must always be aware of their own prejudices and

---

[8] Kohn, "A Historian's Creed For Our Time," *South Atlantic Quarterly*, LII (1953), 344.
[9] *Ibid.*, 345.

group interests. He rejects the distinction that is often made between political historians and historians of ideas on the ground that ideas and politics are closely interlined and interdependent. "History, whether as scholarship or as art or as teaching, represents the meeting, the interaction, the interrelationship of objective and subjective factors. The facts of the past present the objective material; the ethos and the personality of the historian present the subjective factor without which the facts of the past and the past itself remain dead." [10]

Judged on the basis of his own standards, it is reasonable to say that Kohn has earned and attained a position of respect among his fellow historians. A scholar of multiple interests, he has written not only on many phases of modern European history but he has also turned his attention to developments in the Middle East, Asia, and Africa. But it is primarily as a historian of nationalism that he has made his greatest impact on the society of scholars. Especially valuable are his contributions on eastern and central European nationalism in which he was reared and which he understood. His general work on the meaning, characteristics, and development of nationalism is distinguished by a pioneer quality which has given direction to other students of the elusive ism.

At the same time Kohn's general spirit of optimism serves as an antidote to the pessimism of Spengler and his fellow apostles of doom. As historian, Kohn does his best to salvage the great democratic dream of the eighteenth century Enlightenment. He sees large parts of mankind today as impatient with the hard discipline of individual thinking, full of desire to march in masses, as a means of overcoming the loneliness and fear in the growing complexity of the human situation. Twentieth century man has become less confident than his predecessors: he has witnessed the reappearance of fanatical faith, infallible leaders, slavery, massacres, uprooting of whole populations, ruthlessness, and barbarism. But Kohn steadfastly holds to his belief that, against all expectations of totalitarians, Western civilization has proved its power of resistance against fanatic ideologies.

[10] *Ibid.*, 348.

A. J. P. TAYLOR

H. RUSSELL WILLIAMS
Southern Methodist University

"Iɴ ᴛʜᴇ ꜰɪʀꜱᴛ place I know I know." [1] Such is Alan John Percivale Taylor's basic assumption about himself and consequently about the history he writes.* To be sure, he added "In the second place I know you know," but the weight of all he has written and all that is known about him indicates that the first sentiment is the paramount one. It is a simple premise, held with a conviction so genuine it might be touching if it were not so maddening. Much of the world is inclined to remark of him as Lord Melbourne did of an earlier historian: "I wish I was as cocksure about anything as Macaulay is about everything!" [2] Certainty is not granted to most people, and the incredulous majority naturally enough resent the fortunate few who are free from nagging doubts. Resentment is a feeling Taylor has aroused in abundance.

Other factors besides his certainty have, of course, contributed to making Taylor one of the most controversial living citizens of the scholarly world. One of these is precisely his refusal to stay within the prescribed boundaries of that world. Through television appearances which, it is whispered, he actually enjoys, and through writing in most unscholarly publications, including the *Sunday Express*, his has become a household name throughout Britain. This achievement has won him scattered applause, but it may also have cost him the coveted Regius Professorship at Ox-

* Research for this article was made possible by the Graduate Council of the Humanities, Southern Methodist University.

[1] Ved Mehta, "The Flight of the Crook-Taloned Birds," *New Yorker* (December 8, 1962), 130.
[2] David Cecil, *Melbourne* (London, 1955), 342.

ford University and it has undoubtedly earned him the ardent disapproval of many academicians. He has what fastidious Americans might think of as a "Hollywood Image."

In addition to his irritating self-assurance and his envy-provoking success in the world at large, Taylor's personal characteristics and mode of operation have added to the atmosphere of conflict in which his fame and reputation are still being shaped. His current image is much affected by what is sometimes called his irrepressible *gaminerie* or, put more bluntly, his downright perversity.

It was proverbial when he was teaching at Oxford that he would do or say the unexpected. At a time when he was a highly successful lecturer there, he had to say he was happier in Manchester; when addressing a party-line congress behind the Iron Curtain he gave an aggressively conservative speech, although at home he calls himself a socialist and is an active supporter of the Campaign for Nuclear Disarmament; not only must he write in the *Sunday Express*, he must assert that it is a much better paper than the *London Times*.[3] It is abundantly clear that he has worked hard to achieve and perpetuate his reputation as a shocker. This characteristic is very evident in his writings and while it may be judged stimulating on some occasions, it seems irresponsible, insincere, and mischievous on others.

Taylor's background does not explain his craving for paradox or his hostility to orthodoxy. He was born in 1906 in Lancashire, the only son of a well-to-do Radical-Liberal cotton manufacturer. He received his early education at a Quaker school and subsequently attended Oriel College, Oxford, after having failed the entrance examination for Balliol. Oxford legend has it that his rebuff resulted from ostentatious flippancy in his interview; but whether or not this is true (he says not) he was soon sufficiently launched on his career of unorthodoxy to take pride in becoming the only member of the Labor Club in his College.[4] However, his academic career was distinguished. He took first class honors and subsequently studied under the famed A. F. Pribram at Vienna.

[3] Mehta, "The Flight of the Crook-Taloned Birds," 120–22, 131–32.
[4] Edward B. Segel, "A. J. P. Taylor and History," *Review of Politics*, XXVI (October, 1964), 531–46.

Brilliantly trained in the historical discipline and in command of the five major European languages, Taylor now began an eight-year association with the University of Manchester, where he came into close contact with the great Sir Lewis Namier, the most respected British historian of his time. Namier remained, until his death in 1961, one of the most potent influences in Taylor's career, although rumor insists that in 1957 Sir Lewis' word was decisive in obtaining the Regius Professorship for Hugh Trevor-Roper rather than Taylor.[5]

At the time of the appointment Taylor had been at Oxford for nineteen years, having become a tutor at Magdalen College in 1938. He already had two books to his credit: *The Italian Problem in European Diplomacy, 1847–1849* and *Germany's First Bid for Colonies, 1884–1885*.[6] Henceforth, his brilliance as a writer, lecturer, and provocative personality brought him steadily to the forefront of the profession. He also became something of a public figure by publishing, outside the usual scholarly journals, a stream of articles, essays, and reviews. His media beyond the aforementioned *Sunday Express* included the *Observer, Guardian,* and *New Statesman,* about as wide a spectrum as the prominent English press offered. Then, through an academic distinction, another avenue of popular communication opened up.

In 1955 Taylor received the coveted invitation to give his University's prestigious annual Ford Lecture Series. He chose a subject which fascinated him, "Dissent Over Foreign Policy," and which allowed him to display both his sound scholarship and his disturbing conceptualizations. Obviously, he knew a great deal about the ins and outs of diplomacy, but was he right in concluding that the opponents of official policy were always more prescient than those in power? If so, the implications for the present were—and are—startling indeed. Taylor himself was so pleased that he calls the published version of the lectures, *The Troublemakers,*[7] his favorite among his own books.

[5] Mehta, "The Flight of the Crook-Taloned Birds," 66.

[6] Taylor, *The Italian Problem in European Diplomacy, 1847–1849* (Manchester, Eng., 1934); *Germany's First Bid for Colonies, 1884–1885; A Move in Bismarck's European Policy* (London, 1938).

[7] Taylor, *The Troublemakers: Dissent over Foreign Policy, 1792–1939* (Oxford, Eng., 1960).

The Ford Series, delivered in a lively, exciting style for which he was already well known at Oxford, greatly enhanced his reputation as a speaker. Academicians might not entirely approve of what has been called "an histrionic performance,"[8] but the television moguls did (and here we may perhaps assume that it was the delivery rather than the content that counted). Henceforth, Taylor was launched on a new career. Within two years the *New Statesman* saluted him as a real television star, a man whose Sunday afternoon broadcasts brought him regularly into homes all over Britain.[9] Again the disparate elements in his personality and presentations accounted for his success. Alan Taylor—the name by which he is known to British television audiences—could be expected to be exuberant, warm, and oddly charming even—or especially—when he was shredding conventional ideas about history, politics, or whatever he chose to discuss. As both "preacher and acrobat," the "pyrotechnician of history," delighted that broad segment of the public which enjoyed the discomfiture of the Establishment; as an intellectual and a serious historian he appealed to the discerning public which came to resent, however, both his pandering to popularity and the excesses of some of his views, e.g., that the sole purpose of history is to amuse.[10] The net result was Taylor's installation among the acknowledged "personalities" of the time.

It is a tribute to his strength of purpose and character that Taylor did not abandon his scholarly pursuits for the glamor and financial rewards—both of which he enjoys—of the world of popular entertainment. His most controversial as well as his most widely appreciated historical works were published after his television conquests.

Taylor's reputation as an historian had developed simultaneously with his career as a university don and had in fact been the springboard to his fame both as a popular journalist and television personality. Before 1960 he had published eight books, one perhaps his best, *The Struggle for Mastery in Europe*, innumerable essays, reviews, and pamphlets. Since then, six more books, including an-

---

[8] "The Seventh Veil," *New Statesman*, LIV, no. 1385 (September 28, 1957), 376–77.
[9] *Ibid.*   [10] *Ibid.*

other of his best, *English History, 1914–1945*, and his most controversial, *The Origins of the Second World War*, have appeared, as
have two essay collections and one translation from the German.[11]
It seems that his long years of scholarly activity and prodigious
work habits are producing tangible results at an ever-increasing rate.

It is customary and convenient to make a rather arbitrary division of Taylor's works into the categories of national history and
diplomatic history. The collections of essays stand aside from these
groupings and because some of his most interesting ideas appear
in his shorter works, the individual essays may be employed profit-
ably to point up a critical evaluation of the works in the general
categories.

The major national histories are *The Habsburg Monarchy,
1815–1918; The Course of German History;*[12] and *English History, 1914–1945* (1965). These three books cannot easily be forced
into a single mold: Taylor's variations in attitude towards his subjects are enough to insure basic differences in aproaches, treatments, and conclusions. The first and third of these works are
relatively noncontroversial. His Austrian thesis, namely that the
Habsburg Empire became a hopeless anachronism in the nineteenth century and was inevitably fated to collapse, is sanely argued (although undocumented as are so many of his books), and
the conflict of nationalities is presented with an impartiality
which, in light of his subsequent writings, is startling. The thesis
is a significant one in view of its bearing on the philosophy of
history and of the historical importance attached to the territorial
arrangement of central Europe. It has not gone unchallenged.
Nevertheless, it has in the main been received as a stimulating
contribution to nineteenth century European history, and its importance is attested to by the fact that *The Habsburg Monarchy* has been reprinted more often than any other of Taylor's
books.

[11] Taylor, *The Struggle for Mastery in Europe, 1848–1918*, Vol. II of *The
Oxford History of Modern Europe*, eds. Alan Bullock and F. W. D. Deakin
(Oxford: Clarendon Press, 1954); *English History, 1914–1945* (New York, 1965);
The Origins of the Second World War (London, 1961).

[12] Taylor, *The Habsburg Monarchy, 1815–1918: A History of the Austrian
Empire and Austria-Hungary* (London, 1941); *The Course of German History:
A Survey of the Development of Germany since 1815* (London, 1945).

The newest of Taylor's works, the *English History*, occupies the august position of volume XV in the authoritative *Oxford History of England*. It *had* to be restrained, documented, and generally in the pattern established by the earlier volumes. The consensus of opinion up to this point is that Taylor restrained himself admirably. Not that it was easy. As he hints in the preface, the use of the word "probably" throughout the book was the result of outside influence.[13] There are still some disturbing statements: many Englishmen will not agree that David Lloyd George was "the most inspired and creative British statesman of the twentieth century," and indeed after saying this, Taylor makes an analysis of the Welsh Wizard which indicates precisely why he does not deserve the original accolade.[14] It is a fine Taylor-like paradox. In addition, American readers will find a number of gratuitously unpleasant references to the United States, but these surprises are relatively mild; the calm of the historical profession has not been unduly ruffled. One can, perhaps, detect echoing through the groves of academe a slight sigh of relief that this was no repetition of *The Origins of the Second World War*.

Nor did the new work in any way resemble *The Course of German History*. In 1945 this little book had been well received in the English-speaking world, which was not at that point interested in an impartial judgment of Germany. Read today, it is an incredible production. One can only imagine Taylor writing it at the height of the blitz, crouching under a table, bombs raining about him, and with but a typewriter between him and oblivion. Admittedly such circumstances are not conducive to clear reflection and for that reason the professional historian, as distinguished from the propagandist, might be expected either to acknowledge his extreme personal involvement in his current situation or to focus his professional skills on subjects not quite so close at hand. Instead Taylor chose to give us, in his own words, a "serious history" which amounts in fact to a wholesale denunciation of an entire nation.[15]

Taylor's Germans had been going wrong since time immemorial

[13] Taylor, *English History*, vii.   [14] *Ibid.*, 192.
[15] Taylor, *The Course of German History*, 7.

and with Luther they took a particularly bad turn.[16] That reformer, reflecting accurately the German spirit, rejected all the values of Western civilization including its art, culture, and intellectual attainments. From then on, the German spirit was to assert
itself consistently against reason, against civilization, against the
West. Smashing indictments indeed. Under these circumstances
Taylor, reasonably enough, found it advisable to disavow any connection between his own national home and that across the North
Sea: "England and Germany are not only not alike, but do not
belong to the same civilization." [17] He attempted to answer the
charge of anti-Germanism in the preface to the 1961 edition, but
his explanations will hardly convince those who have charged him
with bias against the Teutonic cousin. In spite of their great
achievements in other fields, Taylor insists, the "art of political
behavior has been beyond them." His favorite solution remains a
divided Germany, contained by an Anglo-Russian alliance.[18]

It is not surprising, then, that Taylor's national histories of
England and Germany should be different but, even given the
circumstances under which they were written, the vastness of the
differences is remarkable. The two books illustrate in fact the
bipolarity of Taylor's historical ideas, methods, and achievements.
The German history is a series of striking conceptualizations and
generalizations often startling, often penetrating, occasionally hor-
rifying. The book, fittingly enough, is unencumbered by scholarly
appurtenances. It is an example of what has been called the telescopic approach, although Taylor is supposed to prefer the microscope.

The former method concentrates on the "Big Picture," the
trends, movements, *Zeitgeist,* of an historical period. Of course,
the deductions drawn from observing these major phenomena
should theoretically be supported by the known facts, but in
practice the temptation to select supporting facts and ignore
disturbing ones is well-nigh overwhelming. The devotee of the microscope, on the other hand, is concerned with the "Little Picture,"

[16] *Ibid.,* 18–19.   [17] *Ibid.,* 7.
[18] This edition published by University Paperbacks (London, Methuen, 1961),
pp. vii–x.

with the indisputably documented concrete facts. He eschews intangible forces or ideas. Taylor employs the microscopic approach in the *English History* and perhaps the most telling criticisms yet made of the book concern exactly the narrowness inherent in this method.[19] Thus, in the German history Taylor is long on ideas, short on facts; in the English history, vice versa.

Turning to the second category of Taylor's works, the diplomatic histories, his use of the historical microscope becomes even more important. He is a skilled technician, an impressive craftsman. His knowledge of languages is matched by his familiarity with the archives and literature pertinent to his interests. Moreover, he has the great and rare gift of being able to spin an enthralling narrative out of a mass of dry documents.

More than a quarter of a century separates *The Italian Problem in European Diplomacy, 1847–1849,* his first diplomatic history from his latest, *The Origins of the Second World War.* In between came two studies of Bismarck and, as earlier mentioned, his most ambitious effort in this field, *The Struggle for Mastery in Europe, 1848–1919.* Obviously, Taylor has remained fascinated by the way in which nations—specifically European nations—have conducted their relations with each other. His premise is stated in the title *The Struggle for Mastery in Europe.* For Taylor, nations are basically power units whose behavior is governed by inexorable laws. The Balance of Power principle has served to thwart the natural ambitions successively of Spain, France, and Germany, although it required the intervention of the United States in 1917 to prevent the last challenger from obtaining mastery in Europe. Thereafter, the Balance has ceased to exist as a European phenomenon.

Taylor's overall view, then, is deterministic, as he himself states, but he is rather more interested in how individual statesmen and diplomats actually operated or seemed to operate. His choice of villains and heroes provides an interesting insight into the working of Taylor's mind. Here the essays in *Englishmen and Others*[20] and *The Troublemakers* are valuable.

---

[19] E.g. see Asa Briggs, "Taylor's Own Times," *Encounter* (February, 1966), 66.
[20] Taylor, *Englishmen and Others* (London, 1956).

As might be expected, Taylor admires the diplomatic maverick, the dissenter, the troublemaker. "To my mind Dissent is too normal and sensible to demand explanations," [21] he says. That Taylor himself identifies with this view is too obvious to require comment. Fox, Bright, Cobden, Morley, E. D. Morel he finds most attractive, although he must admit being troubled by Fox's inconsistencies and must entirely disown David Urquhart, whose chronic contention was that Lord Palmerston was a Russian spy. What attracts Taylor to dissent is his conviction that it has performed an essential historical function. Whether the practitioners were right or not he will not argue because, he says, it is not the historian's business to judge right or wrong. However, Taylor does assert that the dissenting opinion has so often been accepted by history that if at any given time one wants to know what will be the accepted policy of the future one should observe the contemporary dissenting opinion. He does not provide a guide as to which dissenting opinion should be chosen, although there is a hint.

All of Taylor's bona fide dissenters were on the left of the officials they disagreed with. He does not ordinarily approve of conservatives, especially Metternich, but he does admire Palmerston (not included among the real dissenters), whose domestic policy in the 1850s and 1860s was the bane of all English liberals then and since. That his foreign policy was considered liberal is redeeming and so perhaps is the very fact of the dichotomy between a liberal tone abroad and a conservative one at home. But even at home Taylor admires Palmerston, Why? Because although he was born and bred an aristocrat, he did not entirely conform. In politics he was a loner, developing influence so slowly that, although he had previously served twice as Foreign Secretary, the Whigs who invited him into the cabinet in 1846 did not realize that the sixty-year-old fledgling had found his wings and would henceforth be a troublesome member of the Establishment.[22] Taylor was delighted that the Whigs had taken "a cuckoo in the nest" and was even more pleased that the crisis of the Crimean War swept him to final power in the same way that other crises produced or were to produce the elder Pitt, Lloyd

[21] Taylor, *The Troublemakers*, 16–17.   [22] *Ibid.*, 38.

George, and Churchill. Palmerston alone of the four retained power after the crisis was over; but, Taylor says, he was a "rogue elephant," politically estranged from his own cabinet and therefore unable to carry out a positive policy. Taylor admired his isolation, courage, flair, and individuality; still, all in all, it is a bit difficult to see how a man who prefers Garibaldi to Cavour can put up with Palmerston. One suspects that Taylor's personal evaluations are highly subjective, but this must not obscure the fact that as a diplomatic historian he is accustomed to doing detailed, sustained research on a very extensive scale.

However, in spite of his undeniable intellectual gifts and his unquestioned diligence in research, Taylor has sustained almost unparalleled criticism for works in the categories of both national and diplomatic history and when using both the telescope and the microscope. His reckless quest for singularity would have insured some of this in any case, but it is noteworthy that his greatest trouble comes when he deals with Germany, especially in *The Origins of the Second World War*. To the historiography of the Second World War this book is what Harry Elmer Barnes' *Genesis of the World War* was to that of the first, and its ultimate fate, although as yet undecided, may be similar. It is not intended here to recapitulate the well-known arguments for and against the *Origins*, but out of the acrid (and on some levels childish) debates surrounding the book a number of significant points emerge which bear on Taylor's position as a diplomatic historian. These points involve the use Taylor made of the documents supporting the *Origins* and the conclusions he drew from them. Both are suspect. It does not matter who won the battle of invective which Taylor and Trevor-Roper carried on in the pages of *Encounter* and over television, the fact remains that Trevor-Roper's charge that Taylor's treatment of his sources was capricious has not been successfully refuted.[23] This is a most serious—even fatal—flaw in diplomatic history, especially when a suspicion exists that the mis-

---

[23] Trevor-Roper, "A. J. P. Taylor, Hitler, and the War," *Encounter* (July, 1961), 88–96; Taylor, "How to Quote, Exercises for Beginners," *Encounter* (September, 1961), 72–73; Trevor-Roper, "A Reply," *Encounter* (September, 1961), 73. And see Segel, "A. J. P. Taylor and History," 542–43; and T. W. Mason, "Some Origins of the Second World War," *Past and Present*, no. 29 (December, 1964), 68–69.

uses were intentionally designed to support preconceived conclusions.

To criticize the *Origins* as an apology for Hitler is to miss the whole point. Taylor was, of course, aware of the moral debate going on in the 1950s in which the question of German guilt for the war and genocide program was being threshed out. The alternatives that emerged (ignoring the moderates who took characteristic refuge in the idea of the interplay of historical factors) were (1) that Hitler and his small band of cronies were guilty of having duped and misled the majority of the German people—a view the Germans themselves were understandably anxious to support; or (2) that Hitler was merely the agent of the desires, values, and aspirations of the German people. It takes no imagination to determine where the author of *The Course of German History* would take his stand. The German people must not be allowed to escape the blame—as Taylor himself admits.[24]

The "whitewashing" of Hitler, then, was only a by-product, and, in spite of considerable protest, Taylor's rationalist, pseudo-scientific approach coupled with his literary persuasiveness succeeded in convincing the reviewers of such respectable publications as the *Observer*, and the *Times Literary Supplement* of the merits of his thesis.[25] Taylor was probably quite pleased. He had managed to condemn the entire German people while appearing to exonerate the worst of the lot! It was a triumph for perversity.

Essentially, what Taylor did was to examine Hitler solely in the light of concrete documentary evidence, eschewing such nebulous factors as the international atmosphere which Nazi Germany created and the larger aspects of Hitler's aspirations. Especially and specifically he eliminated considerations of contemporary morality. For an historian bent closely over his documents and determined avowedly to draw his conclusions solely from what he read there, to discount larger movements was relatively easy. There were, however, troublesome documents, especially the "Hossbach Memorandum" and *Mein Kampf*. Taylor dismissed

[24] Mehta, "The Flight of the Crook-Taloned Birds," 123.

[25] Trevor-Roper, "A. J. P. Taylor," 89. These and other favorable reviews were partially responsible for Trevor-Roper's writing the article.

the former as a paper drawn up primarily to distract internal opposition to Hitler's financial plans, and he largely ignored the latter. Trevor-Roper challenged him on both counts.[26]

The conclusion to which Taylor's strictly rationalist approach (meaning that intangible and/or immeasurable forces are disregarded) leads him is that Hitler was doing nothing more than following traditional German foreign policy. If anything was wrong about that policy, it was the German tradition, not Hitler.

One other and much less well-known instance of Taylor's handling of German matters emerges from his essay on the great German historian, Leopold von Ranke. Taylor professed to admire Ranke, rating him not first, but among the six greatest historians of all times.[27] He then proceeds subtly but surely to demolish him. Ranke's opinions that Bismarck was excessively liberal and that King Frederick William IV of Prussia was the ideal monarch are recounted without further comment. The reader is allowed to draw his own conclusion about the great historian's powers of judgment. Taylor then passes on to Ranke's marked tenderness toward the Habsburgs, a susceptibility that evaporated in the 1850s when Austria sought to challenge the rise of Prussia. At that point, according to Taylor, "Ranke discovered that Roman Catholic Powers did not understand the workings of Providence." [28] The Prussian historian is subsequently described as maintaining that the Austro-Prussian War of 1866 was a defensive war against sinister Austrian designs. The reader is allowed once more to draw his own conclusions about the great historian's objectivity.

What set Taylor off on the Ranke essay was a renewal of German interest in the famous historian. This renascence, Taylor decided, was an attempt on the part of contemporary Germans to evade responsibility just as Ranke had evaded it "by a sort of political quietism—finding God in history in the hope that He will take the blame for everything that goes wrong." [29] Moreover, according to Taylor, Ranke was being revived in order to prove German historical "normality." Taylor had already pronounced

[26] *Ibid.*, 93.   [27] Taylor, *Englishmen and Others*, 12.   [28] *Ibid.*, 16.
[29] *Ibid.*, 12.

against this trait in the Germans. The opening words of *The Course of German History* are: "The history of the Germans is a history of extremes. It contains everything except moderation, and in the course of a thousand years the Germans have experienced everything except normality. . . . Only the normal person, not particularly good, not particularly bad, healthy, sane, moderate— he has never set his stamp on German history." [30] Clearly Ranke had to be shown up. Not that the essay is a total denunciation. Ranke is allowed to retain his stature among the historians, although the qualities that place him there, "gravity and self confidence," are not very convincing. Taylor is too clever a man and too well trained an historian to picture his individual subjects exclusively in blacks or whites. He uses them both, avoiding gray wherever possible because it represents compromises which do not excite him. The paradoxes resulting from the juxtaposition of extremes stimulate him, and they also contribute to the perverse image which he strives to perpetuate. The discerning reader need not, however, be taken in. What he means is scarcely gray either.

In the *Course*, Taylor employed the telescopic approach to castigate the Germans; in the *Origins* he used the microscope, but the result is the same. Historians who place any value on objectivity or impartiality must conclude that, when dealing with the Germans, Taylor is not one of them. Nor will those who believe that some degree of bias is inevitable in any work rest easy. Taylor's is not a conscious, acknowledged, manageable bias; it surpasses any reasonable limits. The result is that on the subject of Germany Taylor may be brilliant and provocative, but he is also misleading and unreliable.

This might not be important if either Taylor or his readers really believed that he wrote, as has been claimed, solely to amuse. But this is nonsense; he is a serious person. Some instances of his ostentatious flippancy, his desire to shock, his vow to write history free from moral or philosophical speculation may be seen as parts of the defense mechanism of a hypersensitive man who not only cares about what he says but cares too much. Other instances are due to his faith in the efficacy of paradox as an intellectual stimulant. Neither situation is either comic or frivolous,

[30] Taylor, *The Course of German History*, 13.

nor is it difficult to find in Taylor's writings a fairly constant set of values.

Perhaps the most persistent principle found throughout his works is his advocacy of individualism. It is trenchantly stated at the conclusion of his joint essay on Macaulay and Carlyle in *Englishmen and Others*, in which Taylor has the opportunity to contrast two opposing philosophies and two divergent styles. His views on Macaulay are especially interesting because either he consciously set out in his career to emulate his great predecessor's style or else he discovered the coincidental similarities later. In either case, he admires Macaulay for being sure of himself and of the differences between right and wrong.[31] Perhaps, Taylor muses, the Whig historians *were* right after all. In the final analysis, however, he concluded that Macaulay's greatness stemmed not so much from his views as from his powers of narration. This may be a comforting thought for him.

Turning to Carlyle, Taylor is devastating. Nothing could be more damning than to say "the hero he worshipped was his own opposite." [32] Taylor analyzed Carlyle as a man who had supreme sympathy for the masses but deserted them during the Chartist agitation and spent the remainder of his life paying for his betrayal. According to Taylor, Carlyle was compelled to lay about him in every direction in order to avoid the necessity of accounting to himself for his social treason. Moreover, this wild compulsion may explain the inchoate nature of Carlyle's thoughts. "His ideas are those of a man of the people who has suddenly become articulate—if only in Anglo-German." [33] Nevertheless Taylor appreciates the force both of Carlyle's ideas and his language. He acknowledges the Sage of Chelsea to be a more powerful writer than Macaulay but concludes that the latter won out in the long run because his cause, freedom of the individual, enjoyed moral superiority over the tyranny advocated by Carlyle.

In another place Taylor excoriates Rousseau's General Will as one of the most dangerous ideas to emerge from the mind of man.[34] Taylor will not, moreover, subordinate the thinker to the thought. Rather, he insists that ideas have no idependent existence

[31] Taylor, *Englishmen and Others*, 20–21.   [32] *Ibid.*, 23.   [33] *Ibid.*, 22.
[34] *Ibid.*, 3.

of their own. "Men make ideas" and not vice versa, he says.

Taylor is not only a stanch individualist, he is vociferously anti-universalist. He deplores the eighteenth century's transformation of men into Man, "a universal simplicity or even simpleton."[35] As usual, the values Taylor abhors he finds present in German history, and universalism is no exception. It has been since Charlemagne, he says, one of the principal—and, of course, unfortunate—determinants both of German history and of the German national character.[36]

Taylor's insistence on individualism appears to be connected with at least two other problems which have fascinated his critics—historical determinism and moral interpretations in history. Taylor considers himself a determinist, which would appear to be in direct contrast to his marked penchant for individualism. He resolves the problem by reserving the deterministic approach for the large view of history, while feeling that his detailed studies permit the action of accident and individual factors. One fairly recent interviewer who wished to probe more deeply into this matter was unable to draw from Taylor any further elaboration.[37] The following quotation seems to represent his stand on the matter: "Two Germanies would have come into existence even if Bismarck had never been born—though their political character might have been different."[38]

Possibly the problem worries Taylor more than he admits. In the essay on Macaulay he seems to indicate that a man cannot be both a statesman and an historian. As the former he may feel the excitement of political activism; as the latter he must realize its artificiality; he must *act* as if his vote in Parliament matters when he *knows* it really does not.[39] Taylor's own career as a moderate activist must carry similar reservations and perhaps the resulting frustration is another source of his flippancy. On the other hand, as one of his critics has pointed out, when Taylor is in a more serious mood he seems to feel that the study of history can improve man's ability to master his own destiny.[40] More specifically,

35 *Ibid.*, 4.   36 Taylor, *The Course of German History*, 16.
37 Mehta, "The Flight of the Crook-Taloned Birds," 128.
38 Taylor, *Bismarck, the Man and the Statesman* (New York, 1955), 37.
39 Taylor, *Englishmen and Others*, 22.
40 Segel, "A. J. P. Taylor and History," 534.

his knowledge of German history makes him an outspoken advocate of the necessity to contain Germany and prevent its reunification.

His views on the historian's duty to make or refrain from making moral judgments are even more blatantly inconsistent than his ideas on individualism and determinism. In one of his essays he says: "I am not a philosophic historian. I have no system, no moral interpretation. I write to clear my mind, to discover how things happened and how men behaved. If the result is shocking or provocative, this is not from intent. . . ." [41] This same attitude of moral neutrality is reiterated later in the "Preface for the American Reader" to the *Origins*.[42] But only a year or so earlier he had said in an interview: "When I judge—perhaps this is the wrong way for a historian to go on—but when I judge events in the past I try to judge them in terms of the morality which then existed, not mine." [43] About all one can make of this is that Taylor does on occasion try to write history devoid of moral judgment but that he cannot, in the final analysis, succeed. In fact, on those occasions when Taylor insists on his moral neutrality, e.g., in the *Origins*, his history comes closest to supporting what are known to be his personal convictions.

The question which torments almost all historians when contemplating their own work or judging that of others is, will it last? This depends of course on what qualities future generations will value most highly.

It is a fairly safe assumption that the brilliance and clarity of Taylor's literary style, the eminent readability of his works, will support any quest for immortality. After all, there are not many men who can write fascinating bibliographies. Some of his wit may fade with time, but the powers of narration should evoke admiration among future generations of students seeking effective ways to organize and present their historical findings. The works of Macaulay's generation have been largely superseded but his are still read. Those of his more academically correct contemporaries are merely outdated curiosities.

41 Taylor, *Englishmen and Others,* 22.
42 Taylor, *Origins of the Second World War* (Greenwich, Conn., 1961), ix.
43 Mehta, "The Flight of the Crook-Taloned Birds," 72.

The twenty-first century's regard for the prophet Taylor can be expected to shine or fade according to what happens to Germany. Should his historical evaluations and warnings about the chronic German danger prove accurate, he may join Burke and Tocqueville among the successful prognosticators of history. If, however, Germany should finally accommodate itself to Europe, as now seems likely, his pronouncements on the subject will seem ridiculous. What will matter then is whether future generations will accept the task of sorting out his work, of retaining those portions of undoubted value, and of forgetting the horrendously biased misjudgments. If they should, Taylor, from whatever regions he may then inhabit, might not be entirely pleased. As he once told his students, "Error can often be fertile, but perfection is always sterile." [44]

[44] *Ibid.*, 138.

J. L. HAMMOND

I T IS A CURIOUS coincidence that so much of importance on the history of Great Britain in the industrial age has been written by three eminent husband and wife teams. The Webbs, the Coles, the Hammonds—each pair in its different way calls up a series of significant contributions that have enriched our understanding of the nature of British life since the seventeenth century. Some enterprising historiographer may one day assay a joint study, not a dual biography but rather a triple dual evaluation. Yet such an analysis may well turn out to have more unity of focus than many works devoted to a single protagonist. The intention here, however, is more modest, a mere survey of the historical accomplishment of one of this remarkable six.

John Lawrence LeBreton Hammond was born in 1872 at Drighlington in Yorkshire, where his father was vicar.[1] After five years at Bradford Grammar School he entered Oxford in 1891. Although his career at St. John's College was not outstanding— he took a Second in Greats in 1895—it did much to shape his future ideas and concerns. His inherited liberalism was perhaps reinforced by his association with such fellow undergraduates as Hilaire Belloc, F. W. Hirst, and J. A. Simon, but it was given a profound social thrust by the influence of Sidney Ball, one of the

---

[1] Details of Hammond's life may be found in the usual obituarial notices, for example, Gilbert Murray's sketch in L. G. Wickham Legg and E. T. Williams (eds.) *Dictionary of National Biography, 1941–1950* (Oxford, 1959), 350–52, and more particularly in R. H. Tawney, "J. L. Hammond, 1872–1949," *Proceedings of the British Academy, 1960* (London, 1961), 267–94. I have relied heavily on the latter.

few Fabian socialists in the academic world of the nineties. Above all, he was thrown into contact with Gilbert Murray, the distinguished classicist who became a lifelong friend of Hammond and, after 1901, of his wife Barbara. Like Murray, Hammond came to nourish his liberalism at the springs of antiquity, and the deep imprint of his classical studies is to be seen in all his later works. Repeatedly, the questions he was to raise about the nature of the good society and the quality of the good life were to be framed in ways that revealed his great debt to the Greek and Roman authors who had posed similar questions about their own contemporary world.

For a time after going down from Oxford, Hammond served as secretary to Sir John Brunner while plunging into the divided world of liberal journalism. From the beginning he took his place in the ranks of those liberals of the Left who were repelled by the supposed attractions of imperialist slogans and policies and were appalled by the drift toward war in South Africa. At about the turn of the century, the *Speaker*, a weekly journal, came into the hands of a group of such young liberals, among them Belloc, Hirst, Simon, G. K. Chesterton, Philip Carr, and Hammond.[2] It was natural that Hammond, whose abilities as a journalist were already evident, should have become editor soon after the Boer War broke out. As R. H. Tawney has commented, his editorship was both successful and characteristic.[3] He spoke out with courage about conditions in the concentration camps of South Africa, vigorously supported the "pro-Boer" position of Sir Henry Campbell-Bannerman, and in general took up causes that were as unpopular as they may have been just.

The *Speaker* was not the only vehicle for Hammond's views. For example, in 1900 he published in collaboration with Gilbert Murray and F. W. Hirst a little collection of essays on *Liberalism and the Empire*.[4] In his own analysis of colonial and foreign policy, Hammond drew a sharp contrast between the leading ideas of liberalism and those of "modern imperialism." Noting the

[2] Hammond, *C. P. Scott of the* MANCHESTER GUARDIAN (London, 1934), 80.
[3] Tawney, "J. L. Hammond," 268.
[4] Hammond, Murray, and Hirst, *Liberalism and the Empire* (London, 1900).

opprobrium which was currently being visited on the heirs of Charles James Fox, he counseled against despair. Trust in morality between nations, respect for the best instincts of true nationalism, a conviction that England could not cut herself off from the highest interests of Europe—these he claimed as the great principles of contemporary liberalism. Bitterly assailing the imperialism of Joseph Chamberlain, Hammond argued that domestic reform, if it were to be more than empirical legislation wrung from the rich by the threats of the needy, offered little hope until the language of England abroad became the language of morality and not the language "of pride, of mastery, of force, of violence, of revenge." Real progress, he suggested, was hardly possible until England once more should win back the respect instead of drawing upon herself the curses of liberal Europe, "till the love of country and the love of liberty, divorced to-day, shall be brought back into their old glorious association." [5]

Although he married Lucy Barbara Bradby in 1901, their partnership did not result in the first of their joint works, *The Village Labourer*, until a decade later. Meanwhile, Hammond wrested time from his journalistic duties to complete a political study of Charles James Fox. [6] As he explained in his preface, the book was an attempt to portray the ideas Fox stood for, to defend the essential consistency of his career, and to appreciate the magnanimous inspirations he gave to politics. It was, therefore, not a biography but a series of essays on Fox's position in relation to the king, to parliamentary reform, to Ireland, to colonies and dependencies, to the French Revolution and the Revolutionary Wars, to the Reign of Terror, to nationalism, to religious toleration. Perhaps not a major work, it is nevertheless worthy of notice as a revelation of its author's almost passionate attachment to the values of liberty and the dignity of individual men. He saw all of Fox's limitations, his frequent inertia, his lack of concern for parliamentary reform or for the redress of economic inequities. But outweighing all the faults were Fox's struggle for domestic freedom in an age of repression and his defense of national lib-

---

[5] Hammond, Murray, and Hirst, *Liberalism and the Empire*, 161, 165, 211.
[6] Hammond, *Charles James Fox. A Political Study* (London, 1903).

erties abroad, whether in revolutionary France or in England's other island across the Irish Sea. Fox, he wrote, "was the valiant friend of freedom, justice, and equal law at home, but his name is still more illustrious because in a nation with great and distant possessions, with subjects dependent on the precarious mercy of the unknown rulers, his arm was always uplifted for the defenceless, and he never watched in a pale silence or a smothered anger the applause or the consummation of a public wrong." [7]

By 1907, when the *Speaker* was transformed into the *Nation*, Hammond had decided that editorial work left him insufficient latitude to do justice to his historical studies. He left the journal and for the next six years held the apparently less demanding position of secretary to the Civil Service Commission. These were the years in which the European state system trembled from crisis to crisis until the assasssination at Sarajevo precipitated a confrontation that was not successfully weathered. In the last days before the outbreak of war, Hammond did what he could to work for the maintenance of peace. But once he was convinced by the German invasion of Belgium that national rights were at stake, he insisted, despite his pacific temper, upon taking up a commission in the Royal Field Artillery. At forty, however, he was too frail to be permitted to serve abroad and in the course of time he went from noncombatant service back into civil life. For a time he worked in the Ministry of Reconstruction; then, after the Armistice, he served as a special correspondent of the *Manchester Guardian* at the peace conference.

Like John Maynard Keynes, Hammond was horrified by what he saw at Paris. For a time he hoped, as he wrote in the *Guardian* of April 12, 1919, that England and America would put their credit behind the victims of war, that they would renounce debts and feed the countries where famine raged, that they would act to stimulate the revival of industry by loans and raw materials. But instead of a generous peace of reconciliation, the victorious leaders at Paris created a settlement marked by an almost callous disregard for Europe's economic needs and by brutality and insolence toward the countries that had suffered defeat. The truth about the peace

[7] *Ibid.*, v, 25–26, 29–30.

conference, he wrote much later, was that during five months of conflict and argument no power made an effective sacrifice for the sake of a permanent peace or the restoration of Europe. "The shadow of famine and revolution was thrown across Europe, but these statesmen, hardened in the atmosphere of war and suffering, scarcely noticed it in the struggle of their dialectics." [8]

Hammond's journalistic reaction to the peace settlement merits some attention in a survey of his historical work because it gives a sharp insight into the spirit that informed his more important writings on the Industrial Revolution. In 1911 he and Mrs. Hammond had published *The Village Labourer* and it was followed in the years of war and peacemaking by *The Town Labourer* and *The Skilled Labourer*.[9] Although *The Village Labourer* was not reviewed in the *English Historical Review*, it was hardly unnoticed: J. A. Clapham criticized it sharply in the *Economic Journal*. By 1917, when *The Town Labourer* appeared, the first volume had been reprinted twice. By 1948 that number had been increased to ten with a total printing of 66,500. *The Town Labourer* was reprinted eleven times in two editions of 43,750 and *The Skilled Labourer*, somewhat less general in its appeal, was reprinted three times in some 6,000 copies.[10] With the completion of the trilogy the influence of the Hammonds was established. Their pessimistic portrait of the consequences of industrialization came to be largely accepted and it has indeed retained widespread popularity to this day. That interpretation was challenged in its turn, particularly by economists and economic historians, who made effective use of quantitative data to present a radically different description of conditions in the early Industrial Revolution. But it is an oversimplification to see the *Labourer* volumes merely as the medium

[8] Hammond, *C. P. Scott*, 266. In this volume, Hammond refers (but without using his own name) to his dispatches from Paris as special correspondent of the *Manchester Guardian*.

[9] Hammond and Hammond, *The Village Labourer, 1760–1832* (London, 1911); *The Town Labourer, 1760–1832: The New Civilisation* (London, 1917); *The Skilled Labourer, 1760–1832* (London, 1919).

[10] The figures are in R. M. Hartwell's introduction to the ninth edition of J. L. and Barbara Hammond's *The Rise of Modern Industry* (London, 1966), xv–xvi. See also Hartwell's "Interpretations of the Industrial Revolution in England: A Methodological Inquiry," *Journal of Economic History*, XIX (1959), 231.

for the view that the English working classes suffered increasingly in the years between 1760 and about 1850.

In the years from 1900 to the First World War, a spate of books on English agriculture appeared in print. The great agricultural depression had finally come to an end, and it is understandable that attention should have been directed back to the eighteenth century when the last fundamental change in farming and in rural life had taken place. *The Village Labourer* was not, however, concerned with technology so much as with its consequences. Subtitled *A Study in the Government of England before the Reform Bill*, it directed itself to describing the life of the poor or, perhaps more accurately, the treatment of the poor by "the governing class that ruled England with such absolute power during the last century of the old regime." After a chapter in which they outlined the concentration of power in the hands of a small group of wealthy landowners,[11] the Hammonds then proceeded to a detailed discussion of the enclosure movement, describing village life before enclosures, analyzing the procedures and stages by which, in their words, "the aristocracy . . . broke the back of the peasant community." [12] Arguing that the enclosures created a new organization of classes in which the peasant with rights and a status gave way to the laborer with no corporate rights to defend, they then turned to the remedies proposed and the expedients adopted to cope with rural distress in the years between 1795 and 1830.

Two chapters, based largely on Home Office Papers which they were among the first to use, attempted to describe the scope and significance of the Labourers' Revolt of 1830 and to assess the reaction which it elicited from the Whig Government of the time. Commenting finally on the sheltered and nurtured elegance of eighteenth century landed society, the Hammonds concluded with an emotional peroration that summed up the main thrust of their argument. "That class," they wrote, "has left bright and ample records of its life in literature, in art, and political traditions,

[11] In the *Guild Books* edition of 1948, the Hammonds make use of Sir Lewis Namier's *The Structure of Politics at the Accession of George III* (London, 1928), 82–93, to reinforce their impressionistic sketch of the governing class.
[12] *Guild Books* edition I, 101.

in the display of great orations and debates, in memories of brilliant conversation and sparkling wit; it has left dim and meager records of the disinherited peasants that are the shadow of its wealth; of the exiled labourers that are the shadow of its pleasures; of the villages sinking in poverty and crime and shame that are the shadow of its power and its pride." [13] To redress the record was the Hammonds' purpose in *The Village Labourer*.

The Hammonds may have been disappointed in the scant attention paid to their chapters on the labourers' rising. From the beginning, discussion and criticism of their monograph centered about two issues. First, it was charged that their picture of the hardships of the rural poor was exaggerated, that outrage and emotion had been substituted for hard data in their account of the village community, that in any case, while there had no doubt been abuses in the system of enclosure, there was little evidence that the process was as devastating as the Hammonds asserted. And second, they were accused of deliberately ignoring the importance of enclosure in increasing the food supplies of the nation at a time of urgent need. On the first issue, the rural standard of life, the Hammonds and their critics were not really as far apart as might have appeared. When Sir John Clapham, for example, published the first volume of his magisterial *Economic History of Modern Britain*, he concluded that on the average the potential standard of comfort of an English (or Welsh) rural labouring family in 1824 was probably a trifle better than it had been in 1794, assuming equal regularity of work. He conceded, however, that there were important areas in which it was probably worse and many in which the change either way was imperceptible.[14] Even this conclusion, J. L. Hammond contended a few years later, needed to be modified. Clapham, who had insisted on the importance of quantifications, placed an inordinate faith in his statistics. The figures for wages in the period under consideration were actually defective and unreliable. Even if this were not so,

---

[13] *Ibid.*, II, 136–37.
[14] Clapham, *The Early Railway Age, 1820–1850*, Vol. I of *An Economic History of Modern Britain* (3 vol.; Cambridge, Eng., 1926), 131.

Clapham had not really demonstrated that his "average labourer" was representative.[15] Clapham in turn made some concessions to Hammond's counter-criticisms,[16] but each scholar held to the basic tenor of his own argument.

On enclosure itself the controversy still continues. At the purely descriptive level, the Hammonds' account of the legal and administrative procedures by which it was carried out was recognized as an important contribution, but about its implications there was conflict. The most telling stricture was that the problems of the rural populace were hardly attributable to the forces singled out by the Hammonds. Traditional village organizations were crumbling in the eighteenth century before parliamentary sanction was given for their reorganization. For many long decades the open-field village had been experiencing profound changes. It was hardly the pre-enclosure paradise that sometimes seems implied in *The Village Labourer*. From another point of view, during most of the period under investigation, the area of land under cultivation increased, rents and profits rose, more intensive farming gained ground—altogether an indication of some agricultural progress. And finally, the enclosures themselves, by fostering improvements which increased the food supply, made it possible to feed and even to improve the lot of an increasingly urbanized population.

There is much in the criticism that calls for acceptance. The weakest point in the study is that it does not go back to the significant changes that were under way long before the middle of the eighteenth century. The authors' tendency to write "as though the fall of man occurred in the reign of George III" has been noted by even so sympathetic a judge as R. H. Tawney.[17] But he has also pointed out that to charge the Hammonds with minimizing the advantageous consequences of enclosures is to misread their argument. They took for granted the technical benefits and addressed themselves to a different issue entirely. Was en-

---

[15] Hammond, "The Industrial Revolution and Discontent," *Economic History Review*, II (1930), 215–19.

[16] These concessions appear in the 1939 reprint, with corrections of the 1930 edition of Vol. I of his *Economic History of Modern Britain*, pp. ix–x.

[17] Tawney, "J. L. Hammond," 276.

closure by private act of Parliament the most efficient and least socially damaging procedure that might have been employed? Many eighteenth century observers thought not. Men like Arthur Young and Sir John Sinclair, strong supporters of enclosure, nevertheless were persuaded that the interests of cottagers might well have been better preserved, and in effect the Hammonds agreed with these predecessors. Too often, it is clear, they and their critics were at cross-purposes. The latter spoke almost exclusively of the long-run economic consequences of enclosure; the Hammonds on the other hand were concerned with the immediate social consequences of essentially political measures.

That concern was equally reflected in the two sequels to *The Village Labourer*. Although they were originally intended to be parts of a single volume, it turned out that *The Town Labourer* was published in 1917 and *The Skilled Labourer* two years later. The former was directed toward the general features of early industrial England, while the latter was intended to present in detail the history of working people in various industries, supplemented by an account of the Luddite movement and a description of the presumably characteristic activities of a notorious *agent provocateur*. The major premise of *The Town Labourer* was the obvious one that the Industrial Revolution was a social revolution, creating a new civilization with problems and a character of its own. The Hammonds set themselves the task of studying these problems and the solutions that were proposed for them, and particularly of investigating the impact of the revolution upon the quality of life in the new society. Above all, they asked, what did the "dominion of man over matter look like to the great population taking part, if a blind part, in its establishment and its exercise?" [18]

The Town Labourer, then, was a study of the fate of the working classes during the first seventy years of the factory system. Beginning with a graphic description of the new power released by the change from an agricultural to an industrial society, the first half of the book attempted to portray the effects of the new

[18] Hammond and Hammond, *The Town Labourer* (1948 Guild Books ed.), I, 16.

power in all its forms upon the urban proletariat of England. The corrosive effects of the new discipline in the factories, the soul-destroying consequences of living in the dirty, disease-ridden, badly governed new towns, the warped administration of justice, and the antiquated enforcement of public order formed backdrops for a long discussion of economic conditions. The Hammonds recognized the role of the long war with France in creating working class distress, but they laid special emphasis on ways in which the new manufacturers used the war to free themselves to treat their workers as they thought fit, on the war waged against the trade unions, and particularly on the harrowing conditions under which children were employed in the new mills.

The chapters on conditions of work came to be the most challenged portion of the whole work, although one may argue that the six following chapters, which concluded the book, were much more important, certainly much more imaginative and original than most of what has been written on the Industrial Revolution. One chapter devoted to the "mind of the rich" described the development of the theory that "if society looked after the capitalist, the capitalist would look after the workman, and that if society took care of the interests of property, the deserving poor would become rich." Another illustrated how the dominant religions of the period, tempered by a measure of private philanthropy, taught a message of resignation, patience, and gratitude, a message nicely suited to easing the consciences of the rich. Then followed what one reviewer called "the superb chapters" concerned with the mind, the defenses, and the ambitions of the poor.[19] In the end, therefore, the study became much more than simply one of wages and conditions of work; it widened into a discussion of the intellectual gap that yawned between the rich and the poor during the early Industrial Revolution and of the consequences of the confrontation of classes at cross-purposes with each other.

In contrast to the broad sweeps of The Town Labourer, its companion volume employed detailed case studies to illustrate the

19 W. P. Hall, review of The Skilled Labourer, in American Historical Review, XXVI (1921), 324.

generalizations already outlined. *The Skilled Labourer* devoted itself to groups of workingmen about whom the Hammonds felt they could draw together the fullest records. Thus they described industrial conditions and conflicts with government among Northumberland and Durham miners, cotton and woolen workers, silk weavers, and framework knitters. In particular, three chapters centered about the Luddite Rising of 1811–14, a movement that appeared to the Hammonds primarily as desperate, unorganized, and sporadic outbreaks against the new machines, but at the same time as stimulated by the underground manipulations of *agents provocateurs*. Finally, they turned to a case study of one of these agents in a thoroughly documented and thoroughly unpleasant dissection of the ambiguous career of Oliver the Spy.

The Town Labourer and *The Skilled Labourer* were above all concerned with the effects of industrialization on the first generation to experience its influence. The pessimistic picture that inenvitably emerges from the pages of these deeply felt studies became, as has already been noted, the accepted version of the impact of the Industrial Revolution for more recent generations of students. Like Arnold Toynbee in 1884, the Hammonds saw growing up side by side great affluence and even greater poverty and degradation.[20] Because their work seemed to be so carefully documented—industrial conditions from Sadler's Select Committee Report of 1832, political activities from the Home Office files—they were judged to have added the necessary ingredient of solid research to the brilliant insights of the prematurely stricken Toynbee as well as to the work of such of his successors as Thorold Rogers and William Cunningham.

In the years that followed, however, the Hammonds' use of their documents came under serious scrutiny. In 1926, for example, W. H. Hutt attacked their reliance on testimony before Sadler's committee, observing that the committee report had been deliberately organized to produce a grossly exaggerated picture of the evils of child labor under the factory system. It included evidence only from Sadler's supporters, he pointed out, and then went on to argue that it was significantly refuted by later reports in 1833

[20] Toynbee, *Lectures on the Industrial Revolution in England* (London, 1884).

and 1834.[21] Many subsequent historians have accepted Hutt's
assertions about as readily as those of the Hammonds were accepted earlier. Yet his analysis leaves at least as much to be
desired as theirs. Because Sadler's committee was rigged did not
mean that the evidence it elicited was basically untrue. And,
despite the fact that in 1833 many felt that the Factory Commission of that year was as heavily weighted on the side of the
employer as Sadler's committee had been on that of the children,
the conditions described in the 1833 report itself lend considerable
credence to the portrait that was sketched in *The Town Labourer*.[22]

As to the Home Office Papers, there has recently been an
ingenious, if not altogether convincing, discussion of the Hammonds' scholarship by E. P. Thompson. He argues that they distorted the meaning of working-class Luddism because they were
so anxious to prove that conspiracy and rioting were the results
of provocation and not in any sense to be regarded as part of a
conscious laboring class attack against the existing order. They
assumed that the various depositions about these activities in the
Home Office materials were false, because any evidence about
revolutionary features of the movement was bound to be false.
Once this was taken for granted, he suggests, "the Hammonds
embark upon the seas of historical fiction." [23] Thompson makes
his own case for a geniunely class-conscious revolutionary movement from such scanty material that it is hardly proved, but it
serves as a stimulating challenge to the case studies in *The Skilled
Labourer*, this time from the Left rather than from historians
somewhat more conservative than the Hammonds. And even
Thompson, who has much to say in support of the Hammonds'
work, notes that their interpretation of Oliver the Spy remains the
most authoritative reconstruction of his career.[24]

Of a piece with the *Labourer* volumes were two others which

---

[21] W. H. Hutt, "The Factory Factory System of the Early Nineteenth Century,"
Economica, VI (1926), 78–93. The article is reprinted in *Capitalism and the
Historians*, edited by F. A. Hayek (Chicago, 1954).

[22] See Tawney, "J. L. Hammond," 284–85, and E. P. Thompson, *The Making
of the English Working Class* (New York, 1966), 336–38.

[23] Thompson, *The English Working Class*, 575–76, 591–95.   [24] *Ibid.*, 650.

quickly appeared in 1923 and 1925.[25] *Lord Shaftesbury* in part was concerned with the tortured inner experience of a lonely man of rigid conscience, in part with his role as a public reformer. The Hammonds did not have access to Shaftesbury's voluminous diaries, but they made full use of the generous extracts from the diaries published (in 1886) by Edwin Hodder in a three-volume life. The Hammonds had little sympathy for Shaftesbury's intellectual narrowness, which they saw as the concomitant of his stiff and inflexible Evangelicalism. At times they appeared puzzled that such a system of belief should go hand in hand with the obvious concern for mankind evident in much of Shaftesbury's public career. Perhaps their puzzlement was unnecessary for, as Élie Halévy once wryly pointed out, love of mankind may surely be as closely allied with the Evangelical dogma of justification by faith as with any more rationalistic Voltairean skepticism.[26] In any event, the main thrust of the biography was to analyze Shaftesbury's leadership of a series of public causes, the reform of working conditions in the mines and the factories, the improvement of public health, the liberalization of lunacy laws, the curbing of chimney climbing by infants and youths. Throughout the book, the Hammonds' passionate indignation against the conditions which Shaftesbury battled evoked an admiration for him that survived their frustration over his egotism and smugness, his dread of trade unions, and his suspicion of democracy. On balance, they concluded, he had opposed the simple revelation of his Christian conscience to the law of indifference and drift, the accepted wisdom of laissez faire. "This was his service to England; not the service of a statesman with a wide plan and commanding will, but the service of a prophet speaking truth to power in its selfishness and sloth." [27]

The Rise of Modern Industry, although the Hammonds intended it for the general reader, had a somewhat more modest sale than the *Labourer* trilogy. It reflected all the characteristic emphases which by now had become the hallmark of their work on the

[25] Hammond and Hammond, *Lord Shaftesbury* (London, 1923); *The Rise of Modern Industry* (London, 1925).

[26] Halévy, review of *Lord Shaftesbury*, in *History*, IX (October, 1924), 257.

[27] Hammond and Hammond, *Lord Shaftesbury* (4th ed.; London, 1936), 276.

Industrial Revolution. In some ways, however, it was the most balanced of their books in this area. Trying to place the Industrial Revolution in history, the Hammonds argued that in the nineteenth century, as once before in the time of Rome, a worldwide economy had come into being. Its origins, in their view, were essentially commercial. In turn they discussed the revolution in the character and scale of commerce as its center moved from the Levant to the Atlantic, the increased employment of capital, the shift in the products consumed. Because the English were in a specially favorable position in geography, in climate, in their history and politics, they became the pioneers of the industrial transformation.

Having written of origins, the Hammonds then turned to a series of case studies of the process of industrialization. Chapters on the revolution in transportation, on the steam engine, on changes in the iron and pottery industries, and a somewhat cursory chapter on cotton flanked two central discussions, which repeated much that they had written in earlier works, on the destruction of the peasant village, and the destruction of custom in industry. In a third part of the volume a rather questionable theory that the use of slave labor in the American colonies had hardened English hearts to the conditions of labor in the factories at home was followed by a not altogether convincing comparison of Roman concern for the "common enjoyment" of all with its neglect in the new industrial towns. Finally, with references to Cobbett and Owen, Shaftesbury and Dickens, they outlined the process by which the new wealth was eventually tempered by the "desire to create a civilization" in which men could live as men and not as things used for production.

These two volumes, then, reinforced the argument made in the earlier *Labourer* volumes, and their conclusions about working class living standards became part of the canon of the "pessimistic" approach to the Industrial Revolution. The response to those conclusions took the form not only of criticism of the evidence so patiently studied by the Hammonds but also of an increasingly searching attempt to test them in the light of new kinds of evidence. One of the most authoritative of the criticisms was of course that of the distinguished economic historian whose comments on their interpretation of rural life have already been noted. In the preface to the first volume of his formidable *Economic History of Modern Britain*, J. H. Clapham wrote somewhat unfairly of the view that "everything was getting worse for the working man down to some date between the drafting of the People's Charter and the Great Exhibition." [28] His attack on the Toynbee-Hammond thesis came after long years of careful research on group after group in English industrial life. Austere, almost arid in its prose, his study, in the words of a later historian of the first rank, expressed "social relations in terms of quantities." [29] Using, in particular, wage statistics developed by A. L. Bowley and G. H. Wood and a cost-of-living index made by N. J. Silberling, Clapham concluded that, except in such dying trades as hand loom weaving, for every class of urban or industrial worker about which information was available real wages had risen markedly between 1790 and 1850.

J. L. Hammond was not slow to rise to the challenge.[30] Writing in the *Economic History Review* in 1930, he suggested that the argument minimizing the oppressive and pauperizing impact of the Industrial Revolution "seems to depend on evidence that is not altogether convincing." [31] Anticipating T. S. Ashton, himself a cautious "optimist" whose sophisticated scrutiny was later to destroy the validity of Silberling's cost-of-living index upon which Clapham had significantly relied,[32] Hammond began by raising questions about the use of averages for standards of living as against data for conditions in particular areas. He tried to show

[28] Clapham, *An Economic History of Modern Britain*, I, vii.

[29] T. S. Ashton, "The Industrial Revolution" (*Studies in Bibliography*. III), in *Economic History Review*, V (1935), 105.

[30] Nor was Barbara Hammond. Her article on "Urban Death Rates in the Early Nineteenth Century" in *Economic History*, I, No. 3 (Supplement to *Economic Journal*, January 1929), 419–28, showed how inadequate was the statistical proof of the improved health of towns in the period involved.

[31] Hammond, "The Industrial Revolution and Discontent," 216.

[32] Ashton, "The Standard of Life of the Workers in England, 1790–1830," *Journal of Economic History*, Supplement IX (1949), 29–30. This is also reprinted in *Capitalism and the Historians*.

some of the "strange results" that emerged from "taking the wage put down for each of the several counties, adding up the figures and dividing the sum by the number of counties, irrespective of the number of labourers each county contained." [33] Basically, however, his argument was not confined to this analysis of the use of figures. Even admitting that so far as statistics can measure material improvement there was improvement, he insisted that statistics could not tell very much about what men enjoy and what they suffer. Referring back with approval to Toynbee's use of classical standards by which to judge a later period, he contended that in Greece even the poor man shared a certain communal fellowship in the contemplation of beauty of city, beauty of building, beauty of literature; or in Rome by the influence of a brilliant municipal civilization creating common tastes and common pleasures and making the magnificence of the city an object of common enjoyment and common pride.

"Common enjoyment" was a phrase J. L. Hammond was later to use again in his Hobhouse Memorial Lecture,[34] and it is the key to the central thesis of his work.

> If you look at the life of the age of the Industrial Revolution in this spirit [he wrote] you are struck at once by its extraordinary poverty. What did Manchester or Leeds offer to the workman? It had destroyed his contact with nature and turned him from a craftsman into a man serving the routine of a great industry. It did not offer to him the beauty of the Parthenon or the beauty of great drama: it did not offer to him the dignity of political rights or the excitement of a share in the government of a great society: it did not offer him the fellowship of common pleasures or common culture symbolized in the magnificence of his city. It offered him one incentive and one only, the hope of becoming rich.[35]

Lack of beauty, lack of fields or parks, lack of pageants or festivals, lack of beautiful buildings, and in their place the ugliness of the new life, with its growing slums, its destruction of nature, its disregard of man's nonmaterial needs—these were criteria of a

---

[33] Hammond, "The Industrial Revolution and Discontent," 218.
[34] Hammond, *The Growth of Common Enjoyment* (London, 1933).
[35] Hammond, "The Industrial Revolution and Discontent," 223.

standard of living as surely as were statistics on wages and on food consumption.[36]

The quality of life became the Hammonds' test of living standards as they answered the criticism levelled against their work. Their increasing emphasis on psychological pressures as against concrete suffering was already long in gestation when J. L. Hammond wrote on "The Industrial Revolution and Discontent." Indeed, when their next monograph, *The Age of the Chartists*, appeared in 1930 its subtitle was *A Study in Discontent*.[37] The subtitle explained the title. There was no attempt to tell the story of Chartism but rather to use the Chartist movement as the symbol of the unrest caused by other forces. The book described the society brought into being by the Industrial Revolution, assessed its spirit including the reasons for the popular sense of wrong, and sketched in the efforts for improvement that were finally made. Harking back to their classical model, the authors introduced their discussion by a surprising chapter on Greek and Roman life. They sought to use ancient history to illuminate the causes of social discontent in the nineteenth century. The Greeks and Romans, they argued, despite a very low standard of life and even despite the incubus of slavery, suffered little in the way of serious proletarian unrest.

The reason, to them, was clear. Classical antiquity was con-

---

[36] The "pessimist"—"optimist" controversy over the standard of living in early industrial England has been as heated and extensive as that over the rise and decline of the gentry in the sixteenth and seventeenth centuries—and sometimes almost as tedious. This is not the place to cite the voluminous literature except to note that the current leading champions appear to be R. M. Hartwell for the optimists and E. J. Hobsbawm for the pessimists. See particularly Hobsbawm's "The British Standard of Living, 1790–1850," *Economic History Review*, second series, X (1957), 46–68; Hartwell's "The Rising Standard of Living in England, 1800–1850," *Economic History Review*, second series, XIII (1961), 397–416; and "The Standard of Living during the Industrial Revolution: A Discussion" by Hobsbawm (pp. 119–34) and Hartwell (pp. 135–46), *Economic History Review*, second series, XVI (1963). Good bibliographical surveys have been T. S. Ashton's article in the *Economic History Review* for October, 1935, already cited and Hartwell's "Interpretations of the Industrial Revolution in England: A Methodological Inquiry," *Journal of Economic History*, XIX (1959), 229–49. The most balanced recent evaluation of the state of the controversy is A. J. P. Taylor, "Progress and Poverty in Britain: A Reappraisal," *History*, XLV (1960), 16–31.

[37] Hammond and Hammond, *The Age of the Chartists, 1832–1854: A Study in Discontent* (London, 1930).

cerned with the common enjoyment, with providing baths and theaters, temples and places for play, so that a large proportion of the population could share in the art and the culture of the society. In contrast, the nineteenth century English worker lived in a world of social incoherence. Treated as a culprit under the New Poor Law, he was cut off from his earlier contacts with nature in the new towns devoid of amenities, badly governed, unsanitary, utterly lacking in those institutions which classical cities had provided to refresh and to stimulate the civic pride of their populations.[38] When he was so denied open air and exercise, or even the hope of serious education, or too frequently the consolation of serious religion, it was no wonder that the English worker should have turned to the beerhouse and the ginshop. It was no more strange that he should have embraced the Charter as the instrumentality of his "imagination in action." To him it represented the hope for a better world and, even when the great movement collapsed in 1848, it had really triumphed because it had promoted the self-respect of the English workman. After 1850, conditions improved. Society as a whole began to take into account the new demands raised by the working class. Gradually, public health measures were developed, the working class itself began to seek education from a flood of cheap periodical literature and fellowship in a spate of friendly societies. Mechanics' institutions emerged and grew more popular. Town after town turned to the provision of amenities for the common enjoyment. Little by little, the "spirit of wonder which had created art and religion, music and letters, gardens and playing fields" began timidly to sprout. "That spirit could not live at peace in the treadmill cities where the daylight never broke upon the beauty and the wisdom of the world." [39]

The Age of the Chartists was more difficult to subject to

---

[38] In his Hobhouse Memorial Lecture, J. L. Hammond put the contrast succinctly: "Whether a nation keep its beauty or not depends on the value it gives to beauty. The Romans, like the Greeks, thought a city should be beautiful; they were ready to spend money lavishly, public and private money, and they took care of their monuments. Our great-grandfathers would have thought it a waste of money and energy to spend the profits of the cotton industry on making Manchester beautiful." Hammond, *The Growth of Common Enjoyment*, 27.

[39] Hammond and Hammond, *The Age of the Chartists*, 365.

quantitative criticism than earlier volumes. As one reviewer re-marked, indignation caused by the growth of slums is not pro-portional to the number of slum dwellers.[40] The Hammonds may have exaggerated the virtues of Rome and Greece as they exaggerated the vices of Manchester and Liverpool. Their feeling for working-class experience in nineteenth century England was to be sure highly subjective and value laden. But it would have been hard, if indeed it would have been at all possible, to refute a judgment that represented not the addition and subtraction of statistics but rather the vision of what the good life for all men might be. The Hammonds had, in other words, qualified their earlier approach to the industrial age and they continued to do so. When they published in 1934 a revised edition of *The Age of the Chartists* under the title *The Bleak Age*, they conceded that the view was probably more or less correct that "most men were less poor when . . . discontent was loud and active than they were when the eighteenth century was beginning to grow old in a silence like that of autumn." [41] Therefore, they insisted, the ex-planation for systematic and widespread discontent had to be sought outside the sphere of strictly economic conditions. But that the age was a bleak age they had no doubt.[42]

With one exception other than an occasional article,[43] *The Bleak Age* marked the end of the joint publication of J. L. and Barbara Hammond. In 1932 they published a rather pedestrian commissioned biography of James Stansfield, the Victorian col-laborator of Josephine Butler in her campaign against the vicious Contagious Diseases Acts.[44] It is not hard to guess that much as they respected Stansfield for his championing of an unpopular

---

[40] T. H. Marshall, review in *English Historical Review*, XLVI (1931), 657.

[41] Hammond and Hammond, *The Bleak Age* (London, 1934). I have used the first Pelican edition of 1947, p. 15.

[42] Hartwell in "Interpretations of the Industrial Revolution in England," p. 245 complains that the chapter on "The State of the Towns" in *The Bleak Age* concentrates on extremes and ignores contrary evidence to be found even in the sources used.

[43] For example, Hammond and Hammond, "Poverty, Crime, Philanthropy," in *Johnson's England. An Account of the Life and Manners of his Age*, edited by A. S. Turberville (2 vols.; Oxford, 1933).

[44] Hammond and Hammond, *James Stansfield: A Victorian Champion of Sex Equality* (London, 1932).

cause, the subject itself repelled them. The book showed little of the enthusiasm that had characterized their earlier studies and has quietly been relegated to a very minor place in the hierarchy of their books.

J. L. Hammond continued to be productive. Two years after the unsuccessful *Stansfield* he published another biography, this one undertaken at the request of the sons and daughter of C. P. Scott, longtime editor of the *Manchester Guardian.* Here the tone was very different. Hammond, who served on the paper for a good part of his professional life, admired Scott and saw in him, it seems clear, the kind of liberal he himself aspired to be. "He was a realist," he wrote, "with a careful eye to practical needs; a man of culture with a sense of the importance of ideas and of the arts that inspire and express them; a man of action ready for bold remedies, and to the end of his life a man of faith who believed that no wrong existed which could not be set right by courage and good will." [45] It might well have been a self-portrait.

Much more notable than the biography of Scott was J. L. Hammond's last major work. *Gladstone and the Irish Nation* appeared late in 1938. It was warmly received by reviewers but attracted only limited attention.[46] Sales were meager, partly no doubt because of its length and high price, partly perhaps because in the catastrophic days of 1939 and 1940, Gladstone must have seemed as remote to many potential readers as Henry II or Hammurabi. Then in early 1941 the remaining publisher's stocks and the plates of the book were destroyed by bomb damage and fire. Because the copyright was held by the Gladstone trustees, who had given him various kinds of help in his work on the book, Hammond felt unable to press for reprinting in the years that followed. After his death, Barbara Hammond was unable to arrange for a reissue and it was not until 1964 that a new impression, published with a revealing introduction by M. R. D. Foot, was made available.[47] The long delay was all the more to be

[45] Hammond, *C. P. Scott,* 302–303.
[46] See, for example, G. M. Trevelyan in *English Historical Review,* LIV (1939), 345–48; P. Knaplund, *American Historical Review,* XLV (1939), 147–49; E. Curtis, *History,* XXIV (1939), 164–65; *Times Literary Supplement,* October 29, 1938, 687–88.
[47] This information is from Foot's introduction to the 1964 edition.

regretted because *Gladstone and the Irish Nation* was Hammond's finest historical work. It was based heavily on the Gladstone Papers, the quarter of a million items that were by 1938 only partly arranged and catalogued. As a result, there were no references to British Museum manuscript numbers that had, indeed, not yet been assigned. Hammond did not examine or did not have the opportunity to examine such collections as the Gladstone family papers at Hawarden, Herbert and Mary Gladstone's papers, or E. W. Hamilton's important diary. He did, on the other hand, see Herbert Gladstone's abbreviated version of Gladstone's diary, and it is clear that it gave him an understanding of Gladstone's psychology and motivation which added enormously to the penetration of his study.

Hammond's concern for Ireland was a contemporary as well as a historical one. In 1920 he had gone to Ireland for the *Manchester Guardian*. His experiences in reporting the bitter Anglo-Irish strife had made him a firm advocate of Irish independence, an advocacy that he had pursued with his editorial pen. It was natural, therefore, that he should have turned to the Irish question and natural also that his own liberalism should have led him to investigate Gladstone's role in the great Home Rule controversy. The rich knowledge of nineteenth century English social and economic conditions that were the harvest of his longtime interests stood him in good stead. He came to understand the landless Irish peasant as he had the English factory worker. He was able to make telling comparisons between the opposition to factory legislation in England and the hostility to land legislation in Ireland. Among many other accomplishments, he did justice to Michael Davitt, whose economic aspirations had been given scant shrift by previous historians, for whom Parnell was the towering Irish figure. But he did equal justice to the latter. He demonstrated, for example, that the Irish leader had gone to great lengths in 1883 and 1884 in trying to obtain large Irish reform without violence, but he also showed that Parnell did not give Gladstone half a chance to collaborate with him when the shock of the divorce strained the nonconformist consciences of some of Gladstone's followers.

With regard to Gladstone, Hammond was able to expose the

hollowness of the charge that he had gone over to Home Rule in 1885 because of his desire for office. Instead, he established how Gladstone's ideas on the Irish question had matured slowly and that, as early as the 1870s, Gladstone's chief colleagues knew that he was moving toward an acceptance of Home Rule. But while important, these interpretations, quarried out of the documents that his wife and Edith Stopford helped him to organize, were not really the heart of his theme. Basically, as G. M. Trevelyan put it, Hammond "in explaining Gladstone's Irish policy and its methods . . . explained Gladstone and his mind." [48] For, like Charles James Fox early in his scholarly career, Gladstone near its end was an exceptionally sympathetic subject. Hammond was most attracted neither by Gladstone's grasp of economic problems or legal issues nor by his astute political sense or striking eloquence in public appearances. He was drawn to Gladstone because he saw in him a man whose moral principles, deeply held and incorruptible, were the bedrock upon which was based his approach to Irish issues. Gladstone's moral sense enabled him, in Hammond's view, to understand the broader questions at stake between the English and the Irish nations. The sources for that sense of responsibility Hammond found in Gladstone's devotion to Homer and Greek civilization, to the Bible and Christianity. In part, too, he saw them in the internationalism of Gladstone's European outlook that enabled him to grasp the contradictions in Britain's position as the supporter of oppressed nationalities while keeping the Irish under rigorous control. Reacting to the easy caveats of the Edwardians who had seen in Gladstone little more than the living demonstration of Victorian hypocrisy, Hammond used the Irish issue as the framework for a deeply reflective assessment of Gladstone the man as well as of his work. He recognized weaknesses in Gladstone, his mistakes concerning the American Civil War, his inability to understand the pressing urgency of social problems. But his final judgment was that the Grand Old Man was a giant, "at once a great politician and a great prophet, a great Englishman and a great European, a great Minister of State and a great minister of justice." [49] The evaluation was not without its flaws

[48] Trevelyan, in *English Historical Review*, 345–46.
[49] *Gladstone and the Irish Nation* (London, 1964) 738.

and some scholars have been unable to follow him in his sympathetic empathy with the liberal colossus in the twilight of Victorian England. Holes can be picked in the details of his work by earnest young students of the nineteenth century as M. R. D. Foot phrases it. But, to continue with his remarks, "knocking chips off the facade leaves the strength and proportions of the intellectual structure unaffected in its grandeur." [50] *Gladstone and the Irish Nation* was an outstanding work of richly satisfying scholarship written by an author whose own concern for human dignity and freedom, like that of its subject, was revealed in its every page.

From a little before the First World War the Hammonds lived outside London in a house near Hemel Hemstead. Here most of the major works were written, as were the many articles J. L. Hammond did for the *Manchester Guardian*. When war came once again, he rejoined the *Guardian* staff on a full-time basis. In September, 1939, the Hammonds moved to Manchester where until the end of the war they lived in what a friend described as a kind of gay austerity.[51] Hammond, whose love for French history and culture was profound, soon came to devote most of his attention to the affairs of France. He responded to her wartime fate with a series of editorial articles that Denis Brogan described as the sanest, best informed, most generous, and so most wise of the journalistic writing on French themes to be published during the course of the war.[52] The articles were rooted in sound scholarship and a firm determination to write with candor and balance. From the earliest, in which he reflected on the consequences of the control of the weapons of modern war by savages and barbarians, to the latest, which mirrored his deep concern lest the Allies believe they could "play the governess" in France, he pleaded that the Allied nations must understand the temper and the problems of France. For he saw the fate of Europe as bound up with hers. Others than Frenchmen would have died in vain, he warned, if

[50] *Ibid.*, p. xxiii. Mr. Foot completed *Gladstone and Liberalism* (London, 1953), which J. L. Hammond had started before his death in 1949. It is one of the volumes in the popular *Teach Yourself History* series edited by A. L. Rowse.

[51] Tawney, "J. L. Hammond," 290.

[52] Hammond, *Faith in France. A Selection of Leading Articles Published in the Manchester Guardian between June 1940 and September 1944, With a Preface by D. W. Brogan* (London, 1946), 8.

victory did not leave her free, united, and strong and ready to take her part in the defense of the West.[53] Collected in a volume and published in 1946 as *Faith in France*, these articles are among the few wartime pieces that can still be read as much for their literary quality as for the sober warmth of their sensitive humanity.

Honors came to Hammond as the significance of his work was recognized. In 1933 he and his wife were awarded the honorary D.Litt. on the same day by Oxford. In 1937 he was made a Fellow of his college, St. John's. A few years later he became a Fellow of the British Academy and in 1944 he received an honorary degree of D.Litt. from Manchester. His firm support of France in her hour of travail was signalized in 1948 by his appointment as an officer of the Legion of Honour. He worked effectively almost to the end, and on April 7, 1949, a few months before his seventy-seventh birthday, this gentle controversialist who "never made a personal enemy or lost a friend" died at his home.[54]

To sum up the work of J. L. Hammond is really to sum up the work of two people. For after his marriage, even those books that bore his name alone were heavily indebted to his wife's help in research and intellectual cooperation. All their work was unusually well written, its classical sense of form warmed by the deep social sympathy that shone from every page. The Englishmen to whom Hammond was drawn are as revealing as the broad issues of social history that interested him. Charles James Fox, whatever his personal shortcomings, redeemed them by the rich love of freedom that was the first tenet of his political faith. James Stansfield and Lord Shaftesbury were admired for their compassion for the weak as much as for their courage in struggling for unpopular causes. For C. P. Scott, who combined shrewd political sense with high principles, Hammond had the respect of a colleague who likewise regarded his journalism as the responsible exercise of public education. Above all, he saw in Gladstone a statesman of great vision because he based his actions upon deeply rooted moral convictions. In assessing Gladstone's Irish policy, Hammond conceded his faults, but he had no doubt that Gladstone's fundamental con-

[53] *Ibid.*, 13, 195, 201.
[54] Gilbert Murray, *Dictionary of National Biography, 1941–1950*, p. 352.

victions and ultimate aims were infinitely more important than any detail of his day-to-day policy.

As for the partnership of J. L. and Barbara Hammond, the great trilogy on the laboring classes in the early Industrial Revolution stands as a monument of historical exposition. No doubt the Hammonds neglected to develop in *The Village Labourer* the economic necessity and long-run value of enclosures. Unquestionably, their emphasis on the physical and moral suffering of the English masses in *The Town Labourer* was only one side of the coin and too heavily based on certain kinds of materials. Perhaps *The Skilled Labourer* made assumptions about the passivity of the working classes that may be overdrawn. But after all the criticisms have been absorbed, the kinds of questions raised by the Hammonds remain crucial. What did constitute the good life for the English masses in the nineteenth century? Granted an upward movement in money wages, did that movement reflect an improvement in the quality of the ordinary man's existence? Was the gap between widespread affluence and widespread poverty not increasingly intolerable as the potential of industrial development began to be grasped? On all of these questions, a contemporary student, whether of modern Britain or modern America, may be somewhat uncertain of the overriding importance of the quantitative evidence concerning working class improvement. He may instead be more inclined to think in terms of comparison among the various groups in society and to reflect upon the imponderables of aspiration and frustration the import of which the Hammonds so clearly grasped. That historians of nineteenth century England are still debating these particular questions is the most eloquent commentary on the lasting historical achievement of J. L. Hammond.

PART TWO

CONTINENTAL PERSPECTIVES

ADOLFO OMODEO
Historian of the "Religion of Freedom"

CHARLES F. DELZELL
Vanderbilt University

IN ITALY THE link between historiography and politics has always been intimate. This connection is certainly visible in the case of the late Adolfo Omodeo, one of Italy's most articulate spokesmen of the idealist school of historiography. Intrigued by thought that inspires meaningful action, he spread his research interests over the millennia from the advent of Christianity to the Italian Risorgimento and modern European intellectual history. A professor at the University of Naples for almost a quarter century, he was well known in Italian academic circles and highly esteemed by most of his peers. Unfortunately, Omodeo remained somewhat less familiar to foreign scholars, partly because he almost never ventured from his native land and partly because few of his works were ever translated. This is doubly regrettable, for Omodeo was not only a historian of considerable talent but also one of a small minority of Italians who refused to compromise their moral integrity during the era of Fascist totalitarianism.

A rather dour and puritanic figure, Omodeo's inner personality remained largely hidden from his contemporaries, with the possible exception of Benedetto Croce, who was to become his most intimate collaborator during the years that Omodeo lived in Naples. The veil that so long shrouded this "tough and merciless, yet penetrating and perspicacious" teacher—to use the apt phrase of Walter Maturi, another topflight Risorgimentalist [1]—has been partially lifted in recent years by publication of letters written by

---

[1] Walter Maturi, *Interpretazioni del Risorgimento: Lezioni di storia della storiografia* (Turin, 1962), 644.

Omodeo between 1910 and 1946.[2] As a result of this correspondence and the recollections and appraisals of fellow scholars, it is now becoming somewhat easier to evaluate the historiographical, political, and moral significance of Omodeo.[3]

Born on August 18, 1889, in Palermo, Omodeo always displayed certain characteristics of Sicilian pride and stubbornness, yet his outlook was not in the least parochial. His father, a tax assessor from Lombardy, migrated to Sicily for professional reasons, and the son was able to visit the mainland often during his youth. It was natural, therefore, that he should become imbued with the sense of Italian nationalism that was rapidly developing in the post-Risorgimento era. More noteworthy was to be the fact that this spiritual son of Mazzini could broaden his horizons to the extent that by World War II he would advocate European federation.

From childhood Omodeo reacted vigorously against the positivist currents of thought that were popular among many Italian intellectuals at the turn of the century. His own bent was clearly religious, though not in the traditionally Roman Catholic sense. His idealist philosophical slant was encouraged by Eugenio Donadoni, his high school teacher in Palermo, and was further stimulated by his studies from 1909 to 1912 in the Faculty of Letters at the University of Palermo.[4] There he worked with Professor Giovanni Gentile, who had formulated a kind of substitute reli-

[2] Adolfo Omodeo, *Lettere, 1910–1946*, ed. Alessandro Galante Garrone (Turin, 1963). Galante Garrone was one of Omodeo's sincerest admirers but was an historian whose philosophy was more eclectic than Omodeo's.

[3] In addition to the perceptive essays by Maturi and Galante Garrone, see the sympathetic and thorough critique by Aldo Garosci, "Adolfo Omodeo. I: La Storia e l'azione," *Rivista storica italiana*, LXXVII (March, 1965), 173–98; "Adolfo Omodeo. II: La Guerra, l'antifascismo e la storia," in *ibid.*, LXXVII (September, 1965), 639–86; "Adolfo Omodeo. III: Guida morale e guida politica," in *ibid.*, LXXVIII (March, 1966), 140–83. Also of value is the special issue of Omodeo's Neapolitan review, *L'Acropoli: Rivista di politica*, II, No. 17/24 (1947), that appeared soon after his death. It contains tributes by Croce, Luigi Salvatorelli, Luigi Russo, and others, as well as a complete bibliography of Omodeo's writings. Marxist critiques of Omodeo are to be found in Giorgio Candeloro, "Omodeo storico del Risorgimento," *Società*, V (December, 1949), 582–601; and Delio Cantimori, "Commemorazione di Adolfo Omodeo," in *Studi di storia* (Turin, 1959), 51–75. Also of use is the essay on Omodeo by Augusto Guerra in *Nuova rivista storica*, XLIX (May–August, 1965), 357–70.

[4] In 1908–09 he studied briefly at the Scuola Normale Superiore in Pisa.

gion ("actual idealism"), based on Hegelianism. Omodeo's somewhat similar philosophy of history was set forth in a penetrating essay written at Palermo.[5] And, of course, it was to be refined and modulated by his later collaboration with Croce.

As early as 1911 Omodeo was able to outline his professional plans to his fiancée Eva Zona, daughter of a Venetian astronomer who had moved to Palermo:

> First I must establish myself firmly in the world of scholarship, and after I have mastered the past, I must tackle the present with all of its problems. A teaching career will enable me to gain a better sense of myself, of what I can do, of what I lack in order to understand and judge people better. . . . As a historian, I want to reveal a life that has become almost completely forgotten by us modern Latins— the world of Christianity in its greatest moments. But along with this I also want to embrace several other activities. I want to study our Risorgimento and gain an understanding of all the repercussions it has for us—which means that I also want my mind to master the present historical moment. The study of history will bring me face to face with the political problems of our own days.[6]

This in fact turned out to be the outline of his career, although the precise sequence of some of his research projects was modified at times by economic necessity and the pressure of his publishers.

Thus, Omodeo's scholarly production consisted of two major parts—the history of the first century of Christianity and the study of modern European, especially Italian history. Although at first glance one might think these categories were neatly separated, they actually were intimately linked in the *forma mentis* of the author as well as by an affinity of themes. For what interested Omodeo in Christianity was not so much the historical milieu, the institutions, or the doctrinal aspects as the great religious leaders in action—men like Jesus, Paul, and John the Baptist. To catch a great leader in the intimate fervor of a personal crisis that leads to action should be the supreme aspiration of the historian, Omodeo insisted. This was for him what he termed "ethical-civil" his-

[5] Omodeo, "Res gestae e historia rerum," *Annuario della biblioteca filosofica di Palermo*, III, No. 1/2 (1913), 1–28. See Garosci's discussion in *Rivista storica italiana*, LXXVII (March, 1965), 177–89.
[6] Omodeo, *Lettere*, 15–16.

tory, the unfolding of the human ethos. Omodeo's strong sense of moral commitment caused him eventually to shift his research to the expansion of liberalism in modern Europe for, in his judgment, here was to be found the expression of "ethical-religious-civil" history most relevant to our own age.[7] As Luigi Salvatorelli, whose own historical research followed a pattern rather similar to that of Omodeo, has observed:

> Christianity is not a dead religion; neither Christ nor Paul are mummies lying in subterranean tombs. In the Christian churches and in today's religious life we still see the propagation and results of the original movement, and these results cut through every aspect of present-day social and political reality. This is particularly true of Catholic countries, and most clearly of all in the Italy of the Risorgimento era, which saw the formation of a nation-state by means of a struggle between Church and State and involved a crisis in the principle of temporal power.[8]

Omodeo's first major publication was his thesis, *Gesù e le origini del Cristianesimo*.[9] Although he never became a specialist in ancient Oriental languages, the youthful scholar was reasonably well prepared for a study of this sort. He was conversant with but often hypercritical of the research done in this field by German Protestant "higher critics." More to his taste was the research of the French scholar Alfred Loisy; indeed, Omodeo later declared himself to be his disciple and wrote a critical essay on him.[10] The Sicilian scholar was primarily concerned with Jesus' contribution to ethics. He contended that Jesus did not originally intend to do more than fulfill Israel's dream for a restored kingdom but, because of the impact of his newly acquired faith, actually went much further. Omodeo was less successful in relating Jesus to John the Baptist and the twelve apostles than he was in analyzing his ethical teachings.[11] The author has also been rightly

---

[7] Maturi, *Interpretazioni del Risorgimento*, 519.

[8] Luigi Salvatorelli, "Gli studi di storia," *L'Acropoli: Ad Adolfo Omodeo*, II, No. 17/24 (1947), xi–xii.

[9] Omodeo, *Gesù e le origini del Cristianesimo* (Messina, 1913). A revised edition in 1926 bore the title, *Storia delle origini cristiane. I: Gesù*.

[10] Omodeo, *Alfredo Loisy storico delle religioni* (Bari, 1936).

[11] According to Salvatorelli, Omodeo succeeded better in this respect in a later, shorter book, *Gesù il Nazoreo* (Venice, 1927). There he condensed the results

criticized for not paying sufficient attention to the canons of well-rounded literary craftsmanship: there is too much space allocated to methodological discussion and too little to clarification of the religious milieu.

The second volume in Omodeo's series of studies on the origins of Christianity appeared in 1920 and was entitled *Prolegomeni alla storia dell'età apostolica*. It was devoted chiefly to criticism of the various Gospel sources. The third volume, published in 1922, was devoted to Paul of Tarsus, while the fourth, undertaken considerably later, was focused on the Gospel according to John.[12] It was in his works on Jesus and Paul, and particularly the latter, that Omodeo was most successful in fulfilling his avowed intention of interpreting great leaders in their moments of personal crisis. The other two books were considerably more philological in nature, while the one dealing with the Gospel of John was more an introductory essay than a rounded-out discussion. Several experts have downgraded Omodeo for going too far in setting Paul apart from the mainstream of Hellenist culture.

In sum, it can be said that Omodeo's studies in the field of early Christian history made a worthy contribution to a difficult subject and were especially notable in a country where there was a paucity of such research by non-Catholic scholars. Neither the indefatigable work of the excommunicated modernist priest Ernesto Buonaiuti nor the youthful publications in this sector by Salvatorelli had resulted in establishing a school of critical studies at the university level.

Italy's entry into the war in 1915 greatly affected the life of Omodeo, who was then a young teacher in the technical school of Cefalù. A deep sense of patriotic duty led him to volunteer at once. After the requisite training, he became a second lieutenant and later captain in the artillery. He took part in the campaigns along the Carso and during the difficult withdrawal from Capo-

---

of his own impressive research and reoriented the account so as to accept Jesus' youthful adherence to the community of John the Baptist. *Cf.* Salvatorelli, "Gli studi di storia," xiii–xiv.

12 Omodeo, *Prolegomeni alla storia dell'età apostolica* (Messina, 1920); *Storia delle origini Cristiane. III: Paolo di Tarso apostolo delle genti* (Messina, 1922), second edition entitled *Paolo di Tarso* (Naples, 1956); *La mistica Giovannea: Saggio critico con una nuova traduzione dei testi* (Bari, 1930).

retto in 1917 managed to lead his battery back to safety. Soon he returned to the front, where he participated in operations along the Piave in June, 1918.[13] He remained in the combat zone until the end of the war and was discharged in January, 1919. The letters that Omodeo sent from the battlefront to his wife were studded with impatient criticisms. Whereas unruly and unresponsive students in the high school had plagued the austere and demanding teacher before the war, it was now his turn to complain bitterly about unimaginative and incompetent superior officers, self-centered and often semiliterate soldiers, "weak and vile" members of Parliament, and unpatriotic civilians rioting in the great northern cities. It is probably just as well that Omodeo did not choose to enter politics at this juncture, for in all likelihood he would then have been a reactionary of the first water.[14]

Nevertheless, it was the wartime experiences, supplemented by his dismay at the establishment of the Fascist dictatorship a few years later, that served to imbue Omodeo with a more democratic attitude and to draw him partially from the academic cloister. Furthermore, his military service inspired him to compile a collection of letters written by officers and soldiers who gave up their lives in the conflict that had ended the "age of the Italian Risorgimento." [15] This epistolary anthology, published in installments in Croce's La Critica after 1929 and then in book form in 1934,[16] was to be the first of Omodeo's works that could rightly be described as "moral teaching" rather than serene historical analysis. He was interested in selecting letters (mostly from officers) that pointed up the Mazzinian ideals of devotion to duty, justice, and freedom—ideals that had motivated him and others like him during the war and that stood in sharp contrast to the Fascist glorification of bluster and bellicosity. It is worth noting that in publishing these letters, Omodeo saw fit to leave out many anti-parliamentary passages that had filled his own wartime correspondence.

[13] See Roberto Montesano, "Nel Giugno '18," L'Acropoli: Ad Adolfo Omodeo, II, No. 17/24 (1947), lxiv–lxx.

[14] Omodeo, Lettere, xxxviii.

[15] Omodeo was to terminate his best-known book, L'Età del Risorgimento (Messina, 1931), with the peace settlement of 1919.

[16] Omodeo, Momenti della vita di guerra: Dai diari e dalle lettere dei caduti (Bari, 1934).

The years from 1919 to 1923 saw the war veteran getting settled again, resuming old themes and studies rather than embarking on new intellectual enterprises. With the help of Professor Gentile, he moved in May, 1919, to the University of Messina to teach ancient history. The following year, however, he decided to return to Palermo, where he became professor of history and geography at the Istituto Tecnico and later at the Liceo Vittorio Emanuele. Meanwhile, publication of some of his early studies on Christianity won for him the coveted prize in philological sciences conferred by the national Accademia dei Lincei. During 1921 and 1922 Omodeo entered the competitive examinations for the chair of ancient history at the University of Padua and the chair of ancient and modern history in the University of Rome's faculty for training women teachers, but in neither instance did he win first place. Instead, he joined the faculty of letters of the University of Catania in January, 1923. Finally, in August of that year, he attained the pinnacle of his academic career when, once more with timely assistance from Gentile (who had become Mussolini's first Minister of Public Instruction), he was appointed to the chair of church history (later relabeled history of Christianity) at the University of Naples.[17] There he launched his courses with a prolusory address on "The Humane Value of Christian History," followed soon by a textbook on the history of religion—a work which revealed his considerable skill in clarifying the links between various religions.[18]

Ten months before Omodeo moved to Naples, Mussolini's Blackshirts marched on Rome. A good many Italians were inclined at that time to look upon the Fascist movement as a party of national regeneration. It would not have been very surprising if Omodeo had also chosen to support the Fascists initially, for his political orientation up to then had been imprecise at best.[19]

[17] Garosci, "Adolfo Omodeo. II: La Guerra," 652–54.
[18] Reprinted in Omodeo, *Tradizioni morali e disciplina storica* (Bari, 1929); *Storia della religione (dalla Grecia antica al Cristianesimo)* (Messina, 1924). Republished with new preface and title as *Religione e civiltà: Dalla Grecia antica al Cristianesimo*, (ed.) Benedetto Croce (Bari, 1947).
[19] As Galante Garrone has noted, it is easier to discern what Omodeo was against than what he was for in politics. Although he stood within the broad Risorgimento stream of liberalism and nationalism, he had no use for Giovanni Giolitti, the major liberal statesman of the early twentieth century. Although

When the First World War came to an end he had expressed disgust with the bankruptcy of Italy's ruling class and the country's social disorder. None of the existing parties had pleased him, and on July 20, 1919, he had written to Gentile (who had joined the Nationalist Party): "I don't see clearly where my battle-station is."[20] Although there were some features in Omodeo's temperament that might have disposed him to cast his lot with the new Fascist movement, he never did so. From the outset he felt suspicions and reservations about it. Nevertheless, he did not line up militantly against Mussolini during the latter's first two years in office—any more than did Croce, who was also willing to wait and see, in the hope that fascism might somehow be tamed and led into the normal pattern of politics. For Omodeo, moreover, the fact that his beloved former teacher Gentile had accepted a post in the government caused him to think that significant and beneficial school reforms would result. The somewhat transitory nature of these reforms, however, soon discouraged him.

But it was the brutal assassination by Fascist thugs of Giacomo Matteotti, the outspoken secretary of the democratic Unitary Socialist Party, on June 10, 1924, that terminated Omodeo's ambivalent attitude toward the new regime. In a letter of June 24 he urged Gentile to lead a purifying movement within fascism.[21] It so happened that a week later Mussolini dismissed Gentile along with two other ministers; but the educational philosopher never turned his back on the Blackshirt regime, despite Omodeo's letters which sought to convince him that fascism did not in the least coincide with Gentile's own dreams of a strong, ethical state. In vain Omodeo argued that the murder of Matteotti provided ample proof that the very essence of fascism was unadulterated "violence," not justifiable "force."[22]

There is no record of any correspondence in 1925 between Omodeo and his former master. Instead, on April 21 of that year Gentile drafted a "Manifesto of the Fascist Intellectuals"—a document that aroused Senator Croce (whose eyes had also been

---

patriotic, he certainly was not ready to join the chauvinistic Nationalist Party. Although a self-styled "son of Mazzini," he was not yet a republican. He felt scorn for the Masons and the radicals and stood at opposite poles from both the clericals and Socialists. Omodeo, *Lettere*, xxxvii.

[20] *Ibid.*, 372.   [21] *Ibid.*, 413.   [22] *Ibid.*, 418–20.

opened by the repercussions of the Matteotti murder) to pen a headed "Reply" that was published on May 1 by *Il Mondo*, the Rome newspaper of the leader of the Aventine secession, Giovanni Amendola (himself soon to become another victim of fascism).[23] This clash over the question of the intellectuals' proper attitude toward fascism was superimposed on years of philosophical feuding over the precise nature of historicism, and it brought to an end not only the once amicable relationship between Gentile and Croce but also the friendship between Gentile and Omodeo, for the latter came increasingly to side with Croce.[24] Omodeo's article in 1926, "Storicismo formalistico," [25] criticizing the readiness of certain historicists to accept the "inevitability" of *faits accomplis*, marked the final breach with Gentile. On May 22 of that year Omodeo wrote to him: "My most bitter sorrow of these days is the thought of seeming harsh and ungrateful to you as I follow a path that I cannot desert if I am to remain true to myself. But you, I am certain, will recognize that I have chosen the more difficult and painful way." [26] Thus, after years of indecision, Omodeo, answering an inner call of moral duty to resist fascism, found his battle-station.

During the late 1920s the University of Naples historian contributed reviews and articles to Luigi Russo's journal *Leonardo*, but after its suppression in 1930 he had to confine most of his writings to Croce's *La Critica*, the only major literary journal edited by a conspicuous anti-Fascist that was never closed down by the dictatorship.[27] Omodeo spent many hours each month helping Croce put together the review. Almost inevitably there were

[23] See Charles F. Delzell, *Mussolini's Enemies: The Italian Anti-Fascist Resistance* (Princeton, 1961), 49, 90–91.

[24] Regarding the complex philosophical dispute between Croce and Gentile and Omodeo's position in it, see Garosci, "Adolfo Omodeo. II: La Guerra," 681–83.

[25] Republished in Omodeo, *Tradizioni morali e disciplina storica*, 249–66.

[26] Omodeo, *Lettere*, 424. A few more letters were exchanged when Omodeo considered preparing some articles for the new *Enciclopedia italiana* but the correspondence ended on December 4, 1929. Because of his unrepentant fascism, Gentile also lost the support of several other former students, including Guido De Ruggiero, Luigi Russo, and Ernesto Codignola. In the summer of 1944 Gentile was shot to death by a Communist partisan on a Florence street.

[27] Presumably Mussolini did not wish to alienate foreign opinion unnecessarily by cracking down on the world-renowned Croce, and there was some propaganda value to be gained by telling outsiders that Croce was able to write unfettered in Italy.

minor points of difference between the two savants, and the stern Sicilian could not conceal his disdain for some of the sycophants who on Sunday afternoons regularly streamed into the senator's sprawling home in the heart of old Naples—a palace that had once belonged to Giambattista Vico.[28] But these irritations were never allowed to overshadow the increasingly similar philosophical and historical outlooks that linked the two men. Indeed, it seems most likely that Omodeo's deep interest in the history of religion and in the relationship of philosophy and religion to history contributed to the sharpening of Croce's own views in this field. With good reason, Garosci has suggested that when Croce in the 1930's defined history as the "religion of freedom," he was more than a little indebted to Omodeo.[29]

After Omodeo's breach with Gentile and the slow evanescence of his dream of preparing a history of the church, he dedicated himself almost completely to studies in the field of modern European and Risorgimento history. In this way he could reveal how the "religion of freedom" was manifesting itself in modern times. The first of these new studies appeared in 1925—a textbook designed for use in the third year of high school: *L'Età moderna e contemporanea*.[30] The book could not be adopted in the state schools, however, apparently because its coverage halted at 1919 and the author did not end with a paean of praise to the Duce and fascism, as was then expedient. Six years later, therefore, Omodeo decided to release it to the general public after making various minor revisions and relabeling it *L'Età del Risorgimento Italiano*.[31] In that format it was to go through no fewer than seven editions and was long to dominate the field. Although the new version was more than a mere textbook, and indeed was one of a handful of truly good Italian histories written by native scholars for the cultured public, it is nevertheless true that the book fell short of being a carefully conceived and well-executed work

[28] Regarding these Sunday open-houses, see Elena Croce Craveri, *Ricordi familiari* (Florence, 1962), 17 ff.

[29] Garosci, "Adolfo Omodeo. II: La Guerra," 667.

[30] Omodeo, *L'Età moderna e contemporanea* (Messina, 1925).

[31] Omodeo, *L'Età del Risorgimento italiano* (Messina, 1931). Editions appearing after World War II were published in Naples by Edizioni Scientifiche Italiane and included a biographical profile of the author by Croce.

of history. In its chronological pattern, arrangement of material, treatment of certain topics and curious omission of others, for example, the work retained telltale traces of the textbook. It continued to be European or world history with special regard to the history of Italy, and there remained "too much of Europe for a history of the Risorgimento, and too much of Italy for a history of Europe." [32]

The *terminus a quo* employed by Omodeo—the Treaty of Aix-la-Chapelle in 1748—seems to have depended on arbitrary curriculum specifications laid down by the Ministry of Public Instruction rather than on any considered judgment by the author. He could have changed the beginning date in the revised version, but he did not. As a matter of fact, in most of his writing, Omodeo was quite willing to accept traditional patterns without much argument. Certainly it would have been much better if he had decided to rewrite the manuscript from start to finish as a history of the Italian Risorgimento in continuous intellectual, economic, political, and diplomatic contact with the rest of Europe. For as it stands, too many aspects of general European history are presented that have little or no relevance to Italy, while some other topics that were germane—for example, Britain's constitutional development and industrial revolution—are inexcusably omitted.

Omodeo began his discussion of the period before the French Revolution with a skillful analysis of the European balance of power, giving particular attention to the strengths and weaknesses of the states in the Italian peninsula. He noted the already well-established sense of nationalism in England and France during the eighteenth century but was perhaps too inclined to detect similar nationalist tendencies in Prussia at that time. Omodeo's section on the Enlightenment, though adequate, rested on the traditional literature he had read in his youth; for him, the Enlightenment was only an accessory element to the theme of political and national change. The interpretation that he accorded to Rousseau was more sympathetic than that given by Croce and underscored the democratic qualities in his thought. Omodeo pointed out that the Italians who participated in the Enlightenment were still

[32] Maturi, *Interpretazioni del Risorgimento*, 521–22.

isolated individuals, "unable to assume the leadership of events and gain ascendancy over the masses." [33]

The author's discussion of the French Revolution and Napoleonic era tended to stand in juxtaposition to that of Italian history but this did not prevent him from pointing out how the French upheaval laid the basis for the Risorgimento by reconstructing Italian society on the basis of the revolutionary principles of the Napoleonic Code, offering military and administrative training to the Italian people, and injuring irrevocably the temporal power of the papacy. Because of all this, the Italians could not participate effectively in the insurrections against Napoleon. Omodeo's interpretation of this period appears to rest on such older writers as Aulard and Sorel, as can be sensed in the sympathetic treatment accorded to the Declaration of the Rights of Man, the Night of August 4, Mirabeau, Danton, and even Napoleon. There is no evidence of familiarity with the socialistic school of historiography inaugurated by Jaurès; and Omodeo's use of pejorative adjectives to describe Robespierre, Saint-Just, Couthon, and Hébert makes them worthy of a rogues' gallery, as Garosci has noted.[34]

In the period of the Risorgimento proper (1815–70) the book focuses on Italy, as it should, but there is generally good fusion with the rest of European history. As Omodeo is quick to point out, the Risorgimento developed in harmony with the liberal and national trends elsewhere in Europe. The long years spent abroad by many Italian patriots strengthened their common ties with other peoples, so that "all the men of the Risorgimento from Mazzini to Cavour, from Garibaldi to Settembrini, were conscious of working and suffering not just for Italy but for a universally human ideal valid for all peoples." [35]

In this section the author once more reveals his skill in describing clearly the shifting balance of power and his flair for shedding light on the thread of ideas running behind events. Thus he presents a good picture of the age of romanticism, and he stresses the nineteenth century's strong faith in the idea of progress. Whereas

[33] Omodeo, *L'Età del Risorgimento italiano* (7th rev. ed.: Naples, 1952,) xiv.
[34] Garosci, "Adolfo Omodeo. II: La Guerra," 670–75.
[35] Omodeo, *L'Età del Risorgimento italiano*, xiv.

Omodeo is somewhat sketchy in his discussion of Masonry and the Carbonari, he is good in his handling of the 1821 revolutions in Italy. In later years the author was to investigate further the political roles of King Charles Albert and the Catholic publicist Vincenzo Gioberti, but he never was inclined to change the essentially hostile judgment set forth in his early work. Omodeo's treatment of Mazzini is generally quite good, although he perhaps let his admiration for the Genoese prophet carry him too far in ascribing so much importance to Mazzini's program in precipitating the 1848 revolutions. As for Cavour, it is evident that as early as 1925 Omodeo recognized he was not a statesman who from the outset had known exactly how he would bring about Italian unification. Although the author's chapter on Garibaldi's invasion of Sicily in 1860 is entitled "The Struggle between Cavour and Garibaldi," Omodeo did not go as far as Denis Mack Smith was inclined to go in later years in emphasizing the conflict between Cavour and Garibaldi. On the other hand, in the 1931 version of his book, Omodeo did include new information regarding friction between Cavour and Victor Emmanuel II as to the question of sending Piedmontese forces into the Marches to head off Garibaldi from Rome.

Omodeo's touch was considerably less felicitous when he moved on to the post-Risorgimento period. Here European history once more became the central theme, but many aspects were omitted, especially in the 1925 edition. In the 1931 revision the author improved his discussion of intellectual history and offered a more optimistic interpretation of Italian history between 1870 and 1915 —almost certainly as a result of Croce's new studies dealing with this period.[36] Throughout this portion one is aware of Omodeo's anti-Teutonic prejudice. With respect to the actions of the Central Powers in 1914, Omodeo's sense of outrage is evident:

> The repugnant Austrian ultimatum to Serbia, so similar to that which was sent to Piedmont in 1859 . . . ; the brutal invasion of Belgium and Luxemburg, the explicit denial to small states of any right to existence . . . ; the methodical employment of brutal "right

[36] Croce's *A History of Italy, 1871–1915*, was first published in Bari in 1927; his *History of Europe in the Nineteenth Century* appeared in book form in 1932.

of war" against unarmed populations aroused no simple emotional response but rebounded strongly against their authors, provoking in the assaulted nations . . . a deep moral reaction. . . . No one could conceive of living in a vast Austria such as Europe would have become under German hegemony; everyone preferred rather to face the ordeal of war.[37]

The section dealing with the war is full of details regarding the Italian campaigns—not surprising when one recalls that the writer had participated in some of them. Whereas the 1925 text tended to repeat the propagandistic theme of "mutilated victory" as regards Italy, the 1931 version conceded that the nation emerged from the conflict in a relatively improved position in the world.[38]

Although *L'Età del Risorgimento italiano* was the most widely read of Omodeo's books, many of his significant contributions to more accurate interpretation of the era appeared in other essays and books. Throughout these works certain typical themes stand out. One of these was the firm belief that the creative moment in history is provided by religious conscience. Omodeo was to make this quite clear in a posthumously published book on Calvin: "It is the great pangs of human conscience that unleash new forces for human edification and achieve profundities unknown to the most brilliant geniuses of war and diplomacy." [39] It was not surprising, therefore, that in his discussion of the Risorgimento, Omodeo should attribute fundamental importance to the work of Mazzini: "We sense how his is the religious experience that stands at the base of the 'third Italy.' Even though we steer clear of certain aspects of his beliefs and do not insist blindly on strict observance of his doctrines, we recognize that he still has something to tell our age." [40]

In addition to the *Leitmotiv* of religious conscience, Omodeo's writings on the Risorgimento were characterized by emphasis on the "circulation of ideas" in European life. This quality enabled him to avoid the unduly ethnocentric interpretation of Italian his-

[37] Omodeo, *L'Età del Risorgimento italiano*, 512–13.
[38] *Cf.* Garosci, "Adolfo Omodeo, II: La Guerra," 679–81.
[39] Omodeo, *Giovanni Calvino e la riforma in Ginevra* (Bari, 1947), 153.
[40] Omodeo, *Difesa del Risorgimento* (2nd rev. ed.; Turin, 1955), 74–85.

tory that Gentile had presented. The latter had sought to disregard as much as possible the impact of both the Enlightenment and French Revolution on the development of Italian nationalism, preferring to stress an autochthonous chain of development that led from Machiavelli through Vico, Cuoco, and Mazzini to Gioberti. Omodeo vigorously objected to this. As early as 1929, in an essay entitled "Primato Francese e iniziativa Italiana," he argued that both the Mazzinian call for a "grass-roots" Italian initiative and the Giobertian dream of a new Italian primacy were developed in full recognition that Italy belonged to a common European civilization and had something meaningful to offer to it.[41] This feeling of tolerant and interdependent nationalism was never so strong as in the period between 1814 and 1848, he continued. No doubt Omodeo was essentially correct as to Mazzini's own outlook, but it must be noted that certain second-generation Mazzinians like Francesco Crispi and Alfredo Oriani were considerably less tolerant in their nationalism.

The question of the relative importance of Gioberti and Mazzini in accelerating the course of the Risorgimento led to another quarrel between Omodeo and his former professor. In 1919 Gentile had assigned to Gioberti a place of parity alongside Mazzini, arguing that the former's *Primato morale e civile degli italiani* (1843) had gone beyond Mazzini's level of abstractions and had stirred Catholic opinion to create a neo-Guelf movement that opened the way for 1848–49. When these revolutions aborted, Gioberti was ready in 1851 to give another boost to Italian unification by writing a second tract, *Del Rinnovamento civile d'Italia*, in which he called upon the Italian people to look to the House of Savoy for leadership.[42]

Once more Omodeo came forth with a rebuttal. In the essay, "Vincenzo Gioberti e la sua evoluzione politica," charged with a crusading spirit of political engagement, Omodeo contended that the Catholic publicist Gioberti had invented the neo-Guelf myth

[41] Omodeo, "Primato Francese e iniziativa italiana," *La Critica*, XXVII (1929), 223–40; republished in Omodeo, *Difesa del Risorgimento*, 17–38.
[42] This thesis was later developed in greater detail by the historian Antonio Anzilotti. See Maturi, *Interpretazioni del Risorgimento*, 476–77, 531.

as a kind of Trojan horse to penetrate the absolutistic, Catholic-minded Italy of the 1840s.[43] Almost certainly Omodeo let his bias get the better of him here, for the neo-Guelf ideal had developed prior to Gioberti and had already become a kind of utopian dream. As both Croce and Maturi have observed, Gioberti's *Primato* could hardly have been effective had it not been preceded by the historic epic of the Lombard League and battle of Legnano (1176), as well as by the work of numerous liberal Catholics.[44] Omodeo stood on firmer ground when he demonstrated that previous writers had oversimplified matters by interpreting Gioberti's *Del Rinnovamento civile d'Italia* as a prophecy of the Risorgimento to be accomplished under Cavour's leadership. After carefully examining Gioberti's correspondence, Omodeo pointed out that as of 1851 the ex-Guelfist thought it most likely that Italian unification would come about through the help of a democratic and social revolution in France. It was Omodeo's conclusion that Gioberti's essay contained a "deliberate ambiguity" and "left the door open for either a fully republican solution or a constitutional monarchical one." [45] In this, Omodeo was probably correct; but it remains a fact that the democratic revolution did not take place in France and instead the Second Empire emerged there, while in Italy a group of patriots, headed by Giuseppe Massari, drew inspiration from Gioberti's document and used it to promote the cause of the House of Savoy.[46]

Omodeo's polemics on the subject of King Charles Albert were important both for shaping the historian's own political future and for rectifying historical judgments. Thus, as an outgrowth of his study of the "crowned Hamlet" of Piedmont, Omodeo was to shift his own orientation from liberal monarchism to democratic republicanism, while on the historiographical plane, Omodeo's arguments were to inflict a death blow to the interpretations of

---

[43] The essay was first published in Turin in 1941; it was republished in Omodeo, *Difesa del Risorgimento*, 86–155.

[44] Croce, *Storia d'Europa nel secolo decimonono* (Bari, 1932), 137; Maturi, *Interpretazioni del Risorgimento*, 523–33.

[45] Omodeo, *Difesa del Risorgimento*, 154.

[46] Maturi, *Interpretazioni del Risorgimento*, 532–34.

Alessandro Luzio, the Risorgimentalist whose views hitherto had dominated the field. Luzio and his followers had sought to present Charles Albert as a veritable king of kings who personified the new Italy, with Mazzini serving at best as a kind of John the Baptist.[47] Omodeo, on the other hand, denied that Charles Albert was a great monarch. He was willing to say only that his "romantic, mystical dreaming, the inadequacy of his talents, his clash with the harsh world, his tragic destiny all made him a historically and humanly interesting figure, if one looks at him without preconceptions." [48] Omodeo's psychological intepretation of Charles Albert made him appear like Alexander I of Russia or Frederick William IV of Prussia, a romantic sovereign full of contradictions.

Even more significant was Omodeo's attack upon those historians who had asserted that Charles Albert's reforms in Sardinia-Piedmont had been designed to lay the basis for the state structure that later formed the Kingdom of Italy.[49] Omodeo contended that Charles Albert's reforms, culminating in the *Statuto Albertino* of 1848, sought only to bring about an administratively improved monarchy that would conform to the principles of the Restoration era. What really was to serve as the nucleus-state of the eventual Kingdom of Italy, he continued, was the structure that had to be rebuilt in many ways by parliamentary legislation after the abdication and death of Charles Albert in 1849.[50] Perhaps Omodeo was not entirely fair, however, for it is not enough to take into account the reforms that subsequently had to be enacted in the Cavourian era. One should view the reforms in the context of their time and realize that they did much to transform the old Savoyard military monarchy into a civilian, administrative realm—as witness, for example, the detachment of the police from the authority of the Ministry of War. Nor should it be denied that Charles Albert's economic reforms were of some help in breathing

[47] See Alessandro Luzio, *Carlo Alberto e Giuseppe Mazzini* (Turin, 1923).
[48] Omodeo, *Difesa del Risorgimento*, 222; cf. his caustic comments about Luzio in *ibid.*, 179–80.
[49] Cf. Luzio, *Carlo Alberto e Giuseppe Mazzini* and Niccolò Rodolico, *Carlo Alberto principe di Carignano* (Florence, n.d.).
[50] Omodeo, *Difesa del Risorgimento*, 156–58 ff.

new life into the country, although doubtless the most important stimulus was provided by England's repeal of the Corn Laws, as Maturi has noted.[51]

Omodeo's research in the field of Risorgimento history culminated in his two-volume study, *L'Opera politica del Conte di Cavour. Parte I: 1848–1857.*[52] In this instance, the author retreated somewhat from his earlier position that the historian should concentrate on a leader in the intimate fervor of a great crisis. Thus, Omodeo did not focus his lens on Cavour only; he also gave ample attention to the entire milieu and dealt carefully with Mazzini and other important figures of the decade. Unfortunately, the work was left incomplete; not even after World War II did Omodeo resume it. A clear picture of his assessment of Cavour can be gained, however, by supplementing this study with Omodeo's other essays dealing with Cavour, from Plombières to his death, now reprinted in the collection, *Difesa del Risorgimento*. Omodeo rejected the viewpoint of such writers as Heinrich von Treitschke, Maurice Paléologue, and Gentile, who stressed the cynical, *Realpolitik* side of Cavour and contended that he was ready to relegate his liberal ideals to cold-storage whenever the national interest demanded it. Following the lead of scholars like Francesco Ruffini, William R. Thayer, and Paul Matter, Omodeo emphasized instead the idealistic, liberal qualities of Cavour. He did not deny the statesman's Machiavellian political and diplomatic skill, but he subordinated this to the liberal side of his character. According to Omodeo, Cavour's high ethical principles were clearly shown by the fact that he was not willing to serve just any regime—for example, he would not support Charles Albert so long as the latter reigned absolutistically. Omodeo was not prepared to go so far as to allege that Cavour was always right. He was willing to concede that Cavour occasionally wavered, improvised, and even committed political and diplomatic blunders.

The most fruitful legacy of Cavour lay in the field of domestic political reform, Omodeo argued. His creation of a parliamentary,

---

[51] Maturi, *Interpretazioni del Risorgimento*, 536.

[52] Omodeo, *L'Opera politica del Conte di Cavour. Part I: 1848–1857* (2 vols.; Florence, 1940).

liberal regime in Sardinia-Piedmont provided the nucleus for the liberal parliamentary system of the Kingdom of Italy. Cavour achieved this modernization only by means of a bitter struggle with Victor Emmanuel II, his appointive Senate, and the forces of clericalism. All of this process of liberalization and laicization is described by Omodeo in masterly fashion, although he did not make use of the Cavour papers in the Museo del Risorgimento.[53]

As for the origins of Sardinia-Piedmont's alliance with Britain and France in the Crimean War, Omodeo was the first to explode the legend that Premier Cavour, acting with a free hand, had brought about Piedmontese intervention and had done so with full intuition of what this would mean for Piedmont in the future. Although Cavour felt sympathetic to the cause of France and Britain, his intervention in the war really took place as the result of strong pressure from abroad and at home, but with no assurance that there would be foreign support for Italy after the war. Thus, France and Britain desired most of all that Austria should intervene in the struggle against Russia, and in order to reassure Austria that her flank would not be attacked by Piedmont, they importuned the latter to enter the war too. The other pressure on Cavour came from Victor Emmanuel II, who was so anxious to join the war that he promised the French minister in Turin that he would dismiss Cavour if he resisted. Cavour gave in and everything went smoothly. This interpretation by Omodeo, based on careful study of Subalpine parliamentary papers, has been reinforced by Pietro Silva's later research in the English documents and Franco Valsecchi's in the Austrian ones.[54]

Omodeo was also respected for his conclusions regarding the interdependent roles of Mazzini and Cavour in the Risorgimento. Building on the work of Luzio but writing with more objectivity, Omodeo stressed that Mazzini's active contribution to the unification of Italy, far from fizzling out after the Crimean War, continued to be of great importance until the plebiscites. Whereas in

---

[53] Maturi, *Interpretazioni del Risorgimento*, 538–39.
[54] *Ibid.*, 540. See Pietro Silva, "L'Alleanza del Regno di Sardegna con le potenze occidentali nello guerra di Crimea," in *Figure e momenti di storia Italiana* (Milan, 1939); and Franco Valsecchi, *Il Risorgimento e l'Europa: L'Alleanza di Crimea* (Milan, 1948).

Luzio's eyes Mazzini had been the pure apostle of unification and Cavour had done nothing more than exploit this at the last minute, in Omodeo's judgment the relationship between the two men was dialectical—that is, of repeated interaction between an idea and its diplomatic development. Thus the activities of Mazzini and Cavour were complementary and equally necessary for the formation of Italy. If Cavour's audacity had failed in the 1850's, all of his labors would have benefited Mazzini and republicanism. If Cavour assured Italy a moderate, liberal type of government, it was Mazzini who added the principle that freedom must constantly be expanded in a democratic sense. And if Cavour obtained Napoleon III's support, it was Mazzini who prevented the French from imposing solid hegemony over Italy.

Omodeo was fair in giving much credit to Napoleon III and the Second Empire for bringing about Italian unification—a theme to be elaborated by another great Risorgimentalist, Salvatorelli [55]— and he recognized that Garibaldi deserved major credit for making 1860 the turning point in the unification process, for his expedition filled a "hiatus in Cavour's policies." But, Omodeo added, it would be wrong to portray Garibaldi as Italy's Washington, for the constructive political talents of the flamboyant Red Shirt commander did not measure up to his military ones. [56]

Omodeo was also fair in his assessment of the contributions made by other men to Cavour's ecclesiastical policy of 1860–61. "It almost seems as if the famous program, 'A free Church in a free State,' was a collective work. With great modesty Cavour assimilated information, listened to everyone, and oriented himself in the problems." [57] Yet in large measure this collective work, which was the flowering of Piedmontese liberalism during the great decade, served to lead Cavour back to the thoughts and studies of his youth when the problem of religious freedom fixed itself in his mind, Omodeo continued. On the subject of church-state relations, incidentally, Omodeo corrected the error of the

---

[55] Cf. Luigi Salvatorelli, *Pensiero e azione del Risorgimento* (6th ed.; Turin, 1960), 161–63.
[56] Omodeo, *Difesa del Risorgimento*, 308, 312.   [57] *Ibid.*, 328–29.

historian Francesco Salata,[58] who had implied that Cavour sought a concordat. Omodeo explained that the project Cavour had in mind was not precisely that but rather an act of separation on the basis of mutual consent, and that Cavour also hoped to see Catholic reforms and a liberalization of the Church ensue.[59]

There are gaps in *L'Opera politica del Conte di Cavour*. While it presents a good analysis of the parliamentary and diplomatic scene, it leaves out a discussion of Piedmontese intellectual life during the 1850's. One does not find in it any analysis of the first great confrontation and clash between Piedmontese society and the wave of political refugees who were rushing in from other regions. Nor is social and economic history fused with that of politics and diplomacy. In short, the book would have been better if the author had allowed himself a broader perspective. These lacunae can be explained in part by the nature of the book's origins, for it grew out of the consolidation of two earlier studies: an introduction that Omodeo wrote for a new edition of Cavour's *Discorsi parlamentari, 1848–50*[60] and an essay that he wrote on Mazzini and Cavour for *La Critica* in 1934–35. Despite its gaps, Omodeo's work stands out as one of the most significant to appear in recent years on Risorgimento history in general and on Cavour in particular. Further proof of its signal importance is shown by the fact that it has caused clerical, royalist, Mazzinian, and Marxist historians alike to shift their ground somewhat, as Maturi has explained.[61]

Omodeo's polemics against socialistic historiography in Italy— and especially that of the short-lived Turinese publicist Piero

[58] Francesco Salata, *Per la storia diplomatica della questione romana: Da Cavour alla Triplice Alleanza* (Milan, 1929).

[59] Omodeo, *Difesa del Risorgimento*, 346–50.

[60] Cavour, *Discorsi parlamentari, 1848–50* (14 vols.; Florence, 1932–69), I, vii–cxv.

[61] Maturi cites, for example, Fr. Pietro Pirri for the clericals; Francesco Cognasso for the monarchists, Giulio Andrea Belloni for the Mazzinians, and Giorgio Candeloro for the Marxists. Maturi, *Interpretazioni del Risorgimento*, 543–44.

Without Omodeo's pioneering work it would have been difficult for Cesare Spellanzon to undertake his multivolume *Storia del Risorgimento italiano* (Milan, 1933—), which is now being continued by Ennio Di Nolfo. *Cf.* Salvatorelli, "Gli studi di storia," *L'Acropoli: Ad Adolfo Omodeo*, II, No. 17/24 (1947), xviii.

Gobetti (who was forced by the Fascists to flee to France, where he died in 1926)—help to explain why the University of Naples professor was not very popular with the younger generation of historians influenced by socialism. These polemics also reveal some of the limitations of Omodeo's scholarship. Reviewing Gobetti's *Risorgimento senza eroi*,[62] he criticized the author for bemoaning the fact that the Risorgimento had not brought about a religious reformation in Italy—a prerequisite for political freedom, according to Gobetti. Omodeo asked sharply where such a reformation could have come from in the nineteenth century; after all, Italy's background was quite different from that of Germany. He went on to point out, however, that the Risorgimento did produce its own religious reform movement, a campaign against Jesuitical Catholicism. And as for Gobetti's criticism that the Risorgimento was brought about by a minority elite rather than by popular revolution, Omodeo replied hotly: "Yes, but they worked for the people. They resigned themselves to the fact that they comprised the nation, just like the seven thousand Jews who, in refusing to kneel down before Baal in the time of Elijah, constituted the true Israel. But their great merit was that they believed in the people and in the nation. . . . If their work was not entirely successful, it was simply because a people cannot be improvised in fifty years; one must establish centuries of tradition. The Italian nation was completely new. They confined themselves to furnishing cadres to serve the people and nation." [63]

In retrospect, one wishes that Omodeo could have shown in 1926 the same tolerance of Gobetti's criticisms of the shortcomings of the Risorgimento that he was to show in 1943 towards the French historian Edgar Quinet's anticlerical criticism of shortcomings in the French Revolution. But in 1926 Omeodo was still a liberal conservative in politics, whereas in 1943 he had completed his drift towards radical liberalism, as was to be shown by his adherence to the new Partito d'Azione, a party which was mili-

[62] Gobetti, *Risorgimento senza eroi* (Turin, 1926); reviewed by Omodeo in *Leonardo*, II (1926), 325–28.
[63] Omodeo, *Difesa del Risorgimento*, 444.

tantly republican and owed much of its inspiration to the earlier writings of Gobetti.

In his criticism of Gobetti, Omodeo declared that Italy's contemporary political calamity derived from "distortions given to the meaning of the Risorgimento rather than from the Risorgimento itself." [64] And he went so far as to concede that the historian could benefit from the help of specialists in economics and jurisprudence (though not from nonidealist philosophers). Thus he was willing to move at least a few steps towards those socialistic and eclectic historians who insisted upon a more thoroughgoing probe of the reasons for the triumph of fascism.[65]

During the mid-1930's, when Omodeo was bowed down by the combined blows of the dictatorship, depression, and the untimely death of one of his daughters, he began to search for a theme that would offer a logical link between his studies of the Church and his new determination to clarify how the "religion of freedom" was still unfolding. At last he found such a transitional period, not in the field of post-Kantian German philosophy but in the years of the Restoration in France (1814–30). Although he possessed very little firsthand acquaintance with France (he visited there only twice—for two months in 1932 and for a few days in 1938), he proceeded to read diligently in the works of Saint-Simon, Lamennais, Madame de Staël, Constant, Thiers, Mignet, Comte, and others who contributed to the intellectual and political debates of that time. More and more he was convinced that the Restoration years marked the birth of "nineteenth-century man" —the type of man who, emancipated from clericalism, was assuming a laic, liberal posture and confronting the problems of modern civilization with a clear sense of history. Those fifteen years opened the way for the transformation of Europe, with this new kind of Frenchman serving as the cultural instructor of the rest of the continent. In due course, these essays were assembled in book form under the title, *La Cultura francese nell'età della*

[64] *Ibid.*, 446.
[65] See his "Il distacco dal Risorgimento," in Omodeo, *Il Senso della storia* (2nd rev. ed.; Turin, 1955), 444–48; *cf.* Giorgio Candeloro, "Adolfo Omodeo storico del Risorgimento," *Società*, V (December, 1949), 582–601.

Restaurazione.[66] Despite the unfinished and somewhat disjointed structure, this book was one of Omodeo's best efforts at trying to discern the ideal inspiration lying behind modern civilization.[67] Socialist-minded historians were annoyed, however, by Omodeo's explanation of the genesis of the theory of "class struggle." In these pages he contended that much of it derived from writers of the extreme Right in France who passed it on to the French Socialists, and they in turn to Marx.[68] It probably would have been better, as Maturi has pointed out, if Omodeo had kept more clearly before his readers the most important factor in the development of this theory—the socioeconomic impact of the Industrial Revolution.[69]

When the disasters of Italian participation in World War II eventually unseated Mussolini in 1943, Omodeo found himself appointed rector of the University of Naples on September 10. Although he was the logical faculty member to supervise the purge of Fascist personnel and practices, he accepted the post with misgivings, as he was reluctant to undertake a task that would certainly involve measures against longtime associates.[70]

By this time he had identified himself with the Partito d'Azione —a party whose title recalled the radical, democratic side of the Risorgimento and whose program demanded the elimination of the bumbling royal dictatorship of Victor Emmanuel III and Marshal Badoglio, and their replacement by a republic. Many of its adherents, though not Omodeo, also insisted on a considerable measure of socialism in the postwar economy. For several months Omodeo became the party's most articulate spokesman in Naples and served in the Committee of National Liberation there. In the

---

[66] Omodeo, *La Cultura francese nell'età della Restaurazione* (Milan, 1946).

[67] Some related essays dealing with Cardinal Consalvi and other topics were published about the same time as *Aspetti del Cattolicesimo della Restaurazione* (Turin, 1946). Another important study was that of the reactionary Count Joseph de Maistre, in which Omodeo revealed that in his youth the Savoyard had been a Freemason. Appearing first in installments in *La Critica*, XXXIV/XV (1936/37), this study was later published as a book, *Un reazionario: Il Conte J. De Maistre* (Bari, 1939).

[68] Omodeo, *La Cultura francese nell'età della Restaurazione*, 82–95.

[69] Maturi, *Interpretazioni del Risorgimento*, 548.

[70] See Giovanni Malquori, "Il Rettore," *L'Acropoli: Ad Adolfo Omodeo*, II, No. 17/24 (1947), lvii–lxiii.

columns of the local newspaper *Il Risorgimento*, in broadcasts over the radio, and in addresses at the university, the rector kept up a drumbeat of arguments in favor of thoroughgoing political change in Italy. As early as September, 1943, he wrote: "Nobody can argue that the twenty years of Fascism conformed to the pattern of the Charles Albert Constitution and the traditions of the Risorgimento. Nobody dreams today that it is possible to have a new constitution handed down from above." [71] He insisted that the Allies must give assurances that Italians would be entirely free to choose their own form of government. By December he had founded a small circle of political and intellectual followers under the label, "Pensiero e Azione." All of these steps had the effect of bringing about a political rupture with Croce, who remained a conservative liberal and staunch defender of the monarchical institution, although he too insisted that the present king, tarnished by long years of collaboration with fascism, must go. [72]

During the spring of 1944 the political situation in the liberated South was drastically altered when Palmiro Togliatti, leader of the Italian Communists, returned from Moscow with instructions that his party join the government of Badoglio and the king for the duration of the war. The Action Party was most reluctant of all the forces in the Committee of National Liberation to participate in such a fusion government but at last felt compelled to do so. In April, Omodeo was awarded the portfolio of Minister of Public Instruction. One of his first decisions was to abolish the regulation that allowed heads of institutes to listen in on what was being said by professors in the classroom. He also reestablished the obligation of the *scuole medie* to schedule the usual examinations, forbade student political demonstrations, and did his best to eliminate clerical influence in the schools. [73]

The liberation of Rome in June, 1944, necessitated the formation of a new government, headed by Ivanoe Bonomi and including members of the Rome Committee of National Liberation.

[71] First printed in the Naples *Il Risorgimento*; reprinted in Adolfo Omodeo, *Libertà e storia: Scritti e discorsi politici* (Turin, 1960), 85.

[72] See Delzell, *Mussolini's Enemies*, chapter 8, for details of this period of history.

[73] See Concetto Marchesi, "In defesa della scuola," *L'Acropoli: Ad Adolfo Omodeo*, II, No. 17/24 (1947), liii–lvi.

Omodeo was replaced by Professor Guido De Ruggiero, a member of the same party but an older man who lacked some of the energy of his predecessor. To Omodeo's annoyance, the new government permitted student demonstrations to resume and ignored some of his other measures as well.

Sensing that he was losing influence, and dismayed by the Action Party's adoption that summer of what seemed to him to be a dangerously Jacobinic and semiauthoritarian posture, Omodeo decided to found his own political and cultural review. Entitled *L'Acropoli: Rivista di politica*, it appeared monthly in Naples during the remaining two years of his life. The choice of title coincided with Omodeo's latest historical research interests, the Periclean age in Athens and Homeric Greece. In this review as well as in other forums, Omodeo, who was now an ardent advocate of European federation, expressed his concern at the nationalistic stance assumed by some Italian governmental leaders during the discussions of the peace settlement.[74] He also made it clear that he still regarded Jesuitical Roman Catholicism as the original form of totalitarianism; if democracy was going to flourish in Italy, liberalization of the church would be indispensable, he insisted.[75]

The doughty university rector never lost sight of the fact that the war was not yet over and that Italians must participate in the unfinished task of national liberation. Ever since September, 1943, he had been exhorting southern students to volunteer for service, and he had become increasingly annoyed at their apathy, which was compounded by British reluctance to encourage a greater Italian role in the war effort. At last in January, 1945, the fifty-six-year-old ex-artillery captain suddenly volunteered and spent the rest of the war with the "Mantova" Combat Group.[76]

In the postwar months, although Omodeo and Croce were no longer in agreement as to many aspects of politics, they remained close friends and shared the same approach to history. Thus it was

[74] See his pamphlet, *La Confederazione Europea* (Naples, 1943).

[75] See Gabriele Pepe, "Il pensiero politico nell'*Acropoli*," *L'Acropoli: Ad Adolfo Omodeo*, II, No. 17/24 (1947), xlvi–lii; and especially Omodeo's "Totalitarismo cattolico," republished in Omodeo, *Libertà e storia*, 332–38.

[76] Guido Bologna, "Nella guerra di liberazione," *L'Acropoli: Ad Adolfo Omodeo*, II, No. 17/24 (1947), lxxi–lxxiv.

logical that when Croce was preparing to establish a postgraduate Institute for Historical Studies in his own residence, he intended to name Omodeo as its first director. But fate did not allow this.[77] On April 28, 1946, undulant fever brought Omodeo's life to a premature end—only a few weeks before the national referendum inaugurated the republic he had so vigorously advocated.

Italy had lost one of her most promising scholars at a critical moment in the period of national recovery. A dedicated upholder of the principle that ideas provide the key to understanding of the past, that true history is always "contemporaneous," and that "definitive" history must remain a fallacy, Omodeo unquestionably made substantial scholarly contributions in his chosen fields of historical investigation. It is equally fair to say, however, that he failed to give adequate attention to the ways in which economics, sociology, science, and technology could also be of assistance in providing new insights and dimensions for our understanding of historical development. In this regard, of course, Omodeo was not much different from the majority of Italian historians, who tended to remain strongly wedded to humanistic traditions. There is considerable evidence that Omodeo was not at his best in the classroom. The humorless scholar could never suffer fools gladly; he much preferred to devote his energies to his own research and publications.[78] Fortunately, these publications proved inspiring and stimulating to many Italian scholars, although not all of his readers were disposed to pursue his rather single-track philosophy of history.

Even if his health had permitted it, this "last great follower of Mazzini"—as Galante Garrone has dubbed Omodeo—was probably too inflexible to have survived very long in the rapidly shifting pattern of Italian politics.[79] But this should not blind us to his very real political and moral significance, for there are brief

[77] Instead, Professor Federico Chabod of the University of Rome became the first director. The scholarships that are now offered by this Istituto Italiano per gli Studi Storici are named in honor of both Omodeo and Chabod.

[78] On July 16, 1934, he wrote to Luigi Russo: "After my delusion with regard to Gentile, I don't believe any more in the schools, only in my own work as a scholar." Omodeo, *Lettere*, 521.

[79] *Cf.* Galante Garrone, "L'ultimo grande seguace di Giuseppe Mazzini," *L'Acropoli: Ad Adolfo Omodeo*, II, No. 17/24 (1947), xxi–xlv.

moments in the history of a nation when what is most important is the example of intransigent, high-minded leadership offered by men who are dedicated to the principle of expanding freedom. It was such leadership and inspiration that Omodeo offered in full measure to his countrymen as they emerged from the long night of fascism.

GERHARD RITTER

WILLIAM HARVEY MAEHL

Auburn University

WHEN FRIEDRICH MEINECKE, the dean of the German historical profession, died in 1954, his mantle passed to Gerhard Ritter. The latter's scholarly output, filling more than half a century and ranging over almost every epoch of German history since the later Middle Ages, was by then so impressive that he had become the gauge by which other contemporary historians were measured. In 1959 G. P. Gooch called him "the most productive of living historians."[1]

Gerhard Ritter was born on April 6, 1888, into a pious bourgeois family in Bad Sooden-Allendorf (Werra) in what had been, before the Prussian annexations of 1866, Hesse-Cassel. Son of a Lutheran minister, he was imbued with a sober evangelical sense of responsibility and a devotion to olden German culture. After having finished *Gymnasium* at Gütersloh (near Bielefeld), Westphalia, Gerhard attended the universities of Munich and Leipzig. At twenty he entered the University of Heidelberg, where Herman Oncken (1869–1946) led him into the field of history.[2]

In the twilight of German ascendancy, the shadow of Bismarck loomed pillar-like and imposing at Heidelberg and Berlin (where Ritter also studied for one semester). All of the historians from whom Ritter learned—Lenz, Marcks, Brandenburg, Hintze, Schmoller and, to no inconsiderable extent too, Delbrück and

---

[1] G. P. Gooch, *History and Historians in the Nineteenth Century* (Boston, 1959), iii.
[2] Ritter to author, December 15, 1966; Ritter's *Antrittsrede* (*gehalten am* 17.6.1944). *Sonderdruck aus Jahreshefte der Heidelberger Akademie der Wissenschaften*, 1943–55 (Heidelberg, 1955), 11.

Oncken—were deeply impressed by the strength and skill of the greatest nineteenth century exponent of *Machtpolitik*, all the more because in the deteriorating international position in which the Reich found itself at the *fin du siècle*, none of his successors seemed able to pull the "bow of Ulysses." Two other Heidelberg savants, Max Weber (1864–1920), the constitutional democrat who thought the Bismarck legend hyperbole and was a sharp critic of the constitution of the Second Empire, and Ernst Troeltsch (1865–1923), the near economic determinist, do not seem to have had any influence on Ritter. It was not strange, therefore, that Oncken was eventually able to direct his student's interest along nationalist channels towards the study of recent political history.

His initial attempt to write a philosophic-historical dissertation on the Renaissance theologian and necromancer Cornelius (Agrippa) von Nettesheim (1486?–1535) having foundered "for external reasons," [3] Ritter acted on Oncken's suggestion to explore the record of the Conservative Party and also aid him in preparing a "life and letters" of Rudolf Bennigsen.[4] Ritter's research now brought him into contact with the aristocratic families of Farther Pomerania and afforded occasion for his first published articles on nineteenth century German political history.[5]

After receiving his doctorate, Ritter sat the secondary school teaching certificate examinations in Karlsruhe in 1912, following which he taught for two years in the Cassel school system. At Easter, 1914, he was appointed *Oberlehrer* in the Magdeburg *Oberrealschule*. At that time he did not yet aspire to a university

---

[3] Ritter, *Antrittsrede*, 12–13. A by-product of this Reformation project was Ritter's very first publication, at the age of twenty-two, "Ein historisches Urbild zu Goethes Faust (Agrippa von Nettesheym)," *Preussische Jahrbücher*, CXLI (1910), 300–24.

[4] Ritter's dissertation was later published as *Die preussischen Konservativen und Bismarcks deutsche Politik, 1858–76*, in *Heidelberger Abhandlungen zu mittleren und neueren Geschichte*, XLIII (Heidelberg, 1913). It was a meticulous vindication of Bismarck's aim, pursued in the face of initial but gradually diminishing opposition from the Prussian Conservatives, of galvanizing the German states and peoples into a nation.

[5] Ritter, "Altersbriefe L. v. Gerlachs. Ungedruckte Briefe des Präsidenten E. L. v. Gerlach an A. v. Thadden und M. v. Blankenburg," *Deutsche Revue*, XXXVI, No. 1 (1911), 43–59, 215–29, 358–70; No. 2, 104–18, 207–15, 304–17; and "Die Entstehung der Indemnitätsvorlage von 1866," *Historische Zeitschrift*, CXIV (1915), 17–64. Ritter also published in 1911 two articles dealing with the intellectual development and aristocratic political views of Thomas Carlyle.

career. Despite strong evidence of an aptitude for research and rhetoric, Ritter felt he lacked the encyclopedic memory for historical detail which he thought a professor should have.[6]

During the First World War Ritter served mainly on the eastern front as soldier and military historian with the infantry.[7] During a forced march in Lithuania in September, 1916, he was handed a telegram that marked a turning point in his life. Upon Oncken's recommendation he had been invited to write a two-volume history of the University of Heidelberg.

After the war Ritter commenced work on his assignment, which many years later yielded only incomplete results. Nevertheless, on the strength of an intensive study of the fourteenth century German scholastic rector of Heidelberg, Marsilius von Inghen (1330?–96),[8] he was appointed *Privatdocent* on the philosophical faculty of medieval and modern history at Heidelberg. There, through lectures and studies in pre-Reformation history, he was able to console his countrymen for their defeat in World War I by reminding them of an older, finer nationalism that had once distinguished the German mind. In a number of solid works Ritter explored the role of scholasticism as precursor of the Lutheran revolt,[9] the influence of humanism upon the schoolmen,[10] the impact of the former upon the culture specifically of the Rhenish Palatinate,[11] and the significance of Martin Luther and of More's *Utopia*.[12]

[6] Ritter, *Antrittsrede*, 13; Ritter to author, December 15, 1966.

[7] See Ritter, *Das Reserve-Infanterie Regiment 210 in den Kriegsjahren 1914–15* (Stettin, 1916).

[8] Ritter, *Studien zur Spätscholastik*, I: *Marsilius von Inghen und die okkamistische Schule in Deutschland. Sitzungsberichte der Heidelbergischen Akademie der Wissenschaft*. Philosophisch-historisch Kl., No. 4 (Heidelberg, 1921).

[9] Ritter, *Studien zur Spätscholastik*, II: *Via antiqua und via moderna auf den deutschen Universitäten des 15. Jahrhunderts*, No. 7 (Heidelberg, 1922); *ibid.*, III: *Neue Quellenstücke zur Theologie des Johann von Wesel*, No. 5 (Heidelberg, 1926–27).

[10] Ritter, "Die geschichtliche Bedeutung des deutschen Humanismus," *Historische Zeitschrift*, CXXVII (1923), 393–453.

[11] Ritter, "Aus dem geistigen Leben der Heidelberger Universität am Ausgang des Mittelalters," *Zeitschrift für Geschichte des Oberrheins*, XXXVII (1922), 1–32; "Aus dem Kreise der Hofpoeten Pfalzgraf Friedrichs I," *ibid.*, XXXVIII (1922), 109–23.

[12] Ritter, "Martin Luther," in Schneider Verlag (ed.), *Kämpfer* (Berlin, 1924), 11–108; see Ritter's translation of the *Utopia* in *Klassiker der Politik*, I (Berlin, 1922).

Illustrative of Ritter's then broad familiarity with the Latin and other sources of the fifteenth century is his *Wesel* monograph.[13] Like the *Inghen* and *Via antiqua* studies, it is heavily encrusted with critical footnotes and reveals considerable knowledge of the fifteenth century status of the great questions of theology, biblical criticism, and hierarchal and papal authority. Ritter's sober proficiency in diplomatics and heuristic is also apparent at points in the *Wesel* monograph. He weighed the authenticity of the recently discovered *Opusculum de auctoritate officio et potestate pastorum ecclesiasticorum* without, however, unquestioningly assigning it to Wesel; evaluated other until then unutilized writings by Wesel (e.g., *Questiones de libris physicorum Aristotelis; Sentenzen-Kommentar,* 1, and *Übungen über alte und neue Logik*) from his *Docent* period at Erfurt; by proposing a separation of the polemical from the purely factual parts of the reports of the court trial of Wesel, strongly pointed to their authorship by a senior lecturer in theology and seven times rector of the University of Heidelberg, Nikolaus von Wachenheim; and, finally, carefully sifted the proceeding of the Heidelberg disputation of June 18, 1501, with the aim of proving that the humanist Konrad Hansel had been present at the trial in 1479 and had been impelled down the path of reformism by Wesel.[14]

Among the more important conclusions to which these postwar studies point is that humanism never superseded scholasticism or mysticism in Germany. Neither the emergence of a "skeptical anti-metaphysical" frame of thinking nor any alleged apostasy of the intelligentsia consummated the ruin of scholasticism or very much altered the pronounced transcendental orientation of the German mind, which persisted to the early seventeenth century.[15] According to Ritter, it was an error to regard the German Reformation as a mere facet of the Renaissance, for Lutheranism was separated from Italian humanism by an entirely different view of

[13] Johann von Wesel was an Occamist professor at the University of Erfurt and later pastor of the cathedral at Mainz. He was condemned in February, 1479, for heresy when he was nearly eighty years old. Although he recanted, his writings were burned and he was imprisoned in a monastery at Mainz, where he died in 1481.
[14] Ritter, *Johann von Wesel,* 31–37, 38–44, and 51–57.
[15] Ritter, "Die geschichtliche Bedeutung des . . . Humanismus," 409.

man and God. German humanism, whose literary output was very meager, was only an episode, not a turning point, in history.[16] Far more consequential was the slow, indigenous, intellectual evolution from Johannes Tauler and Meister Eckhart, through Wesel, Wessel Gansfort, and Johannes von Goch to Reuchlin and Luther. For Ritter, the strongest link in that chain was Wesel, whose biblical and rational criticism was the sharpest that had ever been seen in Germany and who fought exploitation by the Roman curia, denounced slavish obedience to episcopal authority, and labelled the pope "a pious fraud." [17]

After the German revolution of 1918 Ritter did not rush to embrace the new republicanism, as did Max Weber and others, but, on the other hand, he was not anti-republican. Eschewing political action, he reflected intensively upon the causes of the fall of the Hohenzollern monarchy. In one article he attributed the ruin of the Second German Empire to the inner tensions of the Bismarckian system and to William II, who was "neither able to establish supreme responsibility for the attainment of clear political objectives nor guarantee a unified line of foreign policy." Here the author outlined a thesis which he exhaustively developed later in his career: the absence of a strong monarchical hand, such as would have been capable of establishing a true "personal regime" and of holding the reins of both military and civil command, promoted a fateful cleavage between civil and military leadership. Noticeable in peacetime only in "an obvious lack of cooperation in technical preparations for war," this divorce became in wartime "infinitely catastrophic." [18]

A few years later Ritter examined the legend of a rejected proffer of English friendship at the turn of the century. Using the earlier volumes to appear in the official *British Documents on the Origins of the War* (11 vols., 1926–38) in collation with the

---

[16] *Ibid.*, 401, 403–405, 421, 425–27, 452–55; and Ritter, "Humanismus und Reformation. Eine Replik [to J. Haller]," *Zeitschrift für Kirchengeschichte*, XLIII (1924), 150–59.

[17] Ritter, *Johann von Wesel*, 12–14, 16–17, 21, 23, 26, 30, 45–47, 49, 53, 57.

[18] Ritter to author, December 15, 1966 and January 7, 1967; Ritter, "Geschichtliche Wandlungen des monarchischen Staatsgedankens in Preussen-Deutschland," *Preussische Jahrbücher*, CLXXXIV (1921), 233–38, 250–52.

monumental German series, *Die grosse Politik der europäischen Kabinette, 1871–1914 (40 vols., 1922–27)*, he reached the conclusion that Holstein had been in error to think that there had ever existed any serious possibility of an Anglo-German alliance. Here Ritter advanced the notions for the first time that England in 1898–1901 was then, as always, pursuing an "insular" policy in contrast to Germany's "continental" diplomacy, that the historic differences between them are best stated in geopolitical terms, and that the mutual misunderstanding resulting from radically opposing ways of life was profound. It was these divergences that had frustrated all official efforts to build a bridge of friendship from Berlin to London.[19]

In 1919 Ritter married twenty-four-year-old Gertrud Reichardt, who was to be his beloved wife until his death in 1967. Three children were born to the couple. After five years at Heidelberg he was invited to become professor in ordinary at the University of Hamburg, where Max Lenz had been the chief luminary in history. Ritter moved there but stayed only until October, 1925, when, in response to an offer from the University of Freiburg im Breisgau, he became professor of modern history there.[20] In the picturesque town on the rim of the Black Forest, which he came to love, he was destined to spend practically the rest of his life.

While still at Heidelberg, Ritter finished writing a short, popular biography of Martin Luther.[21] This work exhibited in some of its judgments an emotional crudity which was gradually elimin-

---

[19] Ritter, *Die Legende von der verschmähten englischen Freundschaft, 1898–1901. Beleuchtet aus der neuen englischen Aktenveröffentlichung* (Freiburg im Breisgau, 1929), 12–14, 21, 28–29, 33–34, 37–49, 40–43. This essay was an expansion upon an earlier one, *Bismarcks Verhältnis zu England und die Politik des "Neuen Kurses"* (*Einzelschriften zur Politik und Geschichte. Beiträge aus dem Archiv für Politik und Geschichte*, No. 7) (Berlin, 1924). Ritter's interpretation has been rejected recently by Willy Schenk, who contends that it unduly depreciates the responsibility of the Germans themselves for deteriorating relations. See Schenk, *Die Deutsch-Englische Rivalität vor dem ersten Weltkrieg in der Sicht deutscher Historiker: Missverstehen oder Machtstreben* (Aarau, 1967).

[20] Ritter to author, August 16, 1965, and January 17, 1967. Of Ritter's children, one son fell on the Russian front on Christmas eve, 1941, and a second became a Lutheran minister in Baden. A daughter is married to a professor of physics at Erlangen.

[21] Ritter, *Luther: Gestalt und Symbol* (Munich, 1925). Citations are from the sixth (1959) edition.

ated in the course of five subsequent editions. The fourth, fifth, and sixth all reduced the original emphasis upon a theological *Weltanschauung*, which corresponded with Ritter's rearing, and focused ever more sharply on the lasting significance of Luther for a Germany convulsed by two world wars. They reflect specifically not only Ritter's own ordeal under Nazism but a vastly richer understanding of the Reformation, deriving from his penetrating research into the sixteenth century and his work after 1938 as editor of the *Archiv für Reformationsgeschichte*.[22]

Emerging from the Luther study, which is devoid of footnotes or bibliography, is one who is still, in Ritter's judgment, the "central force in German intellectual life." Luther was a "mad bull" but nevertheless the "masculine figure of unforgettable vitality who left an imprint second to none upon the German character."[23] He made the sixteenth century "the most German of centuries" and set the best forces of the nation moving towards one point so as "to produce the most original and significant historical contribution for which the world stands in our debt."[24] By unwittingly destroying the power fundament of the western universal church, however, Luther ensured its subordination to a host of German secular authorities. "The foundation of the German territorial churches, foreshadowed and prepared for several centuries . . . set the formal seal to the political fragmen-

[22] Ritter, *Antrittsrede*, 16. Ritter's views on Luther have since 1925 been expounded in a large number of brochures and articles. See especially Ritter, "Die Ausprägung deutscher und westeuropäischer Geistesart im konfessionellen Zeitalter," *Historische Zeitschrift*, CXLIX (1934), 240–52; "Wegbahner eines aufgeklärten Christentums im 16. Jahrhundert," *Archiv für Reformationsgeschichte*, XXXVII (1940), 268–89; "Luther und die politische Erziehung der Deutschen," *Zeitwende*, XVIII (1947), 592–609; and "Lutheranism, Catholicism and the Humanistic View of Life," *Archiv für Reformationsgeschichte*, XLIV (1946), 145–59. A number of Ritter's articles on Luther and the Reformation were reprinted in his *Die Weltwirkung der Reformation* (Munich, 1959).

[23] Repeating verbatim a passage in Ritter, *Die kirchliche und staatliche Neugestaltung Europas im Jahrhundert der Reformation und Glaubenskämpfe* (Berlin, 1941), the author described Luther in 1950 as "the most profound and spiritual theologian, the mightiest, most resolute prophet of his people, a religious genius of incomparable ardor and mystical faith" (*Die Neugestaltung Europas im 16. Jahrhundert. Die kirchlichen und staatlichen Wandlungen im Zeitalter der Reformation und Glaubenskämpfe* [Berlin, 1950], 73).

[24] Ritter, *Luther*, 9, 14, 21, 23, 75, 91, 96–97, 185, 187, 189; cf. Ritter, "Die geistigen Ursachen der Reformation," *Zeitwende*, VII (1931), 1–2, 13.

158   WILLIAM HARVEY MAEHL

tation of the nation and simultaneously determined the character not only of the church but of the political life of the individual principalities," facilitating the triumph of absolutism throughout the empire. In particular, Luther's failure to unite the country ensured the persistence of ecclesiastical states, which were to constitute the most fateful political heritage from the Middle Ages—"the curse of German history." [25]

Without prejudice to the contributions of the medieval Catholic tradition to good government, Ritter argued that the Wittenberg reformer bequeathed German Protestant principalities a body of Christian ethical teaching that for centuries inspired their rulers with a paternalist concern for justice and the well-being of their subjects.[26] On the other hand, Ritter naturally accepted the scholarly consensus that failure of the Peasants' Rebellion of 1524–25 blasted for many generations the pre-Reformation expectations of the masses which centered upon political recognition and the partnership of all Stände with the nobility for the governance of the German states. Although these dreams were in any case utopian, Ritter contended that Luther's course was at least partly to blame for the ensuing reduction of the German nation to dumb submission to its princes and for the consequent rise of "the Christian police state." [27] At this point Ritter appears to have had second thoughts upon this latter development and to have come to a different and exculpatory verdict: namely, that the rise of absolutism in the Germanies, occasionally benevolent but more often oppressive, was inevitable even without Luther. Thus in another of his works Ritter later wrote: "In highly unjustifiable fashion Luther . . . has been repeatedly charged with having educated Germans to a slave-like obedience towards princely authority and to a political perspective that confines moral-religious commandments to a purely private ethic, while allowing those who wield political authority the license to indulge every act

[25] Ritter, Luther, 38, 48, 75, 94, 133, 158–59, 161, 181, 193–94, 219.
[26] Ibid., 128, 132, 180–81, 209–10, 214.
[27] Ibid., 151–52 et passim. Cf. Ritter, Die Neugestaltung Europas, 109, 113, 118. Ritter has examined these expectations in greater detail in his "Romantische und revolutionäre Elemente in der deutschen Theologie am Vorabend der Reformation," Deutsche Vierteljahrsschrift für Literaturwissenschaft und Geistesgeschichte, V (1927), 342–80.

of violence . . . . It is, however, impossible to assign blame to the
Lutheran faith for any alleged or actual servility on the part of
German nation." [28]

While at Hamburg, Ritter commenced research on the life of
Baron Karl vom und zum Stein. The stimulus to do this came
from the Leipzig professor of history Erich Brandenburg, who
had invited Ritter to prepare a biographical essay for inclusion in
a collection of such sketches. An examination of the three-volume
Stein biography by Max Lehmann revealed to Ritter, however,
that the latter's utilization of documents in the Prussian secret
state archives had been "highly one-sided." To vindicate his own
interpretation, Ritter, who was already profoundly interested in
his subject, felt obliged to write in place of the intended essay
a major two-volume work.[29] In this opus, distinguished more for
its scholarly sheen than for its rhetoric, there is ample evidence of
exhaustive review of a vast reservoir of source materials, the bulk
of them unpublished and untapped. It was the best biography
Ritter ever wrote.

This portrait of Stein is less chauvinistic than that of Lehmann
and the liberal-nationalist school.[30] The Nassau reformer was, to
Ritter's thinking, not an admirer of French democracy, but of
English liberalism, and neither an advocate of the *grossdeutsch* nor
kleindeutsch solution of the German problem. Stein was, however,
the main hope of the bourgeoisie for the restoration of its long-
lost administrative power, the "renovator of German municipal
freedom," and the noblest paladin of the European-wide resistance movement to Napoleon.[31] On the other hand, Stein was

[28] Ritter, *Das deutsche Problem. Grundfragen deutschen Staatslebens gestern und heute* (Munich, 1962), 17.

[29] Ritter, *Stein. Eine politische Biographie* (2 vols.; Stuttgart, 1931). Volume I is entitled *Der Reformer;* Volume II, *Der Vorkämpfer nationaler Freiheit und Einheit.* Citations are from the one-volume, third edition (Stuttgart, 1958). All reviews were favorable, the most incisive being by O. Hitze, in *Historische Zeitschrift,* CXLVI (1932), 349–55.

[30] Various nationalist judgments on Stein were reviewed by Ritter in "Die nationale Geschichtsschreibung und das Stein-Porträt," *Vergangenheit und Gegenwart,* XXII (1932), 1–21.

[31] Ritter, *Stein,* 11, 44, 73, 223–24, 227–28, 255, 267, 321, 336, 357–58. Stein was, according to Ritter, inferior in fiery resolve and temerity to General A. Neithardt von Gneisenau. See Ritter, *Gneisenau und die deutsche Freiheitsidee,* in *Philosophie und Geschichte,* No. 37 (Tübingen, 1922), 12–13, 18–19, 27.

really a successful failure: all of his plans were either sharply modified or ignobly suppressed within a few years after his dismissal; and when Germany was at length united by Bismarck, it was not in harmony with Stein's lofty aims but with the Frederician objectives of the Hohenzollern dynasty implemented by "the concentrated power of the old Prussian authoritarian and military state." And yet, notwithstanding all Stein's failures, Ritter discovered in him an exceptional combination of boldness and prudence, of passion and sobriety, which elevates the true statesman above a thousand mediocrities: "Freiherr vom Stein is one of the very rare examples of the proposition that without sensational external success, inordinate lust for power, or even personal political ambition, a man can by force of character acquire political authority and historical fame. . . . [Stein] has not with injustice been called a moral light house whose beams illumine our own epoch from the idealistic past." [32]

A scrutiny of Ritter's estimate of Stein's moderate liberalism reveals affinities between the *Weltanschauungen* of the statesman and his biographer. Stein, who wished to conserve the economic, social, and administrative authority of the nobility, which class he considered the great shield against despotism and revolution, never dreamed of setting the cause of freedom in opposition to the state. He had absolutely no sympathy for the "principle of the uniform equality of the masses, who recognize no true leadership by the *élite* but are prone to flock after every demagogue." [33] Ritter, no less than Stein, distrusted such concepts as the "general will" and "popular sovereignty," which provided combustible matter for the French Revolution. This carping distrust engendered in Ritter a subliminal élitism that ever afterwards colored his attitude towards radical mass movements. Not without reason, however, did Ritter argue here and in other works that the *levée en masse* of 1793 and the German riposte of the *Befreiungskrieg*, both regimenting the common people, prepared the ground for the modern continental, totalitarian people's states with their

[32] Ritter, *Stein*, 536–37.
[33] *Ibid.*, 63–64, 67, 73, 94, 98, 127–28, 194–96, 198, 223–25.

"politicized" hordes and "levelling materialist philosophies." [34]
The years between 1932 and 1936 saw the publication of three
more important works by Ritter. In 1932 appeared his critical new
edition, based upon archival materials at Friedrichsruh, of Bismarck's *Gedanken und Erinnerungen*. There followed the single
published volume of the history of the University of Heidelberg
and a succinct biography of Frederick II.[35]
The Heidelberg work, which appeared on the five hundred and
fiftieth anniversary of the founding of the university, was a heavily
footnoted piece of original research into the Latin sources. Far
more than a mere chronicle of the university or even a description
of its constitution, curriculum, student body and faculty, it discussed in detail for the first time the teaching activities, lectures,
and disputations of faculty members on the basis of their own
notes and writings. Ritter also showed in this work how the universities came to represent the main ideas of the reforming councils on whose side they ranged themselves. According to him, the
universities, in combating the papacy and Rome and in doing their
best to justify their political origins by disseminating imperial
Roman law in Germany, lost their universal religious character.
They became increasingly oriented towards the territorial princes.[36]

[34] *Ibid.* Cf. Ritter, "Das politische Problem des Militarismus in Deutschland,"
in Ritter, *Lebendige Vergangenheit. Beiträge zur historisch-politischen Selbstbesin-
nung* (Munich, 1958), 163; "Ursprung und Wesen der Menschenrechte,"
Historische Zeitschrift, CLXIX (1950), 233–36, 250–51, 260–63; and correspondence between Ritter and Otto Vossler, in *Geschichte in Wissenschaft und Unterricht*, X (1936), 635–50. Similar conservative perspectives, hostile to egalitarian,
utilitarian, and socialist philosophies, are set forth in Ritter, "Die Menschenrechte
und das Christentum," *Zeitwende*, XXI (1949), 1–12; "Vom Ursprung das
Einparteienstaates in Europa," *Historische Jahrbücher*, LXXIV (1955), 564–83;
and *Vom sittlichen Problem der Macht. Fünf Essays* (Bern, 1948).
[35] Ritter, *Die Heidelberger Universität. Ein Stück deutscher Geschichte*, Vol. I:
Das Mittelalter, 1386–1508 (Heidelberg, 1936); *Friedrich der Grosse. Ein historisches Profil* (Heidelberg, 1936). Subsequent citations are from the third (1954)
edition, the concluding pages of which, "Friedrich und Wir," were completely rewritten because the original purpose of this section—to unmask the hypocrisy of
Hitler when he claimed to be the executor of the Frederician legacy—had been
rendered pointless by lapse of time.
[36] Ritter, *Die Heidelberger Universität*, I, 296, 298, 436, 440. These ideas were
further elaborated in his "Zur Geschichte des deutschen Universitätswesen am
Vorabend der Reformation," *Archiv für Reformationsgeschichte*, XXXV (1938),
141–61. Ritter always regarded the Heidelberg history, the research on which put

Though neither a politician nor a stanch supporter of the Weimar Republic, Ritter opposed the Nazi attempt to seize power. The professor, who as a young *Privatdozent* had once written that "all history degenerates from the minute it is no longer animated by fresh contact with the present," in 1932 organized and led a mass meeting in the large Freiburg convention hall to protest against Hitler's candidacy for the presidency. Both Ritter and Dr. Julius Curtius, who had been Brüning's foreign minister until October, 1931, spoke on that occasion. Placards composed by Ritter appeared on the walls and columns of the city, warning against the Nazi threat.[37]

In the years 1934–36 in lectures given at the universities of Freiburg and Basel, Ritter tried in many a periphrasis to contrast the traditionally esteemed models of German statesmanship with the political ethics of Hitler. He especially sought to draw "a sharp distinction between the old Prussian spiritual legacy and the new German Nazidom." That he was able to get away with this was due to several things: his well-known pride in the Prussian accomplishment and his record as an anti-Marxist disarmed suspicion; his colleagues on the social science faculty at Freiburg were "almost exclusively on the side of the opposition" to Hitler, while at the same time politics was to the rector a mystery; and Ritter's tendentious lectures were couched in phraseology that was unintelligible to the obtuse Nazi underlings who sometimes spied on him.[38]

As time revealed to what extent the Nazi regime was committed to the degradation of the human spirit and the distortion of truth, Ritter moved from a position of hostility to one of ardent hatred for the New Order. The systematic character assassination practiced by Walter Frank, Nazi secretary of the *Historische*

---

him to "immeasurable pains," as his "most learned work." Unfortunately for him, the great Johannes Haller, whose ire Ritter had earlier aroused by a published criticism of the latter's theses on Reformation history, damned *Die Heidelberger Universität* with faint praise in *Historische Zeitschrift*, CLIX (1938), 88–102 (Ritter to author, January 20, 1967).

[37] Ritter, "Geschichtliche Wandlungen," 234; interview with Ritter, October 22, 1966, and Ritter to author, January 17, 1967.

[38] Ritter, "The German Professor in the Third Reich," *Review of Politics*, VIII (1946), 243, 246, 248–49, 251.

Reichskommission, upon Hermann Oncken, its chairman and Ritter's venerable former teacher, aroused the Freiburg historian's ire. Ritter himself, who was, no more than any other German historian of the older generation, a champion of democracy, was in 1935 labelled by Frank "a pronounced liberal" in the same letter in which he castigated Ludwig Dehio as a "half-Jew." [39] While Ritter privately believed that the politically elastic Oncken was something of an opportunist and had criticized Oncken's *Die Rheinpolitik Kaiser Napoleons III von 1863 bis 1870* as excessively nationalistic, he expressed his full support of the Berlin professor in his vendetta with the *Reichswissenschaftsministerium.* In a letter to Oncken of February 5, 1935, he castigated Frank for cynically trying to destroy Oncken's reputation and then rose to a premonitory condemnation of the regime: "Quite apart from the fact that there is no longer a free press, I have the feeling that the mere defensive will no longer suffice. Now in your case the dignity of our profession has been so severely impugned that we should and must all close ranks and pass over to an assault upon the pseudo-history of the Third Reich." [40]

On March 31, 1935, Ritter in another letter to Oncken emptied his vials of scorn upon the German scholarly community for its cowardice and inglorious egotism in the face of abuse by the Nazis and bitterly remarked that the current universal disrespect for German letters was, on the whole, not unmerited.[41] When Frank's *Reichsinstitut für Geschichte des neuen Deutschlands* was founded that same year, Ritter ridiculed it. Furthermore, when at the same time the *Historische Zeitschrift* was placed under Walter Kienast and a new editorial board acceptable to the *Reichsinstitut* and the government, Ritter, by refusing his cooperation, dashed Frank's hopes that the New Order might enlist the solid support of the historical profession.[42] In the years 1935–

---

[39] Helmut Heiber, *Walther Frank und sein Reichsinstitut für Geschichte des neuen Deutschlands,* Quellen und Darstellungen zu Zeitgeschichte, XIII (Stuttgart, 1966), 185.

[40] *Ibid.,* 224.

[41] *Ibid.;* and Ritter, *Die deutschen Geisteswissenschaften im Kriege. Rede gehalten am 10. Mai 1940 an der Universität Berlin* (Hamburg, 1940).

[42] Ritter, *Die deutschen Geisteswissenschaften,* 305–306, 693.

37 Ritter's behavior and carping criticism of the regime took him along the road that ended in the resistance camp. A colleague, Hans Bogner, professor of classical literature at Freiburg and a lukewarm member of the NSDAP, reported in 1937 that he was incensed at the scurrilous conduct of "*Volksgenossen*" Professor Ritter whose "utterances were nearly incomprehensible." [43]

Like Ritter's lectures of the mid-1930's, the biography that he wrote of Frederick II was, under pretense of an exhortation to rational political behavior, a veiled censure of the regime. It merited Andreas Dorpalen's encomium that it was "a very courage-ous indictment of Hitler's irrationalism and recklessness, his ideological fanaticism and insatiable lust for power." [44] Not meant to increase our basic fund of knowledge about the great Hohen-zollern, Ritter's biography is not in the same class with Reinhold Koser's four-volume biography. Ritter's work is a profile of the king. Here he appears as neither a genuine Machiavellian nor a militarist but the foremost and the ablest of the "cabinet despots." According to Ritter, a recognition of the natural limits of royal power and an innate repugnance for war kept "Old Fritz" from trusting blindly to an instinct for might. G. P. Gooch was wrong to call him a "crowned robber." No less than his forebears, Frederick II believed that reasons of state set limits to a ruler's ambitions.[45] He accepted as axiomatic the moral responsibility of the sovereign to promote the welfare of his subjects, even though it is true that he "assigned top priority to increasing the power of

[43] *Ibid.*, 554. Considering this evidence for Ritter's disgust with the regime and that he was soon to join other colleagues at Freiburg (Adolf Lampe, Erich Wolf, Walter Eucken, and Constantin von Dietze) in approaching Goerdeler's resistance movement (Hans Rothfels, *The German Opposition to Hitler* [London, 1961], 99), it is clear that the attacks of East German historians, such as Werner Berthold, upon Ritter's integrity are slander. ". . . *Grosshungern und gehorchen*," *Zur Entstehung und politischen Funktion der Geschichtsideologie des westdeutschen Imperialismus. Untersucht am Beispiel von Gerhard Ritter und Friedrich Meinecke*, Schriftenreihe des Instituts für Geschichte an der Karl-Marx-Universität Leipzig, No. 7 (Berlin, 1960), 71, 78. See further, Berthold, "Der Politisch-ideologische Weg Gerhard Ritters eines führenden Ideologen der deutschen Bourgeoisie," *Zeitschrift für Geschichtswissenschaft*, VI (1958–59), 959–89.

[44] Dorpalen, "Historiography as History: The Work of Gerhard Ritter," *Journal of Modern History*, XXXIV (1962), 9.

[45] Ritter, *Friedrich der Grosse*, 17, 86–87, 91, 132–36, 149, 160, 168, 189, 257–58.

the state." To Ritter's mind, it was Frederick alone who "pushed Prussia into the front rank of nations." Like the *rois connêtables* of old, he exercised both supreme military and political power, and "without his absolutist rule, no step forward would have been taken." [46]

Ritter did not always find it easy to reconcile the startling action of the Hohenzollern king with the wisdom and restraint with which German historians have usually endowed him. Certain aspects of Frederick II's character remained obscure for Ritter, whose estimate of the Prussian ruler underwent some change after World War II. In the 1936 biography it was averred that Frederick II, like Richelieu and Bismarck (but unlike Louis XIV, Charles III or Napoleon) was one of a select coterie of statesmen who were able to detect the elusive border where interest of state leaves off and craving for personal prestige (Hitler) begins; [47] but in his postwar *magnum opus* he said that the attack upon Silesia in 1740 was motivated by Frederick's desire "to make a name for himself." [48] Ritter never did attain certainty as to whether the two major land grabs of Frederick's reign—Silesia and West Prussia— were not betrayal of genuine *Staatsräson*, and in one passage of this sketch he managed to leave the impression of trying to sit on both sides of the question.[49] He conceded that the seizures jeopardized the security of the Prussian people by plunging them into a generation of war to maintain a tragic Austro-Prussian dualism within the Empire,[50] but that nonetheless they were the making of Prussia's fortune and the prelude to her unification of Germany.[51]

Ritter's faith in the existence of moral limitations upon power and his equally firm belief that cannons are the last arguments of

[46] *Ibid.*, 75, 81, 88, 193–96, 213–14, 244.

[47] *Ibid.*, 88; Ritter, "The Military and Politics in Germany," *Journal of Central European Affairs*, XVII (1957), 262; *Das Problem des Militarismus in Deutschland*, Schriftenreihe der Bundeszentrale für Heimatdienst, No. 3 (1954–55), 6–9.

[48] Ritter, *Staatskunst und Kriegshandwerk. Das Problem des "Militarismus"* in *Deutschland*, I: *Die altpreussische Tradition, 1740–1890* (Munich, 1955), 30.

[49] Ritter, *Friedrich der Grosse*, 253–55.

[50] *Ibid.*, 96, 108, 253; Ritter, *Das deutsche Problem*, 7, 24–25. Cf. Friedrich Meinecke, *Die Idee der Staatsräson in der neueren Geschichte* (Munich and Berlin, 1929), 398–99, where much the same thing had been said.

[51] Ritter, *Friedrich der Grosse*, 108, 114, 233, 254–55.

states are, as is always the case with the ethical realist, difficult to reconcile. They lead him into the twilight zone of ambiguity. Thus he denied that Frederick's attack on Saxony in 1756 was motivated by schemes of conquest,[52] and Ritter, with an anxious eye on the growing encirclement of the Reich in 1935, asserted that even preventive war "is always a highly questionable expedient of grand power politics." But an addendum to the book largely vitiated this observation: "Without violation of historical rights and without forcible conquest of power . . . there can be no great policy." [53] And in the 1954 edition of the Frederick biography Ritter again recognized the primacy of military power in the fortunes of continental states: "Whoever will ponder the effects of the Frederician legacy in German history . . . will find ample occasion to reflect upon the significance of the disappearance of the former strong Prussian military power along the eastern marches of the continent of Europe for the present and the future." [54]

Ritter fell increasingly under suspicion of the *Wissenschafts-ministerium* and of the Nazi Teachers' Association, to which agencies it was no secret that he, like Willy Andreas and Hans Rothfels, was fundamentally antagonistic to the regime.[55]

The Freiburg historian came perilously close to crossing swords with the ruling authorities as a result of his public remarks at the International Historical Meeting at Zurich in September, 1938. At that time he criticized the secularization of Martin Luther by Otto Scheel, professor in ordinary of the University of Kiel. Scheel's estimate of Luther did not radically differ from Ritter's, but the latter rejected Scheel's de-emphasis of religion as the key to the reformer's character. More particularly Ritter strongly objected to a depiction of Luther as a "hero and miracle man" and to the interpretation of him in terms of current aspirations. Many of the German historians present were incensed at Ritter's temerity.[56]

Frank, enraged at Ritter, believed he now had the evidence to

[52] *Ibid.*, 98, 100, 119, 128–30, 134; Cf. Ritter, "Kriegführung und Politik in der Geschichte Friedrichs des Grossen," *Militärwissenschaftliche Rundschau*, I (1936), 555–64.

[53] Ritter, *Friedrich der Grosse*, 129, 256.   [54] *Ibid.*, (1954), 8.

[55] Heiber, *Walther Frank und sein Reichsinstitut*, 731; Ritter to author, December 15, 1966.

[56] Heiber, *Walther Frank und sein Reichsinstitut*, 748–54.

remove him from his chair at Freiburg and destroy him. In a letter of September 28, 1938, Frank said that Ritter had damaged the prestige of the Reich. That Ritter "stood opposed to the new course in Germany was generally known," but that he had the nerve to exhibit his contempt in public—and of all things, abroad —"must be assessed as a very serious sign of a stiffening of reactionary tendencies within German historical science." [57]

Although Ritter and Scheel subsequently acted in correspondence to close the breach between them, the *Wissenschaftsministerium*'s suspicions had been aroused by Frank's reports. For some years thereafter Ritter was forbidden to accept engagements outside Germany, and he, like Andreas—also a student of Oncken's, was ignored by the ruling establishment. [58]

When for the second time in a generation Germany wrapped itself in the red cloak of war, Ritter subjected to scrutiny the roles of militarism and power politics in his country's past. In the first edition of the *Machtstaat und Utopie*, [59] published in the year of the fall of France, he could only imply things that could not be spelled out until the appearance of the revised fifth (1947) and sixth (1948) editions. Certain tendentious changes that Ritter made in the third (1942) and fourth (1943) editions antagonized the censors, and no more editions were permitted until after the collapse of the Thousand Year Reich. [60]

Under guise of a philosophic-political discussion of the ideas of Machiavelli and More, Ritter contrasted the power procedures of Germany and England. Returning to the theme he had broached

[57] *Ibid.*, 754. It did not escape Frank that while at Zürich Ritter had been the only German delegate to attend the address of the expatriate "Jew" G. W. F. Hallgarten (*ibid.*)

[58] Ritter to author, December 15, 1966; Ritter, "The German Professor in the Third Reich," 242–44; Heiber, *Walther Frank und sein Reichsinstitut*, 558, 756–58.

[59] Subtitled *Vom Streit um die Dämonie der Macht seit Machiavelli und Morus* (Munich, 1940). Subsequent citations, unless otherwise indicated, are from the sixth edition (1948).

[60] Werner Berthold has sought to discover in the successive editions of the *Machtstaat* a sinister metamorphosis. From a worshipper of brute force and the fascist state and from a long-time foe of the Anglo-American world, Ritter after Stalingrad became the coadjutor of NATO in its hostility towards the USSR. Berthold, (". . . *Grosshungern und gehorchen*," 83–127). See further Berthold, "Des politisch-ideologische Weg . . . Ritters," 959.

in the 1920s, he developed the thesis that German history is an integral part of a strictly continental development which stressed the central role of the state, its military sanction, and of *Staatsrä-son*. Using arguments variously drawn from geopolitics, historicism, and the Prussian school of political historiography, Ritter asserted the existence of an ancient contrast between the "conservative, monarchist" methods of "continental" states, such as Prussia and France, and the "humanitarian, liberal" methods employed by maritime and "insular" states, such as the Netherlands and Britain, whose ideas were engendered by revolutions, the Enlightenment, and capitalism.[61] As Ritter better expressed it elsewhere: "The sword is always more ready to the hand of a continental statesman, who stands in the midst of the fray of European power interests, and must always be armed to counter an attack before it is too late; but the 'insular' statesman, who is in a much safer position, can calmly afford to wait. If only for economic reasons he shuns exhibitions of military power and prefers to rely more upon alliances, diplomacy and persuasion . . . than upon force."[62]

Ritter agreed with the Greeks that power is not without virtue, that no great embodiment of power can exist without a parturition aided by the "demonism of force," and that wholly moral political action is a contradiction in terms.[63] It was this glorification of the state that, to some extent, assuaged the suspicion of the *Reichswissenschaftsministerium* towards Ritter.[64] Yet in all editions of the *Machtstaat* he also argued in the spirit of Goethe that "*in der Beschränkung zeigt sich erst der Meister*." For the Freiburg historian "all political authority rests upon moral bases, upon the natural trust of men, and this erects barriers to the arbitrary actions of even the strongest power." The true statesman is able

---

[61] Ritter, *Dämonie der Macht*, 80–81, 100–101. Karl Dietrich Bracher thinks Ritter went too far in drawing this distinction. See G. A. Ritter and Gilbert Ziebura (eds.), *Faktoren der politischen Entscheidung* (Berlin, 1963), 128. In any case, Ritter had always been disturbed by the antinomy, and in the fifth edition (1947) of the *Dämonie*, 112, he suggested the need for a new political theory that could synthesize the continental and insular mentalities.

[62] Ritter, *Das deutsche Problem*, 27–28.

[63] Ritter, *Die Dämonie der Macht*, 9, 15, 17.

[64] Cf. Berthold, "Der politisch-ideologische Weg . . . Ritters," 970, 974.

to harness the "demonism of power" for higher moral purposes, specifically the establishment of a lasting civic order in consonance with ethical purposes: "[He] must unite the greatest contrasts in himself; he must be passionate, yet circumspect, filled with faith in his mission and yet conscious of its limits; he must be able to stand indomitably against his foes, yet be ready, whenever rationally possible, for reconciliation. He must always be on guard against the temptations of the power he wields, for it is in the nature of the demonism of power that its possession is the greatest of all temptations to which man is exposed." [65]

The policies of the Second Reich, Bismarck's strong sense of political morality notwithstanding, were necessarily sharply marked with Machiavellianism, which "thrusts the struggle for power in the center of all political events and celebrates war as the . . . confirmation of true *virtú*." Mussolini also taught, quite rightly, that the iron law of "might is the precondition of all freedom." [66] But it was not until the time of the Third Reich that the most frightening implications of "continental" methods were realized in Germany. Hitler grotesquely perverted Machiavelli's views on the sound relationship of politics to warfare. With the Nazis, power first became brute force, and military preparedness, unending bellicosity. [67]

In 1941 Ritter's last major synthesis in Reformation studies was published. [68] *Die kirchliche und staatliche Neugestaltung Europas im Jahrhundert der Reformation und der Glaubenskämpfe* was based on a broad knowledge of the sources and monographic literature. The book's appeal lies not so much in its literary qualities, which are not the most arresting features of Ritter's writing, as in the admirable logic of development and the clarity of its propositions. The subject of this work is the impact of political and religious forces upon a slowly expiring medieval order, in which the "authority of the ruler rested not so much upon

[65] Ritter, *Die Dämonie der Macht*, 9, 38, 144, 170–71, 174–75.
[66] Ritter, *Machtstaat* (1940), 42, 57.
[67] Ritter, *Die Dämonie der Macht*, 9, 138–39.
[68] In volume III of *Neue Propyläen-Weltgeschichte*, (Berlin, 1941), 169–472. Citations are from the slightly altered 1950 version, *Die Neugestaltung Europas im 16. Jahrhundert*. Similar, if not identical views, were expressed in Ritter, *Die Weltwirkung der Reformation* (Munich, 1941).

material possessions as almost exclusively upon moral factors . . . and eternal law that transcended the mere will of the monarch and all *Staatsräson*." [69] An important theme is the retreat of these universal Christian legal norms before the determined assault of Machiavellianism and the emergence of a balance of power system. The familiar hypothesis is reiterated that in Germany the Renaissance was a purely pyrotechnical display of insufficient force to cause the country decisively to break with its medieval *Weltanschauung*; rather the Reformation was the result of a long and mainly autochthonous evolution going back to the thirteenth century. [70]

Luther is depicted once again in elemental popular-religious colors: "He is the most profound, spiritual-theological thinker, the mightest, most resolute, prophetic figure of his nation, a religious genius of unprecedented introspective and mystical faith." If Luther had stood only temporarily on the side of the emperor, the great reformer's church would have been lost; as it was, he chose to become the mainstay of the authority of the princes who were undoubtedly the real beneficiaries of the crisis he provoked. [71]

As respects the Treaty of Augsburg (1555), Ritter concluded that it stemmed the Protestant movement at full tide and was, in the final analysis, the consequence of a deficient will to power of the Protestant groups, who, had they only possessed sufficient determination, would still have enjoyed every prospect of conquering Germany for their faith. Another thesis is that the German principalities of the sixteenth century were basically disposed to peace, that they "were without military, and even almost without foreign-political ambition," and that the peaceable, Christian authoritarianism of the princes dominated, with some exceptions, the political life of Germany until the eighteenth century. This introspective statecraft lent a characteristic imprint to the German man—"the loyal, honorable, unpolitical, god-fearing German subject"—and it fundamentally influenced the intellectual life of the nation. [72]

Two other main conclusions deserve our attention. Whereas

[69] Ritter, *Die Neugestaltung Europas*, 22.   [70] *Ibid.*, 5, 12, 15, 19, 119.
[71] *Ibid.*, 73, 113.   [72] *Ibid.*, 185, 213, 303.

divisions among emperor, papacy, and French monarchy sustained the Protestant cause before 1552, it was suspicion of the dynastic, universal, political ambitions of the Spanish Habsburg that nourished it after 1552. Finally, the Catholic Reform is denied the reputation of having been a mass movement but is treated rather as the effluence of a master plan conceived by prelates and princes.[73]

During the war years Ritter continued to conduct small seminars and give hortatory lectures under the eyes of Nazi officials. In 1942 party authorities torpedoed the plan of the national *Wissenschaftsministerium*, which was then more favorably disposed towards Ritter, to have him come to Berlin to edit a large Italo-German edition of Machiavelli's works. This project, if approved, would have been tantamount to revocation of the ban on Ritter's engagements abroad.[74] The following year, however, the party's central offices gave Ritter permission to accept an invitation to lecture in pro-German Istanbul and Ankara. His ostensible circumbendibus of the fundamental issues of the war had deceived informers, but official indulgence is understandable when it is remembered that Ritter was a master of the opaque sentence and that he was only a little less celebrated than Karl Brandi for his nationalist interpretation of German history. Nevertheless, when Ritter returned from Turkey, *Sicherheitsdienst* officers resumed their monitoring of his lectures at Freiburg and submitted regular reports to SD district headquarters in Strassburg. However, neither these reports nor the suspicions of chauvinists led in the end to his arrest on November 1, 1944. It was rather the amazing discovery by the *Gestapo* that he had been a member of the Carl Goerdeler circle which had made the famous attempt on Hitler's life on July 20, 1944, and that Ritter's membership dated back to 1938.[75]

Ritter languished in a Gestapo prison in Berlin, where his wife

[73] *Ibid.*, 143–45, 180, 184, 321, 327.

[74] Ritter, "Der deutsche Professor im Dritten Reich," *Die Gegenwart*, I (1946), 25.

[75] Interview with Ritter, October 22, 1966; Ritter to author, October 10, 1964; Ritter, *Die Dämonie der Macht*, 7–8; *Carl Goerdeler und die deutsche Widerstandsbewegung* (Stuttgart, 1956), 463n7, 511n71, and 528n52; "The German Professor," 242, 245–47.

was occasionally permitted to visit him and bring food, for almost nine months. In January he was permitted to shake hands and say farewell to Goerdeler, who was executed on February 2, 1945. Finally, on April 25, 1945, Ritter was freed by the Red Army.[76]

Returning to his chair at Freiburg, he commenced work on a new book,[77] in which he expressed his displeasure with "fair-weather" patriots who had allowed the Nazi interlude to destroy their love of country, and he protested against the anaemic "neutrality of thought" that had gained dominion in Germany. On the subject of guilt for the Nazi orgy, Ritter repudiated the revisionist arguments of Eyck, Schnabel, Holborn, Kluke, Hallgarten, Rassow, Dehio, and Lehmann. In particular he rejected Meinecke's idea that the nation's recent past was an "astonishing deviation from the main line of European development," which could be traced back to Bismarck, the man who had diverted the stream of German history towards the rapids of dictatorship and war.[78]

In company with A. O. Meyer, C. Becker, Rothfels, Rein, v. Muralt, and Ludwig Reiners, all of whom were then striving to remove Bismarck's star from occultation and confusion with Hitler's, Ritter insisted that although the chancellor had made many mistakes and almost the whole of his policies had been put into question as a result of the destruction of the monarchy in 1918 and the bifurcation of Germany in 1945–46, Bismarck had never been a "militarist." [79] That trait in the "iron chancellor"

---

[76] Interview with Ritter, October 22, 1966; and Ritter, *Carl Goerdeler*, 441, 445.

[77] Ritter, *Europa und die deutsche Frage; Betrachtungen über die geschichtliche Eigenart des deutschen Staatsdenkens* (Munich, 1948). Citations are from the 1962 revision, entitled *Das deutsche Problem*. See F. W. Pick's review of the first edition of Ritter's *Die deutsche Frage*, in *Journal of Central European Affairs*, IX (1949), 30–32.

[78] Ritter, *Das deutsche Problem*, 7, 10, 78–79, 108.

[79] *Ibid.*, 77, 101. See Ritter, "Grossdeutsch und kleindeutsch im 19. Jahrhundert," *Lebendige Vergangenheit*, 112; *Das Problem des Militarismus in Deutschland*, 18; "Das politische Problem des Militarismus," *Lebendige Vergangenheit*, 172; "Das Verhältnis von Politik und Kriegführung im bismarckischen Reich," in Werner Conze (ed.), *Deutschland und Europa, Historische Studien zur Völker und Staatenordnung des Abendlandes* (Düsseldorf, 1951), 70; *Staatskunst und Kriegshandwerk*, I, 202–203, 254, 308, 329. This judgment also appears in Ritter's correspondence with Erich Eyck, which this writer has read, relative to the question of the chancellor's responsibility for the outbreak of the Franco-Prussian war (Eyck to Ritter, July 23, 1950; Ritter to Eyck, August 1, 1950).

to which exception could most legitimately be taken was his "conscious misuse of political ideas and principles for purely tactical ends, with the consequence that the great liberal movement, which he first had fought and later sought to compel to serve him, was intellectually emasculated and reduced to sterile opportunism."[80] Yet, from a larger standpoint, it was untrue that there had been gradual descent from the Bismarckian era into the Nazi inferno. The way had rather been prepared for the Weimar Republic by Bismarck's conscious initiation of broad administrative, juridicial, political, constitutional, and social reforms, which were inspired by Frederician paternalist philosophy and supported by the public.[81]

Ritter believed in Bismarck's basic probity: "That power and the struggle for it was not an end in itself, that the highest and true task of the statesman lies in the guarantee of an enduring system of peace, was self-evident to Bismarck, because in him lived on a genuine Christianity and a clear understanding of his moral-religious responsibility."[82]

While Ritter here again stressed the fundamental and "natural contrast between continental and insular policy . . . which has put unending difficulties in the way of the mutual understanding of peoples," he did not deny that in recent times a peculiar conflict had arisen between the political thinking of Germany and the rest of Europe. However, in harmony with everything he had written, he protested against the parochial view that the origins of German totalitarianism were to be sought in a demonic disposition of the Teutonic mind. On the contrary, a whole series of events, some of them fugacious, some alien, had pushed Germany along the road to a leveling mobocracy (a *"Massenmenschtum"*) and the Nazi *Machtergreifung*. Among them were the docility of the citizenry, the immaturity of political parties and parliamentary leaders, an unwillingness of "a great, strong, and self-conscious nation to accept as final the verdict of Versailles and the division of

---

[80] Ritter, *Das deutsche Problem*, 78.
[81] *Ibid.*, 96, 101. Ritter stressed the constitutional character of the Wilhelmine empire (*ibid.*, 108). He also emphasized the growth of the power of the Reichstag under the Second Empire and insisted that true parliamentary government commenced with the fall of Bülow in 1909 (*ibid.*, 207).
[82] *Ibid.*, 101.

power it endorsed," the decline in public morals following the First World War, the Great Depression, and more remotely but above all, democratizing forces unleashed by the French Revolution. Said Ritter: "The whole world is busily engaged in a hunt for the roots of National Socialism in Germany history. . . . Not any single happening in German history, but the great French Revolution decisively undermined the solid bases of the political traditions of Europe; this [event], moreover, has also coined the slogans and molded the concepts with the help of which the modern people's and *Führer*-state itself were founded." [83]

Under the delayed impact of volcanic forces unleashed by that revolution, declared Ritter further, the old German, Christian, authoritarian state system was gradually transformed into a democratic, materialist *"Volksstaat"*; executive power was critically sapped; the mass "conscript" army was born; the respect that had sustained the ruling classes vanished; the church was pushed out of the center of everyday life and agnosticism commenced its victorious course; duties were supplanted with rights; havoc was played with time-honored institutions and thought patterns of the past; demagogues were apotheosized and statesmen neglected; and unprecedented popular pressure was brought to bear on the formulation of grand policy. In the end a psychological force and a sociological momentum were generated that opened a wide breach in the Chinese wall of the conservative order. Through that hole the totalitarian state, spiritual descendant of the French Reign of Terror, thrust forward to dominion.

If this interpretation of Ritter's borders on hyperbole, the quest for the roots of German militarism and Nazism in some presumed black threads in the national birthweb is pure mysticism. Although Ritter, in the main, underestimated the determinative economic and imperialist motivations of politics, and is to that degree vulnerable to constructive Marxist criticism, he nonetheless performed the worthy service of directing attention to the social forces and psychological drives that helped to manufacture the totalitarian state. He showed that the facile overthrow of aristocratic and bourgeois-dominated governments in the twentieth century is most plausibly explained in terms of egalitarian demands of the politi-

[83] *Ibid.*, 28, 51, 57–60, 69, 79, 196.

cized masses who furnished the mania, might, and motive power for the Siva-like, cosmic dances of destruction that have been the most arresting spectacle of the "democratic age."

Ritter's next major work was a biography of Carl Goerdeler,[84] the promonarchist administrator and *Oberbürgermeister* who had been the mainspring of the conservative wing of the resistance movement against Hitler. This work was the nucleus of a system of satellite studies designed to rehabilitate Germany's honor.[85] It synchronized with similar efforts of Rothfels, Gisevius, Zeller, and Schlabrendorff. The Goerdeler biography, which has been described as "the most significant contribution to an understanding of the problem which has yet appeared and one which has as yet no parallel in the literature [on the movement]," [86] was the product of years of personal contact with the resistance leaders and of exacting research into all known relevant documentary collections on both sides of the Atlantic.[87]

[84] Citations throughout are from the third, enlarged edition previously noted and not from the original of 1954.

[85] Of his ancillary essays, especially noteworthy are: Ritter, "Die Wehrmacht und der politische Widerstand gegen Hitler," in *Schicksalsfragen der Gegenwart. Heidelberger politisch-historische Bildung*, I (Tübingen, 1957), 349–81; "Deutscher Widerstand," *Zeitwende*, XXV (1954), 439–48; "The Military and Politics in Germany," *Journal of Central European Affairs*, XVII (1957), 259–71; and "The Political Attitude of the German Army, 1900–44," in A. O. Sarkissian (ed.), *Studies in Diplomatic History and Historiography* (London, 1961). In the United States the Goerdeler biography was hailed as an important contribution towards the revival of sanity in Allied understanding of the German problem. See reviews by C. Easum, in *Journal of Central European Affairs*, XV (1956), 423–24; H. C. Deutsch, in *American Historical Review*, LX (1955), 894–95; and H. Haeusser, in *Journal of Politics*, XIX (1957), 137–38. Similarly favorable was the review by R. A. Spencer, in *International Journal*, LXX (1957), 122–26, and by Hans Herzfeld, "Zwei Werke Gerhard Ritters zur Geschichte des Nationalsozialismus und der Widerstandsbewegung," in *Historische Zeitschrift*, CLXXXII (1956), 321–32. Werner Berthold, who identifies the thinking of Ritter with that of Konrad Adenauer and Franz-Joseph Strauss (". . . *Grosshungern und gehorchen*," 14) was incensed over Ritter's disparaging treatment of the "Rote Kapelle" and dismissed the Goerdeler book as the effort of "an offensive ideologue of resurgent German imperialism" to prepare the way for "a struggle against the Soviet Union, the Socialist countries and socialism *per se*" (Berthold, "Der politisch-ideologische Weg . . . Ritters," 987).

[86] Herzfeld, "Zwei Werke Gerhard Ritters," 320. Other encomiastic comments are made in *ibid.*, 321, 325, and 332. On the other hand, Herzfeld thinks that perhaps Ritter has over-spiritualized the resistance movement and thrust the military into second place, thereby failing to come to grips with the whole problem of the movement, *ibid.*, 332.

[87] Aside from all pertinent documents in the United States Center at Berlin-Zehlendorf and in the Departmental Records Branch of the United States War

In Goerdeler, who persevered longer than anyone else at the "white hot center of the conspiracy," Ritter discerned the representative of millions of ordinary citizens who did not flee the fatherland and who remained at their posts to the bitter end, risking their lives from day to day in seemingly trivial sabotage and efforts to undermine the position of the lunatic who was dragging Germany towards the abyss.[88] One may sympathize with Ritter's accolade to the faceless civilian opponents of the regime without unquestioningly accepting his view of the paramount influence of Goerdeler and his nonmilitary friends over the plans and course of the resistance movement.

Most scholars would agree with Ritter that the fundamentally "non-political" *Reichswehr* neither forced the downfall of the Weimar Republic nor was directly responsible for Hitler's accession to power.[89] Nor would there be serious objection to the propositions that by 1934 the army's acquiescence had changed into active allegiance to the Nazi regime, or that in 1934–35 it was the prospect of rearmament and the reintroduction of universal conscription that consolidated, at least initially, the alliance between *Reichswehr* and *Führer*.[90] But here most western historians part company with Ritter as he develops the thesis, not entirely untenable, that the General Staff never was, as had been charged at the Nuremberg trials, a "criminal organization for the destruction of world peace," but rather that the generals exercised a moderating influence upon Hitler.[91]

Theses such as, for instance, Gordon Craig's that "the officers

---

Department at Alexandria, Ritter also consulted the hitherto virtually unexplored daily confidential reports of Kaltenbrunner to Hitler respecting interrogations of those arrested in connection with the July 20 attempted assassination and Goerdeler's own notes jotted down during his captivity.

[88] Ritter, *Carl Goerdeler*, 140, 180, 202–203; and see Ritter, "The Military and Politics in Germany," 260–62, 269.

[89] Ritter, *Carl Goerdeler*, 133.

[90] *Ibid.*, 134, 140, 143; Ritter, "Das politische Problem des Militarismus," 180–81; "Die Wehrmacht und der politische Widerstand gegen Hitler," in *Lebendige Vergangenheit*, 192–93, 195; "The Military and Politics in Germany," 269; "Das Problem des Militarismus in Deutschland," *Historische Zeitschrift*, CLXXVII (1954), 47–48; "The Political Attitude of the German Army, 1900–1944," 335–36.

[91] Ritter, *Carl Goerdeler*, 140, 180, 202–203; Ritter, "The Military and Politics in Germany," 260–62, 269.

as a class followed their master to the bitter end" are scarcely tenable in the light of the evidence that Ritter adduced (mainly testimonies of Halder, Beck, Ewald von Kleist-Schmenzin and Friedrich Hossbach, Hitler's adjutant).[92] Ritter maintained that in 1938 the whole officers' corps, but especially Generals Beck, Halder, Fritsch, Blomberg, and Adam von Witzleben, as well as Admiral Canaris and Colonel Hans Oster in the central division of the *Abwehr* of the OKW, tried to prevent an invasion of Czechoslovakia, because it risked a two-front war. Their plans to topple Hitler, he affirmed, were sabotaged by Chamberlain "who was very well informed about the opposition of the German generals to Hitler's war policy" but who nonetheless chose to follow Britain's leaders of 1802 down the inglorious path that led to negotiations with the adversary. By refusing to risk war, Britain helped spin the legend of Hitler's infallibility, so demoralizing the military opposition that "never again was it possible to unite the entire officers' corps of the army behind a decisive move for peace." [93]

Ritter's other theses follow fairly logically. Once the war began, every German military victory diminished the prospects of the opposition. Only when the conflict became hopeless did the bell toll again for the resistance movement. Any euphoria in that camp, however, vanished when the Casablanca unconditional surrender formula became known in Germany, for it figuratively froze the hearts of many generals.[94] Considering the disillusionment with Allied aims, the marvelous thing about the famous July 20, 1944, attempt on the life of Hitler,[95] declared Ritter, was "that the conspiracy reached into such high places that it remained secret despite the fact that almost all higher staffs sooner or later became conscious in some degree of its existence." [96]

[92] Craig, *The Politics of the Prussian Army, 1640–1945* (New York, 1964), 469.
[93] Ritter, *Carl Goerdeler*, 149, 177–78, 180, 182, 196, 200, 202–203. The whole problem has recently been re-explored by Harold Deutsch, *The Conspiracy against Hitler in the Twilight War* (Minneapolis, 1968).
[94] Ritter, *Carl Goerdeler*, 189–90; 263–67, 271–72, 319, 335, 375, 395; Ritter, "The Political Attitude of the German Army," 342–44.
[95] The fullest treatment of the plot is in Germany Bundeszentrale für Heimatdienst, *20 Juli 1944* (3rd ed.; Bonn, 1960).
[96] Ritter, *Carl Goerdeler*, 199; "The Political Attitude of the German Army," 339. See the concurring remarks by Gerhard Schulz, "Über Entscheidungen und Formen des politischen Widerstandes in Deutschland," in Ritter and Ziebura

While Ritter was to have been the minister of culture in Goerdeler's projected post-Nazi government, the former was soberly critical of the inadequacy of the political and economic planning of the resistance movement. Moreover, he seems never to have been quite certain as to the cardinal motivation of the plot against Hitler. In the Goerdeler biography the emphasis is on the overriding moral aims of the resistance. The homicidal action of Treskow, Olbricht, Stülpnagel, Stauffenberg, and the rest, totally unaided as it was by foreign forces, was a rebellion by the German people on behalf of the civilized world against the forces of evil, "an act of pure conscience." [97] Yet in another work Ritter conceded that "national interest" provided the principal stimulus: "The whole sense of the conspiracy in July 1944 was to save Germany from absolute disaster by a timely *Staatsstreich*, for it was realized that politically all would be over for Germany if the destruction of the Nazi regime had to be imposed upon the nation by the victorious Allies." [98] If national interest was the central consideration, it is, of course, fair to ask how many conspirators joined the *Putsch* to spare Germany further destruction and to anticipate a Russian occupation.

After Ritter's revelations, it could no longer be seriously argued that the conspiracy was confined to a "small clique of ambitious officers." [99] On the other hand, neither could it be believed, as do Marxist historians, that the opposition rested upon broad mass support. The close-knit officers' corps, with its long-standing tradition of political independence, loomed as large as it did in the plotting because it alone could provide the cadres and an organizational base from which a *coup de main* might be staged. "Under a totalitarian regime it is simply impossible to mount with any prospect of practical success a political-revolutionary movement.

(eds.), *Faktoren der politischen Entscheidung*, 73–74. Cf. Hans Rothfels, *The German Opposition*, 70, who implies that many officers were passive accomplices before the fact; and Walter Goerlitz, *History of the German General Staff, 1657–1945* (New York, 1953), 465–66, who stresses the vast magnitude of the conspiracy.

[97] Ritter, *Carl Goerdeler*, 280–300, 446–47.

[98] Ritter, "Die Wehrmacht und der politische Widerstand," 204.

[99] See Rothfels, *German Opposition*, 84–98; Bundeszentrale für Heimatdienst, "Der Deutsche Widerstand; seine Motive und seine geschichtliche Bedeutung," in *20 Juli 1944*, 9. Cf. Ritter, *Carl Goerdeler*, 379–88.

For the overthrow an external catastrophe is required, unless a *Staatsstreich*—that is, 'a revolution from above'—can be carried out in time."[100] The close and respected collaboration of Mierendorff, Haubach, Leuschner, Reichwein, and Leber with the Goerdeler group does not alter the critical fact that there was no significant participation by labor unions or socialist factions, and considering Hitler's earlier shattering blows against them, there could not have been.[101] It is not to disparage the sacrifices of the conspirators if, on the basis of Ritter's findings, it be concluded that the resistance movement was molded by precisely those rightist elements which had been the chief thorn in the side of the Weimar governments.

Ritter was a more consequential historian than most of his generation because his thought transcended the limits of cloistered scholarship. A prodigious writer, he was also a patriot who spent much of his life dispelling the view that Germany has always been a militaristic nation. Like Friedrich Meinecke, who had expressed his disillusionment with unadulterated materialist policy in his *Die Entstehung des Historismus* (1936), and like the distinguished Austrian historian Heinrich Ritter von Srbik, Ritter was an idealist. His political perspective had been molded by the rigid moralism and political conservatism of the transcendental Lutheran tradition.[102] It was to be expected that Ritter would argue that for the major part of German history the national current has moved under a mist of idealism and has never ceased to empty peacefully its contributions into the Western cultural sea.[103] Part of Ritter's accomplishment was to cite the evidence in support of this contention.[104]

To vindicate his fatherland it was never necessary for Ritter to

---

[100] Ritter, *Carl Goerdeler*, 102, 446.　　[101] *Ibid.*, 82–89.

[102] The implications of Lutheranism for Historical Idealism were discussed by the late Hajo Holborn in "Der deutsche Idealismus in sozialgeschichtlicher Beleuchtung," *Historische Zeitschrift*, CLXXIV (1952), 359–84.

[103] Ritter, "Zur Problematik gegenwärtiger Geschichtsschreibung," *Lebendige Vergangenheit*, 263. This was based on a lengthy report that Ritter made at the International Historical Congress at Rome in 1955 on "Leistungen, Probleme und Aufgaben der internationalen Geschichtsschreibung zur neueren Geschichte (16.–18. Jahrhundert)," in Vol. VI of *Relazioni del X Congresso internationale di Scienze Storiche* (Florence, 1955), 169–330.

[104] Ritter, *Geschichte als Bildungsmacht. Ein Beitrag zur historisch-politischen Neubesinnung* (Berlin, 1946), 34.

become an expatriate, a shabby "court historian," or an unquestioning apostle of the Historical School. He discovered that a perfectly honest (if not unassailable) reconstruction of the record was Germany's best defense. As early as the Historical Conference at Zurich in 1938 he had rejected the notion that the function of history is to put the past pragmatically in the service of the present, and he had no sympathy for Seeley's dictum that history is only living and vital when it concerns itself with didactic purposes. Ritter warned that the historian must guard against becoming a mere publicist without scientific standing.[105] The "inclination and striving for relative objectivity" enobles him as purity did Sir Galahad. The effort is its own reward: ". . . scientific history, pursued earnestly, emancipates one from the banal clichés, cheap generalizations, apotheoses and condemnations characteristic of daily journalism in that the former teaches, above all, understanding." [106]

Sobered by the traumatic experience of two world wars, Ritter had no choice but to abandon the unsophisticated notion of the German Historical School that freedom is to be sought only within and through the state, a perspective which, in the thinking of Hans Delbrück, Herman Oncken, Otto Hintze, Erich Marcks, Max Lenz, the young Friedrich Meinecke, and even the sociologist Max Weber, argued optimistic confidence in the steady, ordered progression of Germany to cultural leadership and *Weltmacht*. Ritter no longer could countenance the Hegelian notion, which underlay the assumptions of the Historical School, that the history of states was the realization of a transcendental, moral idea, or even the viewpoint of the humanistic Meinecke (*Idee der Staatsräson*) that in the long struggle of ethical and moral values against naked political power western civilization would eventually vindicate its title to world leadership.[107] To Ritter's mind, Oswald Spengler's prediction of the decline of European civilization had

[105] Ritter, "Scientific History, Contemporary History and Political Science," *History and Theory. Studies in the Philosophy of History*, I (1961), 262; Ritter, "Zur Problematik . . . Geschichtsschreibung," 271, 276, 277.

[106] Ritter, "Wissenschaftliche Historie einst und jetzt, Betrachtungen und Erinnerungen," *Historische Zeitschrift*, CCII/III (1966), 584–85.

[107] *Ibid.*, 575, 577, 579, 580.

in the end struck closer to the center of the target than had any of the ruminations of Historicism.

From the confusion and wreckage of the Second World War, Ritter rescued only a few professional "grand illusions." He continued to believe that historical phenomena possess lasting significance but that each situation in time is unique. The historian's task is to demonstrate objectively how the past differs from the present and in what degree the great creations of culture and statecraft "possess enduring validity." [108] Precisely here interpretation must not be confused with interpolation. The historian must conscientiously avoid embrangling the past by superimposing temporally incongruous criteria or personal prejudices; but over his manuscript a reasoned interpretation of his data should hover like a nimbus. It must be remembered, finally, that conclusions may at any time turn out to be vulnerable under the impact of new evidence. Ritter himself was always ready "unconditionally to examine critically his own version of history in the light of incontrovertibly authentic historical data and original sources." [109]

Ritter has often been accused by Marxist historians of contriving the rescue of German imperialism by fusing it with Anglo-American imperialism and, by inference, with western culture of the Economic Age.[110] If this is so, the logical corollary of the proposition of undifferentiation would have to be the unreality of Ritter's national, étatist history. Yet nothing could be further from the truth than the allegation that, through a collectivist empathy, Ritter has submerged every unpleasant feature of the German past into the sea of western history. As both patriot and realist, the Freiburg scholar stoutly defended the fundamentally, but not necessarily exclusively, unique character of German political and constitutional evolution.

Ritter's perspective led him to object to the viewpoint of the global cultural school. For instance, in 1953 at the historical conference held at Bremen he publicly deplored the absorption of

---

[108] Ritter, *Geschichte als Bildungsmacht,* 20–21.
[109] Ritter, "Scientific History," 263, 265–66; Ritter, "Zur Problematik . . . Geschichtsschreibung," 281–82, 279–80.
[110] E.g. Berthold, ". . . *Grosshungern und gehorchen,*" 15–17, 145–46.

many postwar professors with the writing of universal history.[111] He rang the changes on the superficiality of omnibus treatments that were usually based upon insufficient knowledge; and he joined hands with the French scholars J. Droz and P. Renouvin in lamenting universalist tendencies in post-World War II French historiography and in demanding a revival of interest in political history.

Ritter charged the Universalist School with self-delusion. Even while it was striving for a comprehensive harmony on a global scale by organizing "One World," abolishing war forever, and extirpating nationalism and political autocracy ("which is to say every immoderately strong state authority"), the world was actually breaking up into bitterly feuding ideological camps and was less united than ever. Reinhold Niebuhr and Herbert Butterfield were clearly right to insist that the strongest drive in history has always been political assertiveness, the Nietzschean "will to power" with all the varied consequences it entails. The sin of German historicism was to observe the political past through the idealist glasses that Hegel and Ranke had manufactured for it. It would have better served truth, said Ritter, to have discovered the demoniacal-Machiavellian face of grand politics, which remains the same through changing times.[112]

A lifelong critic of the Marxian *Weltanschauung*, Ritter also inveighed against an exclusively socioeconomic interpretation of history. At the World Congress of Historians in 1955 at Rome, where he delivered the final report on modern history to the plenary session, he scored the distortions that had resulted from the invasion of historical writing by Marxist influences.[113] In his opinion, "the widespread notion that political life is primarily determined by economic interests [is] one of the biggest and most dangerous illusions of our times," and one to which modern French historians in particular have succumbed.[114] For Ritter,

[111] In XXII. Versammlung deutscher Historiker. Bremen, 1953 (1953), 33 ff. And see Ritter, "Wissenschaftliche Historie," 584–96 and "Scientific History," 278–79.
[112] Ritter, "Wissenschaftliche Historie," 602.
[113] Ritter, "Leistungen, Probleme und Aufgaben," 167–330.
[114] Ibid., 184–98. And Ritter, "Zur Problematik . . . Geschichtsschreibung," 269.

obviously, economic determinism destroys belief in any kind of genuine ideas and draws a veil over the drives of assertiveness, ambition, cupidity, and will power which, in the long run, are stronger than economic interests. It may be said that at Rome in 1955 Ritter founded a neopolitical historical school.

In 1954 the first volume of Ritter's impatiently awaited *Staatskunst und Kriegshandwerk* was published. It was immediately hailed by Gordon Craig as "the most important treatment of the problem of German militarism that has appeared since the end of the war," one that by reason of its utilization of almost all relevant printed and unprinted military and civil source material, except the Russian, "makes most of its predecessors look superficial." [115]

There are two underlying postulates in this four-volume study: (1) While it is true that militarism is more akin than pacificism to political reality, the task of the state is not to be confused with that of the armed forces; and (2) the struggle for power is only a means to an end, which is to promote the general welfare through establishment of a lasting, peaceful order based on principles of universal law.[116] Guided by this aim, true statesmanship must always regard war as an *ultima ratio regnum*, which seldom—less today than ever before—rewards the investment.

The object of Ritter's inquiry was to determine how it happened that in Germany the balance between statecraft and military concerns, which had obtained in the eighteenth century "cabinet war" era, came in the First World War to be perverted by the encroachments of power-hungry generals, and in the Second by a paranoiac civilian to whom a militarized and politicized nation had entrusted itself.

In tracing the case history of the twentieth century separation of civil from military leadership in Germany, Ritter reiterated his familiar views on the limited and rational nature of Frederician

---

[115] Craig's review of Ritter's *Staatskunst und Kriegshandwerk*, Vol. I, in *American Historic Review*, LXI (1955), 123. Also see reviews by H. Haeusser, in *Journal of Central European Affairs*, XV (1956), 409–10; F. T. Epstein, in *Western Political Quarterly*, VIII (1955), 644–55; T. H. von Laue, in *Erasmus*, IX (1956), 563–66; and P. Pieri, in *Nuova rivista storica*, LXI (1957), 129–57.

[116] Ritter's controversial definition of "militarism" is given in "Das politische Problem des Militarismus," 154, and *Das Problem des Militarismus*, 4.

policy, oriented to peace, not war.[117] Likewise, he again assessed the most enduring legacy of the revolutionary and Napoleonic wars for the modern states system. They demonstrated that "the outcome of hostilities is determined above all by a passionate national will to victory; that the expediency of victory is determined mainly by military concepts of morality, such as 'national honor,' and in accordance with the broadest political motives; and that wartime popular passions steadily mount and strive to encompass ever more extravagant goals." France, sharper than ever, had stressed the militant essence of the state, and from the *Befreiungskrieg* Germany was obliged to draw the lesson that grand politics was only a permanent tension of wills. Within this frame of thinking, war was simply a means of educating the masses to an heroic effort "to force the foe to do our will." [118] For war to be waged most effectively, there was need of a powerful propaganda apparatus which should hammer hatred into the masses with every means so as to render them ever more servile to the fiat of the government. In the end the masses would become so militarized that they themselves would reject half-successes and negotiated settlements.[119]

No German drew more disturbing conclusions from the wars than did the brilliant strategist Karl von Clausewitz (1780–1831). Perhaps unmindful of the fact that some of his concepts did not harmonize very well with the realities of the late wars,[120] he taught ominous doctrine: in peacetime, foreign policy considerations must take precedence over internal; future wars must be fought for political ends; the aim of battle should preferably be the *annihilation* of the enemy's forces; and war should be *fought* by an indoctrinated and inspired nation but *planned and conducted* by professional soldiers, subject in the last analysis to "a guiding political intelligence." [121]

[117] Ritter, *Staatskunst und Kriegshandwerk*, I, 32–49, 50–51, 53, 55.
[118] *Ibid.*, 62, 68, 81.   [119] *Ibid.*, 62.
[120] This applies in the first instance to his concept of *Vernichtungsstrategie*, which, in view of logistical limitations of that time, was impossible of realization, but it also applies to Clausewitz's ideas regarding the training, social background, and degree of responsibility of general officers.
[121] Ritter, *Staatskunst und Kriegshandwerk*, I, 57–58, 68, 71, 73–74, 84, 89–90, 111–12, 119.

According to Ritter, the decisive steps away from the *Rechts-staat* towards the military state was taken during the *Reichsgründung*. At that time the Prussian army leaders successfully attacked the whole traditional political philosophy of the aristocracy and bourgeoisie and forced the conscript people's army upon the state. This new force engineered the military education of the entire German nation and soon achieved an unassailable position in the Prussian constitutional monarchy and through it, after 1871, in the Reich. In time the army came to be "a pure instrument of monarchical power, standing above party conflicts," whose inner structure no parliament dared seriously to disturb.[122] Similarly the great German General Staff, whether under the politically unambitious Moltke the Elder or the scheming Waldersee, increased its power.[123] By the turn of the century it had circumvented the authority of the War Ministry and was gradually moving from a position of complete subordination to crown to one where in time of mobilization the General Staff would assume supreme responsibility for the conduct of hostilities.[124]

In the second volume of the *Staatskunst* Ritter examined the nineteenth century relationship of civil to military authority in France, Britain, Russia, Austria, and Germany. About a third of the book is devoted to German naval and military policy.[125] The ninth chapter rests largely upon research that Ritter had simultaneously undertaken on Count von Schlieffen's Operational Plan of 1905–1906.[126] The tenth and final chapter describes the role of

[122] *Ibid.*, 134, 138, 142–43, 148–49, 152–54, 157–58, 166–67, 178, 196–98, 203, 206.

[123] *Ibid.*, 247–48, 260, 295, 298, 308, 311–12; cf. Ritter, "Das Verhältnis von Politik und Kriegführung im bismarckischen Reich," 77, 79–80, 85–89.

[124] Ritter, *Staatskunst und Kriegshandwerk*, I, 223, 225, 231–35, 237.

[125] Subtitled *Die Hauptmächte Europas und das wilhelminische Reich, 1890–1914* (Munich, 1960). See reviews of Ritter's *Staatskunst und Kriegshandwerk*, II, by F. B. Hollyday, in *Journal of Modern History*, XXXIII (1961), 462; F. T. Epstein, in *Western Political Quarterly*, XIV (1961), 796–97; and G. Craig, in *American Historical Review*, LXVII (1962), 405–407.

[126] See Ritter, *Der Schlieffen Plan. Kritik eines Mythos* (Munich, 1956). See reviews of *Der Schlieffen Plan* by A. Vagts, in *American Historical Review*, LXIII (1957), 908–909; E. Kraehe, in *Journal of Modern History*, XXIX (1957), 396–97; W. Foerster, "Einige Bemerkungen zu Gerhard Ritters Buch 'Der Schlieffen Plan,' " in *Wehrwissenschaftliche Rundschau*, VII (1957), 37–44; and H. K. Rönnefarth, in *Historische Zeitschrift*, CLXXXVII (1959), 398–405.

the general staffs of Austria-Hungary and Germany in the crisis of 1914.[127]

In the first half of this volume the main theme is that nowhere in Europe had the primacy of the military over political leadership been established between 1815 and the outbreak of World War I. Efforts were made especially in England and France to limit the generals and admirals in their independence and make them subordinate to political authority. In France, which had been the cradle of the conscript army, the preponderance after 1815 of the civilian over the military instances was ensured by the repudiation of the Napoleonic tradition, whereas the Prussian military system after 1861 and the Russian after 1874 were closer to the original spirit of the French *levée en masse* of 1793.[128]

In the second half of the book Ritter pointed out that in Germany, after the departure of Bismarck, lack of coordination between military and political authority was cause for increasing alarm because there was a constitutional vacuum at the apex of the state. William II virtually abdicated the unitary authority over conduct of affairs, which the *roi connêtable*, Frederick II, had exercised, and the military were left free to elaborate operational plans whose implementation must imperil the Empire.[129]

The first and most important consequence of the self-imposed isolation of the military establishment in the state, as Ritter saw it, was that it precluded total planning for a supreme military emergency. The second fateful consequence was that it entailed a deep alienation of the officers' corps from the national political life. Worst of all, perhaps, the elaboration of exclusively prepared emergency war plans mortgaged the security of the state.[130] Ritter thought that the exclusion of statesmen from military decisions

[127] On this subject see also Ritter's "Die Zusammenarbeit der Generalstäbe Deutschlands und Osterreich-Ungarns vor dem Ersten Weltkriege," in *Zur Geschichte und Problematik der Demokratie. Festgabe für Hans Herzfeld* (Munich, 1956), 523–49.

[128] Ritter, *Staatskunst und Kriegshandwerk*, II, 15–16, 25–26, 28, 30–32, 34, 51, 55–56, 67, 69, 75, 94, 98, 112.

[129] *Ibid.*, 37, 155–56, 241, 250, 254–56; Ritter, "Das Verhältnis von Politik und Kriegführung," 72–73; and *Der Schlieffen Plan*, 35, 57–58, 93.

[130] Ritter, *Staatskunst und Kriegshandwerk*, II, 156–57, 240; interview with Ritter, October 22, 1966; Ritter, *Der Schlieffen Plan*, 23, 102.

doomed William II and his ministers to become sooner or later the servile coadjutors of the High Command.[131]

The Schlieffen Plan had an even more disastrous effect upon German policy than had been produced by the insensate naval armaments of the first decade of the twentieth century. Preponderant blame for the former must, in Ritter's opinion, be assigned to the prewar chancellors. All of them had neglected to urge the primacy of political considerations or insist upon detailed discussions of the plan with the General Staff. No chancellor had insisted upon an examination of the operational concept from the viewpoint of its impact upon the external image of Germany and her relations with foreign states.[132] Nor could this "shocking capitulation of political reason before the generals" be justified by certainty of success on the battlefield. The Schlieffen Plan, with all its uncertainties and technical shortcomings (exposed in detail by Ritter), was far more a big gamble than a recipe for victory.[133] The generals were no more desirous of war than were the civil leaders but were nonetheless blameworthy. In view of Germany's deteriorating international situation after 1905, it was the duty of the General Staff, "which saw this so clearly," to have bombarded the government with memoranda demanding basic changes in policy. For example, the military should have urged a thoroughgoing review of the proposed violation of Belgium's neutrality and advised Austria-Hungary to deal more tolerantly with Serbia. At the same time the generals should have revised their operational concept to a defensive in the west and an offensive against Russia.[134]

[131] Ritter, *Staatskunst und Kriegshandwerk*, II, 92, 129, 133–35, 143, 147, 155–56, 239–40; cf. "The Political Attitude of the German Army,"

[132] Ritter, *Staatskunst und Kriegshandwerk*, II, 241, 253–55. Theobald von Bethmann Hollweg (chancellor, 1909–17) claimed that he was not consulted in the preparation of the 1914 plan of campaign (*Betrachtungen zum Weltkriege* [Berlin, 1922], II, 7). However, if we are to believe Ritter, Bethmann prided himself on not having interfered with the military ("Das politische Problem des Militarismus," 176).

[133] Ritter, *Staatskunst und Kriegshandwerk*, II, 243–44, 246–49, 252; Ritter, *Der Schlieffen Plan*, 13, 16–17, 19–20, 23, 29–30, 47, 57–58, 61–63, 65–66, 79–80, 103. Gordon Craig thinks that Ritter's "persuasive argument" . . . "should modify the excessive veneration in which Schlieffen had been held even in western service colleges" (*American Historic Review*, LXVII, 406).

[134] Ritter, *Staatskunst und Kriegshandwerk*, II, 252, 282, 291–93, 334, 336, 338; Ritter, "Das Verhältnis von Politik und Krieg," 94.

As it was, a glassy-eyed adhesion to the Schlieffen Plan and its technical imperatives prevented the government from exploring alternate diplomatic and military actions and from exhausting all possibilities of a peaceful solution in July, 1914. The result was that Germany was forced to declare war on France in order to justify invasion of Belgium, even though the policy of the German government had in July, 1914 been basically defensive and not aggressive.[135]

Here and elsewhere Ritter stressed that it was nonsense to seek the origins of the war in some supposed "war lust" on the part of the German General Staff.[136] So far from being anxious to strike at the Russian colossus before it could grow any stronger,[137] the German generals, confronted with the fact of Russian military numerical superiority, showed hesitancy and a clammy lack of confidence. Their diffident posture stood in flagrant contrast to that of the masses who were singing patriotic songs in the streets.[138] During most of July when Bethmann-Hollweg was encouraging Austria-Hungary to take "swift, energetic action against Serbia" while European sentiment still seemed to favor the latter's chastisement, Moltke opposed inciting the Viennese government; yet he was scarcely consulted by the civil authorities.[139] His moment came only when it was assumed that Russian total mobilization was in full swing (late in the evening of the thirtieth). Then, feeling the enormous burden of his military responsibility, he thought he was obliged to counsel Bethmann not to send any more admonitions to the Ballplatz. Since a two-front war had been rendered inescapable by the Russian mobilization, Moltke

---

[135] Ritter, *Staatskunst und Kriegshandwerk*, II, 334–38, and III, 16–17; "Der Anteil des Militärs an der Kriegskatastrophe von 1914," *Historische Zeitschrift*, CXCIII (1961), 72–91. Ritter pointed out that Moltke had also tried to find a way to avoid attacking through Belgium but would only endorse the route through Alsace Lorraine in event of war on condition of a British pledge of neutrality ("Der Anteil des Militärs," 80).

[136] Ritter, "Der Anteil des Militärs," 79–80; Ritter, *Staatskunst und Kriegshandwerk*, II, 282.

[137] This is the view of the well-known student of pre-World I imperialism, G. W. F. Hallgarten (*Das Schicksal des Imperialismus im 20. Jahrhundert* [Frankfurt am Main, 1969], 65).

[138] Ritter, "Der Anteil des Militärs," 79–80.

[139] *Ibid.*, 84; Ritter, *Staatskunst und Kriegshandwerk*, II, 282.

was now preoccupied with denying France sufficient time to wreck the German emergency war plan.[140] Thus, it was "no one else but the General Staff that had, out of purely military considerations, demanded and secured a precipitate declaration of war against Russia." [141]

Before publication of the third volume of the *Staatskunst,* which was to deal with Bethmann-Hollweg and German war aims, Fritz Fischer, a professor at Hamburg, figuratively hurled a bomb between Ritter's legs. The appearance of Fischer's book, *Griff nach der Weltmacht,* coupled with a preliminary article by him, inaugurated a bitter controversy which was to outlast the Freiburg historian.[142] Of all the battles Ritter fought in a career that was, in Herzfeld's words, "noteworthy for having repeatedly championed controversial but for him . . . important values of the past," [143] the principled quarrel with Fischer and his school of thought was the most consequential and the most relentless. Many of the dominant figures of German historical science were drawn into the dispute. Upon its outcome turned the verdict of posterity upon the integrity of the last civil government of the Reich, the justification of the Treaty of Versailles and its "war guilt" article 231, and the tenability of an alleged continuity of spirit and aims from Bethmann through Ludendorff to Hitler.

In a massive attack supported by impressive but top-heavy research in the German and Austrian foreign office and a variety of ministerial archives, Fischer brought two theses, in particular, under fire. These notions had been entertained since World War I by some of Germany's leading historians (e.g., Hans Delbrück, Erich Marcks, Otto Hoetzsch, Otto Volkmann, Albrecht Mendelssohn-Bartholdy, Count Max Montgelas, Hermann Oncken,

---

[140] Ritter, "Der Anteil des Militärs," 90.
[141] Ritter, *Staatskunst und Kriegshandwerk,* II, 338.
[142] Subtitled *Die Kriegszielpolitik des kaiserlichen Deutschlands, 1914–18* (Düsseldorf, 1961). As an adjunct to Fischer's fat, 896-page presentation, Immanuel Geiss published 396 out of a total of 5,000 extant documents bearing on the war aims controversy: *Julikrise und Kriegsausbruch, 1914: Eine Dokumentensammlung* (with an introduction by Fischer) (Hannover, 1963). And see Fischer, "Deutsche Kriegsziele, Revolutionierung und Separatfrieden im Osten, 1914–18," *Historische Zeitschrift,* CLXXXVIII (1959), 249–310.
[143] Herzfeld, "Zwei Werke Ritters," 321.

Adalbert Wahl, Alfred von Wegerer, E. C. Helmreich, and Friedrich Meinecke). They proposed that guilt for the war was nicely divided and that the war aims of Bethmann and other high German civil officers were considerably less rabid than those of Ludendorff and Hindenburg.[144]

Fischer's book largely ignored relevant memoirs, private correspondence, and secondary literature and, according to Hans Gatzke, Ludwig Reiners, and Werner Conze, was from the standpoints of rhetoric and sentence structure "unnecesarily repetitious," "involved," "interminable," and "surprisingly dull." [145] Much of the material presented in Fischer's work is well known, and he contributed very little new knowledge to our understanding of the origins of the war and Germany's purposes in waging it. As the author confined himself (as frankly stated in his preface) to an examination of the motives and aims of German imperialism, and inasmuch as the French, British, and Russian documents for the period since 1914 are not yet accessible to historians, the effect of the *Griff nach der Weltmacht* was to reaffirm the sole war guilt of Germany. Fischer pointed to Germany's misdeeds without giving the reader a peek at the skeletons in the Allied closet.

In what G. W. F. Hallgarten, otherwise a stanch supporter of Fischer, describes as an "unwarranted exaggeration" and the "reverse of the truth," the Hamburg historian's opening chapter ("German Imperialism from Great Power Policy to World Power Policy") postulates that, even before Sarajevo, Germany had deliberately and consistently, out of concern for the expansion of

[144] For a treatment of the attitudes of German historians in World War I see Klaus Schwabe, *Die deutschen Professoren und die politischen Grundfragen des Ersten Weltkrieges* (Diss.; Freiburg i. Br., 1958). Revisionist arguments respecting Germany's World War I aims have been examined by several scholars, e.g., the East German Fritz Klein in "Gli storichi Tedeschi di Fronte alla Prima Guerra Mondiale," *Studi Storici*, III (1962), 730–56, and "Die westdeutsche Geschichtsschreibung über die Ziele des deutschen Imperialismus im Ersten Weltkrieg," *Zeitschrift für Geschichtswissenschaft*, X (1962), 1808–36, and the West German Hans Herzfeld, in "Die deutsche Kriegspolitik im Ersten Weltkrieg," *Vierteljahrshefte für Zeitgeschichte*, XI (1963), 224–45.

[145] Hans Gatzke, review of Fischer's *Griff nach der Weltmacht*, in *American Historical Review*, LXVIII (1963), 445.

her world power, prepared for a general war which the German government regarded as inevitable.[146] From this proposition of malicious intent derive logically all the other major theses of this book: the July, 1914, crisis must be viewed as a link between the "world policy" that Germany had followed since 1894 and the war aims that she pursued after August, 1914; Bethmann, the German generals, and the foreign office all conspired to drive Austria-Hungary into war against Serbia, thereby "deliberately" risking conflict with Russia and France; Bethmann, in fact, reckoned that the Austro-Serbian confrontation would result in a major general war; Bethmann was, as proved by his notorious memorandum of September 9, 1914 (which Fischer unearthed), an extreme annexationist, and he remained so until his fall from office in July, 1917; among his offensive aims, which never changed from the outset of the fighting to the end of his chancellorship, was the elimination of the British Empire and France as future potential military foes of Germany; public opinion, almost all political parties (including the Majority Socialist), the Trade Associations, and the federated states and princes supported maximalist war aims which could be achieved only by victory on the battlefield; the German civil government, as well as the High Command of the Army (OHL) preferred a policy of annexations and detachment of Poland from Russia to one of separate, negotiated peace in the east; Ludendorff's policy was distinguished from that of Bethmann and the civil government only in that the general's "method was harder, less elastic, and . . . more imperious," but it is a myth that there were substantive differences between military and civilian war aims; Germany's most cherished war aim in the west was the annexation of Belgian territory, which precluded the possibility of any separate peace with England; the Reichstag Peace Resolution of July, 1917, signified neither a renunciation nor serious abatement of the war aims of Ludendorff; the realization of the program of Germany's wartime government would have brought about a thoroughgoing revolution in European political and economic relationships; and, finally, the fiction of a purely defensive

[146] Hallgarten, *Das Schicksal des Imperialismus*, 62.

war encouraged the German nation to repudiate the Treaty of Versailles as a *Diktat* and to live against the day when a Barbarossa would rise to lead the country to world power.

While Fischer's views were, as might be expected, generally endorsed by Anglo-American and expatriate historians, they evoked criticism from most German scholars, as was equally to be expected. Objections of varying force were levelled against the "extraordinary German" from Hamburg by Egmont Zechlin, Andreas Hillgruber, Hans Herzfeld, Hans Rothfels, Karl Dietrich Erdmann, Ludwig Dehio, Theodor Schieder, Erwin Hoelzle, Karl H. Janssen, Paul Sethe, and, most of all, by Ritter himself.[147] It did not escape Fischer's detractors that his basic error had been to ascribe, without submitting convincing evidence, aggressive motives to every single major German decision between 1913–18, while ignoring a wide range of factors that often conditioned or determined in decisive fashion the actions of responsible officials— military imperatives, economic necessities, popular (especially) Socialist influences, personal psychological motives, vague collective fears that gripped the whole nation, and a wretched geographic position which made conscience an expensive luxury.

Meanwhile, Ritter was preparing, with the aid of former doctoral students, the third volume of his *Staatskunst*, which, like Fischer's study, was based on an amazing amount of research into diplomatic, military and ministerial documents in the archives in Bonn, Potsdam, Munich, Stuttgart, and Vienna, as well as upon a broad spectrum of memoirs, correspondence, and secondary materials. Even before the appearance of this third volume, however, Ritter felt compelled to enter the lists against Fischer.

In an article appearing in 1962 Ritter flayed Fischer's rhetorical method. It belonged to the style of Fischer's book, said the Freiburg scholar, that it preferred to deal in tendentious statements

[147] For an extremely hostile critique see Erwin Hoelzle, review of Fischer's *Griff nach de Weltmacht*, in *Das historisch-politische Buch*, X (1962), 65–69. Conversely, for reviews that accept all of Fischer's theses with enthusiasm and without demurrer of any kind, see F. L. Carsten, in *English Historical Review*, LXXVIII (1963), 751–53 and G. Barraclough, in *International Affairs*, XXXIX (1963), 78–79. For a more balanced judgment by an American scholar, who, however, is sympathetic towards the Hamburg historian, see Klaus Epstein, "German War Aims in the First World War," *World Politics*, XV (1962), 163–85.

and inferences, which the reader is left to spin into his own conclusions.[148] German imperialism was taken for granted, but Ritter complained that Fischer did not deign to take other imperialists into account.[149] No proof was adduced in support of the statement that the will to war inspired the German army, except for a private letter of Moltke to his wife. In any case, Fischer completely misunderstood Moltke's attitude, which was anything but bellicose. Fischer did not, on the other hand, take cognizance of the sincere efforts of influential civilians, such as Albert Ballin, to forestall war through an understanding with Britain.[150]

In the late July crisis Fischer tried to shift the war guilt from Berchtold to the "vacillating and insecure" Bethmann Hollweg, said Ritter. Fischer's deliberate misinterpretation of the reasons behind Berlin's delay in relaying to Vienna the English warning of July 29 served the purpose of discrediting the German chancellor.[151] "Fischer does not say the chancellor wanted war, but only that he regarded it as inevitable and sought diplomatically to prepare for it—an expression that one may construe as he pleases." [152] In effect, Fischer denied Bethmann the reputation of an honest friend of peace. "I find such a viewpoint irreconcilable with the total picture yielded by the massive source materials that have till now become available respecting the personality and ultimate political motives of Bethmann." [153]

Systematically undercutting the documentary piles on which Fischer's thesis of preponderant German war guilt rests, Ritter demonstrated that Bethmann's and official German policy in the years 1912–14 were fundamentally peaceful. In the light of recent research, Fischer's view that in late July the actions of Berlin proceeded from a burning desire for war must be discarded.[154] Rather, they are to be explained by the fear of the consequences of a tardy

[148] Ritter, "Eine neue Kriegsschuldthese? Zu Fritz Fischers Buch *Griff nach der Weltmacht*," *Historische Zeitschrift*, CXCIV, (1962), 646–68.
[149] *Ibid.*, 650. K. Epstein says much the same thing in "German War Aims," 180–81.
[150] Ritter, "Eine neue Kriegsschuldthese?" 667–68.   [151] *Ibid.*, 663–64.
[152] *Ibid.*, 655.
[153] *Ibid.*, and see Ritter, *Staatskunst und Kriegshandwerk*, II, 313n17, 317–18, and 382.
[154] See Andreas Hillgruber, *Deutschlands Rolle in der Vorgeschichte der beiden Weltkriege*, Die deutsche Frage in der Welt, No. 7 (Göttingen, 1967).

and halfhearted course by Austria, such as would leave the foe time for military and diplomatic countermeasures that would eradicate the moral-political advantage initially enjoyed by the Central Powers as a result of the assassinations of June 28. In the face of two generations of historical research that proves the contrary, Fischer's assertion cannot be sustained that the attack on Serbia was motivated by the Dual Monarchy's fear that to hesitate meant loss of German support; rather, Germany supported Austria-Hungary in order not to lose its last important ally.[155]

Fischer's expressionistic portrait of Bethmann rendered unrecognizable the man of honor and moral scruples, whose greatest character failing was that he was vacillating, wholly without sure political instincts, and tormented by a host of doubts and afterthoughts. For Fischer, Bethmann was only a sly, hypocritical, resolute exemplar of power politics, who frivolously gambled with the fate of Germany.[156] To Ritter, the last straw in Fischer's heap of distortions was his contention that the German chancellor directed his last admonitions to Vienna not on England's account, but out of regard for the reaction of the Social Democratic Party, which had to be convinced of the innocence of Germany and the Dual Monarchy! This, for the Hamburg historian, was the real reason why Bethmann obstinately resisted for so long the demands of the General Staff and war minister for countermobilization to the Russian call to arms.[157]

In 1964 the third volume of the *Staatskunst* appeared.[158] It bristled with ninety-eight pages of footnotes, many of which contained lengthy discussions of the state of various questions, and with a text of over seven hundred pages.[159] This third volume was

[155] Ritter, "Eine neue Kriegsschuldthese?" 659, 662. This is also the opinion of Egmont Zechlin, expressed in *Beilage zu der Wochenschrift "Das Parlament,"* May 17, June 14, June 21, 1961.

[156] Ritter, "Eine neue Kriegsschuldthese?" 667–68.   [157] *Ibid.,* 665.

[158] Subtitled *Die Tragödie der Staatskunst: Bethmann-Hollweg als Kriegskanzler, 1914–17* (Munich, 1964). See especially the reviews of Ritter's *Staatskunst und Kriegshandwerk,* Vol. III by Gordon Craig in *American Historical Review,* LXXI (1965), 226–28; Paul Sethe, "Die Tragödie eines Staatsmannes . . . ," in Hamburg, *Die Zeit,* Jan. 20, 1965, p. 30; and Theodor Schieder, in *Historische Zeitschrift,* CCII (1966), 389–98.

[159] Ritter told this writer in an interview of October 22, 1966, in Freiburg, that out of propriety he had relegated 211 critical responses to Fischer's arguments to the footnotes.

mainly devoted to examining the struggle between civil and military leadership in wartime Germany and to analyzing the methods by which in the end the High Command (Ludendorff) achieved absolute victory over Bethmann Hollweg and cast its somber mantle over the realm.

The central personage in the story is, of course, Bethmann. Ritter recounted how the chancellor in the heady flush induced by the first reports of victory over France subscribed to extremist war aims set forth in the memorandum of September 9, 1914, but how, under the psychological attrition of the years of bloodshed that followed the German check on the Marne, Bethmann passed through a catharsis and came to embrace war aims that were increasingly more moderate than those endorsed by the OHL, and how he was finally, like some noble soul in a Greek tragedy, overwhelmed by stupendous forces beyond all human control.[160]

From a penetrating description of the manifold difficulties that beset Bethmann, Ritter concluded that this "highly estimable statesman" was not animated by extravagant aims of conquest but approached the conduct of the war with moderation. The chancellor was a "statesman who with desperate, but never despairing, efforts strove to free himself from the entanglement of an overpowering wartime destiny and find a road to peace for a nation mired in a hopeless situation." [161]

Ritter did not paint a halo over Bethmann's head. He was, after all, the political leader of all Germans and had, in some practical measure, to be the common denominator of a variety of class war aims. At the outset, according to Ritter, Bethmann's statements gave the lie "to the asseveration of German intellectuals" that the "war was purely defensive for Germany." His aims respecting Belgium, though more restrained than those of the for-

---

[160] Ritter, *Staatskunst und Kriegshandwerk*, III, 46. By the end of 1914, according to Ritter, the chancellor had come to reject the idea of the annexation of Belgium (proposed by the state secretaries of the interior and foreign affairs) and confidentially told the foreign office that Germany could now be happy if she succeeded in merely maintaining the *status quo ante bellum* in a war against half the world (*ibid.*, 52–53).

[161] *Ibid.*, III, 21–22, 32, 38, 42–45, 52–53, 58, 62, 73, 88, 113–16, 144, 285, 585. Gordon Craig thinks that Ritter's interpretation is "the best we possess" about Bethmann's "policies, his dilemmas, and the combination of circumstances that led to his fall" (Craig, review of Ritter's *Staatskunst und Kriegshandwerk*, 226).

eign office or the OHL, obstructed hopes of peace with England and remained to curse the whole German war effort. In the east, too, the chancellor at first opposed Falkenhayn's wish for a separate peace with Russia, at least until the tsarist armies had been expelled from Poland.[162]

Nevertheless, in spite of the "song of hate" that rang through Allied countries, Bethmann, shortly after the Battle of the Marne, abandoned the September 9, 1914, program. Thereafter, beyond doubt, the chancellor's war policy was of a "fundamentally defensive character." [163] By October, 1915, if we are to believe Ritter, a chastened chancellor was beginning to desire a peace on the basis of the *status quo ante* but had to moderate between the annexationist demands of the bourgeoisie and the anti-imperialist desires of the socialist workers. His speech of April 5, 1915, to the Reichstag foreshadowed the government's adoption of annexationist goals in the Baltic area. "With this speech," said Ritter, "Bethmann had taken a dangerous step: a step away from his former cautious position in the question of annexations and in the direction of the irresistible current of the day." [164] Nevertheless, contended Ritter, annexations never enjoyed top priority in Bethmann's thinking. He would not for a moment have let them stand in the way of the possibility of a general peace of understanding or a separate peace with Russia if prospects for either had brightened; and his overall view of the final peace, as was revealed in his letter of April 25, 1915, to Count Westarp, the Conservative leader, in which he dedicated himself to a settlement of "relative moderation, in the spirit of Bismarck," was very different from the outlook of the *Alldeutschen*. Yet he could not afford to disclose his fundamentally continent attitude to the chauvinistic public.[165] It is probable that the contradictions and fluctuations in Bethmann's utterances, to which Ritter pays more attention than

[162] Ritter, *Staatskunst und Kriegshandwerk*, III, 46 and 62.
[163] Ritter, "Bethmann Hollweg und die Machtträume deutscher Patrioten im ersten Jahr des Weltkrieges," in *Festschrift Percy Ernst Schramm zu seinem siebzigsten Geburtstag* . . . (Wiesbaden, 1964), II, 206–207, 209.
[164] Ritter, *Staatskunst und Kriegshandwerk*, III, 116, 143.
[165] This letter is mentioned in Fischer, *Germany's Aims in the First World War*, (translated from German; New York, 1967), 193; Cf. Ritter, *Staatskunst und Kriegshandwerk*, III, 88, 91, 113, 115, 144, 152, 161.

Fischer does, are to be explained on grounds that, unlike Bismarck, the World War I chancellor was not a "fighter." Being malleable, he was not infrequently beaten into a form set by forces harder than himself.

The struggle for precedence between the military and political leadership began in October, 1915, with the confrontation with Chief of Staff, General Falkenhayn. The chancellor brought about the fall of Falkenhayn and, ironically, hoped from his successor— Hindenburg (who was the façade for Ludendorff)—that he would acknowledge civilian leadership.[166] The rope by which Ludendorff and Hindenburg pulled themselves to supreme power was unrestricted submarine warfare. In this struggle against the united army and naval leaders, who were supported by the bulk of the public, Bethmann showed courage and an unsuspected tenacity. "This struggle," wrote Ritter, "offers a virtually classic example of the basic theme of our book, the problem of 'militarism' in Germany." [167] This fight also thrust into the spotlight what "irresistible power, even over purely military decisions, was enjoyed in an age of peoples' war by public opinion with all its preconceptions, passions, and myths." [168] Possessed of a deeper understanding of Germany's situation than Ludendorff, Bethmann showed himself to be no starry-eyed philosopher in his representations to the kaiser. In his greatest memorandum of the war (that of February 29, 1916) the chancellor urged William II to reject unrestricted submarine warfare, which would not force England to her knees but would bring a rupture of relations with the "unneutral" United States.[169] On November 7, 1916, in an acrimonious exchange with Ludendorff, Bethmann sharply reminded the general that he (the chancellor) alone bore the responsibility for the formulation and conduct of imperial policy.[170]

[166] *Ibid.*, 103, 226–39. This is also the view of Karl H. Janssen, "Der Wechsel in der Obersten Heeresleitung, 1916," *Vierteljahrshefte für Zeitgeschichte*, VII (1959), 337–71.

[167] Ritter, *Staatskunst und Kriegshandwerk*, III, 285. See further 328, 367–68, 379, 381–82.

[168] *Ibid.*, 145.

[169] *Ibid.*, 200. See further 166–77 for Ritter's rejection of the myth of American neutrality.

[170] *Ibid.*, 257–58.

As Bethmann came to realize that it was futile to hope for victory on the battlefield, he became more amenable to a peace that largely sacrificed the "securities and guarantees" he had demanded in 1915. In his note of October 27, 1916, to the Prussian state ministry and in his peace note of December 12, 1916, which contained much the same proposals, he drastically reduced his price for an armistice. But the OHL thought an independent Poland, the annexation of Courland and Livonia and the Longwy-Briey mines, and economic pledges in Belgium insufficient booty and refused to endorse Bethmann's peace note. As Ritter remarked, "it was always the weakness of his position vis à vis the OHL that he could never demonstrate the existence of an actually concrete possibility of peace to justify the basic renunciation of annexations." [171] This proved to be the case in December, 1916. When the chancellor's note was, in effect, ignored by the Allies, and Wilson, in whom Bethmann reposed a certain trust, failed him, the hour of the German generals struck. German public opinion would see nothing more in Wilson's peace move than an attempt to postpone the defeat of England by U-boat war,[172] which officialdom, the admirals, and the generals all regarded now as necessary. The hysterical, militarized masses, driven to despondency by Wilson's unneutral attitude and by Allied demands for unconditional surrender, stood squarely behind the submarine offensive.[173]

Bethmann was forced to capitulate to the military in the fateful crown council of January 9, 1917, when in response to excruciating pressure from all sides he was obliged to confess that he could no longer shoulder responsibility for further delay or rejection of unrestricted submarine warfare in view of the position of the German armed forces. For Ritter, this was the "darkest hour in the political career of Berthmann Hollweg, for it was tantamount to the formal capitulation of political authority before the military in the most portentous question of the first world war." [174] This genuflection to overwhelming strength opened the last act of the tragedy that led to Bethmann's fall in July. His continuing fight against an open declaration of annexations in the east (which

[171] *Ibid.*, 335–36, 348, 502.   [172] *Ibid.*, 362, 379.
[173] *Ibid.*, 162–65, 195–98, 211, 215.   [174] *Ibid.*, 381, 382.

would have alienated Austria-Hungary), in a word, his conciliatory policy toward Russia, cost him much domestic support in the last six months of his tenure of office.[175] In the last analysis, however, it was the Allied commitment to total victory that spread Germany, like a conquered country, at the feet of Ludendorff, "the most radical of all militarists." [176]

In the *Griff nach der Weltmacht* Fischer made the egregious error of equating Bethmann with his worst foe, Ludendorff. The author chose to ignore the fact that the chancellor sincerely, if at times obliquely, opposed the extreme war aims of the generals, the Conservatives and the National Liberals, as may be studied in the controversy over unrestricted submarine warfare and seen in Bethmann's memorandum of May 1, 1917, in which he declined to be bound by the OHL's Kreuznach war aims statement of April 23, 1917. Fischer was the prisoner of his initial proposition that Bethmann's memorandum of September 9, 1914, to Clemens Delbrück was not simply a psychological response to the tremendous wave of chauvinism that attended the first German military victories, but was the unswerving policy of the chancellor as long as he remained in office.[177]

Ritter, on the other hand, showed with evidence not cited by Fischer how the German government's war aims shifted over a period of three years, being conditioned at any one time by a myriad of factors. Bethmann, himself, increasingly turned away from rank annexationist aims and towards the bases that might provide a lasting peace, which is to say towards the Majority Socialist position on war aims.[178] When at length military and civ-

[175] *Ibid.*, 535.

[176] *Ibid.*, 243, 247–49, 253, 257–63, 269–70, 273–74, 284–85, 298–304, 307, 314–15, 317–18, 321–22, 325–27, 331, 337–39, 346–47, 398; "Das politische Problem des Militarismus," 180.

[177] Ritter handled this problem also in his "Bethmann Hollweg und die Machtträume deutscher Patrioten," 204–205.

[178] As Karl Dietrich Erdmann, who agreed with Ritter, wrote, a time came when Bethmann "placed peace above territorial accessions" ("Zur Beurteilung Bethmann Hollwegs," *Geschichte in Wissenschaft und Unterricht*, XV [1964], 537). In the long forgotten diary of Karl Riezler, Bethmann's secretary and confidant, Erdmann discovered under date of November 3, 1916, an entry affirming that Bethmann believed that a fruitful foreign policy "could only be pursued with the Left," but that such a policy was utopian because of the opposition of all authoritative political, military and governmental instances (*ibid.*, 529).

ilian leaders came to agree that separate peace with Russia was a necessity, it is plain that the September 9, 1914, program, for the East at least, had been abandoned.

Of course, Ritter did not resolve all the problems that were raised by Bethmann's mercurial behavior. For instance, Ritter did not explain the apparent contradiction between his thesis that the radicalized and militarized masses favored extremist war aims and the fact that the largest popular political party in wartime Germany, the Social Democratic, had from at least July, 1915, adhered to a conciliatory and durable peace program.[179]

When all is said, however, it must be admitted that Ritter has given us a much more plausible portrait of Bethmann Hollweg than has Fischer. The Freiburg historian's interpretation is of a mediocre, honorable, humane, and fundamentally defensive-minded statesman reacting in changing ways to the pull and tug of cyclopean forces he was powerless to control, a man who was not a great political leader but who scrupulously exercised his constitutional power without being corrupted by it.[180] Ritter related Bethmann's fall, as Fischer did not, to the struggle against the German "militarism" and its assault upon the constitution which the chancellor was sworn to uphold. With greater fairness than his adversary, Ritter explained in detail how Bethmann was deprived of the only argument—the existence of a genuine possibility of a negotiated peace—with which he could successfully have combated extremist war aims. His moderate desires were frustrated by "the mighty annexations which the enemy governments not only planned during the war but incorporated in treaties." High on the list of these would be the twelve-point program which, proposed by Sazonov shortly after Tannenberg, was ac-

[179] William H. Maehl, *German Militarism and Socialism* (Lincoln, Nebraska, 1968), 112. The *SPD's* manifesto, which was printed in the central organ *Vorwärts* (July 3, 1914) affirmed that the party had "always unanimously opposed the policy of conquests and annexations" and "now raised anew the sharpest protest against all efforts and pronouncements in favor of annexing foreign territories and oppressing other peoples."

[180] See Ritter, "Bethmann Hollweg und die Machtträume deutscher Patrioten," 206. Cf. Epstein, "German War Aims," 172. The unique mobility and eclecticism of Bethmann was recognized a generation ago by Johannes Ziekursch, *Politische Geschichte des neuen deutschen Kaiserreiches* (Berlin, 1930), III, 218.

cepted by the French cabinet and contemplated the "annihilation" of the Central Powers.[181]

Bethmann, who was a temperate conservative, opposed the constitutional changes which his diplomatic failures had rendered exigent and accordingly alienated all parties in the Reichstag, which now sought Germany's salvation in the institution of parliamentary democracy.[182] His elimination from office almost immediately after the kaiser had expressed his complete confidence in him left a void which was filled not by a responsible ministry but by the military dictatorship of the archannexationist Ludendorff, who now proceeded to emasculate the Reichstag Peace Resolution of July 19, 1917, on which Bethmann had pinned such hopes. Ritter's interpretation of the fateful events of the first half of 1917 was not only the climax of the whole *Staatskunst*—the triumph of militarism over statecraft; [183] it was also a systematic refutation of the alleged continuity of German aims for world domination. Ritter showed that this thesis, which had been advanced by Mario Toscano in 1955 at the International Historical Conference in Rome [184] and had been echoed by Fritz Fischer, is pure myth. So far from being a "clutch at world power," Bethmann's peace efforts were "rather to be likened to the grasp of a drowning man at a plank that might save him." [185]

It is beyond the scope of this essay on the historical achievements of Gerhard Ritter to follow the controversy between him and Fritz Fischer any further. In 1964 the former published a

---

[181] Ritter, "Bethmann Hollweg und die Machtträume deutscher Patrioten," 206. See further 212–13. That Allied war aims did not differ in spirit from those of the OHL was reaffirmed in Ritter, *Staatskunst und Kriegshandwerk, IV: Die Herrschaft des deutschen Militarismus und die Katastrophe von 1918* (Munich, 1968), 14–17.

[182] Ritter, *Staatskunst und Kriegshandwerk*, III, 538–39. Bethmann believed that fundamental structural change of the Reich government in wartime was impractical; on the other hand, he strove for a democratization of the Prussian electoral system (*ibid.*, 539, 541).

[183] Ludendorff's militaristic dictatorship is the cynosure of the fourth, posthumously published volume of the *Staatskunst*. It appeared too late to be analyzed in this essay.

[184] *Relazioni del X Congresso internazionale* . . . , V, 3–50.

[185] Ritter, "Bethmann Hollweg und die Machtträume deutscher Patrioten," 201–202, 212, 214.

short study that summarized his main theses respecting German policy in the First World War, and in 1965 Fischer responded in a series of essays totalling 108 pages.[186] In neither work did the author present any startling new evidence. Each simply refined his arguments and thrust at chinks in the armor of his adversary. In this vendetta, however, time was on the side of Fischer, the younger man. Ritter was beginning to feel the effects of old age and a severe coronary condition.[187]

Since 1956 Ritter had worked at feverish tempo. In that year he had been made *emeritus* at Freiburg but continued during winter semesters to give heavily attended lectures at the university. He continued to add to the total of thirty-one books and one hundred and thirty-seven articles (not counting book reviews), which he had had to his credit by 1956. As vice-president of the *Comité International des Sciences Historiques* he had again in 1958 visited the United States and had spoken in Columbus, New Orleans, and Houston.[188] But in the mid-1960s, although Clio appeared to him as fair and seductive as in his youth, he was forced to husband his energies. He now labored primarily to complete the *Staatskunst* down to 1945. In that connection he was just about to make his last "archival journey" to Bonn when this writer visited him in 1966.[189] Fischer's attacks, however, made Ritter more wary and necessitated his devoting far more space than he had originally intended simply to the last sixteen months of World War I. Thus it was that when the fourth volume appeared, with its ninety-two pages of footnotes (in which issue is often taken with Fischer's methods and his interpretations of events

[186] Ritter, *Der erste Weltkrieg. Studien zum deutschen Geschichtsbild*, Schriftenreihe der Bundeszentrale für Politische Bildung, No. 65 (Bonn, 1964); Fischer, *Weltmacht oder Niedergang: Deutschland im ersten Weltkrieg*, Hamburger Studien zur neueren Geschichte, No. 1 (Frankfurt am Main, 1965).

[187] Interview, October 22, 1966.

[188] Ritter to author, October 14, 1964, and August 16, 1965. He was then also a member of the academies of Heidelberg, Berlin, Munich, Stockholm, Rome (*Accademia Lincei*), as well as of the Royal Society in London and an honorary member of the American Historical Association. He had also been named to the *Friedensklasse des Ordens pour la Mérite*.

[189] The fourth volume of Ritter's *Staatskunst* was originally to have been entitled *Herrschaft, Sturz und Wandlung des deutschen "Militarismus" von Ludendorff bis Hitler, 1917–45*; interview, October 22, 1966.

and documents), it did not contain the originally contemplated coverage of the Weimar Republic and the Third Reich.

On July 1, 1967, Ritter died. A man who had loved his native land above all things save virtue, he had spent almost sixty years exploring almost all phases of its history since the closing of the Middle Ages. He had especially reviewed the grand crises and the Thermopylae in Germany's past in a quest for honest answers to basic questions concerning their effects upon political forms, social structure, public ethics, and concentration or distribution of power in the state. Although primarily an historian of *Machtpolitik*, Ritter recalled to his contemporaries Germany's durable contributions to the religious, cultural, artistic, and institutional heritage of western civilization. As he had grown to understand that the glories of Germany had always been the achievement of men who had exemplified both fortitude and rectitude, the word "German" came to mean for him more than nationality; it came to be his profession. "A great patriot" and " a great historian," in the words of Theodor Schieder, Ritter stood forth as the latter-day champion of the German record, of which, by and large, he was not ashamed.[190] For this knight in the lists, his pen was a lance.

It was Ritter's tragedy that he felt called upon to assist at the resurrection of national and political history in an age that was hostile to both. Although more critical and scientific in his method than Sybel, Treitschke, Delbrück, Marcks, Oncken, or Meinecke, he neither would nor could wholly reject the bequests of nineteenth century nationalism and historicism. Although he did not seek for laws determining the development of peoples and states, he had a profound respect for law as such and for historical institutions, and he argued, with Herder, that the circumstances and influences that determine a nation's history are unique and must be studied objectively without superimposition of a priori preconceptions. Uncharitable critics have seen in this viewpoint of Ritter's merely a cheap effort to exculpate German history from guilt for militarism and Nazism.

Because of his endemic patriotism Ritter was maligned by many

---

[190] Schieder, review of Ritter's *Staatskunst und Kriegshandwerk*, Vol. III, in *Historische Zeitschrift*, CCII (1968), 398.

English, French, American and German expatriate scholars who, still fighting the battles of World War II, regarded the unitary, Prussian-dominated, German state as a blot on the escutcheon of humanity.[191] These critics imputed to Ritter an anti-Western philosophy, which he, in fact, had never had. On the other hand, he was also reviled by Soviet-oriented Marxist historians for trying to resurrect an excrescent German imperialism and merge it with Western, capitalist imperialism. The Marxists accused him of being (as were all leading West German historians, in their eyes) a reactionary who was a stormtrooper of Konrad Adenauer's and Kurt Kiesinger's in their offensive against the Slavs and their DDR shield.[192] The thinking of each of these schools basically proceeds from a repudiation of the ideal of a strong, unitary, and sovereign Germany. While "neo-racists" are inclined to empty every poison in their apothecary upon those who defend the German record, the Russian school of falsification sees in Ritter's vision of a liberal-conservative social order the antithesis of the classless society, and in a reunited Germany the main obstacle in the way of a continental Soviet Russian empire of puppet peoples.

Ritter's sympathy for his countrymen, broken on the rack of mammoth wars, led him increasingly to emphasize the primacy in history of the ideological and individual over the materialist and mass. This perspective, inherited from Kant, Carlyle, and Sybel, planted Ritter unmistakably in the main stream of Western thought. A conservative of moderate views, as were Bismarck and Bethmann Hollweg, he cherished the nineteenth century ideal of an élitist but individualistic society which, seen at its best, was suffused with a paternalistic regard of the ruling establishment for the state and the whole people.

This philosophy of responsible élitism, which Fischer would simply write off as "authoritarianism," excluded sympathy for collectivist methods and mob rule, which were the dubious gifts of the French and Russian revolutions.[193] Ritter's political philosophy forced him narrowly towards the study of great leaders. In the

---

[191] Hallgarten, *Das Schicksal des Imperialismus,* 92–93.
[192] Berthold, "Der politisch-ideologische Weg Ritters," 960, 989.
[193] Fischer, *Weltmacht oder Niedergang,* 97.

course of painstaking research he had had occasion to ponder the fact that without systematic training in history, a political figure must lack real expertise and a *sens de choses possibles*. In the twentieth century, more than ever before, ignorance of history is the precursor of charlatanism. Thus it was that Ritter reviewed the thoughts and deeds of preceptors from the German past in the hope of discovering in the patterns of their lives threads of morally acceptable political conduct. He concluded that policy-making by independent, enlightened civilians, in contrast with *ad hoc* action taken by demagogues in response to military or mass pressure, was what distinguished rational from irrational government.

The man who wrote *Die Dämonie der Macht* was, however, no utopian. Ritter's devotion to Germany, the "state of the European middle," forced him to affirm that the survival of sovereignty within the framework of the continental states system depended upon the sanction of military power. The all-important addendum to this proposition was that true statemanship sets limits to the appetite for aggrandizement. The great political leader wields power without succumbing to it. For him force is merely the ul-timate resort for attaining morally justifiable, circumscribed goals. Responsible statesmanship is guided by ethics and a profound re-gard for law, national and international. To have revealed to his countrymen the postulates and worth of a *Rechtsstaat* may well have been Gerhard Ritter's noblest service.

GAETANO SALVEMINI:
Meridionalista

GEORGE T. PECK

Greenwich, Connecticut

To CHARACTERIZE Gaetano Salvemini as a *meridionalista*, that is, one who was concerned with the problems of his native South, may seem to place undue limitations both on his breadth of vision and his notable achievements as a historian and teacher. Such a characterization may even seem farfetched to the English-speaking public, which is far better acquainted with his work as an anti-Fascist than with the *meridionalismo* of his youth.[1] And yet his political thought and much of the inspiration for his historical work from 1896, the date of his doctoral thesis,[2] until the outbreak of the Libyan War in 1911 was centered around the southern question. During these fifteen years of intense activity he added a new dimension to thought about the South.

Even when he later turned to other interests, Salvemini never attempted to escape the strong direction which his extraordinary southern background gave him. He was born in Molfetta in Apulia in 1873, and despite the poverty and obscurity of his home town, he said with pride: "I am Molfettese to the marrow of my bones." [3]

The Molfetta of the seventies and eighties went through a period of slightly diminished need, carried along by the boom in the production and sale of wine, and the Salvemini family was able to make ends meet. The latter was in many ways typical of

[1] It is indicative that Denis Mack Smith frequently refers to Salvemini's later activity but not to his *meridionalismo* in *Italy, A Modern History* (Ann Arbor, 1959). By contrast, Lelio Basso thinks of the youthful Salvemini as the "best Salvemini," in *Gaetano Salvemini, socialista e meridionalista* (Manduria, 1959), 6–7.

[2] Salvemini, *La dignità cavalleresca nel commune di Firenze* (Florence, 1896).

[3] Basso, *Gaetano Salvemini, socialista*, 19.

[206]

the petty bourgeoisie of the South, drawing its income both from a twenty-odd-acre piece of land rented out to peasants, and from the salary of the father, a part-time teacher. The income was spread thin to raise nine surviving children. In some respects the family was atypical: the mother read a daily newspaper, entered into the frequent political discussions in the home, and read to her five-year-old son the story of Count Ugolino from the *Inferno* —a story which, together with those from the Bible, was hardly calculated to quiet the imagination of the future historian. The uncle, a priest, was one of the three citizens of Molfetta who in 1860 voted against Victor Emmanuel and in favor of the Bourbons—for which he was nearly stoned. It was the uncle who took the education of Gaetano in hand. While, much to the chagrin of the teacher, the student soon abandoned Bourbonism and came to think of the priesthood as a last-ditch alternative to any other intellectual occupation, he became a voracious reader and claimed in later life that he had taken his intransigence from his uncle. He developed into a brilliant student, and none too soon, for one of the disasters which are so common in southern life struck.

The tariff war broke out with France as a result of the Italian protective tariff of 1887. France stopped buying the wines of Apulia and, along with many others in Molfetta, the Salvemini family found itself destitute. In 1889 Salvemini was one of a few students in all Italy to win a scholarship at the Institute of Higher Studies in Florence, and the family was so poor that he had to pay his train fare from his scholarship. In Florence he padded his income by tutoring and sent money home each month. Fortunately for him, another of the patterns of southern emigration entered his life; he was taken in once a week by an Apulian family and given a square meal. Already he was the age-old southern emigrant, finding his place in life in the wide, indifferent world.[4]

On the face of it, such a background may not seem extraordinary, but it was not really until the publication of Carlo Levi's *Christ Stopped at Eboli* in 1947 that the outside world realized

[4] Enzo Tagliacozzo, *Gaetano Salvemini nel cinquantennio liberale* ("Quaderni del Ponte"; Florence, 1959), 3–12. Professor Tagliacozzo was Salvemini's assistant at Harvard from 1940 to 1944.

how remote from modern civilization such southern towns as Molfetta were.[5] As Carlo Levi showed so directly, southern society is divided into the life of the peasants and that of the petty bourgeoisie. This dichotomy had been suggested before, indeed as early as 1880 in the work of Giustino Fortunato and it played a large role in the thought of Salvemini.[6]

Perhaps Salvemini's most important contribution to the discussion of southern problems was his ability to understand the peasants' point of view in any and all circumstances and to express it with piercing clarity. As almost all the other spokesmen for the South were of petty bourgeois background and ideas, and thus on the other side of the social world, his identification with the peasants was almost unique. On the other hand, Salvemini loaded the intellectual petty bourgeoisie with all the opprobrium he could command and thus expressed the existing dichotomy of the society. His sharp insistence on the contrast between these two classes is a central and frequently repeated theme.

> They say that we Southerners are intelligent. And certainly the mass of the rural population, in hourly contact with the painful and arduous reality of life, is very intelligent; at least it is more intelligent than the peasantry of Lower Lombardy or the Ligurian mountains. The proof of this lies in its attitudes toward work and saving, as soon as it has emigrated and found a less wicked environment.
>
> But things change when one considers the bourgeoisie. Visit some summer afternoon one of those "clubs of the civilized" in which is gathered the finest flower of rural laziness. Listen for a few hours to the conversation of that fat gentry with dull eyes, cracked voices, with half-unbuttoned clothes . . . gross and vulgar in word and deed. Notice the stupidity, the nonsense and the unreality with which their talk is stuffed. And then have the courage to say that Southerners are intelligent!
>
> What is the origin of the deep intellectual difference between the "civilized" and the "country" population of the South? I don't know. Perhaps manual labor and the life in the open air saves the peasants from the degeneration which very quickly takes hold of the do-nothing family in that soft and malaria-ridden climate. At least

---

[5] Carlo Levi, *Christ Stopped at Eboli*, tr. Frances Frenaye (New York, 1947).
[6] Giustino Fortunato, *Il mezzogiorno e lo stato italiano, discorsi politici, 1880–1910* (2nd. ed.; 2 vols.; Florence, 1926), 58.

this is certain: that between the *galantuomini* and the *cafoni* of the South there are not only profound and most visible differences in manner of dress, in the dialect, and in everyday life, but also real, actually somatic differences. The peasant is thin, dried up, and a most persistent worker; the "miles quadratus" of Roman times must have been like him. The "civilized" man is corpulent, flaccid, inert, and good for nothing. When the "civilized" man makes fun of the peasant, he tries to disguise his voice, making it bass and masculine, while it is normally falsetto and feminine; he thinks he is satirizing the peasant, but he is really displaying his own degeneracy.[7]

As can be seen, Salvemini applied strong moral judgments to each class. It is not too much to suggest that the moral pattern of his life and work grew out of the life experience in this split society. On the side of the *cafoni* stand directness of speech, simplicity, concreteness, honesty, and hard work; and on the side of the *galantuomini* are rhetoric, complexity, abstractness, corruption, and laziness. These themes of moral judgment, refined by an orderly and immensely learned mind, came to be expressed in precise, schematic verbal form which could encompass any subject. It is perhaps because of such a clear and thoroughgoing moral system that one of Salvemini's most famous and most beloved successors, Piero Gobetti, wrote: "Salvemini is too uncomplicated to understand." [8]

The sharp moral contrasts of the southern class structure and the necessity of not making mistakes, so costly in the struggle for survival in Molfetta, were lessons driven home by Salvemini's university experience. In Florence he discovered Cesare Paoli, professor of paleography, Pasquale Villari, perhaps the leading Italian historian of his generation, and Karl Marx. Of this time, Salvemini wrote: "Almost all these old teachers belonged to that current of thought which is today [1949] disdained as 'positivist,' 'illuminist,'

---

[7] Salvemini, *Movimento socialista e questione meridionale*, in Salvemini, *Opere* (10 Tomes, 19 Vols.; Milan, 1960–   ), Tome IV, Vol. II, 484.

[8] Ernesto Sestan, Armando Saitta, Rosario Villari, Eugenio Garin, and Enzo Tagliacozzo, *Gaetano Salvemini* (Bari, 1959), 151. This book is a collection of commemorative essays by some of Salvemini's outstanding students. Subsequent references to the book will be by name of individual contributor. And see Wilda M. Vanek, "Piero Gobetti and the Crisis of the 'primo dopoguerra,'" *Journal of Modern History*, XXXVII (March, 1965), 2, 7, 8, 13.

or 'intellectualist'. . . . We classified ourselves clearly as believers or unbelievers, monarchists or republicans, individualists or socialists. White was white and black was black. Good was good and evil was evil. Either on this side or that." [9]

Under the guidance of both Paoli and Villari, Salvemini learned well the tools of his craft and developed that strict adherence to the testimony of secure documentation which he practiced, not only as a historian but also as a political writer analyzing tricky newspaper reports to get at underlying truth.[10] Salvemini admired in Villari the use of history to understand contemporary events and the dedication of the citizen and patriot to the welfare of his people. At the time of Villari's death in 1918, Salvemini wrote: "He did not pass by any of our national diseases without a cry of warning—the *camorra*, the *mafia*, brigandage, farm contracts, rural usury, local administration, public health in Naples, the plight of the sulphur miners . . . the treatment of child labor . . . the disorganization of the secondary schools, the campaign against classical studies by a bourgeoisie which wanted to enjoy social privileges but refused to exert any intellectual effort to deserve them." [11]

Villari was indeed a *meridionalista* [12] and Salvemini was soon to take up the cudgels in the same matter. Also from Villari, Salvemini caught the intellectual fire of a great teacher.

It cannot be said that his lectures were really on history and historical method. The other teachers in the Institute provided this. Each of the latter were neat, precise, inflexible. Each took a room

[9] Salvemini, *Che cosa è la cultura?* (Modena, 1954), 55. This is an excellent example of what Garin called Salvemini's "Manichean simplicism," Garin, *Gaetano Salvemini*, 190–92.

[10] Salvemini, *Historian and Scientist* (Cambridge, Mass., 1939), 49–55; Ernesto Sestan, "Gaetano Salvemini," *Il Ponte*, XVI (February, 1960), 182, 183; Elide Guastalla, *Salvemini, l'attualità del suo pensiero storico-sociale* (Rome, 1954), 29–34, 59–63.

[11] Salvemini, "Pasquale Villari," *Nuova rivista storica*, III (March–April, 1918), 121–22.

[12] Villari's first important statement on the southern question was the *Lettere meridionali* (Turin, 1885). And see Bruno Caizzi, *Nuova antologia della questione meridionale* (Milan, 1962), 323–36; Rosario Villari, *Il sud nella storica d'Italia, antologia della questione meridionale* (Bari, 1963), 105–17; Enzo Tagliacozzo, *Voci di realismo politico dopo il 1870* (Bari, 1937), 70–82.

in that unfurnished or badly furnished house which was our culture, and taught us to keep it in order, to mend the crippled furniture, and to change or throw out what was in bad taste. He went into all the rooms, threw open the doors and windows, let in light and air, and even disarranged the order of the others. Officially he taught modern history. In reality, he taught us an infinity of other things too; above all he taught us not to be mummies, but to be men.[13]

Salvemini's own students were to get from him the same intellectual excitement, the same commitment to social injustice, and the same rigorous historical method.

His ideas on the function of history guided him in the selection of subject matter; but once he had thrown himself into the work with all the ardor of his temperament, he treated the subject as a historian, concerned only with clarifying the historical terms, with distinguishing the essential historical features, and with searching out the immediate and remote causes and trends. No one, not even among his many adversaries, was ever able to charge him with writing tendentious history or with adapting the interpretation of the past to the ideas, passions and hopes of the present.[14]

Like nearly all the generation of young intellectuals in the nineties, Villari's students became socialists. Even Benedetto Croce, whose mature thought was so far removed from socialism, flirted with socialism in his youth.[15] As for Salvemini, the doctrines of Marx fitted in with the dichotomy of his southern experience and complemented the positivism of his historical studies. All his life he remained faithful to many of the basic socialist doctrines, just as he remained faithful to the peasants of his native land. During the period of his most active involvement in the southern question, Salvemini was a member of the Italian Socialist Party. In the nineties, the movement had not yet developed the Byzantine rigidity and theocratic pettifoggery characteristic of any aging

---

[13] Salvemini, *Che cosa è la cultura?*, 42–43.
[14] Sestan, "Gaetano Salvemini," 177–78.
[15] Benedetto Croce, *A History of Italy, 1871–1914*, tr. Cecilia M. Ady (Oxford, Eng., 1929), 145–48. Salvemini told a curious story in the Chamber of Deputies about Croce, in which he said that Croce subscribed 1,000 lire to help found the Socialist daily *L'Avanti*. Salvemini, *Dalla guerra mondiale alla dittatura, 1916–1925*, in *Opere*, Tome III, Vol. II, 601–602.

dogma. As Salvemini reminisced in 1955: "This was a happy time, when communist society was being automatically developed in the heart of capitalist society, thanks to the concentration of wealth and the political growth of the industrial proletariat. Whoever spread the gospel of the new civilization was in the central stream of human history, and like the Christians of the first generations, was sure that the Kingdom of God would soon arrive." [16]

Socialism to Salvemini was an emotional and moral commitment, and at this time he thought of the Italian Socialist Party as the channel through which all liberal and progressive forces could express their resistance to the repressive governments of Di Rudinì and Pelloux.[17] His admiration for such Socialist leaders as Filippo Turati, Oddino Morgari, and Leonida Bissolati was profound. He wrote: "The Socialist Party was the tree in the shade of which we dreamed the purest dreams of our youth. The men who founded and still lead [1911] the party were our most effective teachers." [18]

Having received his doctorate in 1895, Salvemini went on to earn his living as a high school teacher, serving in four different schools between 1895 and 1901. The Marxist struggle was the central theme of his rapidly maturing thought and was expressed both in his historical work and his political life.

Salvemini was deeply indebted to Marx as a teacher of historical method. His first great work *Magnati e popolani in Firenze dal 1280 al 1295* was a significant event in Italian historiography.[19] "For the first time Florentine legislation was seen in relationship to economic and social class conflict. . . . In the following years other historians followed the same method, and many books were composed applying historical materialism to the problems of

[16] Salvemini, *Movimento socialista*, 668.

[17] *Ibid.*, 64–67, 306–307. And see Salvemini, *Il ministro della mala vita*, in *Opere*, Tome IV, Vol. I, 5–51.

[18] Salvemini, *Movimento socialista*, 508.

[19] First published in 1899, the work was republished in 1960 by Einaudi and in 1966 by Feltrinelli in the *Opere*, Tome I, Vol. I. See the bibliography in Gene A. Brucker, *Florentine Politics and Society, 1343–1378* (Princeton, 1962), 406–408; Lauro Martines, *The Social World of the Florentine Humanists, 1390–1460* (Princeton, 1963), 387–97.

ancient and mediaeval history." [20] The work won him a full professorship at the age of 28 at Messina in 1901.[21] Though it has to some extent been outmoded by later scholarship, it was republished in 1960 and again in 1966.

While developing his Marxist analysis of mediaeval Florence, Salvemini was using the same technique on his own southern society. The publication of his study of Molfetta in the leading socialist journal, the *Critica Sociale*, in March, 1897, marks his entrance into political life both as a socialist and as *a meridionalista*.[22] Like all his early articles, it was signed with a pseudonym, as writing in socialist journals could cause inconvenience for a young high school teacher. Whatever the pseudonym, here was a new voice and an unmistakable new style, described by one commentator as "aggression with the pen." [23] Salvemini was embarked on a fourteen-year career of forcefully bringing the southern question to the attention of the Left.

The Molfetta article is a clear example of what was later called "concretism"—Salvemini's ability to present the broad sweep of great social movements through precise, specific facts.[24] It was unique in that it analyzed succinctly the social classes of the town from a socialist point of view. Scorning the windy abstractions of political rhetoric, Salvemini got down quickly to the "amorphous mass of little incidents, of stupidities, of vulgarities, of eccentricities which are told by gossiping wives to illiterate husbands . . . of fierce hatreds growing out of the contested possession of a tree or a boundary wall." These were the stuff of class conflict. Of the three classes in Molfetta, fishermen, peasants, and townsmen, he placed his hopes for progress in the peasants.

[20] Tagliacozzo, *Salvemini nel cinquantennio liberale*, 31. And see Ernesto Sestan, "Salvemini meridionalista," *Rassegna storica toscana*, IV (April–June, 1958), 87–91.

[21] Luigi Ambrosoli, "La 'carriera' di Gaetano Salvemini dall'insegnamento ginnasiale alla cattedra universitaria," *Il Ponte*, XX (August–September, 1964), 1051–1066.

[22] "Un commune dell'Italia meridionale: Molfetta," in Salvemini, *Movimento socialista*, 9–26. At the end of his life he came back to the same scene in "Molfetta 1954," *ibid.*, 656–68.

[23] Garin, *Gaetano Salvemini*, 152.

[24] Salvemini, *Il ministro della mala vita*, 425.

The latter, in turn, he divided into four groups: (1) small land-owners, who in true socialist fashion were about to disappear; (2) renters (*fittaioli*); (3) trained agricultural workers (*massai*); and (4) the great mass of day laborers (*braccianti*). The attention of the Socialist Party should be directed to the last two groups; and considering the crushing poverty, the program to be presented to them should be primarily economic—the creation of a union, the fight for better wages, and the abolition of the municipal excise taxes on essential consumer items.

For support Salvemini also looked to the workers among the townsmen, many of whom were artisans while some few were employed in small local food and construction industries. They would not only understand immediately the political appeal of socialism but could also be organized to obtain specific economic advantages, such as better wages and shorter hours, the elimination of graft and tax farming from the municipal administration, free school meals, vocational schools, and perhaps even a consumer cooperative.

The adversary in Salvemini's characteristic dichotomy was the petty bourgeoisie of the town—the *luigini* of Carlo Levi[25]—not the great landed proprietors who hardly existed in Molfetta or in most of the other coastal regions under intensive cultivation.[26] Salvemini knew his adversary well. He described how in the desperate effort to rise from the peasantry, the petty bourgeoisie scrounged to educate children for the liberal professions or government employment, there being little commerce and less industry to employ middle-class people. This led to an elephantine excess of doctors, engineers, lawyers, and bureaucrats, and, consequently, a fierce competition for jobs. The unemployed petite bourgeoisie could easily be converted to socialism, but the Socialist Party should avoid them because they were interested only in getting jobs. A brief history of the political parties in Molfetta drove home the point that, regardless of party label, political activity in the South was merely the struggle of "ins" and "outs", the merciless

[25] Levi, *Christ Stopped at Eboli*, 17–19, 26.
[26] Manlio Rossi-Doria, *Riforma agraria e azione meridionalista* (Bologna, 1948), 28–32.

rivalry of tightly organized clienteles which corrupted political life from the township to the provinces and finally to the national Chamber of Deputies.[27]

While Salvemini was soon to integrate his *meridionalismo* with a large view of national policy, he by no means lost interest in Molfetta. In the winter of 1901–1902, he drew up a specific socialist program for the town and expounded it in three public lectures.[28] The general outline of the program followed typical reformist socialist lines, but he added to it a detailed knowledge of the educational system, arguing that the town should support evening classes to combat peasant illiteracy and that the central government should provide useful vocational secondary education.[29]

Within a year of his publication of the Molfetta article, Salvemini abandoned the doctrinaire socialism of these first *meridionalista* efforts by introducing an important modification of his Marxist stand. As he wrote later: "Small property did not disappear; it was there and he [Salvemini] saw it. The dogma of the concentration of wealth was struck dead."[30] One of the first points which he made in his "Contributions to the reform of the minimum program" (1897) was that small property should not be forcibly suppressed. Since he had become convinced that small landowners, especially in the areas of intensive cultivation, were one of the strongest forces for change and progress, he soon passed over to the attack and urged that small landowners be encouraged to continue their gradual encroachments on the lands of the great *latifondi*.[31] Later history amply justified his judgment.

Then, during the winter of 1898–1899, Salvemini reported that he had "discovered in the municipal library [of Lodi, where he

---

[27] Salvemini, *Movimento socialista*, 9–26.   [28] *Ibid.*, 249–64.

[29] Salvemini's interest in education added to his stature as a *meridionalista*. With Giuseppe Kirner, he founded the union of high school teachers in 1901. In 1906 he was one of a commission of three named by the Minister of Public Instruction to study the problems of secondary education. He and one of the other commissioners, A. Galletti, resigned because they disagreed with the minister. They published their findings in *La riforma della scuola media* (Palermo, 1908).

[30] Salvemini, *Movimento socialista*, 670.

[31] *Ibid.*, 55, 267. The latter reference is a letter to Turati published in the *Critica Sociale* of January 1, 1903.

was teaching] the Lombard political writers of the late eighteenth and early nineteenth centuries, and Carlo Cattaneo, who soared over them all like an eagle. Even today, more than a half century later, I look back to that time with joy and nostalgia as the finest time in my life." [32]

The result of Salvemini's interest in Cattaneo was twofold: first, he began to rethink Risorgimento history by attacking what he called the "hagiography of the victors" and, second, he applied the positivism and federalism of Cattaneo and the republicanism of Mazzini to the southern question. In the "Le origine della reazione" and "I partiti politici milanesi del secolo XIX," which were published in 1899, he analyzed the conflict between the popular national movements on the one hand, and the monarchical, "moderate" (but really conservative) forces behind the Piedmontese leadership on the other.[33] Applying this insight to the situation of 1899, Salvemini argued that the repressive government of Pelloux and the reactionary cliques of the court of King Umberto I were not temporary aberrations but the logical continuation of Cavourian policies. The repressed popular movements of the Milan of 1848 were compared to those of 1898, known as the "Fatti di Milano."

Salvemini saw the history of Milan in the forties and fifties through the eyes of Cattaneo, depending heavily for his interpretation on Cattaneo's two works, *L'insurrezione e la guerra del '48* and *Archivio triennale della cose d'Italia dall avennimento di Pio IX all abbandono di Venezia.*[34] What Salvemini most admired in Cattaneo was his intransigent defense of the achievements of the Milanese insurrection against both the Austrian power and the efforts of the Lombard and Piedmontese aristocracies to use the popular forces for their own limited and selfish goals. He shared Cattaneo's hatred of Piedmontese militarism and administrative centralism, the rigging of elections by bureaucratic violence, and

[32] *Ibid.*, 671.

[33] Salvemini, *Scritti sul Risorgimento*, in *Opere*, Tome II, Vol. II, 6, 13–123.

[34] Cattaneo, *L'insurrezione e la guerra del '48* (Florence, 1949), first published in 1849; *Archivio triennale delle cose d'Italia dall'avennimento di Pio IX al'abbandono di Venezia*, Vol. V of Cattaneo, *Opere edite e inedite*, edited by A. Bertani (7 vols.; Florence, 1881–92).

the suppression of free speech. He also shared Cattaneo's positive faith in the essential wisdom of the people, in the virtues of local autonomy, and in the efficiency of federal union on the Swiss or American model.[35]

Here was indeed a kindred spirit. Both men came from large petit bourgeois families, both had had inspiring teachers, both became school teachers, and both had come to know the sociological details of town life. What we can see now is the striking parallels in their total lives: both founded intellectual weeklies, both mistrusted revolutionary rhetoric, both believed in the fighting qualities of Italian soldiers, both believed in economic progress, both retired from political struggles at critical moments in Italian history, both refused to serve in parliament, both were unwilling to accept the compromises of party discipline, both believed that Austria should become a federation of democratic republics, both tried to tell the truth about Italy to foreigners, both spent many years in exile, and, finally, both returned to Italy in their old age, only to find that history had passed them by.

In 1899 the federalism of Cattaneo fitted into Salvemini's understanding of the struggle between *galantuomini* and *cafoni*. The central government used the very extensive powers at its disposal to intimidate or crush socialist local administrations. Writing of two northern municipalities, Imola and Turin, Salvemini pointed out that no serious improvement in the lot of the common people could be obtained by socialist administrations, unless the latter were willing to fight the central government even if that meant defying the law. There was no use compromising with the state in the manner of the reformist socialists; nor was there any use to talk revolution, wait for the "inevitable" to come and do nothing, in the manner of the revolutionary socialists. Municipal councils should stand up for a democratic program, be dissolved by the prefect, and then be reelected on the basis of the program —until finally the central government would give in to popular pressure. Salvemini urged that the town councillors of the Left

---

[35] Salvemini, *Scritti sul Risorgimento*, 373–92. This is the introduction to his selections from Cattaneo's works, *Le più belle pagine di Carlo Cattaneo* (Milan, 1922). And see Piero Pieri, "Gaetano Salvemini storico dell' età moderna e contemporanea," *Rassegna storica toscana*, IV (April–June, 1958), 94–100.

gather in a national convention in order to give each other confidence and to learn how to fight the state—an extraordinary proposal when one considers that, under the Italian system, town councillors had much less power and sense of their own dignity than Yankee selectmen.

The devil in the piece was the prefect, and in one of his more polemical outbursts, Salvemini wrote: "If Lombroso should prepare a new edition of *L'uomo delinquente,* he should dedicate an entire chapter to that most pernicious form of political delinquency which goes under the name of the Italian prefect." [36] Backing up the prefect were the armies of bureaucrats who were the real rulers of the country.

In the South, where no socialist municipal administrations existed, this machinery held undisputed sway over the lives of the people. The government represented an alliance of great landowners, militarists, and their clienteles, dating from the time of the Unification. The only channel of protest was riot, and in that case, the army was called in to defend the hated *galantuomini.* Nor was that other mechanism of central government, the royal commission, of any use. Writing of Naples, the administration of which had fallen into complete confusion as a result of the rivalries of the *camorra,* Salvemini stated that the royal commission appointed to rule Naples would merely set up one faction of the *galantuomini* in all the administrative and elective offices, leaving the situation virtually unchanged.

At this point Salvemini expressed federalism in its most extreme form. He would have left to the central government only the handling of foreign affairs, the currency, and the tariffs; all other powers would be concentrated in regional, provincial, municipal, and even neighborhood organizations, which would all be chosen by universal manhood suffrage. Naples was to be run like London. This was the period of his greatest faith in the capabilities of the *cafoni.*

As time went on, this faith was gradually dissipated and Salvemini substantially modified his federalism. His inability to

---

[36] Salvemini, *Movimento socialista,* 629. On Imola, *ibid.,* 30–31; on Turin, *ibid.,* 45–48; on the conference of town councillors, *ibid.,* 137–39.

shake the Giolittian machine in the administrative elections of 1902 led him to the conclusion that the army of *cafoni* had no sergeants and that the peasants needed "guides" from all regions to foster their political development. His study of the secondary schools convinced him that only the central government could provide an efficient system. Later on, the more the Giolittian, and eventually the Fascist system, became entrenched in Italian life, the more he lost faith in the peasants. But even at the end of his life, he argued forcibly for greater local autonomy and railed against the "prefectocracy", his arguments buttressed by his experience in Britain and the United States.[37]

How signally this aspect of Salvemini's *meridionalismo* failed is shown not only by the survival of the strong central adminis-tration but also by the fact that in a recent study of it, Cattaneo is not mentioned at all and Salvemini only peripherally. Yet one of his friends was prompted to write "that Salvemini appeared a greater force in Italy when he lost than when he won." [38]

The role of an unheeded prophet was not uncongenial to Salvemini's southern individualism. As he said, "Southerners never agree among each other, and sometimes it happens that a Souther-ner does not even agree with himself." [39] From the very beginning of his career in 1897, his position in the Italian Socialist Party was unique. As one Socialist leader remarked: "Salvemini . . . is a little too batty to tie down." [40] The great argument in the party in 1897 was over the minimum program, supported by the reformists, and the maximum program, put forward by the revolutionaries. He was for neither, believing that the program should be flexibly adapted to particular historical opportunities. On the one hand, he despised the revolutionary wing, led by the Neapolitan Enrico Ferri, whom he thought a mere talker; and on the other hand, he could not share the easygoing, good-naturedness of the reformist leader, the Milanese Filippo Turati.

In the Milanese riots of 1898, Turati did his best to calm the

---

[37] *Ibid.*, 168–73, 181–91, 205–21, 241–42, 621–27, 674, 688.
[38] Robert C. Fried, *The Italian Prefect: A Study in Administrative Politics* (New Haven, 1963), 120, 149; Giuseppe Prezzolini, *Amici* (Florence, 1922), 119.
[39] Salvemini, *Movimento socialista*, 333.
[40] Anna Kulishoff to Turati, quoted in Basso, *Salvemini*, 35.

workers and went to jail for his pains. Salvemini believed that the revolution was at hand and wrote to Turati advising him as to how to capitalize on the riots. Fortunately, Turati destroyed the letter or Salvemini would have been jailed, too. In Salvemini's view, the entire regime was about to crumble because of the narrowness of the constitutional consensus; neither the people nor the clerical reactionaries were represented in the constitutional regime. The Chamber of Deputies represented substantially only one party, and to Salvemini, who always kept the goals of the South in mind, there was little difference between the liberal Giolitti and the reactionary Pelloux. Salvemini consistently called for the union of all leftist parties to fight this monolithic state.[41]

Of course, the revolution did not come, but driven by his interest in how revolutions do come, Salvemini set about composing his finest book, *The French Revolution*, which went through eight Italian editions.[42] What is perhaps most striking about this beautiful synthesis is, on the one hand, the blindness, selfishness, and confusion of the privileged groups, and on the other, a sympathetic understanding of the popular forces. While the parallels to Salvemini's thought on the southern question are obvious, the book stands as an objective historical work. Albert Mathiez described it as the best existing manual on the period: "There is not an important fact which is not brought to light and explained in its causes and consequences; there is not an actor in the drama who is not presented at the right moment. It is wonderful to follow such an intelligent guide and such a pleasant narrator." [43]

Salvemini's vision of the southern question was given new depth by the publication in 1900 of *Nord e Sud*, by Francesco Saverio Nitti.[44] "The wealth of the North," Salvemini wrote, "has been produced by the misery of the South—here is the truth which has been luminously documented in Nitti's book." [45] Nitti established

---

[41] Salvemini, *Movimento socialista*, 52–89, 92–133, 601; Basso, *Gaetano Salvemini, socialista*, 22–35; Garin, *Gaetano Salvemini*, 175–76; Saitta, *Gaetano Salvemini*, 53–58.

[42] Salvemini, *La Rivoluzione francese, 1788–1792*, in *Opere*, Tome IV, Vol. I. The English translation by I. M. Rawson (New York, 1954).

[43] Salvemini, *La Rivoluzione francese*, in *ibid.* And see Franco Venturi, "Salvemini storico," *Il Ponte*, XIII (December, 1957), 1794–1801.

[44] F. S. Nitti, *Scritti sulla questione meridionale* (4 vols.; Bari, 1958), Vol. II.

[45] Salvemini, *Movimento socialista*, 167.

beyond question that Italian national policy favored the North, and after the tariff of 1887, the industrial North, at the expense of the South. In relation to the wealth of the regions, the South paid proportionately heavier taxes; in addition, southern capital, invested in national bonds and in postal savings, flowed north. The national government spent far more per capita in the North on all its services: most military and naval installations were in the North, more was spent per capita on railways and all public works in the North and impoverished Basilicata paid as much per capita in school taxes as rich Lombardy and got back only a fourth as much as Lombardy in school expenditures. In 1904, when the Giolitti government passed special laws to favor the South, the latter were greeted with derision by the *meridionalisti*; Salvemini callel them "shoddy packages at 48 cents apiece"; Antonio De Viti Marco called them "crusts of bread." [46] As it subsequently developed, the special laws were a total failure.

Nitti's argument on tariffs was espoused by Salvemini, who knew from personal experience in his family in Molfetta what a disaster the tariff of 1887 was. The tariff barred the products of intensive peasant cultivation from foreign markets, especially France. However, the large landowners did not suffer, because much of their production was wheat; their political support was bought by the high tariff against American imports. Furthermore, these landowners profited when they were able to acquire for a song the vineyards and orchards which the now bankrupt peasants had spent years developing.

Antiprotectionism became a strong theme in Salvemini's *meridionalismo*. Here he was joined by De Viti de Marco, Luigi Einaudi, and Gino Luzzatto, all of whom were free traders and later wrote for Salvemini's weekly *L'Unità*.[47] Salvemini's particular contribution to the campaign was to urge within the Italian Socialist Party the reduction and eventual abolition of tariffs. He met with strong northern resistance, for the tariffs favored the in-

[46] *Ibid.*, 235, 157–91; Antonio Papa, "Antonio De Viti de Marco," *Belfagor*, XX (March 31, 1965), 196; Villari, *Il Sud*, 388–402.

[47] Antonio De Viti de Marco, *Un trentennio di lotte politiche, 1894–1922* (Rome, 1929); Luigi Einaudi, *Cronache economiche e politiche di un trentennio* (Turin, 1959); Enzo Tagliacozzo, "La collaborazione di Gino Luzzatto all'Unità di Salvemini," *Nuova rivista storica*, XLIX (January–April, 1965), 121–36.

dustrial workers as well as the industrialists and capitalists. The organized workers of the North, and especially the producers' co-operatives, were more interested in their own economic gains than in the welfare of the working classes as a whole; they even went so far as to favor high industrial tariffs and condemn the wheat tariff, the only one that favored the agricultural community in any way, in order that they might have cheap bread. Salvemini commented: "The socialists confined themselves to each cultivating his own garden; and in the rest of the country, the Government preserved intact its ability to smother every movement of administrative opposition and to continue its traditional work of oppression and perversion." [48]

Narrow business unionism condemned Italian socialism to impotency. Salvemini unceasingly argued that the great majority of people in both North and South were agricultural workers and that the support of the latter was needed for the advance of socialism. Yet it was only after the war that the General Confederation of Labor seriously considered supporting free trade, and by then it was too late.

From the high vantage point of the present, after the "Italian miracle" has taken place, it can be seen that the national economic policy of encouragement of industry eventually paid off, to the benefit of both North and South. But Salvemini and his generation are dead and it is questionable that such great sacrifices on the part of the South were really necessary.[49]

While Salvemini accepted the substance of Nitti's argument, he clashed with him vigorously on the subject of federalism, for Nitti looked to the central government as the agent of progress. The general flavor of Salvemini's critique was astringent; later he was to praise Nitti and condemn an excessively critical spirit in Italians and, by implication, in himself.[50]

[48] Salvemini, *Movimento socialista*, 590. On free trade, see *ibid.*, 272–73, 281–94, 354–90, 590–94, 604–607, 616–18.
[49] Rosario Romeo, *Breve storia della grande industria in Italia* (2nd ed.; Rocca San Casciano, 1963), 44–112; Alexander Gerschenkron and Rosario Romeo, "Lo sviluppo industriale italiano," *Nord e Sud*, VIII (November, 1961), 30–56.
[50] In the preface to A. William Salomone, *Italian Democracy in the Making* (Philadelphia, 1945), viii: "If one judges the handiwork of Italian pre-Fascist politicians by the standards of some flawless ideal—the method of the political crusader—there is no politician who would not be sent to Hell."

By contrast, Salvemini never regretted his criticism of Alfredo Niceforo and others who introduced a racist note into the southern question. He and Napoleone Colaianni were among the first to condemn racism unconditionally: [51] "I deny absolutely that the 'character' of Southerners, which differs from that of Northerners, explains in any way the differences in development of the two sections. Race is formed in history, it is an effect of it and not a cause, and it is transformed in history. To explain the history of a country by the word 'race' is for lazy simplists." [52] When these words were written, the physical anthropological school of Cesare Lombroso was in vogue, and Salvemini treated its claims with contempt: "Today fools, camouflaged as anthropologists, go down South, measure a hundred noses, count the ridges on the fingertips of the right hands, study the shapes of the coccyx, and deduce from these the inferiority of the Southern race in comparison with the Northern." [53]

Salvemini went on to remind his readers that the same type of racist explanations were applied to the Lombards in Cattaneo's time. What outraged him most of all was the thesis that life was predetermined by race, climate, or natural forces. Such determinism denied the freedom and dignity of the individual.[54]

Similar to the racists were those who considered the southern peasants as barbarians. In 1910 cholera broke out in Molfetta and the peasants demonstrated against the Red Cross. The newspapers sensationally reported the demonstrations as riots and cited them as examples of southern ignorance and barbarism. Salvemini sprang to the defense of his people. He wrote with great feeling how a peasant woman—mistakenly, no doubt—would defend her family against the medical authorities who had never previously taken any interest in her but who now came to snatch away her beloved ones to what she believed to be certain death in the hospital . . . among strangers. Then they would burn literally every stick and stitch that the family had spent years in amassing; many peasants had no other property but clothes and household effects. Salvemini

---

[51] Villari, *Il Sud*, 431–44.   [52] Salvemini, *Movimento socialista*, 134
[53] *Ibid.*, 167.
[54] Salvemini, *Historian and Scientist*, 158–60; Villari, "Salvemini," 106–107; Garin, *Gaetano Salvemini*, 172; Basso, *Gaetano Salvemini, socialista*, 48–49.

reported with accuracy the bureaucratic stupidity of the Red Cross and the irresponsibility of the municipal administration which, by demagoguery, channelled the fears of the people against the outsiders from the Red Cross.

It was a sad story, only to be repeated the next year on a much larger scale at Verbicaro. The latter town, which later became notorious as one of the most wretched places in all Italy, had its cholera epidemic and was abandoned by almost all the *galantuomini* officials. When a few heroic local doctors begged for aid, the prefect sent in *carabinieri* to restore order. Salvemini commented bitterly: "The 'Government' is respected because it has rifles and sends people to jail. The 'galantuomini' are obeyed because the 'Government' is with them." [55]

To Salvemini, one of the key ways of bringing about progress in the South was to obtain the vote for the illiterate *cafoni*. Universal manhood suffrage was the fourth major theme of Salvemini's *meridionalismo*—next to those of local autonomy, educational reform, and the removal of fiscal and economic oppression. From 1900 to 1911 he hammered incessantly on those four "nails." He wrote in 1900:

> Certainly knowing how to read and write is today an absolute necessity. . . . But this does not mean that the illiterate is incapable or stupid. If that were true, then Italy, which is a country of illiterates, would be a country of idiots. The illiterates do not know how to do addition or multiplication, pen in hand, but they know very well how to do them in their heads. They do not know how to translate their ideas from dialect into the literary language and they don't know how to put words on paper. But they do know how to reason and defend their interest vocally, and many illiterates have a thousand times more common sense than many learned men. To be an illiterate is a misfortune. But this should be no reason to burden the illiterate with the added misfortune of considering him a beast of burden, deprived of intelligence and incapable of protecting his interests or exercising his rights.[56]

The northern socialists objected to universal manhood suffrage because it would not do them any good. Their constituencies

---

[55] Salvemini, *Movimento socialista*, 435–44, 493–97.   [56] *Ibid.*, 177, 413.

consisted mainly of educated urban workers and they feared the influx at the polls of illiterate peasants who were, in the North, very much under the influence of the clergy. While granting the possibility of initial socialist defeats at the hands of the clericals, Salvemini answered that the peasants could be converted to socialism by an active propagandist effort. As for the South, Salvemini brought out a point which few would have made; he affirmed the profound religious indifference of the southerners. At the height of the struggle for universal manhood suffrage in 1910, he wrote: "The priests, who in general come from the same petite bourgeoisie as the lawyers, professional men, the bureaucracts and the displaced persons, and who, in general, have all the vices and baseness of their class, have no prestige and exert no moral leadership. In the eyes of the peasants they are people who perform magical exorcisms to sanctify certain solemn moments in life, to save the crops from accidents and to assure the passage to Heaven in due time . . . but they do not have any authority at all in concrete questions of immediate interest." [57]

By the way, such a comment was factual and does not imply any anticlericalism on Salvemini's part. On the contrary, he despised anticlericalism as a pastime of the *galantuomini,* and welcomed the collaboration of clerics (such as Don Luigi Sturzo) who had the real interests of the peasants at heart. Furthermore, he had a deep respect for religious faith; and while apparently lacking in religious experience, his moral vigor had a firm Christian foundation.[58]

Salvemini's commitment to universal manhood suffrage received a strong reaffirmation during the general elections of 1904. He returned to Molfetta and campaigned for the Socialist candidate Francesco Picca, speaking on street corners to great crowds of peasants, most of whom could not vote. Here he saw for the first time the Giolittian system at work. Giolitti wished to have the Republican incumbent defeated and used the Socialists to help unseat him. In the days, immediately prior to the elections,

---

[57] *Ibid.,* 418. And see Ernesto de Martino, *Il mondo magico* (Turin, 1948).

[58] Late in life, he wrote: "By now I believe only in the *Crito* of Plato and the Sermon on the Mount. This is my socialism." Basso, *Gaetano Salvemini, socialista,* 19.

hired thugs, protected by the police, roamed the streets to intimidate the electors; and Salvemini himself shielded the Republican
opponent from attack. Giolitti's man was elected and Salvemini
concluded: "I played the part of a fool. So began my hatred of
Giolitti. He had made me his accomplice, the captain of his
thugs." [59]

While Salvemini was driven by his hatred of Giolitti, he was
inspired by the example of Mazzini. In 1905 he published his *Il
pensiero religioso politico sociale di Giuseppe Mazzini*, which, like
his study of Cattaneo, cut through the hagiographical mists, and
which was the progenitor of many later historical works.[60] He was
moved by Mazzini's faith in the people as they express themselves
through universal manhood suffrage, Mazzini's fanatical sense of
duty, and his "grand heroic vision of the world, of history and of
life." Though disapproving of Mazzini's highflown and abstract
rhetoric, Salvemini admired, and to a certain extent, emulated him
as a man of action.[61]

Salvemini was not perhaps as full of hope as Mazzini because
he had the characteristic southerner's expectation of the worst.
Occasionally he used the pseudonym "a pessimist," and, like Fortunato, he faced the reality of the South, where the worst was
likely to happen.[62]

On the morning of December 28, 1908, it did. For several years
Salvemini had been teaching at the University of Messina. He had
some time earlier persuaded his favorite sister to come and live with
his family, which by now consisted of his wife and five small children. On that December day, while Salvemini was out of town
all were killed in the earthquake of Messina. On the following
days, Salvemini searched the rubble in the hope of finding his
youngest child alive. The body was never recovered.[63]

[59] Tagliacozzo, *Salvemini nel cinquantennio liberale*, 60, 61.

[60] Republished in 1915 under the simplified title, *Mazzini*, the work is incorporated in *Scritti sul Risorgimento*, 146–251. It has been translated into English
by I. M. Rawson (London, 1956). Other Mazzinian studies are in *Scritti sul
Risorgimento*, 254–392. One of the more notable later studies is that of his
student, Nello Roselli, *Mazzini e Bakounine, 12 anni di movimento operaio in
Italia* (Turin, 1927). See Piero Pieri, "Salvemini storico," 106–12.

[61] Salvemini, *Scritti sul Risorgimento*, 240.

[62] Fortunato, *Il mezzogiorno e lo stato italiano*, II, 468.

[63] The facts were virtually unknown until Tagliacozzo described them, *Salvemini
nel cinquantennio liberale*, 78–79.

In the spring of the following year, Salvemini read of electoral pressures of the Giolittian machine in Gioia del Colle and decided to find out what was happening, saying, "Maybe they will shoot me and that will be the end of it." [64] Arriving in the Apulian hill town accompanied by two newspapermen, he was told to take the next train out of town and when he refused, was all but besieged in his hotel. As usual, hired thugs were in complete control of the streets under the protection of the police, the meeting place of the peasants was locked, and Salvemini was unable to find a single person in town who admitted to being opposed to the Giolittian candidate. Finally he found two members of the opposition hiding in the countryside. They said: "The police are against us. Our opponents are armed and we are not. They arrest us and not them. We tried to go in a group, but the police dispersed us; they take the clubs away from us and give them to them." [65]

Salvemini also succeeded in interviewing the Giolittan candidate and members of his clientele. The result of the election was a foregone conclusion and the new deputy was seated, despite incontrovertible proof of his fraudulent election. Salvemini concluded that the only possible course was to appeal to public opinion and composed his most famous pamphlet, *Il ministro della mala vita*. The "minister of the underworld" was, of course, none other than the most powerful political figure of the time.

> When the crimes committed in Southern elections by prefects, police officers, and governmental rogues are reported in such a precise manner that the Hon. Giolitti cannot dodge the discussion . . . when they are certified in such an incontrovertible manner in every particular that the Hon. Giolitti cannot contest them . . . when they are so grave that the Hon. Giolitti cannot confine his defense to some doltish witticism . . . the Hon. Giolitti suddenly puts on the mantle of a saddened moralist and deplores the fact that political morals have not progressed enough. "I didn't make Southern Italy," he likes to repeat in the Chamber of Deputies.[66]

Salvemini carried on his campaign against Giolitti in the columns of a new Florentine intellectual weekly, *La Voce*, and in the halls of the Socialist congresses.[67] At the Congress of Florence

[64] *Ibid.*, 117.   [65] Salvemini, *Il ministro della mala vita*, 98.   [66] *Ibid.*, 135.
[67] *Ibid.*, 142–62.

in 1908, hatred of Giolitti led him to say that if Giolitti ever proposed himself the introduction of universal suffrage, the Socialists should still fight him. "Systems of oppression and corruption have always been used, more or less, in Southern Italy from 1860 to today. But with time and experience, they have been perfected, and the Hon. Giolitti has made them insuperable. This explains why the Hon. Giolitti is cordially detested by all the honest people in our towns. . . . In fact, no one has ever more cynically, more brutally, and more systematically trampled on our honor and dignity than he." [68]

It was, of course, Giolitti, who in 1911 suddenly proposed universal manhood suffrage. In the previous year, Premier Luigi Luzzatti had introduced an electoral reform bill of his own which would have moderately extended the electorate by granting the vote to those who held a certificate indicating the completion of elementary school. Salvemini fought this bill, and by carefully analyzing Milan and Turin, showed that it would not benefit the Socialists and would deprive them of the propaganda value of their universal manhood suffrage program. Few thought that this slight reform would help the South at all; hence, the argument was directed at the northern Socialists, the "smug Socialists" under the leadership of Ivanoe Bonomi, who supported the Luzzatti government.[69]

After several months of parliamentary fencing, Giolitti pulled the rug from under Luzzatti. By proposing universal manhood suffrage he split the Socialist opposition; by offering the glory of the Libyan War he got the support of the emerging nationalists and thus he easily replaced Luzzatti as prime minister.[70] Salvemini greeted the new electoral law with a sour leader in the *Avanti!*, entitled "Dinner at Eight A.M." and argued that the country was not ready for the law.

Salvemini's campaign was instrumental in creating that atmosphere of public disapproval which eventually drove Giolitti from power. In later years he was to repent his adamant opposition to

---

[68] Salvemini, *Movimento socialista*, 337.
[69] Salvemini, "Il socialismo che si contenta," in *ibid.*, 459–81.
[70] *Ibid.*, 596–98; Salomone, *Italian Democracy*, 73–76, 106–109, 111.

Giolitti and to judge him superior both to his predecessor, Crispi, and his successor, Mussolini. He even admitted that his criticism of Giolitti had helped the reactionary elements and, after the war, the Fascist movement.[71]

The reason Salvemini made such a mistake was that he had a firm faith in Italian democracy. Although he was pessimistic enough to foresee some of the trials of the First World War, he was not so pessimistic as to believe that a reactionary regime, like those of the nineties, would recur in Italy under the guise of fascism. Those who later criticized him for having little faith in the people [72] and those who dismissed his socialism as "youthful infatuation" [73] do not sufficiently take into account his deep attachment to the Italian Socialist Party. He was a thorn in the sides of his best friends, not so much because of a cold and intransigent moralism as because he expected of them the same generosity which was second nature to him. Not unpredictably, he was disappointed.

As the early years of the century rolled by, Salvemini pleaded for the understanding of the North, urged the northerners to forsake their parochial interests for the common good and begged them to come South to lead the *cafoni*. As early as 1899, he wrote: "Northern Socialists should consider Southern peasants as their younger brothers, in need of all their help. . . . In other countries the industrial proletariat has understood that it can do nothing without the help of the rural proletariat. . . . In Italy the difference between urban and rural proletariat is in several respects the difference between Northern and Southern proletariat." [74]

When the governments of Zanardelli and Giolitti came into power after 1900, Salvemini was among the first to understand the danger of Giolittian progressivism to the Socialist Party. It was

[71] See note 52 above. The change of perspective on Giolitti after the Fascist experience is admirably shown in A. William Salomone, "Salvemini e Giolitti," *Rassegna storica toscana*, IV (April–June, 1958), 125–57.

[72] Garin, *Gaetano Salvemini*, 184–91; Saitta, *Gaetano Salvemini*, 44, 92.

[73] Tagliacozzo, *Salvemini nel cinquantennio liberale*, 71. And see Beniamino Finochiario's review of Tagliacozzo's and Basso's books, *Il Ponte*, XV (July–August, 1959), 994–96.

[74] Salvemini, *Movimento socialista*, 89.

clear to him that Giolitti's main purpose was to broaden the ruling class by including in it the working classes of the North. In this way he could tame the Socialist Party; and by 1912, he boasted that he had done it. From the very beginning, Salvemini attacked the tacit support for Giolitti on the part of his reformist socialist friends: "There is no more fallacious or dangerous illusion than this, that a unitary government—even democratic—can solve the Southern question. . . . What happened first to the Right and then to the Left (from 1860 to 1890) will happen to the democratic government—outside a liberal façade and inside the vermin of the *camorras* of both North and South." [75]

As the northern Socialists began to reap the material benefits of Giolittian progressivism, Salvemini exclaimed: "The ministerialism of the Northern Socialists has been for us a continual bloody outrage. . . . We have seen our workers killed without pity at the least sign of disorder, while in the North the police treat the workers most tolerantly and considerately." [76] The whole battery of social reforms which greatly improved the lot of the northern workers was meaningless in the South. For example, the laws regulating female and child labor, and those limiting the hours of work, were irrelevant in the South, where almost any kind of work was a way of staving off hunger. "What do we want to socialize in the South?" Salvemini asked, "Misery?" [77]

What the South needed was political, not social, reform—local autonomy, free trade, universal manhood suffrage, education, and freedom of speech and assembly. Turati and Bonomi answered, rather smugly, that the South was in a precapitalist stage, and that, therefore, Salvemini was talking about the bourgeois revolution. Turati did not believe that socialism could have any appeal in this backward region; and while the socialists of other countries were struggling with the problem of how to deal with the agricultural classes, the subject was all but ignored in overwhelmingly agricultural Italy. [78]

However, at the Congress of Florence in 1908, Salvemini was

[75] *Ibid.*, 189.   [76] *Ibid.*, 316.   [77] *Ibid.*, 313.
[78] *Ibid.*, 248. And see *ibid.*, 268–70, 320–21; Villari, *Gaetano Salvemini*, 115–20; Saitta, *Gaetano Salvemini*, 53–77.

given an oportunity to speak for the South. Though he did not claim to speak for all the South, describing himself as an independent *franc tireur*, he laid his entire program before the delegates. Starting with the theme of antiprotectionism, he charged the northerners with self-interest in their support of industrial protectionism and opposition to agricultural protectionism. Proceeding to his second theme, he showed how the flaccid support for electoral reform contributed to the continuation of the southern condition, where no legal means of opposition were available. His third point was that any efforts at reform on the local level were smothered by the "unshakable" Giolittian machine and the omnipotence of the central administration. Peasant leagues, producers' and consumers' cooperatives, and Socialist municipal administrations, on which the northern Socialists founded their power, were impossible in the South, where the disenfranchised had no chance against the *galantuomini* backed by the power of the state. The crux of Salvemini's argument was that the Socialists of both North and South would be impotent as long as Giolitti controlled the Chamber of Deputies. "How can you expect to dislodge the parliamentary majority as long as Southern political representation is not renewed?"

The resurrection of the South would not be an easy task. The state would have to "modify the taxation and tariff systems, organize technical schools, develop and intensify the road system, the reforestation program, the control of rivers [land reclamation], etc. . . . The world certainly won't change from one moment to the next; we would be foolish and unfair if we hid from you the fact that this will take the period of an entire generation." [79]

Eventually—in the last twenty years—the rebirth did take place, requiring the efforts and investment of the entire nation, but Salvemini wanted it in 1910. Foreseeing that the nation was ready to embark on foreign adventures, Salvemini adumbrated what was to become the central theme of his activity from 1912 through 1925—his concern for a democratic foreign policy. Already in 1908, more and more Italian efforts were going into an attempt

[79] Salvemini, *Movimento socialista*, 341, 391–434, 511.

to become a great power, and the only way of obtaining resources to build the South was by taking them from the military budgets and by fighting the emerging nationalism of the middle classes. No Socialist, with the exception of Leonida Bissolati, Salvemini said, was in the slightest degree ready or willing to combat this danger. A measure of the failure of Italian democratic forces is that the nation seriously turned its attention to the South only in 1945, after the disillusionment of nearly forty years of disastrous foreign adventures.

Salvemini rapidly lost faith in the Socialist Party; he fought the "oligarchism" of the party, only to see it grow more firmly entrenched. "Take care of yourself; I'm taking care of myself. This has been the real program and method of daily action of Italian socialism for the last decade. And so when it is a question of taking care of oneself, always the strongest, the best organized, and the voters succeed in taking care of themselves, and the bill is paid by the weak, the disorganized, and the non-voters."

Finally, after the new electoral law was passed, he abandoned the organization. While this decision grew out of his disillusionment, he perhaps also hoped that he could better educate the electorate of the South and better fight the now more vulnerable Giolittian machine as an independent. He founded his weekly *L'Unità* and Gino Luzzatto later commented: "His independence was extremely useful, because it offered him the possibility of exercising his function far more effectively than in the closed circle of a party. His most characteristic and most valuable function was always that of stirring up new ideas and new energies, and of directing wide attention to several problems which were absolutely vital to the future of our country. With the passing of years he showed himself a true precursor in the stating of these problems, and described tactical attitudes toward their solution which were absolutely unsuspected." [80]

Of the precursors of contemporary *meridionalismo*, Salvemini and Fortunato are perhaps the most prominent. Looking back today, one is inclined to link their names, to think of them as col-

[80] Guastalla, *Salvemini*, 53; Beniamino Finocchiaro, "*L'Unità* di Gaetano Salvemini," *Rassegna storica toscana*, IV (April–June, 1958), 153–78.

laborators in an organized stream of thought; and so it comes as a distinct surprise that they did not even know each other before 1908. Despite the small size of the Italian intellectual class, they lived in two different worlds: Salvemini among teachers, writers, and socialists; Fortunato in the Chamber of Deputies and in the remote hill towns of Lucania. They were isolated voices crying out in the wilderness. Salvemini wrote later: "I have always been sorry that I did not get to know two men sooner, Antonio De Viti de Marco and Giustino Fortunato. My thought would have had ten more years to become more subtle, stronger and richer." [81]

After the war, Salvemini's *meridionalismo* was taken up by Antonio Gramsci and became one of the distinctive features of the new Italian Communist Party. As Salvemini was clearly heterodox from the Marxist point of view, Gramsci ungraciously denied his debt, but it existed none the less. [82] At the same time Salvemini's relations with that other leading *meridionalista* of the 20's, Guido Dorso, were always cordial. In 1925, Dorso considerably deepened the understanding of the sociology of the South by analyzing more closely the processes of the formation of the ruling class, and he directed attention at ways of overcoming the perennial conflict of *cafoni* and *galantuomini*. [83]

Here was the main current of thought which culminated in the transformation of the South in the last two decades—a transformation largely attributable to Salvemini's students and friends. [84] Gaetano Arfè wrote in 1955: "In giving the first impulse to this great movement, an enormous contribution was made by one who nearly sixty years ago undertook with desperate energy his lonely battle for the peasants of the South—the one who had faith in them without demagogy and without mysticism." [85]

[81] Guastalla, *Salvemini*, 12.

[82] Salvemini, *Movimento socialista*, 677–79; Villari, *Gaetano Salvemini*, 122; Villari, *Il Sud*, 535–67.

[83] In *La rivoluzione meridionale* (2nd. ed.; Turin, 1949), Guido Dorso, *Dittatura, classe politica e classe dirigente* (Turin, 1949); Caizzi, *Nuova antologia*, 405–32; Salvemini, *Movimento socialista*, 619–21.

[84] When Salvemini returned to Italy for the European Federalist convention in 1947, he was greeted with a heartfelt tribute from Ferruccio Parri and an ovation from his many friends; Guastalla, *Salvemini*, 22.

[85] Gaetano Arfè, "Il meridionalismo di Gaetano Salvemini," *Il Ponte*, XI (December, 1955), 2013.

In the course of his life, especially during the anti-Fascist period from 1925 to 1944, events and study changed his perspectives. He saw that he had made mistakes, but he was afraid neither of mistakes nor change. Of historians, Salvemini wrote: "Even when he [the historian] errs, he remains an honest man and a scientist." He worked "by moral impulses from which I cannot separate myself; for were they to disappear from my make-up, my whole personality would disintegrate." [86] Even if he was dogged by what Garin called "Manichean simplism," his moral and intellectual clarity was a blessing in a period of Fascist relativism and confusion.

What was important to him was that he was loyal to his people. Reminiscing in old age, he wrote: "One evening, when a group of us were talking at the farm of my best friend under the starry sky, in the mild coolness after a summer's day, a peasant said to me: 'You never tricked us.' These words, spoken in the dark, were fixed in my spirit and never after left it." [87]

[86] Salvemini, *Historian and Scientist*, 84, 126.
[87] Salvemini, *Movimento socialista*, 681.

ERNEST LABROUSSE

PIERRE RENOUVIN
La Sorbonne

D URING THE PAST twenty years economic and social history has occupied a particularly large place in French historical studies.* According to figures recently compiled, 41 percent of the doctoral theses in modern or contemporary history being written in 1961 at the Faculty of Letters of the University of Paris were in this area of research.[1] The growth of this field is without doubt directly related to the intellectual trends and preoccupations of our time. But there is every reason to believe that its expansion would not have been so rapid if the professor of economic history at the Faculty of Letters had not pushed it vigorously. During those twenty years this chair has been occupied by Ernest Labrousse, who was trained in economics as well as in history. Because of his leadership in the domain of methodology, the direction of his research, and his attempts at synthesis, he exerted a strong influence on young scholars. I propose to sum up the principal features of his work.

Labrousse gave brilliant evidence of his gifts as a researcher in two important studies published ten years apart: *L'Esquisse du Mouvement des Prix et du Revenu en France au XVIIIe Siècle*, whose two volumes appeared in 1933, and *La Crise de l'Economie française à la Fin de l'Ancien Regime et au Début de la Révolution*, published 1943. In both books he was mainly concerned with a critical study of sources and interpretive techniques.

---

* Translated by Elaine P. Halperin.
[1] J. Schneider and Philippe Vigier, "L'orientation actuelle des études historiques," *Revue historique*, CCXXV (1961), 397–406.

[235]

Esquisse, with a preface by the economist Roger Picard and the economist Henri Sée, sets out to substantiate and describe, but not to explain, a movement that persisted over a considerable period. The eighteenth century, at least from 1730 on, is a good period for the study of prices and revenues because the value of money was stable, the cost of transportation fluctuated only slightly, and, save for the years 1762–63, the tariff policy was constant. But how does one assemble solid evidence, work out, and verify statistical data? When he studied the price of wheat, Labrousse realized the inadequacy of those sources to which the historian is at first tempted to refer. There are great discrepancies between the "indexes of prices" for a few local markets compiled at the time. As for the "general indexes" elaborated in a report made in December, 1792, by the member of the National Convention, Creuze-Latouche, they indicate neither the source of the figures nor the method of calculation. Such sources are therefore practically useless. On the other hand, the "subsistence bureau" of the Controller General of Finance had performed the important task of making fiscal estimates and determining tariff policy. Twice a month this agency received the "price lists" drawn up by the four hundred subdelegates and based on the *mercuriales* of the places were they lived, and then proceeded to check the figures. In order to correct the discrepancies that resulted from the diversity of weights and measures, it worked out an index based on known facts. This source seemed therefore to be a reliable one. Unfortunately, the "general price lists" for the nation as a whole have disappeared, with the exception of two compiled in 1777 and 1779. The author examined the modalities according to which these two lists had been drawn up and thus determined how reliable they were.

This was a masterly application of the statistical method to the materials of economic history. Labrousse utilized the teachings of William Oualid, Albert Aftalion, and François Simiand, as well as his early gleanings as an instructor of economics at the Faculty of Law in the University of Paris. But he enriched them with the contributions of historical methodology and the exceptional quality of his own documentation. Employing the same techniques, he studied the price of other cereals, of vegetables, wine, meat, and fodder. He also attempted to work out a price index for manufactured goods.

The study of income posed even more complex problems. To calculate income from land, Labrousse relied on rural leases available in the archives of charitable institutions and ecclesiastical bodies. But the various forms of income, monetary and in kind, had to be distinguished. It was even more important to determine the components of such income by examining the situation of farming and nonfarming landowners, of *métayers* and renters, and by distinguishing between agricultural laborers who paid in cash and those who paid in kind. Still another obstacle loomed before Labrousse: the historian does not have at his disposal annual statistics on harvests for the eighteenth century because the statements drawn up by the bureaucracy give only approximate estimates that make it possible to assess productivity but not production. Labrousse tried to surmount this obstacle and almost always succeeded. However, he never concealed the fact that an element of uncertainty remained in the bases of his calculations. All these analyses attest his sureness as well as his ingenuity.

What are the results of this remarkable effort, this penetrating criticism? Labrousse's study established the fact that the prices of all products increased after 1730, that this rise persisted despite cyclical fluctuations until 1817 (it reached 56 percent for wheat), but that the rise was uneven, depending upon the product. Variations were greater for food products of mediocre quality (greater for rye than for wheat, for example). It was therefore the poor who were most affected by the increase in food prices. Income from land, on the other hand, benefited from a rise equal to or even higher than that of the price of agricultural commodities. But the landowner who did not cultivate his land—the nobleman or bourgeois—was far more advantaged than the landowner who did. Finally, the rise in tenant farming, which increased rapidly between 1770 and 1779 and continued until 1790, was considerably greater than the rise in prices. As for wages, their rise averaged 17 to 22 percent—far less than that of agricultural prices. Wages in terms of "consumers' goods," that is to say, *real* wages, thus decreased. During a time when the price of cereals was increasing greatly, wage earners were obliged to reduce their other expenses—beginning with that for apparel. An examination of the statistical data leaves us in no doubt about this: the textile industries were obliged to reduce production, whereas the price of cereals rose rapidly, and the high cost of food resulted in industrial unemployment.

These observations reflect Labrousse's main concern: to measure the "social repercussions" of the fluctuations of prices and revenues. With this in mind he addressed himself to the study of a family budget in a working-class milieu, seeking to determine the proportion spent respectively for food, clothing, and meat. Similarly, he endeavored to establish the cyclical fluctuations of industrial unemployment on the basis of data provided by the reports of the Inspectorate of Manufactured Goods. The economic history of the eighteenth century, to which he gave fresh impetus, assumes its full significance, in his opinion, only when it flows into social history.

But the conclusion of the book opens up still other vistas. It shows the impact of price and income fluctuations on economic doctrines and institutions. The rapid growth of income from land led the physiocrats to regard land as the chief source of wealth. A little later, it impelled the Constituent Assembly to establish a land tax as the basis of a whole new fiscal system. On the other hand, there developed a "growing contradiction" between the fiscal system of the old regime and the fluctuations of income. Because of the tax exemptions enjoyed by the nobility and clergy, the public exchequer did not profit from the increase in land income. The government, for its part, persisted in relying on consumers' taxes even though the yield was poor because real wages were going down. Thus, a study of the economic situation explains the financial crisis that beset the government of Louis XVI. It makes "an experimental contribution to an evaluation of the great interpretive hypotheses of history."[2]

The second book, *La Crise de l'Economie française à la Fin de*

[2] Ernest Labrousse, *Esquisse du mouvement des prix et des revenus en France au XVIIIᵉ siècle* (2 vols.; Paris, 1933), I, xxvi.

l'Ancien Régime, proceeds along similar lines. Here "economic fluctuations" are the central interest. The author addresses himself at greater length to problems he had already tackled in his *Esquisse.* The rise of prices and income from land that he had recorded for most of the eighteenth century did not continue; it was interrupted by a recession from 1778 to 1789 and even by a cyclical crisis. It was on this crisis that Labrousse focused his attention. To ascertain the fluctuations of prices, he supplemented the "general statements" of the *mercuriales,* which he had used earlier, with fresh sources. During these years the office of the Controller General, which served as a ministry of the national economy, expanded its control and received increasingly abundant information. It urged upon the intendants the necessity of punctual and conscientious compliance with its instructions. The sources for historical research are therefore much more precise than those available for the period prior to 1778. In attempting to establish statistics on production, the historian relies on the assessments of harvests that the four hundred subdelegates had to draw up each year on September 15. To follow the population fluctuations, he has only to consult the annual list of births, marriages, and deaths which the intendants after 1772 were supposed to compile.

It is true that a part of this enormous statistical documentation established by the Controller General's bureaus has been lost. But what remains enables the researcher to discover with adequate precision the economic and social fluctuations of the late eighteenth century. To be sure, none of these sources is "irreproachable": doubtless there are numerous errors of detail in these lists. However, the careful analysis to which Labrousse has subjected them in an effort to discover the reasons for such mistakes (for the most part involuntary) and to assess their significance does yield reassuring results. His rigorous examination of the conditions under which these statistical series had been elaborated and checked warrants "in an immense majority of cases" a favorable judgment.

Up to this point the work merely complemented and stated more precisely facts and observations that had already been presented in *l'Esquisse*. But Labrousse did not confine himself to "observing and describing"; he wished to explain, to seek the causes of these economic fluctuations and to measure their consequences. The historian undertakes a quest for causes in a spirit quite different from that of the economist. Whereas the latter endeavors, "in fact, if not in theory," to discover a *law*, the former notes *repetitions* and *relationships*; he sets himself the task of "identifying the stable, recurring concomitants among phenomena, while doubting the element of permanence." He knows that "concomitance sometimes repeats itself only for a brief period," that even if its repeats itself over a long period, "it never does so indefinitely." As for a study of the consequences, it is important to note the extent to which these economic fluctuations modify the material situation of a group or social class, reduce or increase the "social gaps," lessen or exacerbate class antagonisms. When someone's standard of living is affected by an economic crisis whose basic factors escape him, he tends to impute the cause to an individual—the Controller General. "Economic causality retains its old anthropomorphic aspect." Thus the social crisis becomes a political one.

Labrousse could not expect to apply simultaneously these general views and methodological precepts to all the sectors of agricultural and industrial life. He decided first to study the viticultural economy, expecting to undertake other similar studies, which he has never had time to complete. Why did he select vineyards and winegrowers? He did so because at that time the cultivation of vineyards was widespread throughout most of France; because the prosperity or depression of viticultural production was a good indication of the general economic activity; and, finally, because the proceeds from viticulture held an important place in "the income of the rural population."

Application of the methods defined in the first part of the book paved the way for important observations regarding the viticultural sector. The price of wine, after a long period of rise, declined in 1778–80 because of overproduction, but also because of underconsumption (this decline reached 51 percent). Despite some changes due to the quantity and the quality of the vintage, the price generally remained low until 1787; it rose a little in 1787–88 but did not reach the level it had attained between 1760 and 1770. The figures for viticulture as a whole decreased from 1770 to 1791. The income of the winegrower who cultivated his vineyard fell because the cost of production and the price of fertilizer rose. "Viticultural income," that is to say, the income of the winegrower who did not cultivate his vineyard himself, also declined but less markedly. The small winegrowers who cultivated their own vineyards were far more numerous than those who did not. Consequently, "the collapse of viticulture economy weighed more heavily, in absolute terms, on the least resistant social category—in other words, on the mass of winegrowers who cultivated their own vineyards." As for prices and profits, the lowest point was reached in 1786.

This agricultural crisis had political consequences. The small winegrowers constituted among the rural masses a kind of "artisan class" that used techniques better than those of other peasants. They were very sensitive to all the variations of fiscal policy because the taxes that affected the circulation of wines—the *aides*— were a factor in "underconsumption." These winegrowers were also sensitive to changes in tariff policy because they sold their crops directly and therefore understood the importance of external outlets. Hence, it was to the decisions of the government that they tended to attribute responsibility for the crisis. Finally, the winegrowers, who lived in an "open economy" whereas their clients lived in the city, were in a good position to serve as intermediaries between the city and the country, to transmit "urban passwords" to the peasants. Here was an original social milieu in which "a rational and independent élite" was taking form.

Thus, Labrousse, having pioneered in the domain of economic history (he was so well aware of this that he found it necessary to compile a glossary of the economic and statistical terms he employed), opened up broad perspectives in the domain of general history. The interpretations derived from his statistical studies led him to tackle the problem of the origins of the French Revolution. "The economic conjuncture," he wrote, "largely created the revolutionary conjuncture." The reign of Louis XV had been the beneficiary of favorable economic conditions, whereas the reign of

Louis XVI coincided with a "cyclical crisis." Does not this "reversal" have a direct influence "on the most vital internal problems"? The pressure exerted on agricultural income by seigneurial rights and fiscal burdens increased because the profits of tenant farmers and small landowners who cultivated their own lands decreased.

To be sure, historians, even before they possessed such statistical data, had already noted that 1789 was a year of "expensive bread." But Labrousse's work enabled them to describe with exactitude this "pressure of the economic milieu" on political events. It demonstrated that the shortage of agricultural commodities following a very poor harvest in 1788 led to an increase in the price of wheat which reached its height in July, 1789. This increase in agricultural prices produced a crisis in the textile industry—as shown by a comparison of statistical curves (deprived of its customers, most of whom were farm laborers, workers, and artisans, "textiles weakened"). Finally, the economic crisis seriously affected the crisis in public finance. This "thrust" of 1789 had all the more impact on contemporaries because it dealt a blow to an economy that for ten years had been weakened by a long and serious illness, by a fall in profits, and by unemployment.

> Revolutionary events . . . therefore spring, in large part, from the decrease in profits and wages, from the financial embarrassment of the industrialists, artisans, farmers, and landowners who cultivated their land, and from the distress of workers and day-laborers. An unfavorable conjuncture joined the bourgeoisie and proletariat in a common opposition. In this respect, the Revolution appears, far more than Jaurès and Mathiez realized, "a revolution of poverty," even though the eighteenth century, considered as a whole, remains nonetheless a period of expansion. According to Georges Lefèbvre, the great historian of the French Revolution, "Ernest Labrousse's research in economic statistics presents the origins of the Revolution in an entirely new light."

This new and original research had disclosed Labrousse's dominant concern. With the aid of these tables and graphs obtained from the enormous mass of documentation which he had mastered, he aspired to enlarge the horizons of social and political history. This same preoccupation with basic problems is apparent in two works of synthesis whose importance is comparable even though their nature and scope are very different.

The first of these is merely a communication presented in 1948 at the closing session of the congress on the centenary of the Revolution of 1848.[3] It was published under the title *1848–1830–1789 —Comment Naissent les Révolutions?* These three great upheavals, Labrousse says, have some common characteristics: they surprised their contemporaries ("Revolutions occur in spite of the revolutionaries. When one takes place, the government does not believe it. And the average revolutionary wants no part of it!"); they mobilized the masses, whose action was spontaneous; they were "endogenous," that is, they were determined by an *internal* situation (in contrast to the revolutionary movement of 1871 where the determining factor was the influence exerted by the *external* situation). These are "predominantly social" revolutions; therefore they derive in large part from economic facts. If one studies not the remote origins but "the very fact of the explosion," one notes in all three instances the existence of a "state of economic tension."

In 1789 it was the two poor harvests of the preceding years that caused a considerable increase in the price of bread, a considerable decrease in the buying power of peasant producers and urban consumers, and consequently, an industrial crisis.

In 1830 the sequence was analogous: poor harvests in cereals and potatoes in 1827–28; "subsistence disturbances" in 1828–29 that were the direct consequence of these shortages; a crisis in the textile industry that was an indirect consequence of the shortages. Finally, there was a decline of 30 to 40 percent in wages. The situation improved, it is true, at the end of 1829; the political crisis did not equal the paroxysm of the economic crisis; however, it is quite plain that the discontent provoked by the economic difficulties contributed greatly to the coming of the revolution. In 1848 it was the potato blight that caused (as early as 1846) the agricultural difficulties, which in turn again affected the textile

[3] *Actes du Congrès historique du centenaire de la Révolution de 1848* (Paris, 1948), 1–31.

industry. But a fresh crisis was superimposed on this one because the government, owing to the decrease in its revenue, was obliged to curtail the credits that it had granted for railway construction. This immediately damaged the infant metallurgical industry, whose production decreased by one third while wages fell and unemployment spread. This economic crisis consequently produced "social convulsions." The difficulties, however, were attenuated by the end of 1847. The February Revolution of 1848 occurred *after* the critical period. But, Labrousse points out, it was this crisis that "aroused" all the discontent against Louis-Philippe's regime. The newspapers of the period show that public opinion imputed to the government and to the errors of its economic policy the responsibility for the discouraging situation. Doubtless it was not the crisis that filled the more militant opposition groups with revolutionary fervor, but it did sweep along all the undecided, the "floaters." And if, during the February days, the National Guard remained passive in the face of the uprising, did it not do so because the lower and middle bourgeoisie, where it was recruited, had detached themselves from a political regime that they held responsible for the difficulties of the times?

Labrousse realized, however, that this "economic" explanation of revolutionary movements has certain limits: "There are decennial economic crises; there are no decennial revolutions." What, then, are the other causal elements? The historian should not overlook moral factors, national factors, which are preeminently emotional, or idiosyncrasies of certain men; he should neglect "neither the individual nor the role of chance." But above all he must study the capacity of the government to resist. In order to have the kind of "explosive mixture" from which revolution suddenly springs, "the economic crisis must encounter the political crisis." In a political crisis a financial crisis sometimes plays an important role. But the political crisis is essentially a crisis of the regime, "reflecting, to a great extent, anterior social antagonisms that deeply divide the ruling class or ruling classes": for example, the conflict between the bourgeoisie and the aristocracy in 1789 and in 1830; the "triangular" conflict in 1848 between the upper bourgeoisie, the lower bourgeoisie, and the masses. For revolution to break out, still a third condition is necessary: a provocative act of imprudence committed by the government that will cause the "mixture" to explode.

Should one, then, adopt a "unitary" interpretation of history? Labrousse says no. "The economic fact," he observes, "is a major one in our view, but not at all the only one." He is not unaware that in the three cases on which he has dwelt, the economic explanation rests on particularly strong foundations. He realizes that in other revolutionary movements, economic factors have played far less important roles. But even though he has revitalized this domain of research by contributing new methods, he still affirms his conviction that history must "be permeated with sociology." The few concessions he makes to those who contradict him do not shake his certainty. While condemning the "puerile excesses" of certain champions of historical materialism, he remains convinced that the economic interpretation has proved to be "one of scholarship's most powerful and fecund hypotheses."

The second of his works of synthesis, written in 1953, is devoted to *La Société du XVIIIe Siècle devant la Révolution.*[4] There could be no question of contributing new documentary data to a vast subject which had already been treated in numerous studies. What mattered, then, was the personal interpretation of the author. It was expounded with great vigor.

The revolution of 1789, Labrousse says, developed "in the city of the eighteenth century," and was accomplished *by the city.* It was the work of the Third Estate. Why did this Third Estate acquire fresh strength? Because, after 1730, there was a spurt in population growth caused mainly by a drop in mortality rates. This population increase gave rise to a growing demand for agricultural products and consequently to a rise in the price of commodities and in income from land. It also stimulated the textile and building industries. The urban bourgeoisie, which not only engaged in industrial or commercial activities but also had an important share of land holdings, had greatly benefited from the situation; it was prosperous. It played a preponderant role in urban

---

[4] In Maurice Crouzet (ed.), *Histoire générale des civilisations* (7 vols.; Paris, 1953–), V, 345–529.

life because the "semi-proletariat" continued to be a part of its "clientèle." What, then did this bourgeois want? He believed in material happiness; he hoped to "free" economic life from administrative interference and acquire the right to participate in the management of public affairs; above all, he aspired to attain, at the expense of the nobility's privileges, a social status commensurate with his economic role. His demand for *civil equality* was basic. The "real problem" was "the advent of a new society, of a society devoid of orders."

In a few months, the revolution of 1789–90 resulted in "the subversion of the regime." It established this new society, "directed and managed by the bourgeoisie." It brought about the conquest of civil equality and the abolition of feudalism; the conquest of civil liberties (freedom of the press, of speech and political association); the conquest of power by the bourgeoisie (although the tax qualification for voting did not exclude artisans and small landowners from the suffrage, it did make it practically impossible for them to be *eligible* for election); the conquest of "laissez-faire" and "laissez-passer" in the economic domain and the disappearance of the corporative system. To put it briefly, "the functioning of the new system assured the reality of power to the upper and middle bourgeoisie or its representatives."

However, Labrousse continues, these gains were only "provisional in nature." The vanquished—the nobility and upper clergy —did not accept their defeat and began to seek support in the European states whose governments were terrified by the new French institutions. The victors were really divided: the lower bourgeoisie, now allied with the masses, did not regard the revolution as being over, while the upper classes were aware of having been pushed further than they wanted to go: the "forces of resistance" and the "forces of movement" were soon to oppose each other.

The "forces of movement" triumphed in 1792–93 for two reasons. First, the war and the invasion had given rise to a "national sentiment": the French people flung themselves ardently into a struggle that would decide the fate of the new political and social institutions. This passion helped markedly to "radicalize" public opinion and political life. Second, the poor harvest of 1791 and, above all, the crisis in public finance because of its repercussions in the monetary domain, led to a collapse of purchasing power. The crisis in prices was accompanied by a social crisis as early as the winter of 1791–92, and this was even more true the following winter. The masses afflicted by this crisis now had a "revolutionary tool." The two thousand societies, and the clubs with which they were affiliated, assembled "the élite of the regime"; the local "revolutionary committees" kept an eye on public officials and gave their full attention to directing public opinion. These societies and committees were the prime movers of the revolution. "The masses played a major role." Finally, the National Guard became "democratized": it was recruited in part from citizens who did not have the right to vote but who were attracted to it because of the wages. Maintenance of order was thus entrusted to men who had become a part of the "forces of movement." Eminent members of the bourgeoisie were disconcerted by the rise of these "new strata" who wanted access to power.

But during the summer and fall of 1793 the "forces of movement" were weakened by economic difficulties and the measures the government was forced to take against them. Small merchants and peasant landowners were fed up with "the law of maximum" that limited the selling price of consumers' goods. The workers became indignant when this maximum was applied to wages. The failure of the economic system gave rise to hesitancy or disappointment among the masses. "The great collective forces that support the revolution are now tending to falter." When Robespierre fell on the ninth of Thermidor, it was noteworthy that the "working people" were mostly absent and that the call to insurrection launched by the Commune of Paris against the Convention was received "with little enthusiasm." Actually, the forces of order "outclassed" those of the revolution. The bourgeoisie resumed power.

Of all that the ephemeral Year II had achieved—universal suffrage, government by assembly, the separation of church and state, important transfers of property, attempts at social legislation— what remained? "A grandiose glow that illuminated the nineteenth century." From now on, it was the forces of "consolidation" that were to assert themselves; the bourgeois "notables," triumphant, wanted political stability. They feared the reappearance of the Jacobins; they wanted economic stability. To achieve it, they were ready to sacrifice parliamentarianism and even, if necessary, political liberalism, on condition that the gains won in 1789–91 were safeguarded. They were ready to accept the Napoleonic regime whose motto might have been: "Equality, authority, technicality."

In this vigorous interpretation that stressed the "great forces," the center of interest is clearly defined: although this essay of synthesis forms part of a "general history of civilization," in reality it is devoted exclusively to *social* history. In his study of the origins of the Revolution, as in his study of the work of the Constituent Assembly, Labrousse does not dwell on an analysis of current philosophical ideas or concepts of public law. In studying the forces that resisted the Revolution he does not seem to grant a prominent place to religious sentiment. Above all else, he wants to rediscover the "forces of movement" and a general principle of dynamics. Nor does he concern himself with the spread of learning. He also neglects the role of administrative institutions, important though they are in everyday life. His deliberate preferences are related to a specific conception of history: the "balance of social forces" is the center of interest.

The great critical studies and the essays of synthesis are but one aspect of his work. To appreciate its impact, one must know the role that Labrousse has played in the development of historical studies in France during the last twenty years, the impetus he has lent to individual undertakings, and the direction he has given to collaborative investigations for which he has been and continues to be the guiding spirit.

Individual works? Doctoral dissertations have a particularly important place in French historical production for, in many instances, their authors did not hesitate to perform the task of pioneers. The pupils of Labrousse, or those influenced by his work, have often been in the front rank of researchers. Monographs in agrarian history dealing with the Basse-Provence and the Beauvaisis during the seventeenth century have given fresh impetus to a study of methods of cultivation and agricultural techniques. Research undertaken in the archives of banks and businesses have made possible a study of the financing of large-scale industry in the first half of the nineteenth century and of the ways in which an important banking institution expanded between 1863 and 1882. Spanish and Portuguese maritime commerce in the Atlantic during the sixteenth century and commercial relations with China during the eighteenth century have resulted in works of exceptional breadth. A similar impetus was given to very novel research on the growth of large-scale capitalism in Barcelona, on the Parisian bourgeoisie from 1815 to 1848, on Socialist doctrines, and on the French working-class movement from 1914 to 1919. Neither electoral sociology nor the psychology of social classes has been overlooked. The authors of these great theses today occupy the chairs of economic history in French universities.[5]

Although the age limit deprived him in 1965 of his chair at the Sorbonne, Labrousse continues even now to direct the preparation of numerous doctoral dissertations. The list that has just been drawn up at the suggestion of the Association des professeurs d'histoire contemporaine des Facultés françaises [6] bears partial witness to this: five great theses in the domain of industrial his-

---

[5] A partial list of these pupils, their work and their positions includes: Pierre Goubert (Professor, Paris-Nanterre), "Le Beauvaisis au XVIIᵉ siècle," since published as *Beauvais et le Beauvaisis de 1600 à 1730* . . . (Paris, 1960); Jean Bouvier (Professor, Lille) "Le Crédit Lyonnais de 1863 à 1882," since partially published as "Aux origines du Crédit Lyonnais, le milieu économique et financier Lyonnais au début des années 1860," *Histoire des entreprises*, No. 6 (November, 1960), 41–64; Pierre Chaunu (Professor, Caen), "Le commerce maritime Espagnol"; Louis Dermigny (Professor, Montpellier), "Le commerce avec la Chine," and see also *La Chine et l'Occident; le Commerce à Canton au XVIIIᵉ siècle, 1719–1833* (Paris, 1964): Pierre Vilar (who has succeeded Ernest Labrousse in the Chair of Economic History at the Sorbonne), "Le grand capitalisme à Barcelone," which spawned the monumental *La Catalogne dans l'Espagne moderne: Recherches sur les fondements économiques des structures nationales* (3 vols.; Paris, 1962); Adeline Daumard (Professor, Rennes), "La bourgeoisie Parisienne de 1815 à 1848," issued under the same title as volume VIII of the series *Démographie et Sociétés* (Paris, 1963); Claude Willard (Maitre-Assistant, Paris-Nanterre), "Le mouvement guesdiste," has since appeared under the title *Les Guesdistes* (Paris, 1965); Annie Kriegel (Professor, Reims), "Le mouvement ouvrier Français 1914–1918"; and Bertrand Gille (Professor, Clermont-Ferrand), "Le financement de la grande industrie." Bouvier, Dermigny, Gille, and Kriegel have since published substantially in areas related to their dissertations.

[6] Under the direction of J. B. Duroselle.

tory (the coal mines in the Nord and in Pas-de-Calais during the nineteenth century; Lyonnaise textiles from 1815 to 1873; industries in the region of the Cévennes from 1830 to 1914); seven theses devoted to the economic and social history of a French region and four to agrarian structures and rural society. But he is also directing still others on the history of the seventeenth and eighteenth centuries that the list does not include. And all those who work under his guidance value him for his useful advice, his broad perspective, and his talent for providing stimulation.

Collaborative investigations? Labrousse developed his proposals through several bodies: international congresses, the modern and contemporary history section of the Centre national de la recherche scientifique, and the Comité des travaux historiques.

In 1955, at the international congress in Rome, he outlined plans for an inquiry into the bourgeoisie of the eighteenth and nineteenth centuries.[7] He was not seeking to *define* "the bourgeois," preferring to defer this until the study was further along. At the start, he said, it would be enough to give "a brief description" based on occupation and social milieu. Social categories would include officeholders, people with private income, members of the liberal professions, and all those who lived from the "profits of business," from entrepreneurs in industry or transportation to the merchant-artisan. The researchers must compile lists and establish a hierarchy of occupations, then study the framework of social life, cultural activities, ideological choices. They must utilize electoral lists which, in the period of the property qualification, provide important information about fiscal sources (the role of the direct tax); registers of births and deaths and population censuses giving occupations. In addition, they must use the national archives and the records of public servants to assess public opinion. Labrousse evaluated these sources, showing how they could complement each other. He asked his foreign colleagues to compile an analogous inventory, using as their frame a city of medium size—twenty or thirty thousand inhabitants. The immediate benefit was certain: such research would induce governments

7 The report was published in Volume IV of the *Proceedings* of this Congress, pp. 365–96.

in all countries to take steps to insure the preservation of documents. An international team of workers could be organized for a long-term enterprise.

In 1965, at the international congress in Vienna, Labrousse proposed that an "economic balance-sheet of the world in 1815" be drawn up even though the availability of sources varied greatly from country to country. He tried to provide "at least a qualitative glimpse of the fluctuations of national production during a quarter of a century of revolution and war." What are the principal features of his inquiry? Until 1810 a rise in cereal prices occurred throughout Europe, but an evaluation of the quantities produced can yield only presuppositions. Industrial prices rose a little less rapidly than agricultural prices; the amount of goods produced doubtless increased. It can be said that on the whole there was economic prosperity between 1789 and 1800 and that this prosperity declined between 1800 and 1814 because of the extension of the blockade. Landowners benefited greatly. As for industrial or commercial profits, they sufficed to make possible considerable progress in the accumulation of capital. In short, after twenty-three years of war, Europe had, it seemed, "increased its stock of men, products and capital." How different from the Thirty Years' War and World War I! But Labrousse concedes that this general impression must be backed up by a wide-ranging series of researches on a national scale. At least, however, he had paved the way.

Within the framework of the Centre national de la recherche scientifique, the *Rapports de conjoncture*, published annually since 1959, stressed the several directions taken by the research that Labrousse had promoted. In 1960 his research project was an investigation, on the basis of notarial records and tax rolls, into the socio-occupational structures from the beginning of the eighteenth century to the middle of the nineteenth. In 1962 he proposed a methodical utilization of the registers of births and deaths in order to study the makeup of hereditary estates and the distribution of wealth: a study of records giving the names of successive owners makes it possible to ascertain the evolution of inherited fortunes. The inquiry is being conducted in five large cities and for four carefully selected years: 1820, 1850, 1873, 1896. An even vaster project welcomed by both economists and historians, was launched in 1963: a study of economic growth since the sixteenth century with a view to analyzing the "mechanisms of development." The investigation involved prices (in this domain research had already made considerable progress), amounts produced, and population fluctuations. The study of production presented the greatest difficulty. The work plan indicates the sources: land registries, *compoix*, registries of landed property, tithebooks, tax archives, fiscal archives (for consumers' taxes), municipal archives, records of the Inspectorate of Manufactured Goods. The results, although fragmentary, should establish concordances or sequences that will suggest explanations or even make it possible to calculate rates of acceleration or deceleration in production.

Finally, it was the impetus given by Labrousse that led the C.N.R.S. to organize in 1964 the colloquy on the history of the First International. It was attended by sixty specialists from ten different countries.

Through the Comité des Travaux historiques, where he presides over the modern and contemporary history section, Labrousse is attempting, by a program of joint undertakings, to spur and coordinate the activities of local historical societies. In the domain where university and local scholars meet, his immediate concern is to compile the list of questions that figures annually in the agenda of the Congrès national des Sociétés Savantes, to indicate to individual researchers the direction they might follow to make their work effective, to help them by having specialists prepare bibliographical and research guides. It is a vast field of action and the initial results are already apparent.

The influence of Labrousse as a teacher must not be overlooked. The most striking things about Labrousse's courses were the strength of his convictions, the vigor of his words, the warmth of his expression, the richness of his vocabulary—even when discussing the most technical matters—the constant effort to see things with a fresh vision. I am thinking, for example (to take only the last few years) of the series of lectures he gave on the mentality of the French bourgeoisie in the middle of the nineteenth century or the social structures of the peasantry.

And this effort will continue to bear fruit. Labrousse, in collaboration with Fernand Braudel, is directing the preparation of a collaborative four-volume economic and social history of France since the sixteenth century. The publication of this great work will begin shortly.

In this rich and varied productivity that bears the imprint of a strong personality, the talents of an erudite and an historian assert themselves with equal vigor. As an erudite, Labrousse always shows the sharpness of his critical faculties and the quality of his judgments when assessing the value of historical sources; he also reveals the attraction exerted upon him by methodological problems. All this is likewise attested by the investigations he has directed. As an historian he has enlarged the horizon of statistical studies and manifested an intellectual curiosity, a breadth of outlook, an imagination that make it possible to establish new working hypotheses and open up new avenues of research. This is also true of his essays in synthesis. Nevertheless, the general orientation of his work has changed. In the beginning, Labrousse classified himself as an economic historian. He did not limit himself to this and, at every opportunity, evidenced a desire to point out the social consequences of economic transformations. But the statistical study of prices and income was the core of his interest. Later, social history—the history of social structures and social movements—became his major preoccupation. One must add that despite this deviation there is a profound unity: for Labrousse, the economic fact is generally the stimulating agent of great historical developments. But the economic always implies, when it affects history, the intervention of the social and the psychic. This requires time; for the social lags behind the economic, and the pyschic in turn lags behind the social. From his report of 1948 to the present, Labrousse has always wanted to write history that is at once economic, social, and sociological. But in fact, he attaches the most importance to economic explanations. Speaking personally, I am strongly tempted to express some reservations about this, for I remain convinced that in the behavior of human groups, motives are never so simple that it is possible to attribute a preeminent validity to *one* explanation. But I pay homage to the significance of his writings, the impact of which has, without doubt, greatly influenced the present orientation of historical study in France.

FEDERICO CHABOD
Portrait of a Master Historian

A. WILLIAM SALOMONE

University of Rochester

F EDERICO CHABOD: an historian's historian. Few other twentieth century craftsmen in Clio's workshop have so deservedly gained with similar unanimity the homage implicit in that characterization. Those outside Italy who first heard of Chabod as president of the International Committee of Historical Sciences in 1955 and perhaps later came to know of him through one or another of the very scanty number of his works available in languages other than Italian undoubtedly found it easy to share the admiration that had led the representatives of the world community of historians to elect him as their most eminent spokesman.[1] Obviously, the initiates' admiration developed before that election and even before the publication four years earlier of his masterpiece—the *Storia della politica estera italiana dal 1870 al 1896: Le premesse* (1951).[2] In fact, that admiration derived from

[1] So far as I know, to date [1968] the following are the only works by Chabod available in languages other than Italian: *L'Italie contemporaine*. Conférences données a l'Institut d'Études Politiques de l'Université de Paris (Paris, 1950); an Italian edition of the Parisian lectures, *L'Italia contemporanea* (1918–1948). *Lezioni alla Sorbona* (Turin, 1961), appeared in English as *A History of Italian Fascism*, translated by Muriel Grindrod (London, 1963); *Machiavelli and the Renaissance*, translated by David Moore, with introduction by A. P. d'Entrèves (London, 1958); *Italien–Europa: Studien zur Geschichte Italiens im 19. und 20. Jahrhundert*, with foreword by Rudolf von Albertini (Göttingen, 1962). Von Albertini's anthology contains extensive excerpts from Chabod's writings on the "idea of Europe," on method, on the "mission of Rome," from the *Storia della politica estera italiana dal 1870 al 1896: Le premesse* (Bari, 1951), from an article on Italian foreign policy between 1870 and 1915, and from *L'Italie contemporaine*. As this volume goes to press (1971), a fine anthology of six of the most original Chabodian studies has been edited in French by Henri Lepeyre, under the title of *De Machiavel a Benedetto Croce* (Geneva, 1970).

[2] A second edition, apparently made from the original plates, was issued in Bari

[255]

a cumulatively growing impression among Italian and European historians that Federico Chabod, who was born in the Val d'Aosta on February 23, 1901, epitomized both in his person and in his work one of the most original and creative historiographical innovations brought to an ancient craft by the generation of historians born after 1900.[3]

Twice within less than a decade—first in 1951, following the publication of Chabod's acknowledged masterpiece on the "premises" of Italian foreign policy after the Risorgimento, and then again in 1960, this time under the shadow of his tragically premature death—historical criticism was almost "forced'" to forego, though for different reasons, a full-fledged appraisal of the connections between the great historian's life and his work. In practically all of the major or more sustained assessments of Chabod's *Storia: Le premesse* (1951) which were made in Italy and abroad during the first two years after it appeared, there seems to be evidence of a kind of fundamental assumption that that work was almost literally a *tour de force*. Its merits were so outstanding, so patently exceptional that its author must of necessity be regarded as if he were already legendary and therefore beyond all but the most generic characterization as a human being. The work was so accomplished a piece of historical writing that it was felt the man behind it, the person and the mind of the historian, could paradoxically be "left out" of consideration. The "initiates" knew him, of course, but since Chabod had never engaged in any kind of self-advertisement, no matter how high his position, the so-called general public was puzzled even as it stood in distant admiration.[4]

---

in 1962; a pocket edition in two volumes in the Universale Laterza (UL) was published in 1965, but the notes are transferred to the end of chapters. In both the text and the notes of the present essay Chabod's *Storia della politica estera italiana* . . . in its 1951 edition will be referred to as *Storia: Le premesse* or simply as *Storia*.

[3] Sir Charles Webster, "Federico Chabod: An International Figure," *Rivista storica italiana*, LXXII (1960), 625–28.

[4] The following represent a sampling of reviews and opinions on Chabod's *Storia: Le premesse* which appeared within the first two years after its publication: A. M. G. [Alberto Maria Ghisalberti], review in *Rassegna storica del Risorgimento*,

For, quite ironically, Federico Chabod was both renowned and unknown, in part as a consequence of his consistent refusal through a whole generation to encourage any cult of personality— his own, first of all—and in part now, in the early 1950s, as a result of the awe which his masterpiece inspired. Thus not only his personal life—not in question here—but his spiritual development, his intellectual antecedents, and professional career through more than a quarter century since the mid-twenties, when he had published his first "Machiavellian" essays, seemed now relegated to a strange sphere lying somewhere between legend and mystery. In the eyes of his contemporaries, Chabod's biography seemed at that moment to have been completely absorbed into his historiography. If a variation on Fustel de Coulanges' famous dictum may be hazarded, it could be said that it appeared not as if Chabod wrote history but as if history "spoke" through Chabod! Of even greater relevance was the fact that such an impression was bound to lead to a distorting concentration upon the "result" rather than the course, the "product" rather than the process, the "destination" rather than the journey of Chabod's intellectual and spiritual life.[5]

In 1960 and immediately after, under the impact of the incredibly swift manner by which a cruel personal fate had come to deprive the Italian and European "society of intelligence" of one of its most creative historical minds, an analogous phenomenon occurred, though naturally for different reasons and with different tonalities. Now, the tributes were understandably tendered to Chabod the man, perhaps, more than to Chabod the historian.[6]

XXXIX (1952), 867–72; Gaetano Arfé in *Movimento operaio*, IV (1952), 861–64; Giovanni Cottone, in *Belfagor*, VII (1952), 233–39; Alberto Caracciolo, in *Rinascita*, VIII (1951), 606–607; Luigi Salvatorelli, "Idea e uomini della terza Italia," *La Stampa* (Turin), April 22, 1952.

5 For two sustained analyses of the *Storia* which redress at least in part the teleological interpretations of the 1951–52 reviews, see Armando Saitta, "Genesi del giudizio di Chabod sulla classe dirigente italiana," *Rivista storica italiana*, LXXII (1960), 756–73; Gennaro Sasso, *Profilo di Federico Chabod* (Bari, 1961), 145–86.

6 My judgment on the nature of the tributes is not, of course, equally true of all the following pieces: Furio Diaz, "Federico Chabod," *Il Ponte*, XVI (1960), 1232–44; A. M. G. [Ghisalberti], "Amici scomparsi: Federico Chabod (Aosta, 23 febbraio 1901–Roma, 14 luglio 1960)," *Rassegna storica del Risorgimento*, XLVII

Now, in a sense, it was no longer merely the great historian exalted but an intellectual and moral "leader" prematurely dead. At least in part it now seemed as if Chabod's historiography had been merely a large function of his biography.

As we look back from the perspective of time and historical and historiographical vicissitudes, a question arises concerning not merely the character of Chabod's "contribution" but also concerning the nature of its connection with the historian's own life and times. What were the activating motives behind and within his work? What was the vital process which conditioned or guided his mind toward the achievement of the structure and meaning he gave to *his* history? Reduced to simpler or perhaps wider terms, the essential question therefore may be thus formulated: How, through what vital experience, through the combination of what interior and external elements, psychological efforts and intellectual stages did Chabod attain such "results" as he did in his historical vision and historiographical work? Difficult as the search may be, tentative as the answers must be, the question itself is certainly worth posing. Even more important, such a question may be called exquisitely Chabodian, exactly of the kind which Chabod himself implicitly—and frequently explicitly—posed or raised for himself in practically all his own biohistorical studies, whether he delved into the life and work of Machiavelli or Guicciardini, of Giovanni Botero or Paolo Sarpi, of Meinecke or Croce.[7] In a word, such a

(1960), 404–408; Delio Cantimori, "Federico Chabod," *Belfagor*, XV (1960), 688–704; Raffaello Morghen, "Federico Chabod (23 febbraio 1901–14 luglio 1960)," *Archivio storico italiano*, CXIX (1961), 462–67; Fernand Braudel, "Auprès de Federico Chabod," *Rivista storica italiana*, LXXII (1960), 621–24; Alphonse Dupront, "Federico Chabod," *Revue historique*, LXXXV (1961), 261–94; Vittorio de Caprariis, "Un grande storico," *Il Mondo*, XII (August 2, 1960), 9; Raffaele Mattioli, *Istituto italiano per gli studi storici: Commemorazione di Federico Chabod* (Naples, 1960); Rosario Romeo, *Federico Chabod* (Naples, 1961); Chabod, *Italien–Europa*, 5–10.

[7] For Chabod's approach to each of these men as persons and thinkers, see his successive essays as now contained in *Scritti su Machiavelli* (Turin, 1964), particularly the use made by the historian of the personal-psychological factors as tools of philological and hermeneutic analysis in retracing the dating of the composition of *Il Principe* (pp. 184–92); on Guicciardini, Botero, and Sarpi, see the studies in Chabod, *Scritti sul Rinascimento* (Turin, 1967), 225–39, 271–374, 462–587; on Meinecke, see the two quite different articles written by Chabod twenty-eight years apart, "Uno storico tedesco contemporaneo: Federico Meinecke," *Nuova rivista storica*, XI (1927), 592–803, and "Friedrich Meinecke," *Rivista storica italiana*, LXVII (1955), 272–88; on Croce, see "Croce storico," *Rivista storica italiana*, LXIV (1952), 473–530.

question, if it is adopted as a guide to a quest for understanding beyond the purely "personal," the obvious, and the superficial in a historian's life and work, seems to be of the very essence of Chabod's own method and of his approach to an exceptional human personality.[8]

Chabod's maturity of life and work paralleled almost exactly one of the most tortured and tormenting eras in the history of modern Italy. He himself has left us an incisive and enlightening sketch of the involution of Italian politics and spiritual life which occurred in the midst of that age through the rise, rule, and fall of fascism.[9] For most members of his generation the Fascist period in Italy, particularly after the Matteotti crisis of 1924, was a time of almost inescapable decision—a veritable "either-or" between compliance and resistance to the dictatorship.[10] Almost incredibly, Chabod *appears* to have chosen not to choose openly and thus to have eluded the iron grip of the deadly dilemma at least until the coming of the Second World War to Italy. At that time he joined the Party of Action and played a splendid part in the resistance movement in northern Italy, in Piedmont, and then made a truly special contribution toward the saving of his Val d'Aosta from the machinations of a strange but strenuous "irredentist" group from among the French crypto-nationalists (1944–46).[11]

For almost twenty years before the coming of the explosion of the Partisan War against the Nazi-Fascists in North Italy, Chabod had been able to devote himself undisturbed to his historical research and to his teaching and writing. Although we have no memoirs or diary—all his friends speak eloquently of Chabod's persistent, almost congenital "silence" about himself—and his correspondence is not yet available, it does not seem too bold to

[8] See Chabod, "Croce storico," 486, for Chabod's interpretation of Croce's own interpretation of the difference between "personal" and "spiritual" biography; a few pages earlier (481), Chabod remarks that in his essay on Marchese Galeazzo Caracciolo, Croce "had captured in the drama of a soul the drama of an age and of a generation."

[9] Chabod, *L'Italie contemporaine.*

[10] Chabod, *A History of Italian Fascism*, 64–65, contains his rather laconic description of the Matteotti crisis; for comments on Chabod's presentation of the crisis, see Leo Valiani, "Lo storico dei propri tempi," *Rivista storica italiana*, LXXII (1960), 788–89.

[11] See Valiani, "Lo storico dei propri tempi," 789–92, for remarks on Chabod as participant and historian of his own times.

guess, on the basis of his colleagues' recollections and, of course, of inference from the very nature of his work during the Fascist period in Italy, that the young historian had quite early realized what his true "vocation," his real "mission," was in a time of trouble. And he remained almost unswervingly faithful to the commitment that self-knowledge implied and involved for him both for good and ill. Like his Machiavelli in another age of Italian calamities, Chabod, too, appeared to have had a vision of the *verità effettuale* concerning his time and world; he, too, seems to have built his *castelluzzo* (his "little castle") as to how he could best help lift the burden of the present—perchance through his secret unshakable faith in and through his pursuit of the liberating function of historical truth. What the study of politics had been for Machiavelli, the study of history was to be for Chabod—the "food" which would be his alone.[12]

One of Chabod's closest early friends at the University of Turin in 1919–20, the well-known literary critic Mario Fubini, recalled immediately after the historian's death how during their student days the young man from Aosta talked "passionately" about the Florentine Secretary and quoted him almost ceaselessly by heart in tones which betrayed an "identification with his author, as if he felt his [Machiavelli's] drama as his own."[13] And, as Fubini remembered, there was, above all, young Federico's predilection for the impassioned passage in which Machiavelli cries through the mouth of *his* Fabrizio Colonna: "What can I promise them by which they might with reverence either love or hate me when, the war being over, they shall have nothing further to share with me? . . . By what God or by what saints shall I ask them to swear their loyalty?"[14]

---

[12] In practically all his essays on Machiavelli, Chabod cites or makes some reference to the Florentine's famous letter of December 10, 1513, to Francesco Vettori, in which the expression occurs; see Chabod, *Scritti su Machiavelli*, 12, 31–33, 184, 186–87, 249–50, 374–75. For an excellent translation of Machiavelli's letter, see Allan Gilbert (ed.), *The Letters of Machiavelli* (New York, 1961), 139–44.

[13] Mario Fubini, "Federico Chabod studente di lettere," *Rivista storica italiana*, LXXII (1960), 635–36.

[14] *Ibid.*, 636, 642. The passage Chabod loved to quote is from Machiavelli's *Dell'arte della guerra*, Book VII; see the passage in its full context in Niccolò Machiavelli, *Opere*, edited by Antonio Panella (2 vols.; Rome, 1939), II, 660–61.

"By what God and by what saints," we might ask, could the young student from Aosta have helped *his* Italian compatriots— free citizens, not "mercenaries," for whom a Great War had almost completely shattered the tenuous national unity—reaffirm "old" values of freedom and justice now being mocked and engulfed by the corrupting influence of nationalist passions and emergent Fascist violence? He did not possess the single-minded fervor for politics of his friend Piero Gobetti, nor the activistic dedication of Carlo Rosselli, nor the revolutionary temper of Antonio Gramsci—all of them working in the Turin of his student days.[15] Thus from the very start Chabod took his stand with the study of history and he could do no other. But if he did not thereby expose himself to the risks of direct ideological and political warfare neither did he engage, as some of his contemporaries were to do, in that "betrayal of the intellectuals" which the dawn of the totalitarian age was to precipitate in Italy and elsewhere in Europe. True that in the Turin of 1919–22 to which he first came—the Turin in which so many new currents and undercurrents of intellectual and philosophical renovation were stirring, young Chabod appears to have remained aloof, almost a "stranger" to anything that was not directly connected with his studies of history and of his Machiavelli—the Florentine Secretary looming in the foreground of another but distant crisis of Italian politics. And yet, such impressions of the young student could be deceiving if taken out of larger context.

In 1924–25 Chabod went to Florence to study with the most "notoriously" anti-Fascist professor then still teaching at an Italian university—Gaetano Salvemini.[16] Still more revealing, it seems to me, is the extraordinary fact of which Chabod himself never wrote or spoke, not even after the fall of fascism when it became almost

[15] Cf. Fubini, "Federico Chabod," 29–30. On the relations between Gobetti, Rosselli, and Gramsci, see Barbara Allason, *Memorie di un'antifascista, 1919–1940* (Rome-Florence-Milan, n. d.), 17–21.

[16] From a vast literature on Salvemini, most of which I have discussed or utilized in section two of my *Italy in the Giolittian Era: Italian Democracy in the Making, 1900–1914* (Philadelphia, 1960), 117–69, see the articles by Gaetano Salvemini, Ernesto Rossi, and Piero Calamandrei in the photostatic reproduction of their clandestine anti-Fascist periodical (1925) *Non Mollare* (Florence, 1955), 4–112.

"fashionable" to be known as a "Salveminian," that in August, 1926, he actively participated in the successful "plot" to help Salvemini, who had eluded the Fascist police, escape to freedom by crossing over to France at the Little St. Bernard Pass.[17] This at the risk of compromising his professional career, just then at its promising start—he had recently published his much acclaimed first Machiavelli essays—by participating in an "anti-State activity."[18] In the fall of that year, Chabod went to study with Friedrich Meinecke at the University of Berlin, again to be openly associated with a renowned master who, however, at that moment, was certainly not the most popular teacher in Germany. Indeed, as we now know, Meinecke was being singled out, with few other outstanding figures in German academic life, as one of the chief intellectuals whom the nationalists and militarists regarded as the fathers of the "treacherous" Weimar Republic.

In 1928 Chabod accepted the "patronage," if such it may be called, of the actualist philosopher Giovanni Gentile, who was regarded as the major official theorist of Fascist doctrine, at that time the director of the *Enciclopedia Italiana*. In accepting the editorship of the section on modern history of the *Enciclopedia* Chabod was neither asking nor receiving any favors. He was already the most outstanding younger Italian historian, whose interpretation of Machiavelli was subtly but, for the wise, unmistakably critical of the corruption of political and ethical values by the Italian "princes" of the Renaissance who had been largely responsible for the coming of the "barbarians" to Italy. Thus Chabod was appointed for the brilliance and promise of his scholarly work and no partisan demands were made of him either by Gentile or his immediate subordinates. Moreover, Gentile undoubtedly was aware that Chabod was a young favorite of Benedetto Croce, who had been and was now more than ever the most

---

[17] Salvemini, *Memorie di un fuoruscito*, edited by Gaetano Arfé (Milan, 1960), 28.

[18] Chabod, "Del 'Principe' di Niccolò Machiavelli," *Nuova rivista storica*, IX (1925), 35–71, 189–216, 437–73. The 1925 study was Chabod's doctoral dissertation and was published in 1926. See Chabod, *Scritti su Machiavelli*, 5–27, 31–135; and *Machiavelli and the Renaissance*, 1–29, 30–125.

formidable adversary of Gentilian actualism.[19] As one of Chabod's colleagues at the *Enciclopedia* was to recall many years later, the feeling and attitude at the historical section was that while Gentile gave them their "material bread," Croce gave them their "spiritual bread." [20] Finally, against the recollection of the old Fascist historian Gioacchino Volpe (who had been a truly good friend of the Valdostano) that at some indeterminate moment in the early 1930s Chabod was "proffered" and most reluctantly accepted the "party-card," [21] there stands the testimony of Walter Maturi. This stanch old friend and confidant of Chabod was to write that "at the time of Fascism everyone knew on which political side the sympathies of Chabod lay," despite the fact that the Valdostano was *"prudentissimo."* There was at any rate, Maturi added, that dangerous public outburst of impatience and protest made by Chabod against Mussolini's "unhappy idea of nationalizing" in his own Fascist fashion Chabod's native Val d'Aosta. "In all the wars of Italy," Chabod had exploded, "the Valdostani have always fought like other Italians, indeed better than others, and what does it matter if instead of crying V*iva il re* they love to cry V*ive le roi?"* [22] Chabod's eminent and excellent Valdostani friends Alessandro and Ettore Passerin d'Entrèves recalled also the historian's intercession in behalf of his humbler compatriots who sought him out in Rome during the 1930s and obtained his help against the Fascist regime's policy of "italianization" of the Piedmont.[23]

The outbreak of the European war in 1939 and then Mussolini's intervention in 1940 brought Chabod in the active fight against fascism. At first he moved cautiously, through his review *Popoli*

[19] For a concise description of Gentilian actualism, see my article in Joseph Dunner (ed.), *Handbook of World History: Concepts and Issues* (New York, 1967), 7–10.

[20] Arnaldo Momigliano, "Appunti su F. Chabod storico," *Rivista storica italiana,* LXXII (1960), 644.

[21] Gioacchino Volpe, *Storici e maestri* (Florence, 1967), 488.

[22] Walter Maturi, "Chabod storico della politica estera Italiana," *Rivista storica italiana,* LXXII (1960), 746.

[23] Alessandro and Ettore Passerin d'Entrèves, "Federico Chabod e la Valle d'Aosta," *ibid.,* LXXII (1960), 795–96. And see John K. Wildgen, "The Liberation of the Valle d'Aosta, 1943–1945," *Journal of Modern History,* XLII (1970), 21–41.

(1941–42),[24] and then openly, as a militant in the Piedmontese partisan formations of the Party of Action, and later (1944–46) as the indefatigable defender of the Italian character of the Val d'Aosta against French annexionists and some of their Valdostani sympathizers.[25] After 1946 Chabod justly gained the homage as the father of the autonomy of the *valle* within the new Italian democratic state.

One of Chabod's first and enduring technical contributions to modern scholarship on "the puzzle of Machiavelli" consisted in his having established, with rare precision, the dating of the writing of *Il Principe* by Machiavelli (between August and December, 1513) and the relationship between such a dating and the "intentions" behind the famous treatise. Leaving aside the "heated controversies," the almost scholastic debates among historians, to which the problem of dating Machiavelli's two principal works *Il Principe* and *I Discorsi* has given rise since Chabod successfully challenged Friedrich Meinecke's interpretation (both master and "pupil" to the very end of their lives maintained their original positions), [26] the question may be taken as emblematic of a crucial

---

[24] Chabod and his close friend Carlo Morandi were coeditors of *Popoli*. See the brief description of the short-lived review in Luigi Firpo, "Bibliografia degli scritti di Federico Chabod (1921–1961)," *Rivista storica italiana*, LXXII (1960), 825.

[25] D'Entrèves and d'Entrèves, "Federico Chabod," 796–806.

[26] As Chabod points out in his "Sulla composizione de 'Il Principe' di Niccolò Machiavelli," in *Scritti su Machiavelli*, 139n1, Meinecke's thesis, sustaining the contention that the first eleven chapters of *Il Principe* were composed before December, 1513, while the other fifteen chapters were worked out later, had been advanced by the German historian in *Der Fürst und kleinere Schriften* (Berlin, 1923) and then more briefly in *Die Idee der Staatsräson in der neueren Geschichte* (Berlin-Munich, 1924). Eric W. Cochrane, "Machiavelli: 1940–1960," *Journal of Modern History*, XXXIII (1961), 133, calls attention to the fact that in the English translation of *Staatsräson*, which was being prepared shortly before his death, Meinecke inserted the words "I was not convinced" by the critics of his interpretation of *Il Principe*'s problem of dating—first and chief among those critics, of course, being Chabod. Almost similarly, though in a different context, Chabod wrote: "Despite the ingenious and often over-subtle arguments put forward, I do not find it is possible to accept the foregoing hypotheses. I remain of the opinion that the opening sentence of Chap. II of *The Prince* is a precise reference to the *Discorsi*, that it is not a subsequent addition, and that, as a consequence, when Machiavelli began work on *The Prince*, he had already written at least a part of the first book of the *Discorsi*." See Chabod, *Machiavelli and the Renaissance*, 32n2; Chabod, *Scritti su Machiavelli*, 32n1.

task which all serious historical criticism must at some moment face. For in its wider context the problem concerns the relationship not only between chronology and biography but also between *both* of these and historiography. The particular cultural structure and psychological context which at a given moment of his intellectual life the historian possesses or utilizes prove to be important, often decisive, points of reference for an understanding of what, how, and why his work is done. The philosopher and the artist, by the very nature of their purely contemplative or creative activity, can sometimes be comprehended, or at least "appreciated," even in isolation from a biocultural context. The historian, on the other hand, even in his highest or "purest" exemplars—a Ranke, Burckhardt, Meinecke, or Croce—remains as time-bound as his subject, and frequently he finds himself almost suspended between *the time of his history* and the *time of his historiography.*[27]

Contrary to general impression, which is perhaps derived from a misunderstanding of that other characterization—"pure historian" —often associated with Chabod's name, he did not escape, even if like the great masters he ultimately succeeded in dominating, the pull between the time of his subjects and the time of his reconstruction. Though they pose no problems as such, the dates of composition (and publication) of practically all of his major books or essays are very indicative, if not necessarily substantive, elements of their biographical significance. Therefore, if we leave aside purely pedagogical pieces (programs of lessons, study-plans, outlines, bibliographical aids) and often not even them, nothing that Chabod ever wrote may be judged as completely unrelated to some intimate urge in him to convert it into a "rational" historiographical transcription of a state of mind, of a spiritual problem, itself somehow connected with his own historical milieu. Even the apparently fortuitous and occasional aspects in the "practical" background of some of his principal works can be shown through careful internal evidence to have been directly or indirectly, and then enduringly, turned into functions of Chabod's pre-existent in-

[27] On these "two kinds" of time, see the wise discussion in the chapters respectively entitled "The Encountered Past" and "Historic Time" in Paul Weiss, *History Written and Lived* (Carbondale, 1962), 59–94, 141–56.

clinations, of some acutely felt and persistent query concerning his time and world. Most of the historian's major works cannot be totally divorced from his own historical moment, from the activating motives behind his immediate labors.[28]

Of course, it would undoubtedly be easy to fall into a schematizing trap if the relationship between context and "creation" were to be too rigidly or unimaginatively pursued. But it would be equally distorting to seek to understand Chabod's works as if they had been produced in a cork-lined room whose insulated silence and limited perspective permitted his writing history as a Proustlike "remembrance of things past." If, by the very nature of its occasionally excessive documentary substructure,[29] Chabod's historiography is more than time-past "purely" remembered through disciplined association of "memories," his historical consciousness nevertheless derives from the subtle clash in him between the past's irresistible fascination and the present as experience turned into thought. He perhaps never fully accepted the more superficial implications often seen in the Crocean view that "all history is

[28] I have made a careful examination of the following originally "pedagogical" pieces by Chabod and it seems to me that in all cases there is evidence of a double relationship: first, to a pre-existent, sometimes long-ranging, historical interest and, second, to some newly risen or emerging problem directly or implicitly connected with a "present" question—but I should like to insist that by no stretch of interpretation of this relationship can Chabod be turned into a "presentist" historian; see Chabod, *L'idea d'Europa* (Bari, 1961), 3–4, 193–204 (Appendix); *L'idea di nazione* (Bari, 1961), 87–186, containing the "variants" and the Appendix; *Lezioni de storia moderna: Carlo V* [Università degli Studi di Roma. Facoltà di Lettere e Filosofia. Anno Accademico, 1948–49] (Rome, 1949); *Lo Stato di Milano nella prima metà del secolo XVI* [Università degli Studi di Roma. Facoltà di Lettere e Filosofia. Anno Accademico, 1954–55] (Rome, 1955); *Alle origini dello stato moderno* [Università degli Studi di Roma. Facoltà di Lettere e Filosofia. Anno Accademico 1956–57] (Rome, 1957); *Questioni metodologiche* [Università degli Studi di Roma. Facoltà di Lettere e Filosofia. Anno Accademio 1959–60] (Rome, 1960). The last four titles listed above are lithographed editions for students of Chabod's courses at the University of Rome. Chabod's *L'Italie contemporaine* (1950) is likewise a lithographed edition of the lectures delivered at the Institut d'Études Politiques of the University of Paris.

[29] Ernesto Sestan (who, according to Momigliano, "Appunti su F. Chabod storico," 646, "can really say that he has known Chabod") comments in his preface to Federico Chabod, *Per la storia religiosa dello Stato di Milano durante il dominio di Carlo V. Note e documenti* (2nd ed.; Rome, 1962), xv: "It would not be too far from the truth to point out that the most beautiful among Chabod's beautiful pages are those in which he lets himself go a bit; at a glance, these are those which contain a lesser substructure of notes, when from the ascertainment of the facts rigorously, scrupulously documented, he passes on to their historical evaluation." Cf. the remarks on the same point, Sasso, *Profilo*, 35–36.

contemporary history," but he certainly felt, indeed he knew that the "objective reality" of the past "can be grasped only through ourselves"—through experience, sensations, which the historian's thought critically elaborates and refines.[30]

Chabod's twenty-year-long effort to remain "disengaged" from his present—that is, from the practical politics of Fascist Italy— was perhaps after all only a strenuous struggle not for isolation from his time, from neutrality in his world, but for preservation of his authenticity within and yet against them. As we have seen, he did not avoid participation: his connection with the "expedition" to put Salvemini beyond the grasp of the Fascist police, his explosions against the regime, his very reserve when open adherence could have brought him only rapid advancement, and, of course, his wartime engagement against Nazi-fascism in northern Italy, these and more, all testify as to which "political side," as Walter Maturi put it, Chabod's sympathies lay. But almost in each case that participation was for something recognizably "concrete" in the best sense of the word, whether it involved a political personage like Salvemini, the obscure Valdostani who sought his aid in Rome, or *palpable* ideas. In his life as in his historiography Federico Chabod could not and would not commit himself to abstract principles, to theories of political science or ideology, to *systems* of ideas, no matter how attractive (or abhorrent) they might be to his spiritual personality. In all his writings he gives a special place to the word *valori* (values) as against all other practical and historical concepts. The essential link between Chabod the man and Chabod the historian, it seems to me, must be sought in the never-theorized operation in him of a subtle humanistic motivating force.

On the basis of what he had written and how he had written about *his* two major figures of Renaissance Italy—Machiavelli and Guicciardini—Chabod may be said to have been "Machiavellian" in intellectual passion and "Guicciardinian" in psychological inclination. This fascinating dualism can be retraced in the contrasting approaches he adopted throughout his life to the two great Florentines. His biographical and critical essays on them through

[30] Chabod, *Questioni metodologiche*, 25.

more than a half century may have changed in emphasis but not in essence.[31] More indirect but certainly more revealing is the internal evidence concerning his divided outlook which can be abstracted through careful study of his masterpiece, the *Storia: Le premesse.* For in this, as against the more obvious indications of that dualism in his biographies of Botero, Sarpi, Giovio [32] and the sketches he wrote for the *Enciclopedia italiana,* one finds not only an "objective" reconstruction of a crucial moment of post-Risorgimento history but also a subtly "subjective" bio-spiritual "document," a mature elucidation and summation of Chabodian "ideal-types" among historical personalities whose thought and action he investigates. If we momentarily shift the focus of our attention for this purpose only to the great *Storia,* we may discover some extremely interesting and suggestive elements that concern the historian as much as his history.

Cavour, the unique Machiavellian hero of the Risorgimento is not in the *Storia.* Indeed, the greatest modern Italian practitioner of creative statecraft, the man who had incarnated a truly unique balance between political genius and sheer vital force, was never an object of Chabodian biography.[33] This simple fact, it seems to

[31] See the various articles on Machiavelli in Chabod, *Scritti Su Machiavelli;* on Guicciardini, *Scritti sul Rinascimento,* 226–37. See also Chabod's preface to Rudolf von Albertini, *Das florentinische Staatsbewusstsein im Übergang von der Republik zum Prinzipat* (Bern, 1955), 5–9, *passim.* Most interesting, it seems to me, is the fact that in his very last academic year at the University of Rome (1959–60), Chabod, *Questioni metodologiche,* 77–78, enjoined the utilization of the Guicciardinian concept of *particulare* as a kind of psychological and empirical historiographical instrument.

[32] See Chabod, *Scritti sul Rinascimento,* 315–18, on the accentuation in Giovanni Botero, theorist of *ragion di stato,* and Sarpi of some of the worst features of both Machiavelli and Guicciardini, or at least the misuse of valid concepts as the two had originally presented them; see *ibid.,* 586: "Now, if his *particulare* had induced Guicciardini to love the greatness of the popes, the *particulare* of Sarpi induced him toward the exact opposite. 'Fortune' had placed Guicciardini in such condition as to have to desire the greatness of Leo X and Clement VII, and to have to labor in their behalf; 'fortune' or rather to use his own words, 'occasion' had placed Sarpi in a condition to have to struggle against the papacy." And see *ibid.,* 247–50, 259, 260–62, for Chabod's use of Machiavelli and Guicciardini as "norms" by which to judge Giovio's psychological and historiographical attitudes.

[33] The exhaustive bibliography of Chabod's works compiled by Luigi Firpo, "Bibliografia degli scritti di Federico Chabod (1921–1961)," *Rivista storica italiana,* LXXII (1960), 815–34, and "Supplemento alla bibliografia di Federico Chabod," *ibid.,* LXXIV (1962), 356–61, does not reveal any direct writing by Chabod on Cavour.

me, was not a mere accident. The explosive vitalism behind the "balance" of the Cavourian political personality was perhaps alien less to Chabod's historical *forma mentis* than to the "temperamental," the psychological substructure of his historical-mindedness. Thus, in the *Storia*, Cavour is off-stage, whether as an active but "distant," almost myth-enveloped point of reference for the main "actors" or only in the footnotes.[34] Of course, Cavour had been dead almost ten years when Chabod raises the curtain on his great historical "play" under the official time-and-place setting of Italy, 1870. But the original, larger locale is not merely Italy but Europe and the time is the vast nineteenth century crisis of politics and culture of which 1870–71 is both watershed and mainstream. At any rate, Chabod had extraordinary talent for exploiting the "flashback" technique to bring much of pre-1861 political and intellectual history to the proscenium when he thought it necessary to heighten and sharpen his historical drama. Cavour is not in the *Storia* obviously because Chabod wishes to spotlight his real protagonists, the Cavourian successors who are presented as interpreting and fulfilling his "legacy" in the conditions and atmosphere of the post-Risorgimento. If, however, our analysis is at all correct, there may be seen another, a deeper reason for Cavour's absence in the Chabodian masterpiece.

The purely Machiavellian character of Cavour's political action had asserted the predominance of *virtù* as passionate, almost vitalistic defiance of the caprice of fortune (*fortuna*) and the iron vise of necessity (*necessità*), and it had prevailed in the making of a national state. But that "action" gave the historian a glimpse on his own historical grounds of that "demonic" element in history which, in less creative and constructive guise than its Cavourian incarnation, could shatter that "Guicciardinian" balance which, despite all its defects, Chabod regarded as a kind of "ideal-type" of historic life.[35]

[34] For examples of how Chabod utilizes Cavour and his policy as "points of reference" rather than for direct critical appraisals, see Chabod, *Storia: Le premesse,* 111, 119–20, 148–49, 200–01, 334–35, 370–75, 402, 413–14, 468–69, 554–55, 559, 563–66, 591, 603, 606.
[35] In the *Storia* Chabod makes a very complex presentation of the major protagonists on both the European and the Italian historical "stages" of 1870–71

Chabod had experienced such a shattering twice over: once, vicariously, as a student of the crisis of Renaissance Italy and then again as a contemporary witness of the Italian and European crisis of the twentieth century. However different, at the heart of both crises Chabod had discovered a metamorphosis of values (*valori*) that had led to the victory of egotistical and vitalistic urges (personal and collective, individual and "national," Italian and European) over the ideal balance (cultural, intellectual, and spiritual) between life and the "demons" of politics. Chabod's hardly concealed admiration for the efforts of Charles V to maintain the unity of the empire, the balance of national evocations of French life and culture during the Restoration period after the fall of Napoleon; and, finally, in the *Storia* itself, his historical sympathy for the post-Cavourian liberalism of the Moderate elite, which had successfully guided united Italy through the dark passage of the early Bismarckian era, all testified to the "Guicciardinian" bent of his psychological and spiritual inclinations.

All the main actors of Chabod's masterpiece on the post-Risorgimento are "Guicciardinian" figures in the sense I have sought to suggest. Emilio Visconti-Venosta is the center of a constellation constituted, among others, by such "Guicciardinian" figures as Costantino Nigra, Marco Minghetti, Quintino Sella, Giovanni Lanza, and Count di Robilant. Neither Mazzini, the defeated messianic figure, the lonely prophet, the fallen ideologue, who died in "exile" at home in 1872, nor Garibaldi, who survived in pathetic agitationism until 1882, appears as active protagonist. Their "heir" and former disciple Francesco Crispi, the former fiery and impetuous conspirator now become the conservative Jacobin monarchist in action, is a Chabodian "anti-hero." [36] Perhaps it may not

---

and its aftermath. However unlike each other they were—and Chabod is only too keenly aware of dissimilarities in every other respect—Bismarck and Crispi nevertheless, each in his fashion, incarnate for Chabod the worst features of the "Machiavellian" political personality. The Cavourian "successors" (Visconti-Venosta, Nigra, Lanza, Minghetti, Count di Robilant) appear to have tempered those qualities with Guicciardinian *discrezione*. For comparative purposes, see Chabod, *Storia: Le premesse*, 86–106, 125–39, 165–67 (on Bismarck); 76–79, 111–13, 545–62 (on Crispi); 563–618, 625–53 (on Visconti-Venosta, Nigra, Lanza, Minghetti, and di Robilant).

[36] On Crispi, see Chabod, *Storia: Le premesse*, 53–55.

seem too bold to assert that had Chabod been adult, as two of his "masters" (Salvemini and Croce) had been, during Italy's strenuous *belle époque* before 1914, he would have been a cautious Giolittian.[37] Guicciardini, Visconti-Venosta, and Giolitti may well be taken as an emblematic trio who, together, formed or appear as as a projection of a Chabodian biohistorical "ideal-type."

Chabod's experience of 1944–46 in direct political action as a leader of the Piedmontese resistance movement and then as a major "diplomat" of the liberty of his *Valle* proved to be more than a mere episode in his life. It was rather a turning point, representing at the same time his first and only participation in active national and international politics and a relatively long interruption of his historiographical but not of his "historical" work. A truly cathartic moment in his life, it contemporaneously brought him fulfillment and disenchantment. Most of the details of that strenuous period have been recounted by his excellent Valdostani friends Alessandro and Ettore Passerin d'Entrèves. For our purposes of searching out the man behind the historian Chabod, an attempt to appraise, even on the basis of so meager and indirect a documentation as we now possess, that unique experience may perhaps help to highlight certain important features not merely in his historical personality but also in his historiographical work.

During those two years Chabod fought for and won the autonomy of the Val d'Aosta within the then still tentative structure of the Italian post-Fascist state. We know now that this has proved to be a permanent contribution the historian made toward the reconstruction of both his native region and resurgent democracy in Italy. Yet the price he personally paid for his success seems to have been almost disproportionately high in terms of the "hurt"—of the contumely and defamation, the threats and accusations—he had to bear during those years, not only from the "external" French annexionist agitators and propagandists but, infinitely worse, from some of the very beneficiaries—the Francophile wing of them—of his disinterested and heroic activities

---

[37] Cf. *Storia*, 200n4, 478, 546, for references to Giolitti.

in behalf of his native *valle*.[38] That hurt was apparently so great, so grave, that it led Chabod to a self-imposed, physical alienation from the region he loved and for whose freedom he had fought practically to the point of self-destruction. For ten years after October, 1946, Chabod did not return to the beautiful *montaignes Valdotaînes* where, during earlier days of peace, he was wont to spend serene days of respite and work. He never explained and his friends never asked, the reasons for his long absence from "home." On this, his silence was even more impenetrable than on other personal matters.

Speculation is perhaps wholly vain, and it would have to force open portions of a man's soul in which no biographer or historian has any legitimate business. And in this, too, Chabod himself set a "model" worthy of emulation. For no matter how acutely he had delved into the spirit of the works and the minds of the historical personages he studied, Chabod had always respected the intimacy of his subjects' private conscience. The fashionable attractions of psychoanalysis and depth psychology never crept into his conception of historical science; great psychologist that he was in his own historiographical right, Chabod left them in their proper sphere as practical and useful sciences in the medical and pathological fields.[39] With his vast and profound knowledge of all kinds of documentary materials, he could have made "sensational" revelations concerning many high personages in modern and contemporary Italian and European history. But he was not a writer of best-sellers and he never chose to be a superficial amateur in an alien field when he was so refined a master in his own. In his brilliant reconstruction of the life of Costantino Nigra in the *Storia*, Chabod penned an incisive and illuminating portrait of the handsome and talented Piedmontese diplomat.[40] He had had access to Nigra's love letters and, no less important, to the love letters written to the sophisticated ambassador (who had successively been at the courts of Paris, St. Petersburg, London, and Vienna), letters written him by many a high-born woman not al-

[38] Alessandro and Ettore Passerin d'Entrèves, "Federico Chabod e la Valle d'Aosta," 798–800, 804–805, 807–808.
[39] *Storia: Le premesse*, xiii.   [40] *Ibid.*, 600–18.

ways unattached to very important officials. Yet Chabod published nothing, not even an excerpt from any of them. For Chabod, biography was a kind of "sacred" art exactly because it dealt directly with the human personality.

Now, the Val d'Aosta had, in a deep sense, been Chabod's love affair not merely with a geohistorical "fact"—his native corner of Italy"—but with an "idea." The fact was of concern only to him, to his private life, to the prerogatives of his intimate, perhaps "sentimental" attachments to a vital personal commitment. That is why he felt under no compulsion to speak of it, and those who were closest to him and understood knew that they had no right to ask why he did not return to the native region he loved so much. The idea, on the other hand, however elusive it may seem, does belong to a realm which is legitimately the province of the biographer's and the historian's effort to understand. This, too, is clear from the way Chabod had treated his own subjects.

Even while the war was still raging and national disaster enveloped Italy as a result of the sterile pursuit of power to which the blind nationalistic policy of fascism had been reduced, Chabod lectured at the University of Milan. It was the winter of despair 1943–44 and the historian lectured on the "idea of Europe" which had now overtaken the old "idea of nation." [41] He spoke to an audience which could see its nation shattered and Europe in travail—and he offered a glimpse of hope. After reviewing the European expressions of the idea of nation and emphasizing that, amid its variety, it had originally embodied efforts toward the fusion of culture and liberty, Chabod concluded: "There thus came the wild outburst in every part of the earth of 'nationalism,' the contest of 'imperialisms' struggling against one another. And the nation, which a century before, even in the thought of Herder, had not been associated with political force nor with capacity for real action, became a portent of action, indeed ended by incarnating the principle of action for the sake of action." [42] Only a superior "idea"—the "idea of Europe"—had contained orien-

[41] Cf. the enlightening Prefaces by Armando Saitta and Ernesto Sestan to both Chabod, L'idea di nazione, v–xi, and L'idea d'Europa, v–xi.
[42] Chabod, L'idea di nazione, 82.

tations and directives which might have led and could still lead Europeans to avoid the anarchy of "naturalistic" passions stirring behind nationalistic activism.[43] The actualization of a unifying structure of "supreme values, moral and spiritual, which are the creation of our European civilization" might have spared the descent into the abyss of annihilation. For it was to this that the "internal barbarians" had exposed Europe. Now there stood before it the prospect of a reduction to political impotence and spiritual frustration, face to face as Europe was with the hegemonic victory of a coalition of momentarily friendly, gigantic but contrasting forces held together during the war by the common threat of Nazi-fascism. But those forces, too, by the very momentum of their victory and their power, if not of their origins and historic cultures, would prove alien to the actualization of the idea of Europe—of a United States of Europe. And yet, that idea was the last hope and it had to be realized. Again and again Chabod returned to this theme which, as he liked to put it, was "particularly dear" to him and stirred in him "a profound moral and spiritual resonance." In the postwar lectures at the University of Rome he insisted on retracing the historical *iter* of European civilization as he passionately sought an answer to the query as to "how and when our ancestors acquired the consciousness of being Europeans." [44] For Chabod, Europe had become a faith.

In 1946 Chabod did not leave a field of battle in order to enclose himself in an ivory tower. If he returned to his "buried notebooks" and to his meditations and work on history he also plunged, before that year was out (and through almost a decade and a half) into the many-sided labors of his teaching at the University of Rome, the directorship of the Croce Institute in Naples, the editorship of the *Rivista storica italiana,* and in 1955 the presidency of the International Committee of Historical Sciences. Meanwhile, he engaged in one of the most richly productive periods of his historiographical activity, of which the *Storia: Le premesse* (1951), was only the most marvelous fruit. If this immense activity, too, required an engagement of all his vital energies, these now were integrally part of his profession, of his historian's craft. Political

[43] Chabod, *L'idea d'Europa,* 203.   [44] *Ibid.,* 3–14, 196–99, *passim.*

action was perhaps of no less importance or urgency. But for him it had proved erosive of the work for which he "was born." He had now returned to his real "mission," and to the very end of his fertile career he never again abandoned it. Through fourteen brief but intense and creative years he rededicated all of himself to the rigor of that mission's intellectual discipline and he glimpsed its magnificent promise of spiritual fulfillment.[45]

In the vast and varied corpus of Chabod's historiographical production, there were four dominant but related themes—Machiavelli and the Renaissance, Italy and Europe during the age of Charles V, the Reformation as a crisis of the Italian conscience, and post-Risorgimento Italy in the crisis of modern Europe. He wrote on much else besides, but there were the truly grand themes of Chabodian historiography. They can be isolated with relative ease, but the stages and threads through which they were developed amount to one of the most difficult problems faced by any serious higher criticism. By higher criticism nothing more esoteric is implied than the sustained effort to understand critically for one's self first and then to seek to conjure a sense of that understanding for others. Neither summary transcription nor the most accurate paraphrasing can really advance genuine comprehension of a historian's meaning. In dealing with Chabod's work as, for that matter, with that of any other truly great historian, the serious critical student faces a double dilemma.

On the one hand, the student is compelled to attempt to do Chabod full justice as one of the most brilliant and sensitive historical minds of the twentieth century. Certainly no greater violence could be done to either the man or the historian than to reduce him, for whatever plausible reasons, to the dimensions of merely another outstanding writer of history, let alone to cut him down to the size of those blissful souls who seem to avoid pain but also real joy by viewing history without problems—their own or history's. For Chabod would unquestionably have agreed with Boris Pasternak's "Hamlet" when he says that "life is not a walk across an open field." Because history is part of life recaptured

45 Vittorio de Caprariis, "Un grande storico," *Il Mondo*, August 2, 1960, p. 9.

and understood, to write it is not just to survey the past as if it were an open landscape once and for all fixed, objectively distant, and neatly finished. No further elaboration is needed at this point to emphasize how far such a view of life and history was from Chabod's vision of the human world.

The other face of the dilemma posed by Chabodian historiography is no less acute, if of a different kind. All four of his major historical themes reveal a very curious "formal" fact. Whatever the apparently "accidental" factor in Chabod's initial undertaking to deal with an historical problem, once he plunged in he never really let go. Even more significantly, he returned to it from different points of view and sought to turn it directly or indirectly into a function of a coherent and consistent historical interest within a larger structure of understanding. Thus, in Chabod, the interplay of theme and variations constitutes one of the most arduous challenges that historiographical critique can encounter. Almost exhaustive bibliographical documentation would become merely the first step toward proper exegetical summarization and this, in turn, might become the basis for a full-fledged critical analysis. Obviously, necessary as it would be, such procedure is precluded here and an attempt at it will be presented elsewhere.

Throughout his life Chabod wrote six major studies on Machiavelli,[46] five on the Renaissance,[47] four on the State of Milan in the Empire of Charles V,[48] three directly or implicitly relating to the religious and spiritual crisis of the sixteenth century,[49] one

[46] They are now all collected in Chabod, *Scritti su Machiavelli*; in *Machiavelli and the Renaissance*, 1–148, only the essays of 1924, 1925, and 1952 have been included.

[47] Now in Chabod, *Scritti sul Rinascimento*; the essay on "The Concept of the Renaissance" in *Machiavelli and the Renaissance*, 149–246, is a revision and expansion, with an exhaustive bibliography, of the Italian originals of 1942 and 1948.

[48] *Lo Stato di Milano* (1934); *Lezioni di storia moderna: Carlo V* (1948–49); *Lo Stato di Milano nella prima metà del secolo XVI* (1954–55); *L'epoca di Carlo V*, Vol. IX of *Storia di Milano* sponsored by the Fondazione Treccani degli Alfieri (1961).

[49] *Per la storia religiosa dello Stato di Milano* (1938, 1962); "Calvinismo" and "Calvino" in *Enciclopedia italiana*, VIII (1930), 470–78, now reprinted in *Scritti sul Rinascimento*, 722–38; *La politica di Paolo Sarpi* (1950–51), now in *Scritti*

major and two lesser works on the post-Risorgimento,[50] and one on contemporary Italy.[51] There is an almost countless number of minor essays, biographical sketches, and brief articles, (particularly those in the *Enciclopedia italiana*) and a variety of review articles. To compound critical difficulties, it is not always easy to categorize Chabod's works into a tidy major and minor classification. Chabod's brief entries in the *Enciclopedia* under "Machiavelli," "Guicciardini," "Calvin," "Boulainvilliers," "Borghesia," "Illuminismo," and a few others are, in my opinion, major, truly great, perhaps in a sense in which his huge, fantastically rich and elaborately documented *Storia di Milano: L'Epoca di Carlo V* (1961) is not great. His *Storia: Le premesse* is, by general admission, a masterpiece, but so also is the lesser known long "essay" *Per la storia religiosa dello Stato di Milano* (1938). To make matters even more complicated for any synthetic overview, there is the question of structure, form, and style in Chabod's historical writings, whether major or minor—a question to which we shall pay some attention directly. In a word, Chabod's historiography never intended to facilitate the critic's labors but rather to stimulate his intelligence and powers of understanding. Chabod's work eludes both the metacritical and the microscopic approach and neither will be adopted in the economy of this limited essay. In the remaining section of this essay, therefore, we will seek merely to highlight the unity of vision behind the variety of perspectives, the consistency of view amid the diversity of emphases, and the logic of "idea" within the multiplicity of "facts" as they emerge from the major themes of Chabodian historiography.

---

sul Rinascimento, 461–588; *Giovanni Botero* (1934), now in *Scritti sul Rinascimento*, 271–458. On Chabod as historian of the sixteenth century religious crisis, see Delio Cantimori, "Chabod storico della vita religiosa italiana del '500," *Rivista storica italiana*, LXXII (1960), 687–711.

[50] *Storia: Le premesse* (1951); "Considerazioni sulla politica estera dell'Italia dal 1870 al 1915," in Gabriele Pepe *et al.*, *Orientamenti per la storia d'Italia nel Risorgimento* (Bari, 1952), 19–49; "Croce storico," *Rivista storica italiana* (1952), 473–530.

[51] *L'Italie contemporaine* (1950). *L'idea di nazione* (1961) and *L'idea d'Europa* (1961) perhaps could be "subjectively" included under the category of contemporary, although "objectively" and structurally they do not treat directly the twentieth century developments of those two portentous "ideas."

If for Benedetto Croce all history was contemporary in motivation, for Chabod all contemporary historiography must be monographic in structure.[52] Only the depth of the monograph and, therefore, its capacity, under the guidance of an expert and imaginative mind, to recapture a moment, an aspect, a problem of past fact and idea, constituted a kind of methodological insurance toward discovering historical reality *in sè e per sè* ("in and for itself").[53] For Chabod, "historical reality" *in sè e per sè* was evidently short of the Rankean view of *wie es eigentlich gewesen* but also beyond the Machiavellian sense of *la verità effettuale della cosa*.[54] The potential abstraction in Ranke's *es* and the limiting concreteness of Machiavelli's *cosa* may be said to have represented the extreme poles between which Chabod's historiographical endeavor sought to find its balance and its consistency. For, paradoxically, while Ranke's unlimited *it* of past actuality was too elusive, Machiavelli's restricted *thing* of past reality was too pragmatic for the historian's vision to be properly focused. For the one could lead to almost "cosmic" or purposeless reconstruction of history "as *it*[?] actually was" and the other could become a "blind" or empirical appraisal of "the real truth of the *thing*[?]"—that is, of history as a field of examples useful for practical action but not for disinterested historical comprehension.[55]

The Chabodian monograph—and, we repeat, *all* his work is essentially monographic—was a sustained, long-range and recurring, attempt on his part to escape the permissiveness of the unbounded Rankean *es* and the constriction of the Machiavellian *cosa* in human history. With its distillation of the general in the particular, the Chabodian monograph could not but be almost continuously

[52] Chabod, "Croce storico," 527, for the historian's acceptance without qualifications of Croce's own insistence on the "substantially monographic" character of every true historical reconstruction.

[53] *Ibid.*, 525.

[54] Cf. Chabod, *Machiavelli and the Renaissance*, 151, for his direct comment on the Rankean view that "any movement or event should be considered in itself, as possessed of a precise but limited individuality" as against the non-Rankean view of "present-day historians" who detect "living and active individuality against the general background of human history."

[55] Chabod *Questioni metodologiche*, 83–84. See *Storia: Le premesse*, 62–63, 93–102, 135, 189, on the uses and abuses of history by German (Treitschke, von Sybel, Droysen) and French (Renan, Taine, Albert Sorel) historians after 1870–71.

experimental, complete *in sè e per sè* both in form and in substance and yet partial in so far as it represented only a "moment of
general value," a period of investigation, a stage of intellectual
striving toward a higher level, at least toward a larger historical
unit of understanding. For this reason, practically all of Chabod's
works are, and were regarded by him as such, both "unitary" and
"unfinished." Historical truth was neither the abstraction of the
theorist nor the datum of the empiricist; it was neither brute fact
alone nor pure idea, neither a fixed absolute nor a relative fiction
of the mind. It might be only certainty but it was the only certainty
that the historical mind *as such* could be certain of.[56] Abstracted
chiefly from his actual works of history rather than from his scanty
theoretical pronouncements, and even so concisely distilled, these
theoretical historical concepts were at the heart and constituted
the inner character of Chabodian historiography; they are functions of its fascination but also irreducible aspects of the challenge
it poses for genuinely critical understanding.

Chabod wrote no narrative history, neither in its classic nineteenth century tradition nor in its varied twentieth century ver-
sions. From beginning to end, all of his professional writing seems
to have been predicated upon the assumption that selective and
intensive concentration through the monograph on a particular
historical problem of "universal" significance is the ideal structure
within which the search for historical truth must be conducted in
the twentieth century. If he was thereby attempting to escape the
legacy of the system-builders of the nineteenth century, he was too
sophisticated not to be keenly aware that the seventeenth century
tradition of erudite history was anachronistic. All of his recognizably major works, whatever their forms, are characterized by an
attempt to view and reconstruct some question of large historical
import through the close study of a special problem conducted on
the basis of original research and reinterpretation of sources. Thus,
for instance, he studied and returned again and again to Machiavelli's works, particularly *Il Principe*, neither as an abstract formulation of political theory nor as a mere challenge to philological

---

[56] Chabod, *Questioni metodologiche*, 24–25, 75–78, from which I have abstracted my own characterizations.

science. For Chabod, the thought of Machiavelli cannot be disassociated from the agonizing historic crisis of Renaissance Italy.[57] Before that thought can be seen in the perspective of its European and universal significance—that is, as one of the first and most crucial expressions of a transvaluation of values in the Western conscience vis-à-vis the problem of politics conceived beyond the Christian doctrine of good and evil—it must be studied as a biohistorical transmutation of consciousness of "reality" in the mind of Machiavelli, within the context of his historical reality. Wherever it eventually led as a novel concept of power in the history of the West, Machiavelli's meditations on politics must first be reconstructed as an immediate problem, at whose origins lay the confrontation between an exceptional mind and the crisis of Renaissance Italy.[58] A similar or at least analogous genetic process must be reduced to historiographical procedure toward the understanding of the concept of Renaissance, of the emergence of the idea of Europe, of the function of the myth of Rome in post-Risorgimento Italy, or of the idea of progress in nineteenth century Europe. In all of these and in other ideational [59] phenomena, the methodology of reconstruction must be historical before it gives way to the legitimate demands of universalizing concepts or theories concerning self-reflecting human consciousness face to face *in history* with "the brutal realities of things."

Evidently Chabod had a fairly well-defined theory of history, even though all his life he recoiled almost with horror from any ascription that it corresponded to a "philosophy of history." His theory of history was in fact a function of a rigorous methodology of historiography.[60] Quite elaborately in all his university courses

---

[57] "Del 'Principe' di Niccolo Machiavelli," in Chabod, *Scritti su Machiavelli*, 90; *Machiavelli and the Renaissance*, 105: "Thus *The Prince* is at once a synthesis and a condemnation of two centuries of Italian history; and far more than its supposed immorality, what should have stirred the emotions of the commentators was the thought of the boundless misery which was overtaking our civilization."

[58] Chabod, *Scritti su Machiavelli*, 108–35, contains Part VII entitled " 'Il Principe' e l'antimachiavellismo" which has not been included in the translation of the 1925 essay in *Machiavelli and the Renaissance*.

[59] Particularly in his earlier works on Machiavelli and the Renaissance, Chabod tends to use the word *ideologico* and its variants to mean "ideational" rather than "ideological"—that is the passage from *realtà* to *idea*, from *cose* to *coscienza*.

[60] Chabod, *Questioni metodologiche*, 26–27.

and very concisely in the prefaces of his major works, he devoted time, space, and direct attention to questions of methodology. There was often in his lessons a kind of repetitious over-scrupulousness concerning methodological questions that seemed to be almost compulsive. Again and again in his lessons he explicates, illustrates, exemplifies in an insistent manner that occasionally must have appeared unnecessary to specializing students and perhaps superfluous to the general auditor—or to the hurried and harried readers of the university *dispense* of his lectures. In the advanced seminars at the Croce Institute his approach was dialogical, Socratic, and one of his most brilliant students, Vittorio de Caprariis, himself prematurely dead, has left us a rare portrait of the master at work. The explanation for Chabod's insistence upon problems of method, according to de Caprariis, lay in the master's feeling that rigorous attention to "the humblest part of the historian's work" justifies or at least testifies to the claim that work might make to the highest values as a search for truth. For Chabod, method was "a moral fact." [61]

But there are methods and methods. For the historian, what counted was, in essence, the attitude of constant self-vigilance, the ceaseless search for the balance between the documents and the instruments of work and, above all, the mind's mastery over them through knowledge of their uses and abuses, the consciousness of the distinction between means and ends as one strove toward certainty, perhaps toward "truth." On a higher level, however, historical method required an understanding of the sphere proper to its application and again of the ends sought. Beyond the "humblest" stages of analysis, methodological anatomy (*notomizzare*) ceases and historiographical creation (*vivificare*) begins.[62] And it is at that point that the "science" of instrumental methodology gives way to the "art" of substantive historiography. To use a frequent Chabodian characterization, which is equally applicable to the historical process itself and to historiographical reconstruction,

[61] Vittorio de Caprariis, "Chabod Direttore dell'Istituto Italiano per gli studi storici," *Rivista storica italiana*, LXXII (1960), 672.

[62] See Chabod's review [originally in *Nuova rivista storica*, XIII (1929), 336–39, now in *Scritti sul Rinascimento*, 702–705] of a book by E. Mehl, *Die Weltanschauung des Giovanni Villani* (Leipzig, 1927).

at that point "things" become transformed into "facts" and "facts" are transmuted into "ideas," underlying concepts that guide the disciplined play of the historical imagination.[63] Method has served its function; style now makes its claims felt. Style, historical style, is a function of a metamorphosis at whose beginning all "lessons" stop. This not only because "to teach" style is to reduce it to what it cannot be but also because style in its highest reaches completes the cycle—by returning to the man. "The 'concreteness [*corporeità*] of intuition' remains as the first canon of the historian. As is evident, at that point no methodological rule serves anymore and theoretical principles have nothing further to say. Now the only 'actor' is historical sense, the instinct, I would say, the 'scent' of the individual historian, and the sole guide is Guicciardinian 'discretion' [*discrezione*]." [64] In Chabod's works, particularly in his masterpiece on the post-Risorgimento, that historical sense, that instinct and scent are his style, and style is the man.

There is, however, another significant aspect in Chabod's historiography which, through the fusion of thought and practice, transcends methodology and re-encompasses from a different side his theory of history. In a sense, it may be designated as his own historical style par excellence, a function of his uniqueness as a European master-historian among other master-historians. This may perhaps be best approached through the comparative perspective, which will also serve to delineate the "influences" he felt, accepted or rejected, within the historiographical community itself.[65]

The characterizations of Federico Chabod as an historian's his-

[63] In his masterly study on *"The* Composition of *The Prince"* (1927), in *Scritti su Machiavelli*, 186–92, Chabod gave a marvelous example of how, even in a work of apparently "pure" analysis, a moment arrives when philology and historiographical hermeneutics must give way to historical imagination seeking to reconstruct "the live process of creation."

[64] See Chabod, "Croce storico," 505; "Metodo e stile di Machiavelli," in *Scritti su Machiavelli*, 383–87; *Machiavelli and the Renaissance*, 142–47, on style as "imagination," "vision," "intuition," "interior illumination"—"the imagery of one whose emotion [*passione*] is still tempered by faith."

[65] For Chabod's "encounters" with a number of contemporary historians, see Sasso, *Profilo*, 12–13, 25–28, 70–75, 97–100, 106n15, 107–109, 125–29, 138–39, 155–57; Momigliano, "Appunti su F. Chabod storico," 649–50.

torian and as a pure historian are correct in so far as they capture outstanding qualities of his historical craft. On the other hand, they become, at best, mere expressions of a kind of terminological stenography and, at worst, falsifying simplifications if they are not understood within their proper contexts. Something has already been suggested as to how and for what reasons those contexts must be kept in view in appraising the connections between Chabod's biography and his historiography. Here it remains to emphasize that Chabod's methodology was neither pure technique nor a mere instrument of rebellion against the systematizers of past and present in Italy and abroad. For, as we have already seen in another sense, if throughout his life Chabod did not answer the siren calls of pure philosophical history neither did he succumb to the anti-rhetorical rhetoric of varieties of fashionable pragmatic history. The quest for the laws of history he probably regarded as a vain neopositivistic aberration not worthy of serious attention. He did believe, however, that facts are not mere shadows reflected against the wall of a Platonic cave. For him, facts are the elemental constituents of forces in history which are themselves powerful but not necessarily inescapable. Neither Renaissance Italy nor the Empire of Charles V, nor Liberal Italy before fascism *had to* succumb to the forces that were bent upon their destruction and there are no "original sins" in history unredeemable by the "grace" of historic human choice. For no less integral but no less decisive among the forces of history is the force of consciousness as self-reflection and action. What men do with facts, how they are affected by them, at what point and in what manner they translate them into ideas, or into beliefs, faiths, myths, and motives for action (for "free" historic action) ultimately proves more important than the inert "force of things." Human history is "free" not because men are "naturally" free to make history at will but because men are not, need not be, prisoners of geography, circumstances, tradition —or of history itself. For Chabod, history is "free" in so far as men are conscious of the limits but also of the potentialities of their *freedom to make it.*[66]

As practically all members of his generation, Chabod had been

[66] Chabod, *Storia: Le premesse*, xiv.

much influenced by Benedetto Croce and he had at least been exposed to the teaching, so essentially different, of Gaetano Salvemini. Although in a sense he was infinitely more "Crocean" than even tendentiously "Salveminian," ultimately Chabod remained almost equidistant from both Italian masters. His very structure of personality stood against acceptance of Salvemini's incorrigible moralism stirring behind the old historian's eclectic empiricism.[67] At the same time, Chabod stopped short of accepting Croce's secular providentialism re-emerging, particularly during the philosopher's last phase, from beneath his "absolute historicism."

Chabod had been a student of Friedrich Meinecke at the University of Berlin and, despite interpretative disagreement on Machiavelli, he held the German historian in a kind of special veneration. For him, Meinecke's *Die Idee der Staatsräson* (1924) was one of the supreme masterpieces of twentieth-century European historiography.[68] But Chabod would not and did not adopt Meinecke's method of dealing with the history of political ideas. Above all, and especially at the end, Chabod could not accept the almost overwhelming role which Meinecke had assigned to *Fortuna* in the making of the tragedy of German history. For, in his re-examination of the German conscience after the unspeakable Hitlerian convulsion, Meinecke had gone back to *Fortuna*, that exquisitely Machiavellian "woman" who could be subdued by the strong and the bold, and he had turned her into the dominant "abstract" combination of uncontrollable accident, of unexpected chance and almost unforeseeable and irresistible "force" that had led to the "German catastrophe" and Europe to the brink of annihilation.[69]

On a different level and for different reasons, Chabod could not accept the French varieties of historical "structuralism." He was

---

[67] Momigliano, "Appunti su F. Chabod storico," 649. Negligible seems to me to have been the influence of Salvemini on Chabod. On what I have called Salvemini's "eclectic empiricism," see my *Italy in the Giolittian Era*, 144–47.

[68] Chabod, "Friedrich Meinecke," *Rivista storica italiana*, LXVII (1955), 287.

[69] *Ibid.*, 286–87. On Meinecke and Chabod, see Valiani, "Lo storico dei propri tempi," 786–87; Sasso, *Profilo*, 126–32.

a close personal friend and admirer of Fernand Braudel and had great respect for the group of the *Annales*, but he could not follow nor would he emulate them in their rigorous but eclectic socioeconomic and cultural typological history.[70] For, as he pointed out with gentle but firm irony in the preface to his *Storia: Le premesse*, Chabod could not quite see how "the secret of history" could be captured by "so-called psychologism" or by that great expectation of a certain kind of "very recent historiography" which believes that the "secret" can be contained within "statistical tables, percentages, medians, graphs, and diagrams." [71]

Lastly, though Chabod, too, like so many of his own teachers and contemporaries, had "started" with the old master of political history par excellence Leopold von Ranke and, in a sense, never ceased doing him homage as a demiurge of the historical method, he ended under the influence or at least the renewed attraction of the historiographical nonconformist and master of cultural-spiritual history Jacob Burckhardt. Indeed, during the last years of his life Chabod became almost "ideally" reconciled with Meinecke in so far as he pitted, so to speak, Burckhardt against Ranke—the Burckhardt who had peered into "the future" of European history. One of the students who was very close to Chabod at the Croce Institute reported that, during the last years of his life, Chabod "had a number of times occasion to say that if he could have rewritten his book [the *Storia della politica estera!?*] he would have devoted still more space to Burckhardt and his 'prophetism'." [72] But it was to Burckhardt the seer of the contemporary crisis of values, not to the historian of *The Civilization of the Renaissance in Italy*, that Chabod would have wished to return. On the nature and meaning of the crisis of Renaissance Italy, Chabod had, since his youth, discovered a more direct, surer guide than even the Swiss historian himself—Niccolò Machiavelli. And for a reappraisal of the crisis of contemporary Italy through which *they* had *both* lived and suffered, Federico Chabod returned to the histori-

---

[70] For suggestions of mutual professional as well as personal sympathies, see Braudel, "Auprès de Federico Chabod," 622–24.

[71] Chabod, *Storia: Le premesse*, xiii.   [72] Sasso, *Profilo*, 166–67.

cal works of his great friend and unofficial master Benedetto Croce who had died in 1952, when the "young man from Aosta" was at the height of his own career and renown.

1950–1952: these years marked a *triennium mirabile* in Chabod's historiographical labors. In January, 1950, he delivered a series of lectures on contemporary Italy at the Institut d'Études Politiques of the University of Paris, and that same year there appeared his rich critical essay on "Gli studi di storia del Rinascimento" in the Antoni-Mattioli *Festschrift* dedicated to Benedetto Croce. During the fall-winter term of 1950–51, he gave at the University of Rome those lectures which became the basis for his biographical study on Paolo Sarpi. The year 1951 saw the publication of his great *Storia della politica estera italiana: Le premesse.* In May, 1952, he delivered his beautiful swan-song on Machiavelli with his lecture at the Palazzo Strozzi in Florence. In the fall of that year, following the death of Benedetto Croce, he began the composition of his minor masterpiece entitled "Croce storico." Practically all the major themes of Chabodian historiography were present, and they were re-elaborated or developed in new form during a period which, as we now know, was to see a choral climax of a splendid career.

In all those works the dominant chords were unmistakably clear, revealing a maturity and lucidity never before attained by Federico Chabod. But it was his *Storia: Le premesse* that truly made historiographical history within the European community of historical scholarship. There is neither the intention nor the opportunity here to analyze the particulars of that extraordinary work but before a few conclusive comments are made on the historian, at least a general characterization of his major work seems necessary.

In Chabod's reconstruction of the post-Risorgimento, facts and ideas, society and consciousness, politics and culture, biography and historiography constitute the counterpoints of an intricate and subtle treatment of a grandiose theme. The recurring variations are suggested in the very first part and they return with different tonalities throughout, to the very end of the book. The beginning of Italy's national life, Chabod insists, occurred in the midst of a great European crisis of politics at the center of which lay the full assertion of a policy of force and a new consciousness of power by Bismarckian Germany. In the wake of the "fact" of power, as it had asserted itself in the battlefields of 1870–71, Europe undertook a readjustment of its traditional political, social, and spiritual life. To survive or be overwhelmed was of the essence of the new age. Chabod's principal theme is concerned with the understanding of the stupendous problem of how the conflicts engendered at home and abroad by the Italian national revolution, particularly during its Cavourian phase, were placated, if not resolved, by the liberal-moderate ruling classes of post-1870 Italy. The major task of these classes and their political leaders, as Chabod sees it, appears to have been a search for a delicate balance between the ideals of liberty which had inspired the Risorgimento and the realities of power which dominated the policy of both old and new European states after 1871. For, even as in the course of the final crisis, Italy had "conquered" Rome and joined the community of European states, both the universalistic idea of Rome and the idea of Europe, whether as a *corps politique* or as a commonwealth of peoples, had been shattered. "Qui parle Europe a tort: Notion géographique," Bismarck was to annotate on a diplomatic dispatch.[73] Just as Metternich a generation earlier had regarded Italy a mere "geographic expression" and, therefore, the principle of nationality a dangerous chimera, so now after 1871 under Bismarck Europe had become a fiction and national power the sole reality. In an international community in which power had become the principal arbiter, the new national Italy of the post-Risorgimento, confronted as it was with gigantic internal problems and limited resources for external influence, might founder or be overwhelmed. Chabod's *Storia* is the history of the strenuous but successful passage which, under the guidance of the post-Cavourian successors of the "Historical Right," chief among them Emilio Visconti-Venosta, Italy achieved through the perilous realities that had emerged after the waning of "old Italy" and also of "old Europe." Intended to be the first of four volumes, the *Storia: Le premesse*

[73] Chabod, *Storia: Le premesse*, 168–69.

is also a kind of "prehistory" of how liberal Italy eventually came to play an active role in the new Europe taking shape during the latter part of the nineteenth century.

On a different level, Chabod's *Storia* is documentation and evocation, historical reconstruction and spiritual reflection, fact and idea, but so masterfully wrought through the discipline of a rigorous method, so finely fused through the uniqueness of style, that ever since its appearance it has tended to defy most traditional classifications. Those who like to think of history as a "science" have seldom seen an exemplar in which archival documentary materials have been so fully explored [74] and the principles of the so-called scientific method so carefully observed. And yet, to subject the book to mere scientific analysis would certainly result in one's missing its subtle beauty of form and the rich nuances of its substances and structure. Those who may believe that history is chiefly a "work of art" or an aesthetic experience can perhaps find very few contemporary examples of so exquisitely fine a use of the resources of the Italian language as a vehicle of historical expression. Yet they would soon discover that history reduced to stylistic *virtuosismo* was completely alien to the severe personality of the Piedmontese historian. Those who might be ideologically inclined and perhaps eager and ready to dissect the book as merely another Crocean *laudatio temporis acti* full of nostalgic sweetness and light on the Liberal era may find superficial satisfaction in catching here and there Chabod's subtle sympathy for the ideas and men who had worked with an Italy not in the "kingdom of the moon" but in a particular Europe at a particular historic moment.[75] But then not even the most obdurate ideologues could miss the play of light and shade in the Chabodian history of a time of difficulties and dangers not merely for one class of Italians but for the survival of Italy herself as a new, poor and weak, modern nation in a stronger and richer modern Europe. Lastly, those who have a predilection for philosophical history, for history as critique of pure thought, might soon discover that rarely has in-

[74] Chabod was one of the editors of the vast collection of Italian diplomatic documents—*I Documenti diplomatici italiani*—which eventually will span the long period from 1861 to 1943.

[75] Chabod, *Storia: Le premesse*, xi.

tellectual history been treated with similar intelligence and, in particular, that never has the history of an idea, "the idea of Rome," been so sensitively reconstructed and retraced as a function of both Italian and European spiritual life. And yet the "pure intellectual" would ultimately have understood very little if he did not see how Chabod never let ideas become alienated from other "facts," other "realities," and actions and passions of the human condition at a particular moment of modern Italian and European history. The incontrovertible fact is that Chabod's *Storia: Le premesse* brought about the infrequent critical "miracle" of being unanimously hailed as a masterpiece *sui generis*— and it has not since been denied the unique honor connected with that achievement. In Chabod's *Storia*, historiographical ripeness was all.

Both as man and craftsman Chabod's standards were almost impossibly high. But he never irresponsibly compromised with even the least demands of those standards. An "inner" loneliness appears to have been his lifelong companion and, particularly during the last years of his life, when he was at the height of his career and fame, the physical suffering caused by the insidious malady which prematurely cut him down on July 14, 1960 was unrelenting. The silence about himself, to which even his most intimate friends testify, was perhaps a function of that loneliness, and then certainly of that suffering. Yet he never sought to weigh in his favor the anguish in the labors as against the joy intrinsic to the fulfillment of his calling. For, in a profound sense, it was that calling which Chabod pursued as his profession, as his mission.

Despite the homage that continues to be done to his name at home and abroad, it sometimes seems as if, like his life, Chabod's work, too, has tended to remain splendidly isolated, almost inaccessible to those who for whatever reasons may believe that history is "a walk across an open field." Amid the not unrelated cascades of popular history and the whirlpools of esoteric history, Chabod's work pays no tribute to the idols of the market place. His historiography may, therefore, be called "aristocratic" in the very best sense of the word. Severe with himself, Chabod was unbending in his quest for historical truth as his intelligence, his self-training, and experience led him to discover and envisage it. An "historian's historian," therefore, in so far as he was not everyman's historian. But his interests were universalistic and his monographic concept of historiographical endeavor should not be mistaken for what it was not. Chabod was not a pedant writing only for the erudite. On the contrary: on the basis of documented facts, history, for Chabod, deals with life, and through the force of ideas those facts assume meaning and give a sense, a real consciousness of life in the past. For at the core of Chabod's historical thought stirred a vital intellectual passion striving to lay bare the hard bedrock of "brutal fact" in order the better, the more illuminatingly to re-trace the course of Western ideas during the modern period of Italian and European history. Although he seemed to have worked only for "the happy few" who would not shirk his demands, he struggled all his life to loosen some of the tightest knots tied by modern political and intellectual history—knots whose grip few men escaped during the European age of world history.

The rigor which characterizes Chabod's work was an aspect of the self-discipline with which he shaped his life. That is why, de-spite the difficulties often encountered in finding the true points of fusion between them, his life and his work should not be viewed as two separate islands. The relationship between the unity of his historical vision and the multiplicity of his historiographical labors perhaps ultimately lay in Chabod's having discovered the secret of the delicate balance between that rigor of work and that disci-pline of life. Though that secret may forever elude the student's search and the critic's pursuit, it must be subsumed as the quintes-sential element in the consistency of Chabod's historical mind and in the structure of his spiritual personality.

THE FRANCE OF M. CHASTENET

WILLIAM SAVAGE
*Louisiana State University
in New Orleans*

ALTHOUGH HE IS not a professional historian, Jacques Chastenet de Castaing has done more than any living writer to awaken the interest both of scholars and laymen in the history of the Third Republic of France.[1] For more than a decade after the fall of France, the republic lay in the shadow of its humiliating defeat, the record of its past occasionally illuminated by a significant monograph but more often distorted by the flood of polemic this controversial regime inspired. Chastenet was the first writer to attempt a large-scale evaluation of the Third Republic. His seven-volume *Histoire de la Troisième République,* published between 1953 and 1963, offered a masterful and gracefully written synthesis of all aspects of history, joining to the narrative of politics and diplomacy an informative and often provocative account of the intellectual and social life of France between 1870 and 1940. The *Histoire* was written for the educated public rather than the scholar, and it quickly found a large and appreciative audience among Frenchmen, who were grateful for a comprehensive history of an epoch whose issues continued to dominate politics but whose events already had become vague even to the older generation.

Professional historians at first were inclined to dismiss the *Histoire* as another ambitious popularization of history from the ranks of the Académie française. The elegant style and wit coupled with an old-fashioned emphasis on civic virtues and patriotism seemed

[1] This essay concerns itself solely with Chastenet as an historian of the Third Republic. His writings on England and Spain are not treated here.

to confirm this judgment. But in recent years, with the publication of the final volumes, the *Histoire* has won increasing respect from scholars who appreciate Chastenet's perceptive analysis of France's recent past. Even more important from the viewpoint of historians, the *Histoire* offered that rare and valuable account of an epoch written by one who lived through those years and whose study was based on an extensive personal knowledge of the men and events of his time.

Few historians with the ambition to write the history of their own times have been so favored by the circumstances of birth, education, and career. Born in Paris in 1893 not far from where he presently resides on the Faubourg St. Honoré, Chastenet has spent much of his life close to the heart of French politics, only a short distance from the Elysée palace, the embassies, and the Palais Bourbon. He became familiar very early with these halls of government, for his family was deeply involved in the political life of the republic from its birth. His maternal grandfather was a member of the National Assembly in the 1870's and his father Guillaume Chastenet for many years represented the Gironde as a conservative in the Chamber and Senate. The Chastenet home was a frequent meeting place of deputies, senators, and high government officials, and as a youth Jacques Chastenet had the opportunity to meet many of the republic's statesmen. Some of them —Briand and Poincaré, for instance—he was later to know well in his own right.[2]

Chastenet's education befit the position of his family and one who seemed destined to continue the family tradition of service to France. After secondary studies at the Lycée Condorcet, an episode of his youth he always recalls with great fondness, he attended the Sorbonne, the Faculté de Droit, and the École des Sciences politiques. He was an excellent student and earned in rapid order the *licence ès lettres*, honors in Finance and Foreign Affairs, and the *Doctorat en Droit*. During these years in the finest of French educational institutions, his fervent patriotism, which was instilled in him by his father and which infuses all his writings on France, was reinforced by a thorough study of his country's

[2] Chastenet to author, November 3, 1966.

past. Although attracted increasingly to research in finance and foreign policy, his lively interest in history and the arts remained undiminished and helped fashion the rich culture which has made him one of the most talented and versatile writers in France today.

Chastenet completed his formal education in 1914, on the eve of the First World War. He was called into service almost immediately. During the war, he rose to the rank of captain of artillery and served as liaison officer with the American Second Division, an experience which gave him an opportunity to observe both the political and military operations of the conflict. His service earned him the *croix de guerre* with five citations and the Legion of Honor *au titre militaire*.

Shortly after demobilization, Chastenet passed the *concours* of Foreign Affairs and entered diplomatic service. He was thrown immediately into the midst of the frenzied postwar diplomatic activity. His first appointment was as secretary-general to the Inter-Allied High Commission for the Rhine territories in Coblenz. He used this valuable opportunity to study at first hand the controversial question of the Rhineland, which figured prominently in French foreign and military policy. Returning to the Quai d'Orsay, he was assigned to the secretariat of the Conference of Ambassadors under the direction of Jules Cambon and René Massigli. During 1922 and 1923 he attended several international conferences where he came into direct contact with such important figures of the diplomatic scene as Briand, Poincaré, Curzon, Sforza, and Beneš. By the time he was thirty, Chastenet had acquired a thorough grasp of the complex issues of postwar French and European diplomacy.[3]

For personal reasons Chastenet chose to abandon what promised to be a brilliant future at the Quai d'Orsay. Combining a career in banking and journalism, he joined the reputable conservative journal *Opinion* as diplomatic correspondent, at the same time attracting attention for his articles in the *Revue des Deux Mondes* and the *Revue de Paris*. Within a decade Chastenet reached a

[3] Christian Melchior-Bonnet, "L'Historien," *Livres de France, Revue littéraire mensuelle*, xiii (1962), 5–7; Wladimir D'Ormesson, "Jacques Chastenet," *ibid.*, 3–4.

position of prominence and even of influence in both journalism and politics. In 1931 he was named a codirector of the powerful daily *Le Temps*. Although the venerable *Temps* was no longer an institution, as it had been before the First World War, it continued to be one of the most respected and influential newspapers in France. It was still possible for an observer in 1937 to repeat what was said of *Le Temps* in 1914: enter any other paper's editor's office at five o'clock and you will find him clipping articles from *Le Temps* for his own newspaper.[4] Many of these articles were written by Chastenet himself. Although burdened with administrative responsibilities, he often wrote the *bulletin du jour*, the paper's widely read editorial commentary on the issues of the day.

During his tenure as editor of *Le Temps*, Chastenet continued to devote attention to foreign affairs, and many of his articles were concerned with the crucial developments of the last decade of peace. A persistent advocate of a strong France, he deplored the decline of French power at a time when the rest of Europe was girding for war. It was the Popular Front's failure to strengthen France's military forces, as well as its association with the Communist Party, that made Chastenet a severe critic of Léon Blum's government. In 1938 Chastenet, alarmed at France's military weakness, became an ardent defender of the Munich Accords, arguing that the risks of war outweighed France's treaty obligation to Czechoslovakia. After Munich, Chastenet continued to press for French rearmament. At the same time, as it became clear that the German appetite for territory remained unsatisfied, he urged his countrymen to lay aside their differences and strive for the national unity necessary for the trials ahead.

Although Chastenet dreaded war—few had a better understanding of the ravages the war of 1914–18 had brought to France and Europe—he faced the opening of the conflict convinced that France's cause was just. His patriotism and his faith in the future of France left no room for despair even in May and June, 1940, when French resistance melted in the face of the German *blitz-*

---

[4] Raymond Manévy, *La Presse de la Troisième République* (Paris, 1955), 213–14.

krieg. When it became clear that Paris could not be held, Chastenet moved *Le Temps* to Lyons where, in spite of incredible difficulties, he was able to resume publication on a limited basis.[5]

Like the vast majority of his countrymen in the dark days of 1940, Chastenet turned to Pétain as the leader of a much-needed moral and political reorganization of France. But these hopes were deceived as it became clear that French independence was a fiction and that Vichy was less interested in reconstructing the new France than in exorcising the demons of the old. In late 1942, when the German invasion of the Free Zone ended the Vichy experiment, Chastenet chose to suspend *Le Temps* rather than continue publication in occupied territory. What was intended as a temporary interruption was in fact the demise of the newspaper which for many years had set the standards of intelligent commentary on French diplomacy and politics. Towards the end of the war, the liberation government banned all newspapers and journals which had continued to appear after the Allied landings in Africa. Chastenet bitterly resented the ban because of its implication that *Le Temps* had favored collaboration. In reality, he contended, the government's decision was inspired by political jealousies and personal animosities dating from the Third Republic. In any event, Chastenet refused to expend his time and energies in recriminations. He quickly turned to other pursuits and he now regards the incident as "ancient history" and a closed chapter of his life.[6]

Even before *Le Temps* ceased publication, Chastenet had embarked on a profitable and successful career as a historian and writer. Between 1941 and 1966 he published more than a score of books on the political and social history of France, England, and Spain, at the same time continuing to write for newspapers and revues. Hardly a year passed during this quarter century without the appearance of a new volume by Chastenet. He proved to be a master of the art of writing history for the educated public, winning a large following among Frenchmen and the praise of critics for his knowledgeable and eloquent treatments of such diverse subjects as William Pitt, European diplomacy, and eight-

[5] Chastenet to author, November 3, 1966.   [6] *Ibid.*

eenth century Spain.[7] Honors accompanied financial and critical success. In 1947 Chastenet was elected to the Académie des Sciences morales and in 1956 he joined the "immortals" of the Académie française.[8]

Almost half of this impressive literary and historical accomplishment deals with the Third Republic and it constitutes the heart of Chastenet's work as a historian. Like his writings as a whole, it is characterized by a rich diversity. In one or another of a dozen books and numerous articles and essays published over a period of twenty years, Chastenet wrote with equal authority and clarity on almost every facet of the republic, including politics, diplomacy, and social and intellectual history. If historical synthesis proved to be his forte as a historian, he also displayed in *Raymond Poincaré* a genuine talent for biography.[9]

No appreciation of Chastenet's voluminous writings is possible without an understanding of the way he defined his role as a historian of modern France. To some extent, of course, he wrote France's history because of that insatiable curiosity about the past one finds in all successful historians. But Chastenet also saw a purpose in history. A patriot deeply concerned for the future of his country, he believed his countrymen could profit from a knowledge of the forces and events that had determined France's fate since 1870. This preoccupation with the "lessons of the past" is evident in all of his work. His role was to interpret the past, to reveal these lessons to a generation removed in time and experience from the Third Republic.

This attitude toward history helps explain why Chastenet, unlike many Frenchmen who lived through the thirties and forties, was not content "to publish his memoirs in two volumes *chez* Plon." He consciously chose the historian's path, fully aware of the pitfalls that lay in the way of one who chose to write the history of his own times but who was convinced it must be written and confident that the task could be accomplished. In the debate over whether contemporary history is actually history, Chastenet embraced the affirmative position.

[7] Chastenet, *William Pitt* (Paris, 1941); *Vingt ans de diplomatie, 1919–1939* (Paris, 1944); *Godoy, prince de la paix* (Paris, 1963).

[8] Chastenet to author, November 3, 1966.

[9] Chastenet, *Raymond Poincaré* (Paris, 1948).

The value of Chastenet's work on the Third Republic derives in part from the realism with which he confronted the difficulties faced by the writer of contemporary history. Writing of the recent past, he once remarked, is always a Sisyphean labor.[10] No sooner has the historian gone through the available memoirs and documents, than more appear. The accumulation of standard sources will never be complete in his lifetime. The historian must write of his own time with the realization that his work is necessarily incomplete and that future historians, armed with new evidence, will alter and revise his account. Even so, the contemporary historian can make a lasting contribution to historical knowledge. Chastenet was convinced that one who wrote the history of his own times possessed advantages denied future historians.[11] Personal experiences and direct contact with men and affairs was at least as useful as more conventional sources and added a quality to the account that not even new evidence could diminish. Chastenet recognized that in this respect the work would be an important addition to the historical literaure on the Third Republic. His life spanned all but a generation of France's history since 1875 and his family had been involved in politics since the beginning of the republic. His personal papers and notes, which covered the decade before World War II, were an invaluable source of information equal to many an archive. Even more important, Chastenet believed, only a person who had lived through the epoch he wrote about could furnish future generations with an understanding of the many intangible characteristics of the period, the features of society which would never be collected in archives or deposited in museums. Only a contemporary could recreate for posterity the "atmosphere of the times," could capture the elusive *parfum* that reflected the public spirit of a bygone era.[12]

The importance Chastenet attached to "the spirit of the times" offers an interesting insight into his ideas on the forces that determine human history. Like most so-called "conservative" historians, Chastenet assigned a major role to ideas and psychological factors. The philosophy of history that depicts mankind the helpless vic-

---

[10] Chastenet, *Histoire de la Troisième République* (7 vols.; Paris, 1953–63.) Introduction to vol. I.

[11] *Ibid.*, V, 7.   [12] *Ibid.*, VI, 7.

tim of impersonal historical laws was foreign to him. To Chastenet, a people's fate was determined, not by historical laws, not by economic institutions or social structure, but by ideas, the collective mentality of a people, what they believed, the values they cherished, the myths they accepted, the hopes that inspired them to action, the fears that rendered them immobile. This public spirit was what enabled a people to surmount its difficulties or, conversely, to be subdued by them. Chastenet's conviction that a people ultimately controls its destinies is pervasive in all he wrote. Thus the proper study for the historian is the people; not a class, but the nation as a whole. This attitude explained Chastenet's emphasis on public opinion and his constant search to understand the psychological makeup of his countrymen. No doubt this outlook created some major defects in his history of the republic—he tended, for instance, to attribute France's growing economic inferiority to lack of daring and he failed to recognize the importance of the lack of raw materials—but it revealed vistas rarely explored by more conventional historians. No other writer worked so diligently to humanize the history of modern France, to know and make understandable his fellow countrymen, individually and collectively.

Chastenet clearly demonstrated his talent as a historian in his first major work of contemporary French history, the biography of Raymond Poincaré published in 1948. It was indicative of Chastenet's attitude toward his role of historian that he chose not to write a conventional biography. Less interested in providing a detailed account of Poincaré's life and career than in capturing for his readers the essential traits of his subject, Chastenet contented himself with a résumé of the more important chapters of Poincaré's life, focusing attention on the events which formed his personality, values, and ideals.

Chastenet could not have chosen a more difficult subject among the statesmen of the republic. Few Frenchmen equaled in tenure Poincaré's career in politics and none could match his record as an officeholder. Deputy and senator for most of half a century, many times a minister, thrice premier, president of the republic during the First World War, active in diplomacy and finance as well as politics, Poincaré left an indelible mark on many of the republic's institutions. Yet, no other of the republic's leaders was so little known in his lifetime. Austere and impersonal, formal in his relations even with his close associates, he possessed few of the attributes that make the popular hero. He had none of the glamour of Gambetta or the personal magnetism of Jaurès. Poincaré was popular, but it was a popularity of respect and consideration rather than the love the people have for their idols. He possessed qualities that inspired not so much love as confidence, and this to a degree rarely enjoyed by any other French leader. He had many political adversaries and rivals, but he had few detractors or enemies, and his ardent admirers and loyal supporters were found in the ranks of both the left and right. In part, Chastenet believed, the exceptional confidence Poincaré inspired resulted from the image he projected to the French people: "a man cast in a single mold from bronze and steel, the combatant without fear or reproach." [13] Although he was much more complex than this trite formula reflects, it was widely accepted among Frenchmen. In time, Chastenet believed, Poincaré himself was influenced by it, and, "through a mimicry of which History offers many examples, it finally became almost exact." [14] In time of crisis, when other of the republic's leaders seemed incapable of governing, it was to Poincaré that the nation looked for leadership. After 1914 only he was able to establish a degree of unity and stability midst the turmoil of French politics.

Perhaps no one was better suited than Chastenet to undertake the difficult task of making the man and the image comprehensible to later generations. An ardent admirer of the former president, he knew him well and had followed closely his career for many years. Having had the opportunity to observe Poincaré in action, Chastenet was able to add his own knowledge and insights to the information he obtained from other sources. He did not limit his research to the usual documents, official papers, and parliamentary debates. He consulted many of Poincaré's former colleagues, including former ministers, diplomats, and parliamentarians, and he read Poincaré's private correspondence for clues to his

[13] Chastenet, *Raymond Poincaré*, 296.   [14] *Ibid.*

subject's personality. Poincaré's family provided Chastenet with little-known information about his subject's private life.[15]

Given the limitations of a single volume, *Raymond Poincaré* accomplished admirably what Chastenet set out to do. It was a portrait which reproduced faithfully the weaknesses as well as the strengths of its subject. Chastenet penetrated the mask of reserve to find a Poincaré who was tenderhearted and sentimental. Beneath the Poincaré of steel and bronze, he discovered a flesh and blood politician often hesitant instead of single minded, ambitious as well as dedicated, and sometimes lacking in courage when it came to political decisions.[16] Poincaré's intelligence was great, but it was an intelligence without imagination, more given to argumentation than to decision. Although dedicated to public service, he often failed to see that new situations required new methods and approaches. If he possessed to an outstanding degree the qualities that make an exceptional administrator, he lacked the vision that history requires in its heroes. To Chastenet, Poincaré remained all his life what he was as a young man: a product of the nineteenth century with a mind fashioned *nul varietur* by the scientism and positivism of the France of his youth. He professed a blind faith in certain abstractions. Science and *La Patrie* were his gods; liberty and perfectibility of the human race his creeds. These ideals, because they were abstractions, often created a barrier between Poincaré and individuals and between the statesman and his countrymen. His sense of justice was incorruptible but it was more often applied to categories, to "the people," than to individuals. His liberalism was real and profound but it, too, was "nineteenth century." Liberty, as Poincaré conceived it, was the aspiration of an elite and rarely related to the needs of the masses.[17] Even his patriotism—the fierce patriotism of the Lorrainer—lacked the human quality and had as its object the fatherland rather than the French people. Because Poincaré loved France with a passion (it was his only passion, Chastenet explained), he conceived of her almost as a real person, "a sort of radiant and helmeted Valkyrie, entirely distinct from the French people." It was this vision of France and his obsession with Alsace-Lorraine that accounted

[15] *Ibid.*, 11, 12.   [16] *Ibid.*, 181.   [17] *Ibid.*, 59, 295.

for the chapter of his life that was, at the same time, the most glorious and the most tragic. These were the war years, when Poincaré as president helped lead France to a magnificent victory, but a victory bought with the lives of more than a million and a half Frenchmen. His conception of France and his determination to regain Alsace-Lorraine led him to resign himself to four years of slaughter without once lifting a hand to stanch the flow of blood. All for the greater glory of France, for Poincaré had no higher cause than *La Patrie*. Europe and humanity remained unknown to him, emotionally if not intellectually.[18]

Ironically, some of the qualities that formed a barrier between Poincaré and his countrymen helped create the legend that made him the symbol of statesmanship. To Chastenet, the readiness with which Frenchmen turned to Poincaré in time of crisis could not be explained by the reflex of calling a conservative to office to rescue France from the ravages of leftist fiscal and economic policies. Nor could this respect be attributed to his exceptional abilities as an administrator. Poincaré was more than an orthodox economist and more than a capable minister. He exemplified probity and seriousness, two qualities that Frenchmen appreciated in their leaders but which were often lacking in French politicians after the "Republic of Pals" had introduced new men with new moral values into the French political system.[19] When Poincaré entered office, whether as premier or as minister, Frenchmen knew that there would be no deals, no scandals, no sordid transactions. Careless of friends, colleagues, and constituents when his duties were involved, he came to personify the incorruptible statesman. Even his petty economies—his close surveillance of the ministry's stamp box, for instance—and his refusal to *tutoyer* his colleagues emphasized his propriety and respectability. He became the symbol of the Sacred Union during the war. In 1926 his reputation, rather than any specific economic policy, sustained the watery franc. The "Poincaré miracle" was all the more striking because it was never repeated. His departure from office signaled the end of the "years of illusion" for France and Europe and the beginning of the time of troubles. Whether or not Poincaré could have

[18] *Ibid.*, 295.   [19] *Ibid.*, 296.

dealt with the crisis of the thirties Chastenet refused to speculate. In any event, the men who followed him could not. To Chastenet, Poincaré will always serve as a model for those who aspire to lead France.[20]

Raymond Poincaré was followed a year later by *La France de M. Fallières*.[21] The striking differences between the two books demonstrated Chastenet's remarkable versatility as a historian. In *Raymond Poincaré*, he identified the life and career of a single individual with a long period of the republic's history as the setting. In *La France de M. Fallières*, Chastenet undertook a comprehensive survey of French society in the decade before World War I. Yet, there were important similarities. Both were, in a sense, "psychological" studies. In the biography, Chastenet had been primarily interested in explaining the mind and personality of the statesman and his public image, and the extent to which this image reflected the values of Frenchmen. In his survey of prewar France, he again was concerned with analyzing the attitudes of the French people.

La France de M. Fallières is a deceptive book. At first it appears to be less a serious work of history than a sentimental tribute to the France of Chastenet's youth, the years of the Lycée Condorcet, the Sorbonne, and the École des Sciences politiques. Even the title contributes to this impression. For that matter, Chastenet saw no reason why the historian should be forbidden "to toss flowers on the tomb" of the epoch he chose to study.[22] But just as his admiration for Poincaré had not blinded him to the frailties of his hero, his nostalgia for prewar France did not prevent his subjecting this period to an even-handed analysis. Popular literature had long represented the decade as a bygone time of stability, prosperity, and contentment, the last flowering of nineteenth century civilization. Chastenet saw it as the meeting ground of past and future rather than the graveyard of the nineteenth century. In fact, Chastenet insisted, the *Belle Époque* had much more in common with the twenties than with the *fin de siècle*.[23] The movements which appeared so startlingly novel in the post-

[20] *Ibid.*, 299.   [21] Chastenet, *La France de M. Fallières* (Paris, 1949).
[22] *Ibid.*, 379.   [23] *Ibid.*, 10.

war era—feminism, cubism, the emphasis on sports and speed, the decline of the belief in progress, the triumph of intuition—all emerged in the years before World War I and gave the *Belle Époque* a character markedly different from the *fin de siècle*, when positivism was only beginning to be challenged, when abstract ideas and faith in progress still reigned supreme, when figurative art and descriptive literature still dominated French culture. A major theme of *La France de M. Fallières* was the questioning of old values and ideals foreshadowing the "revolutionary" twenties.

To document and describe this change in all areas of French life required a vast amount of research in such diverse fields as art, literature, philosophy, science and invention, popular tastes and public opinion, to say nothing of politics and diplomacy. The book is a mine of information for the social historian of the pre-war decade. Chastenet searched through hundreds of works to bring together in a single volume a multitude of facts about French society, including typical family budgets for various income levels, a description of the living conditions of France's forgotten proletariat, the fishermen, and even the development of sports as a national pastime. Nothing escaped Chastenet's sharp eye. He scrutinized and dissected the values and foibles of France's *gratin* as well as the peasants, the demimonde as well as the bourgeoisie.

A second important theme of *La France de M. Fallières* was the resurgence of nationalist and patriotic sentiment in the decade before the war. In this regard, it foreshadowed Eugen Weber's study of the nationalist revival in France,[24] although Chastenet was much less systematic in his political treatment of this aspect and much more daring in tracing its manifestations throughout French society. While Weber limited his study to politics and literature, Chastenet found manifestations of the nationalist revival in many areas of French public life. In parliament, deputies and senators who recently had been vehement critics of the military became the army's most ardent champions. Indeed, the army and the soldier began to enjoy a respect and popularity unknown

[24] Eugen Weber, *The Nationalist Revival in France, 1905–1914* (Berkeley, 1959).

a decade before. French diplomacy stiffened and sought a strengthening of alliances. France's allies Russia and England came increasingly into favor, as the success of royal visits attested. In literature, Péguy and Barrès led a chorus of praise of *La Patrie* that added fuel to the flames of national feeling. Even art and music reflected the resurgence of patriotism. If Wagner was not completely displaced at the Opera, Debussy found a popularity that could not be attributed solely to the vagaries of musical taste.[25] At the Châtelet, the overnight success of the Ballet Russe owed something to the increasing popularity of the Franco-Russian alliance during these troubled years. If the *Salon d'automne* and the *Indépendants* were immune to the new patriotic climate, canvases depicting military and battle scenes were in increasing favor at the official salons. On the popular level, the low opinion most Frenchmen had of sports in the late nineteenth century gave way to the awakening of interest among all classes in athletic competition and physical culture, a development due as much to patriotism as fashion. "Where better to prepare to retake Alsace-Lorraine than in the stadiums?"[26] Equally indicative of the changing climate in France was the country's sudden preoccupation with its youth. This was especially true in 1912 after Agadir had provoked a fresh quarrel with Germany. In French newspapers and revues there was a vogue of *enquêtes sur la jeunesse*, which Chastenet attributed to the anxiety of Frenchmen to determine the attitudes of the nation's future soldiers.[27] Even though these inquiries touched only a restricted group, for the most part the bourgeoisie, they revealed an unmistakable increase in patriotic feeling among French youth. All these manifestations on the resurgence of patriotism and nationalism contributed to the creation of an atmosphere of tension and defiance. Chastenet, who remembered quite vividly the last years of peace, recalled that there was a kind of electricity in the air that quickened the pace of life. It rendered the laughter more strident and the quarrels more bitter. And if the new mood did not so much glorify war as make it acceptable, more and more Frenchmen came to anticipate the adventure. In August, 1914,

[25] Chastenet, *La France de M. Fallières*, 314.   [26] *Ibid.*, 329.
[27] *Ibid.*, 361.

they rushed off to war as if they feared they would be too late to win the laurels of victory. In retrospect, this innocent acceptance of war has added a tragic quality to the *Belle Époque,* for none guessed that the war spelled the end of the France and the Europe they knew.[28]

The same year *La France de M. Fallières* was published, Chastenet began work on the monumental *Histoire de la Troisième République.* His original plan was to write the *Histoire* in six volumes, each ending at a significant date—1879, 1893, 1906, 1918, 1931, 1940. But as he began his examination of the thirties he realized that the controversial last months of the republic warranted a fuller treatment. Thus he ended the sixth volume with a detailed review of the Munich crisis and devoted a seventh to the twenty months between September, 1938, and July, 1940, when the remnants of the parliament voted virtually dictatorial powers to Marshal Pétain. This last volume was published in 1963, fourteen years after the first was begun.

What motivated Chastenet to undertake such an ambitious and difficult project? Was it the desire to restore luster to the tarnished reputation of the Third Republic? This consideration undoubtedly had some weight with Chastenet for if he was not an apologist for the defunct regime, he nonetheless was convinced that the republic had been unjustly maligned by many of its detractors. A more important consideration, however, was his conviction that a knowledge of all the republic's past was necessary to an understanding of any part of it. No examination of the controversial last decades could be fruitful without an awareness of the forces that had formed the republic in its earlier years.

Although Chastenet did not envision the *Histoire* as a major revision based on extensive original research, he was not content to rely either on the knowledge he had accumulated from his earlier writings or on the works of other historians. The *Histoire* occasioned much fresh research over the entire seventy-year period. He scrupulously incorporated information from recently published monographs and memoirs. Whenever it was appropriate, he consulted unpublished materials, such as the *Souvenirs* of Lucien

[28] *Ibid.,* 12.

Lamoureux, the *Notes* of Félix Faure, and the correspondence of Alexandre Ribot. [29] For his account of the republic's early years he had access to the family archives of such prominent French names as Decazes and d'Audiffret-Pasquier.[30] As in his previous works, Chastenet did not hesitate to use his personal knowledge and his papers but he carefully checked this information against other sources.

A work of seven volumes written over a period of fourteen years is not easily reduced to a few pages. While it is difficult to single out parts of the *Histoire* as more important than others, certainly Chastenet's treatment of the question of France's decline and collapse has attracted the most attention. Because it is such a personal interpretation and because it reflects most accurately Chastenet's ideas on French history—and human history in general—it deserves special emphasis.

Whereas most writers have attributed this catastrophe to material factors—the losses of the war, the depression, the inherent weakness of the constitution and the parliamentary system, the inferiority of France's economic position vis-à-vis other powers—Chastenet searched for the psychological causes. He believed France's crisis was a moral one, a failure of men and not of institutions.[31] Why did the French people lose its purpose as a nation? What psychological changes came over France as a result of the war and were made fatal by the depression? These were the questions, he thought, that went to the heart of the problem of the decline and collapse of the Third Republic.

In Chastenet's opinion, the most important ingredient of the public spirit of prewar France, and the one which suffered the greatest loss of vitality after 1918, was patriotism. To Chastenet, patriotism was the "cement" which held together a nation badly divided on a myriad of social, political, and religious issues.[32] Patriotism was a unifying factor in the nineteenth century in spite of the varied and apparently contradictory conceptions Frenchmen had of *La Patrie*. Obviously, Jacobin patriotism was markedly different in spirit from the patriotism of conservatives and national-

---

[29] Chastenet, *Histoire*, V, 8; VII, 8. [30] *Ibid.*, I, 9. [31] *Ibid.*, VII, 315.
[32] *Ibid.*, II, 331.

ists. Even within republican ranks, men like Ferry and Clemenceau disagreed violently on what constituted "true" patriotism. Nevertheless, Chastenet insisted, there was a factor which gave these conceptions a common focus before 1918. It was summed up in the word *revanche*.

Chastenet's acceptance of the *revanche* thesis—that the refusal of Frenchmen to accept the loss of Alsace-Lorraine was a decisive factor in French politics—differed significantly from the popular view of an enraged French people impatient for a chance to renew the struggle with Germany to recover the lost provinces. Like patriotism, Chastenet contended, *revanche* was diffused and manifested itself in many ways. It was less the desire of Frenchmen to fight another war with Germany than the need to compensate for the humiliating defeat at the hands of Prussians. The French people, wounded in their pride by the debacle of 1870, felt impelled to prove to the world and to themselves that France still was a great nation. This desire to achieve self-respect and to earn the respect of others influenced many areas of French public life in the years after 1870. Although the remarkable economic recovery after 1870 could be explained in part by the fundamental soundness and stability of the French economy, the recovery was given impetus by the desire to demonstrate that France was herself again. If the acquisition of a large empire could be attributed in part to accident, it also owed something to politicians, colonial officials, and adventurous officers who sought to increase French prestige. The empire could never be a substitute for Alsace-Lorraine, but it could restore French pride. In diplomacy, the Franco-Russian alliance testified to the desire of Frenchmen to recover France's position of influence in Europe, a goal impossible to achieve in isolation. In politics, it inspired a *sens de l'état* in French politicians and statesmen, a dedication to public service not always characteristic of French officials in the past—or in the future.

Inevitably, the spirit of *revanche* lost vitality with the passage of time, as the memory of Alsace-Lorraine dimmed and as new preoccupations arose to distract leaders and people. But after 1905 and Tangier the memory of the lost provinces and the humiliation was evoked again and grew stronger as Franco-German relations worsened. Many outsiders and, for that matter, many Frenchmen, deceived by the violent controversies into believing French unity was shattered, were amazed at the unanimity with which Frenchmen rallied to the Sacred Union.

History is fertile in ironies and one of the most tragic for France was that the victory of 1918, by avenging the defeat of 1870 and restoring Alsace-Lorraine, robbed France of the cause which had given the nation a purpose. It was inevitable, Chastenet concluded, that patriotism would suffer. Its goal achieved, spent after four years of war, it became conventional, less ardent, and, in certain quarters, even unfashionable. The "cement" began to crumble. Chastenet admitted that DeGaulle may have been right when he said: "Perhaps a people must have some great national goal to sustain its activity and maintain its cohesion." [33]

Chastenet realized, of course, that the decline of patriotism could not alone account for the moral crisis of France after 1918, a crisis of such dimensions that it often seemed to immobilize the entire people. The pressing problems facing postwar France in the economy, in matters of security, in foreign relations, in social policy were dealt with, if at all, in a haphazard fashion. In foreign policy, France alternated between intransigence and conciliation toward Germany, between strict enforcement of Versailles and a willingness to come to terms with the former enemy, between the policies of Poincaré and Briand. In fiscal matters, French governments vacillated between orthodoxy and experiment, between liberalism and protectionism. In the area of social reform, cabinets brought forth reforms which were generous in principle but miserly in application. Finally, there was a contradiction between a military policy essentially defensive in conception and a foreign policy based on alliances that made France the protector of eastern Europe.[34]

Could this lack of policy direction and organized purpose be ascribed to the material devastation and spiritual exhaustion resulting from the war? Chastenet concluded that while privation, destruction, and death were important, there were more decisive reasons. One was the novelty of the problems facing France after

[33] *Ibid.*, V, 261–62, 317.　　[34] *Ibid.*, 315–16.

1918. To most Frenchmen, the "social question" had never been more than a theme for noble discourse, and the *grand soir* only a dream in the feverish minds of a handful of exalted revolution- aries.[35] After the Bolshevik victory of 1917 universal demands for social change ceased to be visionary or academic, but the response of most Frenchmen and their leaders was to turn their backs on the changed scene in the hope that the new vision was merely a specter that would vanish by itself. The precipitate decline of the franc was equally shocking to a nation which had considered its currency as unchangeable as the meter and the gram and which recalled the words of a prewar Baedeker that the "banknote of the Bank of France is negotiable everywhere on a par with gold." Surely this disaster, likewise, could not be real but must correct itself once peace had automatically restored the true nature of things. Frenchmen had been insulated from the economic and social crises that had beset other countries before the war, and they wished only to perpetuate the security they had known. Moreover, the victory encouraged them to believe that a return to the past was possible and engendered all sorts of other illusions: that France could impose her will on Germany; that the League of Nations would preserve peace; that the wartime alliances would last; that the world order had not been changed, and that the war had been only a bloody episode which, when ended, would leave France unchallenged in Europe and Europe unchallenged in the world.[36]

Chastenet concluded that, given these illusions, the perpetual tardiness of response to events, the hesitations, the inconsistencies, and the contradictions followed each other almost automatically. Not even the depression, which ended these "years of illusion," resulted in a realistic appraisal of the country's economic and military situation. By 1931, when the universal economic decline finally struck France with full force, the nation had been so demoralized by the prolonged habit of turning its back on reality that it was incapable of a systematic, determined response. Just as the French bourgeois, overwhelmed by an unaccustomed eco- nomic insecurity, comforted himself with nostalgic recollections

[35] *Ibid.,* 316.   [36] *Ibid.,* 313; VI, 264.

of the golden age of a stable franc, he sought sanctuary from the rumors and shadows of war in the old dream of eternal peace. Frenchmen continued to place their hopes in the League of Nations long after that organization had proved itself to be "nothing but a tribune for harangues and a center of intrigues." [37] It was a similar nostalgia for democracy that inspired some French leftists to advocate support of the republican cause in Spain when such a policy was clearly against French interests. Even the riots of February, 1934, could be explained by a longing for past glories that found its expression in an attack on those held responsible for the decline of France—the parliamentarians.[38]

In Chastenet's opinion, Munich was the ineluctable consequence of these years of inconsistency and contradiction, of illusions and nostalgia. He recognized the persistence of controversy surrounding the Munich settlement even a quarter century after the event. In volume VI of the *Histoire* he devoted a chapter to a thorough review of the crisis, examining with great care, in the light of recent evidence, the alternatives France had. He concluded in 1962 as he had in 1938 that France had no choice but to act as she did. Having missed so many opportunities to crush Germany when the latter was weak, it would have been folly to go to war when Germany was strong and when France could depend only on halfhearted support from England. A war, and Chastenet remained convinced that Hitler's challenge was no bluff, would almost certainly have been fatal. Hence the necessity of the Munich Accords—"sad and inglorious, but not dishonorable." [39] The impartial historian, Chastenet insisted, could not fault France for avoiding a war she was almost certain to lose.

The catastrophe France avoided in 1938 she suffered in 1940. The respite afforded by Munich saw little change for the better in France's military position. Rearmament picked up pace, but the declaration of war found France unready and her people divided and uncertain. Ill-prepared militarily, refusing to see the logic in "dying for Danzig" when it had not been necessary to fight for Czechoslovakia, fatigued by so may false alarms, torn by conflicting ideologies, prey to outside influence—from England, Germany, Italy, and Russia, the French nation entered its hour

[37] *Ibid.*, V, 314.   [38] *Ibid.*, VI, 266.   [39] *Ibid.*, 206, 210.

of trial in profound disarray. Was the military debacle fore-ordained? In number, French forces were not negligible compared with those of Germany; in quality, the difference was great. French soldiers were not only poorly trained, they were older and less resistant to fatigue and illness than their enemies. The response to the mobilization decree also revealed an ominous lack of military ardor. There were few incidents or disorders, but Frenchmen went to their posts with more resignation than fervor. Nothing could be more revealing of the change since 1914, when Frenchmen had marched to war with spirit and anticipation. The difference between French and German military capabilities extended to the High Commands. There was no single authority in France as there was in Germany; worst of all, there was an unshakable attachment to the defensive strategies learned during the First World War. These defects on all levels of the French military establishment combined to create the catastrophe of May and June, 1940.

The military collapse was only the prelude to another debacle—the death of the republic a month later. Who was to blame? Chastenet's answer was implicit in the title of his last chapter, "The Suicide by Persuasion." Chastenet believed that there had been no need of a large-scale conspiracy to destroy the regime. The moral crisis that afflicted France went far beyond the designs of one man or of many men. By 1940 parliament, weakened from without by the attacks of its critics and from within by the inertia, skepticism, and even the corruption of some of its members, was no longer able to stand up against those who welcomed the end of the regime they had come to despise. Paralyzed by the military defeat, deprived of the leadership of those who had departed for Africa, swayed by the sometimes seductive, sometimes menacing words of Laval, under the spell of the prestige of Pétain, parliament was also overwhelmed by a sense of guilt stemming from its own incapacities and by the realization that most Frenchmen desired a reformation of the state. If Laval was able to deliver the coup de grâce to the Third Republic, it was only because the republic had been abandoned by many of its citizens.[40]

The regime that had been born with few expectations ended

40 *Ibid.*, VII, 270–90, 314.

with few regrets. Historians with a fondness for the ironies of
history have delighted in pointing out that the end of the republic
was appropriate to its beginning. But for Chastenet the republic
could not be measured by either the accident of its birth or its
melancholy demise. In the *Histoire*, he had sought to portray the
epoch with complete honesty and objectivity, bringing into relief
both its defects and its triumphs. What was his final judgment?
Chastenet concluded that the regime merited neither the excess of
honor accorded by its apologists nor the wholesale condemnation
of its enemies. The Third Republic's failures were more obvious
than its triumphs, but they should not lead Frenchmen to for-
get that it had solid accomplishments to its credit. In art, philosophy, and invention, the republic had written chapters as brilliant as any in France's long history. In economic development
and in social reform, the record was not impressive, for the republic had echoed the virtues and defects of its citizens—prudence,
conservatism, lack of imagination, and a fear of risks. Still, for
most of its long life, it had provided its citizens the prosperity and
economic security they valued so highly. The regime's most conspicuous failure was in politics. But here again, the fault lay in
the people and not in the institutions. Repelled by authoritarianism, Frenchmen nonetheless had failed to achieve a workable
parliamentary system. Parliamentary government had remained a
foreign import precariously rooted in French soil. But the darkness
of the republic's political life was not without relief, for over the
years the regime had displayed a constant regard for law and for
human rights. In a world where democracy and liberty had suffered
many indignities and defeats, Frenchmen had remained free.
For these accomplishments the Third Republic deserved to be remembered with indulgence and respect.[41]

With the completion of the final volume of the *Histoire* in
1963, Chastenet could take satisfaction in having accomplished
the goal he had set for himself. He had aspired to write a comprehensive history of the Third Republic for educated Frenchmen and he had acquitted himself brilliantly. His years of labor
had produced the most thorough and far-reaching appraisal of

[41] *Ibid.*, VII, 315.

modern France to come from the pen of a single writer. Although Chastenet had aimed at clarity rather than originality, the *Histoire* went beyond "popular" history and the genteel retelling of the nation's past. Incomplete and destined to be revised by future historians, the *Histoire* possessed qualities that will make it endure as an important addition to the historiography of modern France. Certainly one of the most important of these qualities is the personal information and knowledge Chastenet brought to his account. By enriching the *Histoire* with his experience as a participant and observer of events, he made an important contribution that not even the emergence of new evidence can diminish. At the same time, Chastenet added immeasurably to the value of his contribution by his knowledge of the historian's craft and by the observance of a rigid historian's code. From the beginning he had been guided by his determination to discover the truth. He had not avoided judgments, for they were part of the historian's *métier*. But he had made them with honesty and only after careful investigation. The result was the treatment of even the most controversial episodes and personalities with a moderation and balance that marks the serious work of history.

Undeniable though these qualities are, future generations may consider that Chastenet's greatest contribution was to have written a history of the French people rather than a history of France. By never separating history from its human context, he produced the portrait of an age. His knowledge of men and his desire to make them understandable offered an insight into the French mind that sheds a valuable light on the past. Years from now, students of the republic will turn to Chastenet's pages for an understanding of how Frenchmen under the republic lived and what they thought. Perhaps Chastenet would consider this his most important accomplishment, for he believed that the goal of the historian was not merely to discover the truth and reveal it, but to bring life to the past.[42]

Although Chastenet was in his seventieth year when the *Histoire* was completed, he gave no thought to retirement. An alert

[42] Pierre Dominique, *La Commune de Paris*. Texte de Présentation de Jacques Chastenet (Paris, 1962), 5.

mind and an exuberant spirit left no room for inactivity. Publications appeared at the same rapid pace, with Chastenet adding to his previous works on England and Spain. In 1967 he broadened his historical repertory to include the United States with an account of the westward expansion of the American people.[43] But always he was drawn back to France. In 1966, at the request of a Paris publisher, he agreed to write the history of the Fourth and Fifth republics as the final volume of a multivolume history of France. Admirers of Chastenet look forward to his applying to the France since 1945 the same clarity, intelligence, and wit with which he illuminated the Third Republic.

[43] Chastenet, *L'Angleterre de'aujourd'hui* (Paris, 1965); *La Vie quotidienne en Espagne du temps du Goya* (Paris, 1966); *En avant vers l'Ouest: La conquête des États-Unis par les Américains* (Paris, 1967).

GIOACCHINO VOLPE

EDWARD R. TANNENBAUM
New York University

G IOACCHINO VOLPE was Italy's most eminent nationalist historian; he was also the most important Italian historian to champion fascism. While Croce and Salvemini opposed that regime openly, the majority of the others disregarded it as best they could and went on with their normal scholarly pursuits. Volpe differed from most nationalist historians everywhere in his emphasis on the economic and social base of politics. Kings and statesmen played a minor role in his conception of the making of the Italian nation before Mussolini. Of all the nineteenth century Italian leaders only Crispi attracted him; Cavour, Garibaldi, and Mazzini left him cold. Insofar as Volpe had a "hero," it was that minority of Italians who had molded the dynamic urban environment of the medieval commune, conquered commercial colonies in the Near East, created the literary and artistic masterpieces of the late Middle Ages and the Renaissance, and, beginning in the eighteenth century, fostered an economic and social reawakening that ultimately led to political unification, which in turn facilitated further economic and social gains until 1915. The nationalism that prompted Volpe to embrace fascism was conservative not radical. He believed that the First World War had at last brought the great mass of Italians into the mainstream of the nation's life and that Mussolini's regime alone could lead them to the new levels of unity and glory implicit in the heritage of the past.

Born on February 16, 1876, at Paganica, in the Abruzzi, Volpe went to the University of Pisa at the age of twenty and studied under Amadeo Crivellucci. A historian of the political-diplomatic school that stemmed from Ranke, Crivellucci translated Ernst Bernheim's *Lehrbuch der historischen Methode* in 1897 and instilled its rigorous canons of criticism in his students. He was also the founder and editor of *Studi Storici,* which died with him in 1914. In this journal Crivellucci published a number of his prize student's articles including Volpe's first, in 1898, "Alessandro VI e Cesare Borgia," and, in 1901, "Pisa e i Longobardi," which was part of Volpe's doctoral dissertation on the precommunal period in Pisa. In 1902 the publication of *Studi sulle istituzioni comunali a Pisa* (in *Annali della Reale Scuola Normale Superiore di Pisa,* Vol. XV, 1–423) established Volpe as a leading authority on the medieval commune. Four years later he became professor of modern history at the Accademia Scientifica-Letteraria of Milan. From 1924 until 1940 he was professor of modern history in the faculty of political sciences at the University of Rome. He was also a deputy in parliament from 1924 to 1929 and, along with Giovanni Gentile, a member of the commissions studying constitutional reform. From 1929 to 1934 Volpe served as secretary-general of the Reale Accademia d'Italia. In Rome he also headed the Scuola di Storia Moderna e Contemporanea, where his associates included Federico Chabod, Alberto M. Ghisalberti, Walter Maturi, Ernesto Sestan, and Franco Valsecchi.[1] Volpe was the managing editor of the *Rivista storica italiana,* the *Archivi Storici di Corsica,* and the medieval and modern section of the *Enciclopedia italiana.* In 1940 he finally received the chair in medieval history in the faculty of letters at the University of Rome.

In 1943 the fall of Mussolini brought an end to Volpe's public and academic career but not to his activities as a historian. Within the next few years Volpe completed the three-volume *Italia moderna* (1815-1914), his main work of synthesis. He also continued to write articles on modern history. Since 1959 the Florentine publishing house of Sansoni has been reissuing all of Volpe's major works with the author's collaboration. When I visited him

---

[1] *Studi storici in onore di G. Volpe* (2 vols.; Florence, 1958). This was a *Festschrift* to which thirty-two historians contributed essays, including those mentioned above, as well as Mario Toscano and Ettore Rota.

in the summer of 1965 he was still alert and still helping to prepare new printings of his earlier studies.

In the eyes of most of his colleagues, Volpe's close collaboration
with fascism has not diminished his scholarly and human merits.
Gaetano Salvemini, whom the Fascists hounded into exile, called
Volpe the greatest Italian historian of his generation (with the
same "Alas!" that Léon Blum used when describing Victor Hugo
as France's greatest nineteenth century poet), but Benedetto
Croce and Giovanni Mira taxed him for failing to recognize moral
forces in history. Although this charge was certainly justifiable regarding his medieval studies, in the 1920s and 1930s Volpe consciously played up the "spiritual values" in modern Italian politics
and diplomacy. One may prefer Croce's and Mira's liberalism to
Volpe's nationalism and still see the moral content of both. Volpe
the man was warmhearted, generous, and loyal to his friends and
students, especially those who incurred Mussolini's displeasure. In
a letter dated October 17, 1938, he asked the Duce's permission to
acknowledge in the introduction to his book on the Triple Alliance
that his former student Leo Wollemborg had done a large part
of the documentation; Volpe wanted to list Wollemborg as co-
author but admitted that this was not possible because of the
"unexpected racial laws." [2] Only in his *History of the Fascist
Movement* (1939) did Volpe consciously stoop to pure propaganda. His scholarly reputation rests on his pioneer work in
medieval history, and, although he does not rank with Henri
Pirenne, Alfons Dopsch, or Marc Bloch, his studies in the first
decade of this century on the Italian commune were to guide
further research for almost forty years.

About 1900 Volpe, Salvemini, and Croce (in his theoretical
writings) all broke away from the antiquarian, "philosophical,"
approach that dominated Italian historiography in the late nineteenth century. Local history burgeoned at that time; every
province and every town of any size had its own historical society
and journal. The main activities of local "historians" were textual

[2] Files of the *Segretaria Particolare del Duce*, T-586, Job 108, microfilm frames
29760–72 (National Archives, Washington, D.C.).

criticism and the editing of old documents. Even in the writing of national history erudition predominated over interpretation, and the Italian Historical Institute, founded in 1883, became the stronghold of the "collectors of facts," especially facts about politics and diplomacy. Croce's strictures against this type of history are well known, Salvemini's and Volpe's less so because they have not been translated.

For all three men, Marx's historical materialism served as the catalyst for a new approach to history. Croce's flirtation with Marxism lasted only from 1895 until 1900, but Volpe acknowledged the influence of the Neapolitan philosopher's *Materialismo storico ed economia Marxista* on his own thinking.[3] Salvemini's *Magnati e popolani* (1900) explained the rise and fall of classes in medieval Florence in Marxist terms, and, although Volpe said that this work was too grossly materialistic for his taste,[4] Emilio Cristiani, his main critic today, insists that Volpe was strongly influenced by it.[5] Volpe did concede that he had been much impressed by Antonio Labriola's *Del materialismo storico* (1896) and Giovanni Gentile's *La filosofia di Marx* (1899). He himself had no philosophical bent and he never studied Marx systematically, yet a modified kind of historical materialism served as the main frame of reference for his medieval studies, all of which he wrote before 1914. Salvemini developed his own "positivist," sociological mode of historical analysis, whereas Croce later turned to an "ethical-political" interpretation of history. Until the First World War Volpe called his approach "economic-juridical."

Volpe wanted to study the total situation in any particular period, to see the connections between political, social, economic, religious, and cultural phenomena, always emphasizing the material conditions upon which these were based. He was primarily interested in societies in transformation, like the Italian communes

---

[3] Volpe, *Toscana medievale: Massa marittima, Volterra, Sarzana* (Florence, 1964), xiv. Volpe mentions the 1906 edition of Croce's *Materialismo storico*, but the original edition—a collection of Croce's articles in French Socialist reviews —appeared in 1899.

[4] Volpe, *Toscana medievale, ibid.* The preface to the 1964 reissue contains Volpe's reminiscences of his whole life as well as a cogent attempt to appraise his own work.

[5] Emilio Cristiani, *Nobiltà e popolo nel comune di Pisa* (Naples, 1962), 15.

in the twelfth century and the Kingdom of Italy, which he found to be "on the move" beginning in the 1890's. Volpe was a "materialist" in stressing the economic basis for social change, but he believed that institutions, once established (like the medieval commune and the united Kingdom of Italy), have as much force as economic factors. His interest in the whole texture of life plus his concern with the kind of behavior that was possible under any given conditions made him think of himself as a "realist"— especially in opposition to Croce's "idealism" and Salvemini's "sociologizing." None of these labels is very helpful; Volpe is best described as a social historian who turned to political and diplomatic history when the Fascists were in power.

Like Croce, Volpe wanted history to be taught and written as "past everything." In 1907 he published in Croce's review *La Critica* a series of proposals for reducing the compartmentalization of the Italian university curriculum. Volpe suggested borrowing the approach of Henri Berr's *Revue de synthèse* as the best way to make history a broad, all-inclusive subject.[6] He argued that the existing compartmentalization—especially the chasm between the faculty of law and the faculty of letters—was wrong because it went "against the full vision of the relations between the activities and products of thinking and acting man in history, against the feeling of the unity of life, against the organic systematization of knowledge."[7] Volpe wanted to reform the teaching of history in the universities not only for the benefit of budding historians but also for future politicians and professional people, who needed to be shown how history is relevant to all of contemporary life. Some of his proposals were incorporated into the Gentile law on education in 1923. This law did not overhaul the curriculum, as both Volpe and Croce had wished, but it did give more freedom to teachers in curriculum matters. Unfortunately for its sponsors, Gentile's educational reform, like all other Fascist reforms, was soon perverted by state interference. In 1923 Volpe also proposed a cooperative historical study of all aspects of Italy's past but Croce

---

[6] Volpe, "Insegnamento superiore della storia e rifoma universitaria," *La Critica*, V (1907). After this initial publication the essay was reprinted in Volpe, *Storici e maestri* (Florence, 1924), 11–13.

[7] Volpe, *Storici e maestri*, 15.

refused to participate, and Volpe soon became too busy with other matters to develop his own proposal.

Throughout his career Volpe always maintained that his interest in a particular period in the past was stimulated by the events of his own time. He later said that the peasant and working-class uprisings around the turn of the century "aroused in me and in the young people of my generation, even if not actually socialists, the idea that [our] society was transforming and renovating itself in all its manifestations, as it had eight or nine centuries earlier." Hence, Volpe became interested in the eleventh and twelfth centuries "as an age of social fermentation, the motive force of a new political order." [8] Then the noisy nationalist and irredentist movements of the immediate prewar years aroused Volpe's "patriotism" and turned his interest toward the last century of his nation's history. He and his fellow nationalists "shrugged our shoulders somewhat scornfully at the older generation, the self-styled epigones [of the Risorgimento], whom we reproached for having governed a great Nation like a small private business and for having frustrated the hopes of their fathers." [9] Volpe and the other interventionists viewed the First World War as "the last war of the Risorgimento." Three years after it was over, Volpe became a Fascist and concerned himself with the history of Italy's struggle to become a great power. He later argued that his public activities during the 1920s and 1930s made his historical works of those years more vital.[10] They did indeed in Fascist terms. But Mussolini's disastrous war effort on the side of Nazi Germany exposed the inadequacy of Italy's economic base for such an effort—a "factor" that Volpe prided himself on always taking into account— as well as the moral resentment of most Italians against being forced to fight aggressive wars in the face of losing odds—a "force" that Volpe never seems to have understood. Despite his historical "realism" and his interest and participation in current events, Volpe remained a traditional Italian professor with little sensitivity to the feelings of the masses of his own time.

[8] Volpe, *Toscana medievale*, xiv–xv.

[9] Volpe, "Motivi e aspetti della presente storiografia italiana," *Nuova Antologia*, CCCLXIV (December, 1932), 291.

[10] Volpe, *Toscana medievale*, xx.

For Volpe the origins of the Italian nation lay in the Middle Ages, not in ancient Rome. According to him, "the history of Rome is essentially the history of a city-state and a world empire."[11] The revival of urban life and Roman law in the eleventh and twelfth centuries did, in a certain sense, restore something of the ancient world and did reflect an unconscious reaction against the barbarian invasions and the institutions—especially feudalism—they had imposed on the peninsula; these invasions, however, also played their part in the renewal and rapid progress which marked the true beginnings of Italian history and without which this history would be unthinkable.[12] Volpe discarded the traditional search for the Latin and Germanic roots of modern Italian (and European) history. Instead he examined the new society that was evolving after A.D. 1000. Its origins lay in the social fermentation that moved the center of economic, political, and cultural life back to the towns, thus creating a climate of thought that made it possible for Roman conceptions of law, property, and liberty to become intelligible and assimilable again and to give something of their tone to the new order. As for the people who created this new order, they were neither "Lombards" nor "Romans" but descendants of both. Already by the eighth century the separation of functions was becoming more important than ethnic differences in the emerging Italian society. By then some conquered Romans had already been absorbed into the Lombard feudal aristocracy, and by the eleventh century some "Lombards," particularly the lesser vassals, were proudly calling themselves "Romans" in their struggle to free themselves from the tutelage of their feudal lords.[13]

Volpe saw the revival in the eleventh and twelfth centuries as an original creation by new people. A new petty and middle landed aristocracy emerged among the former retainers of the great lords and included even some men who had risen from a servile status;[14]

---

[11] Volpe, "Albori della nazione italiana," in *Momenti di storia italiana* (Florence, 1925, 1952) 7. This article was originally published in the Roman review *Politica* in 1924.

[12] *Ibid.*, 58.   [13] Volpe, *Toscana medievale*, xii.

[14] Volpe, *Il Medio Evo* (Florence, 1965), 178. The original edition was published in Florence in 1927.

these people fought the bishops and the feudal lords in promoting the autonomy of the towns. Another new "aristocracy" arose among the merchants, traders, and shipowners. Together, these two groups of new leaders built a new world of walled cities in which men regrouped themselves in free associations, transformed public and private institutions, created and exchanged new forms of wealth, and reopened the seaways all around the peninsula. These activities and the accompanying clash of political passions produced a specifically urban and bourgeois style of life, elaborated by forms of law, language, thought, art, and religious expression which became "the hallmark of the Italian people, the most characteristic and distinctive modes of its existence, the necessary base of its national life." [15] Between the eleventh and thirteenth centuries, according to Volpe, all the elements of modern Italian history appeared for the first time: capitalism, the state, the moral and economic unity of the peninsula, and humanism.

In 1905 Volpe outlined his general views on the origins and development of the commune, which he believed to have been Italy's greatest contribution to the beginning of modern times.[16] He considered as only half true the notion that the renewal of medieval society through the creation of the commune was the work of the bourgeoisie. "The bourgeoisie came later; it was the main army that followed the advance guard of diggers, sappers, and builders." [17] This advance guard of military men created the conditions for a new urban culture to which the merchants were to give substance and form between the thirteenth and sixteenth centuries. Even these vassals and other lesser feudal nobles did not act alone; they were aided in their conspiracies against the greater lords by the agitation and rebellions of the peasants themselves who, by the tenth century, were increasing in numbers and avid for more land and freedom.[18]

Volpe listed seven basic points regarding the formation and early development of the communes.[19] First, they exhibited a wide

---

[15] Volpe, "Albori della nazione italiana," 58.
[16] Volpe, "Questioni fondamentali sull'origine e svolgimento dei comuni Italiani," in Volpe, *Medio Evo italiano*, 3–40. This essay was originally published in Pisa in 1905.
[17] *Ibid.*, 7.   [18] *Ibid.*   [19] *Ibid.*, 12–22.

variety of forms, depending upon their geographical location, the social and economic experiences of their inhabitants, and their early political history. Aside from the major difference between the areas under Germanic and Byzantine rule there were important distinctions in external appearance and in the relations among social groups in the communes of Lombardy, Tuscany, and Piedmont. Still, Volpe's second point is that there were only two fundamentally different types of commune: one was rural and very simple, consisting of a free association of farmers bound together as equals; the urban commune was composed of a complex of clearly differentiated social elements juxtaposed against each other in a variety of ways. In the towns sometimes only one of these social elements formed the commune, but the others all had relations of one sort or another with the central nucleus. Point three is that the communes and their institutions were something new, and point four, that economically they were the product of an increase in wealth and an incipient money economy. Juridically, according to point five, the commune was born as a voluntary association whose members bound themselves together by an oath; Volpe sees this form of association as growing in all fields of endeavor in eleventh century Italy. His sixth point is that the most important communes—those that appeared at the seat of a bishop or count—had an aristocratic origin and physiognomy, that they comprised mainly large landowners and vassals, and that their formation went hand in hand with territorial encroachment on the surrounding countryside. In this connection Volpe emphasizes the newness of this early urbanized aristocracy and the fact that its property was almost always usurped from feudal lands and ecclesiastical benefices. Point seven is that each commune originated as a private or semi-private association; it bound together only those people who had spontaneously joined it, and its rules applied only to its own members. The other inhabitants of the town and its district remained outside the commune; only in the early twelfth century did it begin to acquire a truly public, governmental character and to impose its jurisdiction and protection on nonmembers.

Volpe gave a detailed analysis of the political development of the commune of Pisa from the mid-twelfth to the mid-thirteenth century in his *Studi sulle istituzioni comunali a Pisa*. This was "the period of the full flowering of consular institutions and of their first transformation into a government by a *podestà*—a change that was preceded and accompanied by other broad and deep changes in the whole internal social structure of the city, from top to bottom, from the roots to the newest branches." [20] By saying "preceded and accompanied" rather than "caused," Volpe tried to avoid the charge of determinism. Nevertheless, he clearly assumed that economic change causes social change and that new social groups inevitably seek political change.

Toward the middle of the twelfth century, Volpe tells us, Pisa was ruled by an aristocracy of shipowners, traders, landowners, and knights. Their expeditions to Calabria, Sardinia, and North Africa had promoted the development of the political institution of the commune and the political-corporative Consulates of the Sea and of the Merchants, through which they usurped the public powers of the bishops and the feudal lords.[21] But the commune had not yet become a fully public institution. Vestiges of its private origin remained and many merchant ships and warships were still under private control. The leaders of the commune and of the Consulate of the Sea got willing support from the rest of the population until the end of the twelfth century, when the mercantile bourgeoisie and the craft guilds increased in numbers and challenged the leadership of the aristocracy, which became an ever smaller minority of the growing population. These new people, especially the craftsmen, formed political "parties" seeking control of the government. Unable to achieve this directly, they accepted the temporary services of a new official, the *podestà*, as a more representative and impersonal arbiter of political differences than the consuls.[22]

During the thirteenth century, according to Volpe, the old warrior aristocracy exhausted itself in the Guelf-Ghibelline clashes and lost its political power to the middle classes.[23] While the

[20] Volpe, *Studi sulle istituzioni comunali a Pisa* . . . (Annali della Reale Scuola Normale Superiore di Pisa. Filosofia e Filologia, Vol. XV [Pisa, 1902]), vii.

[21] *Ibid.*, ix.   [22] *Ibid.*, 123, 130, 276.   [23] *Ibid.*, 415–16, 421.

craftsmen, military companies, petty merchants, and other members of the *popolo* continued to organize themselves and to try to influence public policy, the major orders of the bourgeoisie formed a new executive body with an elected Prior to run the city.[24] This new body was the *signoria*. It enforced laws that weakened the economic and political power of "the old feudal nobility, with one foot in the city and one in the countryside," thus assuring bourgeois domination of Pisa.[25]

After having set the pattern for research for more than forty years, Volpe's studies of the medieval commune have recently been subjected to a number of criticisms. Enrico Fiumi argues that the Italian commune originated as a democratic organization with a large lower-middle-class elite that can in no way be confused with Volpe's urbanized feudal nobility. According to Fiumi, the democratic organization of the commune lasted until the early thirteenth century, when families or rich merchants transferred their rivalries onto the political scene.[26] This extreme position is not shared by Emilio Cristiani, who takes Volpe to task on other matters. Through a Namierite study of noble families, Cristiani shows that the old nobility was still very active in the affairs of Pisa in the early fourteenth century and that after the 1320s it cooperated closely with the *popolo* in running the *signoria*.[27] David Herlihy attributes this change to the efforts of Pisan "capitalists" to make an economic adjustment to the rise of Florence: "Their old allies the artisans and their old enemies the aristocrats fused in opposition." [28] Herlihy accepts Volpe's main ideas but argues that in the late thirteenth century it was the *popolo*, not the capitalists, that gained control of the commune and broke the aristocrats' monopoly over urban property.[29]

Neither Volpe nor his critics have been able to define satisfactorily the terms aristocracy, bourgeoisie, and *popolo* for any

---

[24] *Ibid.*, 393.
[25] Volpe, "Pisa, Firenze e impero al principio del '300," *Studi storici*, XI (1902), 201.
[26] Fiumi, "Fioritura e decadenza dell'economia Fiorentina: III. Politica economica e classi sociali," *Archivio storico italiano*, CXVII (1959), 487, 492.
[27] Cristiani, *Nobiltà e popolo nel comune di Pisa*, 322.
[28] Herlihy, *Pisa in the Early Renaissance* (New Haven, 1958), 185.
[29] *Ibid.*, 28.

specific period. Volpe himself uses aristocracy to mean the ruling elite before the bourgeoisie allegedly came to power but fails to tell us how the merchants in the old aristocracy differed from those in the new bourgeoisie. Herlihy says that the new capitalists in the late thirteenth century differed from Pisa's older trading families in that their orientation was to their rural home, whence they brought wool to the city to be manufactured and exported.[30] He follows Volpe in equating aristocracy with old native families and democracy with newcomers. In this way, the older artisans, who certainly belonged socially to the *popolo*, are included in the political aristocracy. Elsewhere Herlihy says that "the *popolo* was that one of many 'states within a state' which eventually reduced the others to subservience, seized the *signoria*, the sovereign power, and became the State." [31] Cristiani, on the other hand, says: "The average and rich bourgeoisie (with the latter associating itself ever more closely with the noble-magnate class) had never relinquished the principal levers of power." [32]

Out of this welter of contradictory assertions it is difficult to distinguish between the social and political character of the aristocracy, the bourgeoisie, and the *popolo*. Volpe's great merit was to have shown how economic change and population growth created new social groups that sought to take political power from the older ones. But in Italy, as in the rest of Europe, the bourgeoisie—however one defines it—was far from being the dominant class after the thirteenth century. The Black Death, the rise of the Italian despots, the centuries of economic stagnation, and foreign domination between the High Renaissance and the Risorgimento, all created an immense gap between the bourgeoisie of the communes and the bourgeoisie of the united Kingdom of Italy.

Volpe possessed a keen insight into the functioning of medieval institutions on the day-to-day level. He distinguished with great precision the differences in early medieval Italy between the serfs who worked on the manors and the freemen who farmed their own strips of land. He saw that the guilds grew out of informal cooperation among craftsmen in a specific occupation long before

[30] *Ibid.*, 179.   [31] *Ibid.*, 55.
[32] Cristiani, *Nobilità e popolo nel comune di Pisa*, 229.

they acquired a formal juridical status. In discussing the distinction made by German economic historians between *Naturalwirtschaft* and *Geldwirtschft*, Volpe pointed to the difficulties in dating the transition from a barter economy to a money economy, particularly because of the resistance of many Church-owned economic enterprises.[33]

Yet on economic as well as social matters Volpe lacked the power of conceptualization. He especially admired Werner Sombart's *Die Entstehung des modernen Kapitalismus* and argued that Henri Pirenne's examples of capitalist activity in the twelfth and thirteenth centuries in the Flemish cities, Venice, Florence, and Augsburg, merely modified Sombart's thesis without invalidating it.[34] Volpe accepted Sombart's idea that medieval commerce was a small-scale affair conducted by merchant-artisans who were incapable of realizing large profits and who lacked the capitalistic spirit. But along with many others, he denied Sombart's assertion that the first capital formation came from rising ground rents in the towns. According to Volpe, "the houses and the land would not have increased in price without those same efficient causes that gave life to commerce, that is, the growth and concentration of population, with the relative rise in needs of all kinds of demand, production, exchange, etc., that is, in the last analysis, of capital." [35] He was correct in describing the obvious reasons for the rising value of urban property but he missed the point of what captial *is*, namely, savings reinvested in economic expansion. "Demand, production, exchange, etc." are not capital.

In his one major study outside the field of economic-juridical history, his *Movimenti religiosi et sette ereticali nella società medievale italiana: secoli XI–XIV*,[36] Volpe extended his frame-

[33] Volpe, "Per la storia giuridica ed economica del Medio Evo," in Volpe, *Medio Evo italiano*, 226–43, *passim*; 255; 272. This article was originally published in *Studi storici* in 1905.

[34] Volpe, "Un Congresso internazionale di scienze storiche" (at London, April, 1913), in Volpe, *Storici e maestri*, 105. This article was first published in 1914 in the *Archivio storico italiano*.

[35] Volpe, "Questioni fondamentali sull'origine e svolgimento dei comuni Italiani," 30–31.

[36] This work was originally published as "Eretici e moti ereticali dal'XI al XIV secoli nei loro motivi e riferimenti sociali," in the Milan review *Rinnovamento* in 1907; it was then expanded into a book (Florence) in 1922. The version cited here is a reprint (Florence, 1961), without revisions, of the 1922 book.

work of class conflict to the religious and heretical movements of medieval Italy. According to him, the main importance of these movements was that they reflected conflicts between "proletarians and bourgeois, between country people and townsmen, between the low and high clergy, between the feudal world and the urban world." The new movements especially expressed the desire of urban people outside the feudal and clerical orders for new rights and status. Volpe ventured one of his rare generalizations in saying that "new people" always express new religious feelings: "Every great historical upheaval is basically an onslaught of new classes, with their own new practical activities, forms of wealth, etc., with their own new moral and spiritual needs and conceptions or intuitions of life and of the world." [37]

Unfortunately, Volpe's preoccupation with the perennially rising bourgeoisie beclouded his otherwise excellent portrait of the various Italian heresies and evangelical sects. On the one hand, he maintained that heretics like the Cathari, who approved of lending money at interest, attracted a significant number of merchants, many of whose activities were regarded as sinful by the church and by ordinary people. On the other hand, he argued that the urban and feudal aristocracies turned to anticlerical movements in their struggle against the new bourgeois factions when these people allied themselves with the local bishop and the pope.[38] Volpe characterized the medieval heresies as "the first form of [mass] 'protest' in Catholic Europe and the only one that Italy had ever had." [39] At the same time he viewed them as indications of an individualist spirit that constituted a distinctive sign of the beginnng of the modern era.[40] Indeed, he treated Arnold of Brescia as a combination of the Abbé Sieyès and Michael Bakunin. Volpe described this twelfth century revolutionary as "a free man of the Italian Commune, who first participated in movements of towns-

---

[37] Ibid., viii, 37. [38] Ibid., 99, 103.

[39] Ibid., ix. The "only one," that is, before the upsurge of the Popolari (Christian Democrats) and Socialists immediately after World War I. Volpe's fear of these "demagogic movements" (ibid., xii–xiii) was undoubtedly a major reason for his adherence to fascism; it probably also explains why he eliminated any mention of Arnold of Brescia or the impact of the medieval heresies from his general history of the Middle Ages (Volpe, Il Medio Evo, 1927 edition).

[40] Ibid., viii.

people against the bishop-lord and then left his restricted municipal environment, breathed the air of France and Paris [as a disciple of Peter Abelard], became interested in philosophy and dogmatics, broadened his intellectual outlook and raised to questions of principle those issues that behind the walls [of the towns] were the focus of daily partisan battles, to questions of morality those issues that touched only economic and political interests." [41]

Arnold of Brescia's ultimate fate belies Volpe's effort to tie religious heterodoxy to any social or political interest. After Arnold led a revolt in Rome against the popes, Emperor Frederick Barbarossa executed him as a heretic and used Pope Adrian IV as a tool in his struggle against King William of Sicily. Volpe did not neglect the evangelical protest against the worldliness and corruption of the church hierarchy but in his effort to link this protest to the merchant class he missed much of its popular character. Although the decline of the heretical movements in the thirteenth century may have been partly the result of the "calming of the [political] waters," the work of the Franciscans and Dominicans in reaching the masses again was more important. [42]

For Volpe the Renaissance, like the religious movements of the Middle Ages, was primarily an expression of social and political developments. Its starting point was the "city-state, urban culture, the bourgeoisie." [43] By this Volpe did not mean the civic humanism of early fifteenth century Florence but rather the gradual secularization of life in the communes beginning in the eleventh century. Just as the merchants revived the Roman law in their effort to liberate themselves from the bishops and the feudal lords, so the humanists used classical literature and thought in their struggle against clericalism and scholasticism. Volpe rightly challenged Burckhardt's conception of the Renaissance as a clear break with medieval civilization; he also understood that classical antiquity provided only the models, not the creative force, for Renaissance art, literature, and thought—that the humanism and

[41] *Ibid.*, 33–34.   [42] *Ibid.*, xvi.
[43] Volpe, "La Rinascenza in Italia e le sue origini," in Volpe, *Momenti di storia italiana*, 163. In 1904 Croce had admired this article and published it in *La Critica* under its original title, "Bizantinismo e Rinascenza (a proposito di un scritto di Karl Neumann)."

"paganism" of Petrarch and Valla expressed basic changes in their own immediate environment.[44] He went too far, however, in portraying the Renaissance as the triumph of the free commune and bourgeois values over those of the Church and the feudal aristocracy. He underestimated its intellectual and cultural achievements as well as the non-"bourgeois" uses to which these were put.

Volpe refused to see the aristocratic and princely character the Renaissance was acquiring by the late fifteenth century. Once it ceased to express "bourgeois" interests, it lost its originality in his eyes. But where does such a view leave the works of Raphael, Da Vinci, and Michelangelo, most of which were commissioned by princes and popes? (Lorenzo de Medici and Lodovico Sforza were no more "bourgeois" than Popes Julius II and Leo X.) Were Ariosto's Orlando Furioso and Castiglione's The Courtier not expressions of the aristocratic outlook of the High Renaissance? And was Machiavelli's The Prince not the most telling description of Renaissance politics? It will not do to say that "after the fifteenth century, the creative power of the first [i.e. fourteenth-century] Renaissance grew increasingly feeble . . . aside from the original productions of artists with fourteenth-century vigor, like Michelangelo, and of the new scientific literature." [45]

After 1913 Volpe did no more original research on the Middle Ages and he never wrote a work of synthesis on any aspect of medieval history. He had outlined his theories on the commune in 1904 ("Questioni fondamentali . . .") and had amplified some of these in long review articles thereafter, but his study of Pisa was his only full-scale work on communal institutions. In the period 1907–12 he concerned himself with church-state relations in the Italian cities but, again, never wrote the synthesis. Instead, in 1913 he published a short monograph, "Per la storia della giuris-dizione communale e dei rapporit fra Stato e Chiesa nelle città medievale: Massa Marittima," in Studi storici. In that same year he wrote two other short works on small Tuscan cities but these were not published until 1923. Volpe's monographic studies of individual communes, his Movimenti religiosi e sette ereticali, and his short pieces on church-state relations constitute the bulk of his

[44] Volpe, "La Rinascenza in Italia," 158–59.   [45] Ibid., 160.

research in the medieval field. His *Medio Evo italiano* (1923) is a collection of earlier articles and essays; his *Il Medio Evo* (1927) is a popular work for students and teachers, not a scholarly synthesis.

The First World War heightened Volpe's nationalism and absorbed all of his energies. He was an active member of the Milanese Democratic Liberals for Italian Intervention during the ten-month period of Italian neutrality.[46] After having participated in several war rallies in April and May of 1915, he left his professional chair for the army and was later decorated for bravery. Like the radical nationalists—Enrico Corradini, Luigi Federzoni, Gabriele D'Annunzio—Volpe viewed the war as the final phase of the Risorgimento, not only in gaining *Italia irredenta* and making Italy a great power in international affairs for the first time in her history, but also in solidifying diverse social groups into a true national community. From then on he was to devote himself to the realization and preservation of these three goals, as a writer, teacher, and Fascist dignitary.

Italy was not the only country where nationalists wanted an imperialist war as an antidote to international socialism, but, unlike those in Austria, Germany, Russia, and even France, many Italian nationalists also viewed the war as a means of rejuvenating what they considered to be a spineless and ineffective political regime.[47] From the beginning, interventionism was an ideology rather than a mere policy for them. After their shock over Caporetto and their disillusionment at Paris, they felt that the only way to justify this ideology was to overthrow the political leaders who had failed to make their dream of a powerful, unified Italy come true. Surely, fear of disorder and of Bolshevism attracted many Italians to fascism, just as its own violence attracted others. Nevertheless, Volpe himself admitted that "in the second half of 1921 and more so in 1922 . . . the general condition of the country had im-

[46] John Alden Thayer, *Italy and the Great War* (Madison, 1964), 413.
[47] By making militant nationalism "official," Poincaré, Barthou, and Clemenceau were able to steal the thunder of antiparliamentary nationalists like Maurras and Barrès far more successfully than Salandra and Sonnino *vis-à-vis* Corradini and Mussolini.

proved . . . and the infatuation for . . . Bolschevism [*sic*] was in a decline." [48] He embraced fascism because it seemed to carry the implications of interventionism to their logical outcome: national regeneration, imperialism, dynamic leadership. In the immediate postwar years Salvemini, who had also been an interventionist, said that he would not have taken that position if he could have foreseen that it would give rise to fascism. Volpe remained mesmerized by the "Radiant Days of May," 1915, for more than twenty-five years.

Volpe's interpretation of the effects of Caporetto on the Italian people implicitly contradicts his claim that, except for the socialists and a small group of neutralist intellectuals, "the most conscious section of the Italian people" eagerly wanted their country to enter the war: [49]

> Caporetto served as a rude awakening to a half-asleep people, as a call back to reality whose abandonment had led to false images of things. . . . The current of aware Italians attracted, dragged along, and absorbed not a few refractory or inert elements. Not only did the willing ones experience a revival of energy and determination but a jolt was also given to that vast majority of Italians who partly because of preexisting and historical conditions and partly because of the way we entered the war were still living morally on the margins or outside of the war itself. [50]

Undoubtedly Caporetto rallied the Italian people to save their country from total defeat, but it was wishful thinking to believe that the war itself was *popular*.

Volpe himself recognized the fact that wartime unity quickly gave way to heightened class conflicts and a potential revolution. In addition to the emergence of mass movements like the Socialists and the *Popolari* he noted the dramatic appearance of daring groups of individuals who could form a true elite. Volpe turned to the Fascists as the one elite that would quell these demagogic

---

[48] Volpe, *History of the Fascist Movement* (Rome, 1939), 82.

[49] Volpe, *Il Popolo italiano tra la pace e la guerra* (Milan, 1940, but written sixteen years earlier), 145ff.

[50] Volpe, *Octobre 1917. Dall' Isonzo al Piave* (Milan, 1930), 183.

movements, dissolve class antagonisms, and concern itself with an exclusively political approach to national affairs.

This new preoccupation with strong individuals and elites colored Volpe's approach to history throughout the Fascist period. Except for his studies on the history of Corsica, culminating in *Storia della Corsica italiana* (Milan, 1939), he all but abandoned his previous interest in anonymous masses and forces for the study of men and politics. As the historian of the regime he wrote *Lo sviluppo storico del fascismo* (Palermo, 1928), *Guerra, dopoguerra e fascismo* (Venice, 1928), and *Storia del movimento Fascista* (Milan, 1939). He also published *Francesco Crispi* (Venice, 1928), *Il popolo italiano tra la pace e la guerra* (Milan, 1940), and *L'Italia nella Triplice Alleanza, 1882–1915* (Milan, 1939), which is a collection of diplomatic documents with an unfavorable commentary on Italy's membership in the Triple Alliance.

Like the Fascists and most nationalists, Volpe showed little interest in the Risorgimento. He insisted on its indigenous national origins but played down the achievements of the Cavourian liberals. While Mussolini ruled, it was the anti-Fascist historians who developed the study of the Risorgimento along new lines. Luigi Salvatorelli, Adolfo Omodeo, Cesare Spellanzon, and Croce emphasized its European aspects and its rational and liberal political ideals. A few months before the regime fell in 1943, Salvatorelli's *Pensiero e azione del Risorgimento* pointed up the democratic side of Risorgimento and clearly implied that fascism was the antithesis of everything Mazzini, Garibaldi, and Cavour had hoped to accomplish.

Despite his devotion to fascism, Volpe did not distort Italy's history in order to make it all seem like a necessary prelude to that regime. In 1925 he said that since the time of Frederick Barbarossa, the Italian nation had been in the making,[51] but three years later, in *Italia in cammino*, he insisted that the few patriots

---

[51] This statement was made in "Italia é Europa," Volpe's inaugural lecture in his course on modern political history at the University of Rome. The lecture is reprinted in Volpe, *Momenti di storia italiana*, 438.

who led the Risorgimento were the first to make "the great mass of Italians, still amorphous, indifferent, and diffident," see themselves as a nation.[52] In his introduction to this work, his best during the interwar years, Volpe characterized the Fascist period as an "overcoming and synthesis" of the "phase" between 1861 and 1915.[53] Although this language smacks of Hegelian and Marxian determinism, Volpe placed the origins of fascism in the Great War, not in the Italy of the Postrisorgimento.

The first edition of *Italia in cammino* appeared in the spring of 1927, six months before Croce's *Storia d'Italia dal 1871 al 1915;* the former gave a nationalist, the latter a liberal interpretation of the forty-five-year period preceding the war. Both works have an essentially political framework, with Volpe's giving more space to foreign policy and Croce's more to "ideals." Whereas Croce tried to see the history of that period as the gradual triumph of liberalism, Volpe tried to see it as the movement of the nation toward power and greatness. Croce praised Giolitti's return to *trasformismo* after 1901 as the best way of overcoming the antagonism between the extremes of Left and Right—as "a unifying transformation of their ideals." He also saw the extension of the franchise in 1912 (at which time he had viewed it with misgivings) as evidence of democracy in the making.[54] For Volpe, Giolitti's laissez-faire liberalism was simply an excuse for lack of leadership of the *nation* in the making.[55]

Aside from this basic difference in interpretation the two books reflected the different interests and temperaments of their authors. Whereas Croce described Italy's economic growth briefly and impersonally, Volpe devoted a long chapter to "Gli Italiani al lavoro," in which he gave evocative examples of all phases of economic life as well as a revealing analysis of the effects of mass

[52] Volpe, *Italia in cammino* (Milan, 1928), 2. In his expanded version of this paragraph in volume I of *Italia Moderna* (Florence, 1946, but written in early 1943), Volpe added (p. 5) the following sentence: "Nothing [is] more false than that banal image . . . of an Italy always, for centuries, fixated on the idea of unity, vibrating with the spirit of independence, but always bound by her chains, despite her every right."

[53] *Ibid.,* ix.

[54] Croce, *Storia d'Italia dal 1871 al 1915* (3rd. ed.; Bari, 1928), 225–26, 267.

[55] Volpe, *Italia in cammino,* 79–80.

emigration at home and abroad. Croce criticized Volpe's "materialistic" preoccupation with social issues such as population movements and class conflicts and decried his neglect of moral questions.[56] Volpe tried unconvincingly to justify the "morality" of Crispi's imperialism (which Croce deplored) by reminding his readers that the poet Giosuè Carducci (whom Croce admired) had enthusiastically supported this policy.[57] Croce, on the other hand, gave full credit to his own philosophical and critical efforts to revitalize Italian culture after 1902, especially in his review, *La Critica*.[58]

In their histories of the prewar Kingdom of Italy, Volpe and Croce gave Italian historiography an ideological stamp that it has not yet overcome. Volpe's view of Italy as continually "on the move" was particularly congenial to the Fascists. Croce therefore defended the Italy created by Cavour's parliamentary regime and took special interest in the ideas and activities of the political elite that had reaped the fruits of the Risorgimento, namely the anticlerical liberals. After the fall of fascism Volpe's interpretation was repudiated by most of his former students, but Croce's also came under fire from radicals, Marxists, and Catholics. Twenty years after the end of the Second World War, Volpe expressed his disapproval of the new generation of social historians (both Marxist and non-Marxist) who tried to project the social upheavals of their own time into the past—especially into the so-called *rivoluzione mancata* of the poor during the Risorgimento.[59] He still maintained that in the mid-nineteenth century Italy's main problem had been to become a nation. In his criticism of the view of Antonio Gramsci and his disciples, Volpe found himself in accord with two "Crocean" liberals, Federico Chabod and Rosario Romeo, but he continued to doubt the ability of the pre-1915 liberals to make their institutions work.

Yet in his last major work, the three-volume *Italia moderna*, Volpe painted a more balanced (in some instances almost nostal-

---

[56] Croce, *Storia della storiografia italiana* (2 vols.; Bari, 1939), Vol. II, 236–37
[57] Volpe, *Italia in cammino*, xvii.
[58] Croce, *Storia d'Italia*, 253–57.
[59] Personal interview in Rome, July 24, 1965.

gic) picture of the liberal monarchy than he had in *Italia in cammino*. His defense of the historical role of the monarchy undoubtedly reflected his ultimate disillusionment with Fascist policy, particularly Mussolini's ill-advised entry into the Second World War.[60] In his brief treatment of the Risorgimento he said: "The monarchy gave the unity, the continuity, and the necessary force in a country that had the Papacy, which usually looked unfavorably on unification." [61] Volpe softened his earlier criticism of Cavour's successors, the men of the *Destra* in the 1870s.[62] He acknowledged their lofty idea of the state governed by an educated elite, their determination to instill this idea in the masses, and their recognition of the state's social responsibilities to the poor.[63] After lamenting the ineffective rule of the *Sinistra*, especially in foreign policy, Volpe presented Francesco Crispi as a strong leader favoring the monarchy as a force and symbol of unity and giving his countrymen national prestige by means of astute diplomacy.[64] The social unrest of the 1890s created a severe rift between the nation and the monarchy, but in 1900 the advent of Victor Emmanuel III brought a new period of unity behind the king,—from the conservatives through the Socialists—even though this unity was soon fractured by another wave of strikes.[65] Although Volpe still disapproved of Giolitti's laissez-faire tactics in handling the 1904 general strike, he noted that the monarchy itself continued to gain popularity, offering as evidence the "magnificent" (most people would say monstrous) monument erected in Rome in honor of Victor Emmanuel II.

In volume III (1910–14) of *Italia moderna* Volpe gave detailed stress to colonial and foreign policy, irredentism, and nationalism but on the whole, he was fair to the liberals and socialists. He showed more sympathy for the Giolitti of the immediate prewar years than he had previously. Volpe conceded that Giolitti was often able to get parliament to pass reforms that other prime ministers were unable or unwilling to obtain. While maintaining that his decision to conquer Libya was prompted in part by a de-

---

[60] Volpe, *Toscana medievale*, xxi.   [61] Volpe, *Italia moderna*, I, 45.
[62] Volpe, *Italia in cammino*, 35–36.   [63] Volpe, *Italia moderna*, I, 109–12.
[64] *Ibid.*, 315.   [65] Volpe, *Italia moderna* (Florence, 1949), II, 38.

sire to disarm his right-wing critics, Volpe expressed admiration for the way in which Giolitti made this decision at the time when the other powers were preoccupied with the second Moroccan crisis.[66] In a recent article, the eminent Socialist historian Leo Valiani agrees with Volpe that Giolitti took good advantage of the favorable international situation in the summer and fall of 1911, even though Valiani regrets the fact that the Libyan adventure triggered the Balkan Wars of 1912 and the holocaust of 1914.[67] Volpe depicted Italy in 1914 as "on the move"—more prosperous, more cultured, and, most important of all, more patriotic than ever. Indeed, he added, Italy seemed like a country that was better than its government and (in an irrepressible allusion to Mussolini) worthy of a better government. He recognized the persistence of class divisions and frustrations but noted that conservatives like Sidney Sonnino, along with the nationalists, had hoped that Italy's entry into the war would give the nation its moral consensus.[68]

Although Volpe clung to his militant nationalism as an antidote to revolutionary socialism, by 1952, when he finished volume III of *Italia moderna*, many Italian historians were experiencing "the end of ideology." In that year the editors of the Resistance-oriented monthly review *Il Ponte* lamented the fact that "a big industrialist" had given Volpe a large cash prize, which they interpreted as an effort to rehabilitate a former Fascist.[69] Volpe himself had denounced the Resistance movement as divisive, but after Mussolini's overthrow in 1943 he had put his faith exclusively in the monarchy and rejected the Italian Social Republic set up by Mussolini under German sponsorship. This gesture did not spare Volpe from the wrath of the Resistance forces, which destroyed his library and deprived him of his university chair and his pension. Nevertheless, as in France, the postwar government of Italy soon abandoned its purge of former Fascists. In the Italy of the mid-1950s both fascism and anti-fascism had ceased to be burn-

---

[66] Volpe, *Italia moderna* (Florence, 1952), III, 315–42, *passim*.

[67] Valiani, "Le origini della guerra del 1914 e dell'intervento italiano nelle ricerche e nelle pubblicazioni dell'ultimo ventennio," *Rivista storica italiana*, LXXVIII (Sept., 1966), 596–97.

[68] Volpe, *Italia moderna*, III, 645–47.

[69] *Il Ponte*, VIII (Oct., 1952), 1340.

ing issues and communism was apparently becoming domesticated. Under these conditions Volpe's former students and colleagues forgave him his close collaboration with Mussolini's regime. (After all, they themselves had had to work under it, even though most of them had disliked it.) Their tribute to him took the form of the two-volume *Festschrift* mentioned at the beginning of this essay.